Inside the Hearts of Bible Women

TEACHER'S and ADVERTISING MANUAL

Katheryn Maddox Haddad

Katheryn Maddox Haddad

Other Books by this Author

CHRISTIAN LIFE
Applied Christianity: Handbook 500 Good Works
You Can Be a Hero Alone
Worship Changes Since 1st Century + Worship 1sr Century Way
The Best of Alexander Campbell's Millennial Harbinger
Inside the Hearts of Bible Women-Reader+Audio+Leader
The Lord's Supper: 52 Readings with Prayers

BIBLE TEXTS
Revelation: A Love Letter From God
The Holy Spirit: 592 Verses Examined
Was Jesus God? (Why Evil)
365 Life-Changing Scriptures Day by Date
Love Letters of Jesus & His Bride, Ecclesia (Song of Solomon)
Christianity or Islam? The Contrast
The Road to Heaven

FUN BOOKS
Bible Puzzles, Bible Song Book, Bible Numbers

TOUCHING GOD SERIES
365 Golden Bible Thoughts: God's Heart to Yours
365 Pearls of Wisdom: God's Soul to Yours
365 Silver-Winged Prayers: Your Spirit to God's

SURVEY SERIES: EASY BIBLE WORKBOOKS
→Old Testament & New Testament Surveys
→Questions You Have Asked-Part I & II

HISTORICAL RESEARCH BIBLE
for Novel, Screenwriter, Documentary & Thesis Writers

HISTORICAL NOVELS & STORYBOOKS
Series of 8: They Met Jesus
Ongoing Series of 8: Intrepid Men of God
Mysteries of the Empire with Klaudius & Hektor
Christmas: They Rocked the Cradle that Rocked the World
Series of 8: A Child's Life of Christ
Series of 10: A Child's Bible Heroes
Series of 8: A Child's Bible Kids
Series of 10: A Child's Bible Ladies

GENEALOGY:
How to Climb Your Family Tree Without Falling Out
Volume 1 & 2: Beginner-Intermediate & Colonial-Medieval

Copyright © 2017 Katheryn Maddox Haddad
NORTHERN LIGHTS PUBLISHING HOUSE

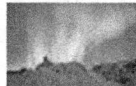

Cover design by Sharon A. Lavy. Images from DepositPhotos.
Scriptures taken from the HOLY BIBLE, NEW INTERNATIONAL VERSION.
Copyright © 1973, 1978, 1984 International Bible Society.
Used by permission of Zondervan Bible Publishers.
ISBN-978-1-952261-10-7

Printed in the United States, First Printing 1994, Second Printing 2017

Table of Contents

Other Books by this Author 2

HOW TO USE THIS TEACHING MATERIAL 8

HOW TO USE THIS ADVERTISING MATERIAL 20

DARE TO BE THAT STAR 78

MOVING AGAIN ~ SARAH 80

Lesson One: Packing 80
- Cope with Being Uprooted 80
- Know How to Say Goodbye 80

Lesson Two: Traveling 89
- Keeping Children Content on Long Trips 89
- Seeing the Good Side of Moving 89

Lesson Three: Settling In 98
- Adjusting to a New Community 98
- Keeping Up Courage When All Seems Futile 98

HOMOSEXUAL BUT NOT SO GAY ~ LOT'S WIFE 110

Lesson One: Protecting our Morals 110
- GUIDE YOUNG PEOPLE TO RIGHT DECISIONS 110
- LIVE UNTAINTED AMONG THE IMMORAL 110

Lesson Two: Compromising Our Morals 122
- Understand the Militancy of Homosexuality 122
- Understand our Creator's Hatred for it 122

Lesson Three: Losing Our Morals 134
- Know What is Wrong with Homosexuality 134
- Learn When to Get Out of a Bad Situation 134

NOT MY CHILDREN ~ REBECCA 145

Lesson One: Family Confrontations 145
- Identify Problems Between Siblings 145
- Help Siblings Get Along 145

Lesson Two: The Irrevocable Act 154
- DON'T BE A "CONTROLLING" MOTHER 154
- DEAL WITH DECEIT 154

Lesson Three: Falling Apart 164

- ♥ Cope When Your Children Do Wrong 164
- ♥ Maintain Faith When Your Family Falls Apart 164

UNBEARABLE LOSS ~ JOB'S WIFE 177

Lesson One: Loss of Possessions 177
- ♥ Face Financial Setbacks 177
- ♥ Face Challenges to Faith 177

Lesson Two: Loss of Loved Ones 188
- ♥ Cope with Death of Children 188
- ♥ Cope with the Grieving Process 188

Lesson Three: Loss of a Personal God 206
- ♥ Understanding Euthanasia 206
- ♥ Deal with Shattered faith 206

SECOND TIME AROUND ~ RUTH 219

Lesson One: Letting Go 219
- ♥ Adjust to Widowhood 219
- ♥ Understand Widowhood 219

Lesson Two: Single Again 230
- ♥ Make Social Adjustments 230
- ♥ Make Economic Adjustments 230

Lesson Three: Readjusting 240
- ♥ Choose a Godly Second Husband 240
- ♥ Blend Two Lives with Habits Already Formed 240

ABUSED ~ ABIGAIL 252

Lesson One: Enduring Abuse 252
- ♥ Maintain One's Self-Esteem 252
- ♥ Have Patience in Trials 252

Lesson Two: A World of Abuse 266
- ♥ KEEP OUR OWN VALUES SORTED OUT 266
- ♥ ESTABLISH COMMUNICATION 266

Lesson Three: Abuse and Affliction—The Triumph 275
- ♥ Create Courage From Trials 275
- ♥ Utilize a Support System 275

BEGUILING OCCULT ~ WITCH OF ENDOR 286

Lesson One: The Susceptible Ones 286
- ♥ Understand Why We Help Others 286
- ♥ Understand Why We Want to Know More than Others 286

Lesson Two: Masquerade or Mystique ... 297
- Draw the Line in Seeking Answers to Life's Mysteries ... 297
- Be Careful People Don't Think We are Proponents of the ... 297

Lesson Three: If It Were True ... 311
- Know that What is Not of God is Against God ... 311
- Follow God's Way to Reach the Spirit World ... 311

VIOLATED ~ TAMAR ... 325

Lesson One: Innocent Trust ... 325
- Avoid Rape Situations ... 325
- Know How Far to Trust ... 325

Lesson Two: Betrayal ... 336
- Be a Comfort to the Victim ... 336
- Console One's Self ... 336

Lesson Three: Evasive Consolation ... 346
- Recover from Rape ... 346
- Handle Urges for Revenge ... 346

UNFAITHFUL ~ GOMER ... 358

Lesson One: Beginnings of a Shaky Marriage ... 358
- **KNOW THE FOUNDATION OF MARRIAGE** ... 358
- **WORK TO BUILD A SOLID MARRIAGE** ... 358\

Lesson Two: Coping with a Tumultuous Marriage ... 369
- Face Unfaithfulness ... 369
- Try to Hold It Together ... 369

Lesson Three: Salvaging an Impossible Marriage ... 377
- Know the Price of One's Soul ... 377
- Cope with Marriage Breakdown ... 377

BEAUTY AND THE BEAST ~ ESTHER ... 386

Lesson One: Commoner ... 386
- Be An Example to Others in Difficult Times ... 386
- Make Sure We Really Want What We Wish For ... 386

Lesson Two: Queen ... 394
- Keep Up Our Health During Stress ... 394
- Understand the Value of Fasting ... 394

Lesson Three: Hero ... 404
- Understand the Value of Tact ... 404
- Stand from the Crowd for Unselfish Reasons ... 404

WHEEL SPINNING - MARTHA ... 415

Lesson One: Getting Organized 415
- **Learn What Gets in the Way of Hospitality** 415
- **Understand Impulsive Behavior** 415

Lesson Two: The Agenda 425
- **Get Control of Our Time** 425
- **Accept Ourselves Without Complaint** 425

Lesson Three: Selfless Giving 434
- **Set Priorities** 434
- **Remain Cool, Calm, and Collected** 434

TRUE TO THE END ~ PRISCILLA 442

Lesson One: The Price of the Search 442
- **Search the Scriptures for Ourselves** 442
- **Sift Out Our Own Religious Pre-Judging** 442

Lesson Two: The Price of Sharing 457
- **Courageously Stand for Christian Unity** 457
- **Help Others Read the Bible for Themselves** 457

Lesson Three: The Price of Salvation 470
- **Sacrifice for Jesus in Some Way Every Day** 470
- **Stick with the Church (Body of Christ) No Matter What** 470

THANK YOU 481
ABOUT THE AUTHOR 482

BUY YOUR NEXT BOOK NOW 483
CONNECT WITH THE AUTHOR 484

Get A Free Book 484
JOIN MY DREAM TEAM 484

How to Use This Teaching Material

FRIENDLY WARNING

This material is not for you if you don't feel comfortable using Jesus' methods, for as the Great Physician, he sought out and touched the spiritually sick (Mark 2:17). Nor is it for you if you don't feel comfortable with Jesus' fighting spirit, for he didn't come to bring peace [with Satan] but a sword to actively fight him (Matthew 10:34). It's not for you if you don't feel comfortable acting like Jesus did, for he associated with sinners of all kinds (Luke 5:30). It's just not for you if you don't feel comfortable being what Jesus is, for peacemakers are called children of God (Matthew 5:9).

THANK YOU

It would be so much easier for you to teach simple fill-in-the-blank lessons, or ones that deal with just general Christian principles. *INSIDE THE HEARTS OF BIBLE WOMEN* is meant to get down to the nitty-gritty of our everyday lives as they relate to our human struggle between Satan and God, right and wrong. It is not a study for the faint-hearted. But I guarantee you that, as a result of your courage, your Christian life will never be the same again. So, on behalf of everyone you will be courageously reaching out to with the unconditional love of God, thank you.

WHO SHOULD TEACH THIS?

The main requirement is that you be a woman. If there is even one man in the class, no matter how sensitive, it becomes a mixed class. Men and women do not open up around each other very well, and perhaps it should be so.

You do not have to be a Bible scholar in any sense. The research has been done for you. Supportive Bible verses have been located for you. Possible answers have been provided for you.

You do not have to be a psychologist. If there were more caring Christians around reaching out in friendship to each other, we might not need so many psychologists. Sometimes all people need during difficult times is a friend. No one can solve their problems for them—not you or a psychologist or their family. What they need most from you is moral support.

The main requirement of the woman who teaches these lessons is that you be sensitive to the feelings of others. Just relax and concentrate on reaching out to your ladies with that love you already feel for them.

WORKING WITH

THE NARRATIVE

Periodically through the student book's story of each Bible woman, there will be a footnote. That footnote is for them to stop for a discussion. Your discussion questions are numbered to coincide with the footnote numbers.

Suggested Types of Classes

SUNDAY AM OR WEDNESDAY PM

You will have to be most careful in this arrangement to time everything so your class is at a stopping point when time is up. Sundays are good if you want to attract members who do not attend the rest of the week. Wednesdays are good if you want to attract ladies who attend church somewhere else on Sunday mornings. (Many denominations do not have Sunday night or Wednesday night assemblies.)

WEEKDAY

Classes which meet independent of other activities of the church are most flexible. I have found that even an hour and a half, if let out right on time, is comfortable for ladies in this setting. This applies to both day or evening times.

BEFORE WORK OR NOON

If you want to reach ladies with whom you work, here is a perfect chance. Companies normally do not care what the employees do on their own time. However, you would have to get permission to use their facilities such as cafeteria or conference room. If you cannot, how about reserving a room at a nearby restaurant once a week during lunch or right after work?

ANY TIME AT HOME

If you can get just two neighbors and friends interested in coming to your home during the day or evening, you have enough. Don't worry. They will invite their friends as soon as they find out how helpful your discussions are.

SATURDAY LADIES DAY

An all-day session would bring in people from the neighborhood. However, they won't come automatically. You would need newspaper coverage, radio spots, telephone calls, flyers handed out door to door along with registration cards, letters, and so on. Each type of public relations gets different responses. For instance, for every hundred flyers you mail out, you will get perhaps 2 to 4 responses.

RETREAT

Line up a campsite or hotel. Use this to unite the ladies of your congregation, or help mothers and daughters draw closer. If you have a lot of university or military ladies in your community, this would fit them very well. It's also a possibility for the teenage girls in your congregation.

Suggested Schedules

The purpose of your class will not be to turn it into a detailed problem-explaining or -solving session. Below are suggested schedules depending on the time allotted for your class.

In most cases, you will not be able to discuss all the questions. Select or ask your class to select the questions of most interest to everyone. These schedules allow 5 minutes to discuss each question, which should be your average.

Only one suggested schedule allows you to play the MP3 in class. I feel they would be much more beneficial and heard better if played by each member on their own time. I have included a pause chime in the readings where questions come up for class use if so desired.

If you have a short class time and feel a need to cover more material than the slower discussion method allows, you could bring up each question, have a class member read the applicable scripture, then answer the question yourself. You could cover probably twice as much material this way, even allowing for comments from the class.

Otherwise, the short schedule below reflects the discussion question format. I have reduced the number of questions that can be covered rather than eliminate the good work. I feel very strongly about including the good works. Please do not eliminate them unless your group can only meet for about a half hour, such as at people's place of employment. WE MUST TEACH FOR LIFE CHANGE!

The 90-minute session, of course, is for ladies who meet during the weekday or evening independent of other classes. I have found that in an exciting class people hardly notice the time. You probably won't need a break, but I've inserted one just in case.

If you would like to use this material in a retreat, treat each day as a separate all-day ladies day. The retreat is primarily for church members, and the ladies day is primarily for community outreach. My suggested schedule includes a continental breakfast and lunch. If possible, ask the men of your congregation to set up, serve, and clean up lunch for you. (You promise to "rise up and call them blessed" if they will!)

In your all-day session, whenever you play the MP3 disc, you may wish to have a power point presentation or make transparencies for an overhead projector. Take photos of people in your congregation in modern clothes doing modern versions of what the Bible people are doing in the story. Go to your next picture every time you hear the tone on the tape.

At the end of an all-day program, stand at the door and give everyone a flower, small scripture plaque or some other memento—anything to encourage them to come back on Sunday and begin worshipping with you.

Whatever you do, START ON TIME. Do not reward late comers; reward the early birds. If you begin to wait just a minute or two, people will come just a little later than that. You could end up starting your class ten minutes late each time. Also, END ON TIME.

30-Minute Session:

  5 Minutes   Introduce Lesson
20 Minutes   Discuss 4 Questions
  5 Minutes   Conclusion and Prayer

45-Minute Session:

  5 Minutes   Welcome
                 Acknowledge Visitors
                 Announcements
  5 Minutes   Introduce Lesson
25 Minutes   Discuss 5 Questions
10 Minutes   Good Work and Prayer

60-Minute Session:

  5 Minutes   Welcome
                 Acknowledge Visitors
                 Announcements
  5 Minutes   Introduce Lesson
30 Minutes   Discuss 6 Questions
10 Minutes   Good Work
  5 Minutes   Song
                 Quickie Questions
  5 Minutes   Prayer Requests and Prayer

90-Minute Session:

  5 Minutes   Welcome
                 Acknowledge Visitors
                 Announcements
10 Minutes   Introduce Lesson
25 Minutes   Discuss 5 Questions
  5 Minutes   Break to stretch and refill coffee/tea
25 Minutes   Discuss 5 Questions
10 Minutes   Good Work
  5 Minutes   Song
                 Quickie Questions
  5 Minutes   Prayer Requests and Prayer

2-Session Class:

SESSION I:

  5 Minutes   Welcome
                  Acknowledge Visitors
                  Announcements
10 Minutes   Introduce Lesson
25-40 Minutes   Listen to Tape and Discuss 3-5 Questions
  5 Minutes   Prayer Requests
                  Prayer

SESSION II:

  5 Minutes   Welcome
                  Acknowledge Visitors
                  Announcements
20-35 Minutes   Listen to Tape and Discuss 2-4 Questions
10 Minutes   Good Work
  5 Minutes   Song
                  Quickie Questions
  5 Minutes   Prayer Requests
                  Prayer

Ladies Day or Retreat:

9:00   Registration and Continental Breakfast

10:00   COMMON ASSEMBLY
                  Opening Announcements (Explain Agenda)
                  Song
10:15   Introduce Lesson I
10:30   Over loud speaker, play tape and show power point covering Lesson I (time this ahead of time)
10:50   Dismiss to small groups
11:00   Groups discuss 6 questions
11:30   Dismiss
11:45   Lunch

12:30   COMMON ASSEMBLY
                  Song
12:35   Introduce Lesson II
12:45   Over loud speaker, play tape and show slides covering Lesson II (time this ahead of time)

1:05   Dismiss to small groups
1:15   Groups discuss 6 questions
1:45   Dismiss

1:55	COMMON ASSEMBLY Song
2:00	Introduce Lesson III
2:10	Over loud speaker, play tape and show slides covering Lesson III (time this ahead of time)
2:30	Dismiss to small groups
2:40	Groups discuss 6 questions
3:10	Dismiss
3:20	COMMON ASSEMBLY Song
3:25	Final encouragement and invitation to attend worship with you on Sunday
3:30	DISMISS

USE OF AUDIO

I have read each story onto an MP3 audio. I did this for two reasons. (1) People don't read much anymore. Most feel they're too busy. Most don't read their lessons before class. With an audio, they can listen going to and from work, or while fixing dinner. (2) It helps view the Bible woman as a real person who laughed and cried, whispered and shouted, got sad and excited. A tone is inserted periodically for two possible uses. (1) Combine the audio with power point or opaque projection to be changed at each tone for a larger assembly. (2) The written narrative indicates where each "Thought Question" belongs as indicated by endnote numbers in the text for private reading.

SMALL GROUPS

The questions should be discussed freely by everyone. Groups of about five ladies seem best, for this gives everyone a chance to say something. If you do decide you want to divide up in your class for the discussion portion of the lesson, do the following:

1. Photocopy the part of your manual that includes the questions, related scriptures, and "Possible Class Response."

2. Select enough ladies before class that you have one leader for each group. Give her a copy of the scriptures and answers you photocopied.

3. Give her enough small pieces of paper that she can write down the applicable scriptures to each question to give members of her group to read at the appropriate time.

VISUAL AIDS

I have included charts, signs and graphs to use when you introduce each lesson. They are further explained in TODAY'S WORLD and BIBLE WORLD. If you are good with PowerPoint, use that. If you have an overhead projector available, make a transparency from them with a photocopier. If you do not have an overhead projector, hold up the sign I provided you while you talk. Other alternatives are to copy them onto poster board or the blackboard, or make photocopied handouts for everyone in class.

TODAY'S WORLD

Current research was done on how prevalent each Bible woman's problem is today in the twenty-first century. I did this specifically to show your congregation the odds that people you worship with and people in your community are suffering with this problem. Since we Christians are bad about admitting to each other that we have problems, these statistics will play an important part in your decision on what to study. The women in your congregation and community usually suffer these things silently, thinking they are the only ones. Also in this section, modern methods of solving these problems are sometimes shared. Use this information to whatever degree you wish. Don't feel obligated to use it all.

BIBLE WORLD

When writing the story, I drew some conclusion that you may wonder about. Often my conclusions came from other scriptures in the Bible referring to this person or this problem—how it was viewed in those times. Sometimes I hinged something on the Greek or Hebrew if the English translation was vague. I also did research in Bible dictionaries, ancient books such as those by Josephus and Eusebius, and so on to find the geographical, social, and customs setting during which each Bible woman experienced her problems.

SCRIPTURES

Along with each question is at least one support scripture. Write them out on small slips of paper to hand out as the ladies arrive. This way they can already have them looked up and marked when it is time to read them. Your manual includes the scriptures, but their workbooks do so only occasionally. Encourage your class to write the scriptures in their workbooks whenever you ask for one to be read.

INTRODUCING THE LESSON

Read the background material in TODAY'S WORLD and BIBLE WORLD, and look over the visual aids. Give your ladies statistics of how prevalent a problem is. This will help them not be embarrassed to speak up for fear they're the only ones with a particular problem. It will also help those who have no idea the problem may be in your congregation to see what the possibilities are that it is. The statistics are of the general population, which means the problems will not have touched "Christians" as much. But the world does infiltrate the church, doesn't it?

You may prefer to spend more time than listed in the suggested schedules above. Use whatever time you feel is necessary to get across to the class that the problem is here and needs to be addressed.

POSSIBLE CLASS RESPONSE

These are discussion questions and have no right or wrong answers. However, sometimes people have no answer because they don't understand what the author is getting at. Another reason I included possible responses is to warm your class up and get them started responding. Read one or two from those I listed, or come up with your own response. These are just ideas. Your class may have different needs than I addressed in the possible responses. You may never need to refer to them at all. Be sure, when you ask a question, to pause and leave a moment of silence for the ladies to think. Someone probably will speak up if, for no other reason than, to break the awkward silence. Remember too, if you expect them to reveal secret parts of themselves, you'll have to do the same as their example.

GOOD WORK

Teach for LIFE CHANGE! These good works should be included in all classes except perhaps the all-day or 30-minute ones. Jesus taught more by example than preaching. How many Christians attend worship and classes year after year, yet their lives and those around them are no different? Hebrews 10:24f says we are to assemble in order to encourage each other to have love and good works.

I feel so strongly about this that I wrote another book entitled *APPLIED CHRISTIANITY: A HANDBOOK OF 500 GOOD WORKS*. It is over 200 pages explaining just about every possible type of good work for just about every type woman, regardless of age, health, or location.

Does your community admire your congregation because it reaches out to people with care and love? Your class's good work is one way to show them how much God cares for them through you—his mouth and hands and feet. Don't worry about whether or not it will do any good. God said, "My word will not return to me void" (Isaiah 55:11). Just do your good work and God will give the increase (1 Corinthians 3:6).

You may wish to collect change from the ladies at each class to pay for the postage. I strongly suggest that you, as the teacher, mail the notes yourself. Human nature has a lot of good intentions that never get done.

CLOSING REMARKS

There will be times when your discussions get a little emotional. People don't need to return to their normal daily routine like this. That is the reason for the summary quickie questions. The answers are obvious. With an enthusiastic smile, as though you are saying "Eureka! I've got it!" quickly go through the questions.

Have someone selected for the prayer before class. Ask for prayer requests if you have time, or ask that they be written down and handed to the prayer leader ahead of time. Always remember those whose lives are touched with the problems discussed in your lesson.

GOSSIP

Occasionally remind everyone that what is said in class is to GO NO FURTHER. No one is to tell things class members have confessed about themselves or their families to anyone else, even husbands. This will encourage discussion. The only exception is when we feel a non-class member could help her. In that case, she must give her permission to tell that specific person. Gossip will destroy your class. Emphasize loving trust and confidentiality.

MEMBERS WITH NEEDS

Tell your class that if they notice tears coming to the eyes of someone they're sitting near, feel free to put their arm around her. If this happens and no one notices, you might say, "I believe _____ needs a little extra love from someone right now." Then go on with your class.

Before class, you may want to find out who might have time to meet with anyone who opens up during class and needs someone to talk to afterward—just as a friend, not a counselor. Then, if someone wants to talk about their problems during class, just suggest to her that you (or someone else) can spend some time with her after class (there, out for coffee, one of your homes).

Then go on with your class. When you do meet her later, explain that you have no answers for her other than what is in the Bible. Reassure her that you want to be her friend and can at least listen while she works things through.

If she goes deeper than you feel comfortable with, refer her to your minister or elder. But keep her as a friend; don't drop her. Remember the last time you had a problem and no one to confide in because your friends quit coming around?

Ask her if the class can pray for her the next time you meet. If you feel comfortable doing so, pray with her whenever she talks to you about her problems. It will give her a sense of release. Just a short prayer is fine.

SUPPORT GROUPS

If two or more ladies come to you about the same problem, get permission to tell them about each other so they can exchange phone numbers and create their own support group. In so many problems of life, we just need to ride out the storm, and can use reassurance while we do. They may even decide to meet once a week in one of their homes, or go out for coffee just to offer the mutual encouragement only those going through the problem can understand.

HOW THE STORIES WERE WRITTEN

The three lessons for each Bible woman typically are divided up as follows: (Lesson 1) The woman as she was normally; (Lesson 2) What happened to get her into her problem; (Lesson 3) How she handled her problem—right or wrong.

IT IS A COMMENTARY IN NARRATIVE FORM. At the risk of people thinking I was "adding to the Bible" I wrote this. I wanted so very much for each Bible woman and her problems to come alive and leap off the page right into the heart of the reader. I wanted you to laugh when she laughed and cry when she cried. I wanted you to not only know her logically, but to feel what she must have felt deep down in her heart. I wanted you to develop a sister relationship with her as God intended.

As I wrote, I put myself inside each Bible woman's skin and imagined how I would feel with such things going on in my life. As I wrote, sometimes I laughed out loud, and sometimes I could hardly see the words because of my tears. The more intense stories I had to schedule to write when there weren't many important responsibilities in my own life, because I knew it would take an emotional toll on me.

Throughout the writing, I felt as though each woman was standing up off the page and shouting across time and space, "Hey! I was a real person! I had feelings just like you! I hugged people I loved and cowered from those I feared just like you. Look at me! Really look at me! God let me go through all this as an example to you. That's why he included this difficult part of my life in his Word. He really and truly cares about you. Look at me! Listen to me! Try to love me if you can! Don't cause me to have lived through all this in vain."

CLASS VISITORS

Although these lessons are as much for your regular church members as non-members, it will take a little added effort for the visitors. No, it will take a LOT of added effort.

First, you should offer child care if possible. Refreshments also act as an ice breaker. Have name tags for everyone. If possible, you might make them say, "Hello, my name is _____ and I love you!" or "Hello, my name is _____ and God loves you."

Have registration for everyone if you did not register them going door to door or by phone. Let them fill out the cards themselves to avoid embarrassment over answers and name spellings. Besides name, address, and phone, you may want also to have squares to check presence in the home of husband and children/ages. Also ask for church affiliation and have squares to check how often they attend (once a year, twice a year, once a month, weekly, haven't been for years). Then have a "Comments" section.

Tell your regular class members ahead of time that this will not be the time to decide with each other when to get together for lunch next week, etc. That time must be unselfishly given up so members can sit by and spend time visiting with the visitors—those with lost souls. At the end of class, you older members should ask the visitors to write their phone number on their name tag and give it to you. Then call them during the week.

You may attract ladies to your class from the community whose very expressions look beaten down, and they may not even try to dress themselves up anymore. Look at it as temporary. That beaten expression will soon leave with a big dose of the love of God. If they don't show up in nicer clothes after a few weeks, someone might show them a closet with some clothes in it (hung on hangers with dignity) to give away.

If a visitor has more problems than you can handle, ask an elder or minister or other ladies to help or take over for a while. Beware of the victim-rescuer-persecutor triangle/cycle which I explained in my book, *APPLIED CHRISTIANITY: A HANDBOOK OF 500 GOOD WORKS*.

FOLLOW UP FOR CONVERSIONS

As your visitor works through her problems by learning what the Bible tells her, she will become curious about other things in the Bible.

Someone should approach her after her second visit to see if she'd like to study the Bible in her home on whatever subjects she desires. Tell her you'll learn together and bring your concordance. Bible studies always lead to talk about salvation, so be ready to ask her if she'd like to see how the first-century people became Christians. Then be prepared to go through the conversions in Acts and all the Bible verses on baptism.

After about a month of attending, turn your new class member from just a visitor-learner to a learner-teacher. Encourage her to tell her friends about what she's learning in class and the private Bible studies. EVEN IF YOU HAVE ONLY ONE VISITOR to start out, your congregation will grow. Use that visitor as your NUCLEUS. She knows people your congregation doesn't know. As she tells her friends and brings them in, members (men and women) in your congregation can be on the standby to start teaching them and becoming their special friend.

By then turning her into a learn-teacher-recruiter, your visitor will gradually let go of dependence on you, and you can move on to helping someone else.

ADVERTISING

A friendly warning: Do not get involved with bringing people in from your community unless your group decides ahead of time two things: (1) You're willing to put in the time to create your advertising campaign, and (2) You're willing to temporarily sacrifice old friends so you can sit with in class and associate with outside of class strangers you may not have chosen to be part of your social group.

A note about associating with strangers. Sometimes we Christians don't see each other during the week. We love each other, and we look forward to class time. But, if we're going to bring in strangers from the community to try to save their souls, we're going to have to do some substituting. We may have to arrive before the visitors so we can do our talking, or call each other more during the week. If visitors don't make new friends among people in your group, they will not come back and your advertising efforts will have been wasted. Sacrifice time with your old friends for a little while, and the soul you save will be eternally grateful.

Suggestions and instructions are given for use of each advertising and public relations item included in this manual. You may photocopy whichever portions you need; but we ask you do so only for your group. All materials are given in alphabetic order by the woman's name, Abigail being first and Tamar last.

Advertising and public relations has one basic difference: Advertising you pay for, public relations you do not pay for. There is some of both in this manual. If something does not appear that you'd like to try, write and I will try to put something together for you, and perhaps include it in the next published advertising manual.

LIMIT PERIOD OF STUDY

If you are planning to use this material as a community outreach, remember, people are busy. They will give you a few weeks, but will not give you eternity.

Your student book is actually three books in one. Originally, each book had twelve lessons from four women. Therefore, it may be beneficial to only offer one Bible woman series of three lessons at a time. Your survey will tell you which issue are most wanted in your community.

Once the lessons on the one Bible woman are completed, it gives busy people a chance to drop out and for you to advertise another woman. By advertising one woman at a time, it gives you more opportunities to advertise.

When you quote statistics, rather than use those that are national, you may wish to quote statistics of your community or your state.

How to Use This Advertising Material

ANONYMOUS SURVEY

This survey was developed to help you decide which Bible women to study. You may use the same survey in your congregation as in the community. It is also a form of advertising.

When you hold the survey in your congregation, you should try to reach your Sunday-morning crowd. If possible, ask that the closing announcements include the request that all the women remain seated a few minutes while the men leave. Have women lined up to quickly pass out the surveys in each row.

They are self-explanatory, so do not read the directions already on the form orally and tie up their time any longer than necessary. Just announce that they will be collected at the door by one of your ladies. Human nature and good intentions being what they are, don't expect them to fill out the forms and turn them in later.

You can also take a survey of your neighborhood by calling a sampling of about 35 ladies. Identify yourself by name and as being from the church of Christ.

"We are doing a random survey of women in our neighborhood. Is there a lady there I can speak with briefly?"

"We're doing a random survey by phone number only, and do not know your name. We're not trying to sell anything. Do you have a couple minutes to answer 12 quick yes-no questions? [If yes,] Have you or a friend experienced any of the following: [read questions]."

"After we tally up the survey, our ladies will be offering some free classes on some of these subjects. Would you like us to notify you when we do?"

If a conversation starts to get lengthy, ask if you can call her back.

Dear Christian Sister: We want to serve you better in areas that would help your daily Christian living. Therefore, please help us by checking applicable items below. Do NOT sign your name.

I or a friend have had problems with:

_____ My young/grown children
_____ Having been raped or an incest victim
_____ Having to move all the time
_____ Being widowed and/or remarrying
_____ Talking to people about Christianity
_____ Working hard and hardly getting anything done
_____ Homosexuality among family or friends
_____ Suffering and death of a loved one
_____ An unfaithful mate
_____ Why people don't understand the Bible alike
_____ An abusive mate
_____ Obstacles in the way of my dreams
_____ The occult

_____ Other_____

_____ Other_____

Ladies Bible Classes will be offered in the future dealing with issues most indicated by ladies in our congregation and their friends.

Please fold in fourths and hand in to woman at the door as you leave.

May be photocopied

RADIO SPOT

Prepare your radio spot by selecting the radio blurbs for each woman you will be studying. Each blurb is approximately 5 seconds long. Insert them at the beginning of your announcement and end with our suggested conclusion. It should err on the short side of 30 seconds; never on the long side. So read it over and over slowly until you have 28-30 seconds.

Then record it onto an MP3 disc. One of the ladies should read it with one or more ladies humming "Amazing Grace" or "Just As I Am" or some other hymn that is easily recognizable in the first few bars. The station may wish you to re-record it on their equipment, but at least your original tape will give them an idea what you want.

Select a variety of radio stations—easy listening, rock, classical, country, talk—to reach different kinds of people. Also, you may run into prejudice against your topics of study at some stations. Call them to see if they give charitable organizations free 30-second spots. Explain yours is about some social problems and sponsored by your congregation and is free. If they do, ask who is in charge of it.

Take in person or mail the radio spot to them, both in writing and on cassette. Then call in a couple days later to see if they received it.

Request that it be run a week before your class begins.

30-SECOND RADIO SPOT

Insert blurb of first woman to be studied here

Insert blurb of second woman to be studied here

Insert blurb of third woman to be studied here

Insert blurb of fourth woman to be studied here

A free 3-week series is being offered to help women cope with these problems. Come to the Church of Christ at [give a landmark, as people don't memorize addresses] starting [date and time]. Remember, the Church of Christ at [landmark of location], at [date and time]. We care.

RADIO SPOT BLURBS

ABIGAIL Each year an estimated six million women are beaten by the men they love.

ENDORA Out of the nearly 50,000 witches in America are white middle-class women. One-fourth of Americans believe in witchcraft.

ESTHER Morally, American women are superior to American men according a national survey. Yet they are paid only 75% of what men are doing the same job.

GOMER About 50% of America's married couples commit adultery. Yet only 17% of the men and 10% of the women plan to leave their spouse

JOB'S WIFE One-fourth of America's households are touched by a crime. One out of every six funerals in America is for a young person.

LOT'S WIFE It took only 3 years for 24 US cases of AIDS among homosexual men to expand to 7,000 victims. It took only 7 more years to explode into 180,000 victims. Why is it spreading?

MARTHA Only about half of Attention Deficit Disorder children grow up to lead work around their problem and lead productive lives. Time management is nearly an impossibility for these adults.

PRISCILLA There are thousands of denominations in America. Is the Bible that much harder than our court system or the IRS rules and exceptions?

REBECCA Over a million minors leave their homes every year. Two-thirds run away because their parents are physically and/or sexually abusing them. One-third leave because they are abusing their parents and were asked to leave.

RUTH Nearly 20 percent of all former homemakers are having major problems being accepted back into the workforce, regardless of their education.

SARAH Nearly half our population moves at least once every ten years.

TAMARA A woman is raped every six minutes in America. 70% were planned in advance. Two-thirds are molested by a close family member..

RADIO TALK SHOW

This is not as scary as you might think. There is usually some radio station in each community that has short 15-minute interviews with people representing causes of general public interest. Often these are held around noon, late at night, before or after the news, or weekends.

If you do not know a radio station that does this, call around to several until you find one. If you live in a large community, you may wish to try to get on radio stations with different type listeners.

When you call, ask to speak with the general manager if you don't know if they have such a talk show. If you do, ask to speak with the producer of that show. First, state a couple of the statistics on the issue your class will be talking about. Second, tell them that your group is offering a free series on _____. Offer to send or bring them further written material you have on the subject. You will get this material from the TODAY'S WORLD, BIBLE WORLD, and visual aids to your lessons. Then ask what it would take for you to be a guest on their talk show.

If they like the material and decide to invite you to be a guest, tell them you will make out a list of questions for the program host to ask you.

Practice ahead of time answering the questions. Being radio, you can keep all the notes you want. However, do not write your answers out word for word. If you do, you'll be tempted to read them and it will come across that way. So just jot down word reminders in the form of a list of what you want to say in answering each question.

Your station may be willing to record your session with the host ahead of time in order to cut sections with possible glitches.

A VARIATION of this would be to call a PHONE-IN TALK SHOW while on the air and tell them about your series. Again, first emphasize the statistics. At the end tell about the series that is free and open to the public. It's easy to get on these.

PUBLIC-ACCESS TELEVISION

By law, television cable companies must allow free air time to the public on their specified channel, often found in the 50s and 60s on your dial. Programs can be developed in their studio or out in the community.

On such channels, you are likely to see college courses, city council meetings, religious programs, cooking, guitar or exercise classes, clubs explaining why they exist, musical or drama groups trying to get experience and hoping to be spotted by a talent scout. This is a non-profit channel for non-profit organizations and individuals.

Public-access programs cannot carry advertising or request money. The moral code is very strict, with the allowance of absolutely no obscenity or indecent material.

The person(s) using the TV equipment must take a month-or-two course—usually at night for a couple hours a week. Participants are taught to (1) use the TV camera in a studio and in the field, (2) use the microphones and audio deck in a studio and in the manual, (3) use lighting in a studio and in the field, (4) work the video and sound panel when using more than one camera and microphone, (5) edit (dub and splice) film, (6) and write/produce a show overall. Everything is free. Some grants are available if you want to make a different backdrop, etc.

For your show, you could play the Heart-to-Heart M while showing PowerPoint of people in modern clothes acting it out. Or you could have an interview-type show with the teacher explaining the problems your class will discuss; or with people who've experienced these problems explaining how God helped them. Use your imagination. (Also use the men in your congregation if you need more manpower.)

Allow about two weeks lead time after production is completed to get your show worked into the programming schedule.

Katheryn Maddox Haddad

NEWS RELEASE

A separate mini-article is included in your manual for each of the twelve Bible women currently part of this series. Select the appropriate mini-articles matching the Bible women you will be studying. Insert them in the news release as shown.

Next decide on a headline. They may not use your suggestion, but it will give them a hint on how you'd like it to read. If you will be studying four Bible women in the quarter, make it read something like, _____, _____, _____, _____ ARE TOPICS OF FREE SERIES. I have changed the mini-article topics of some of the women to gear them more toward public interest. For instance, Priscilla's "True to the End" would appeal to Christians, but "Christian Unity" would appeal more to the general public.

Type your article in the format given, double spaced, listing number of words. Allow at least one-inch borders all the way around to give editors room to write instructions to the typesetters, layout people, etc.

Newspapers love PHOTOGRAPHS. It enhances your possibility of being published. So take a photo of your ladies planning the class or the lady teaching it, or the group leaders. Send that along with the news release. Write full names of everyone in the photo on the back, along with a caption telling what you're doing.

Call a newspaper and find out the names of both city editor and religious editor. Some newspapers will consider your news release religious news and other city news. Ask the switchboard for the correct spelling of their names, and make sure you get their title correct. Also get the newspaper's mailing address.

Mail your news release to each of them by name about two weeks before your class begins. Then call them to see if they received the story and are interested. If not, try another newspaper.

Name of Church

Address
Phone
Contact Person
_____ Words

FOR IMMEDIATE RELEASE

Insert Mini-Article of First Bible Women to be Studied Here

Insert Mini-Article of Second Bible Women to be Studied Here

Insert Mini-Article of Third bible woman to be Studied Here

Insert Mini-Article of Fourth Bible woman to be Studied Here

Beginning [date], the ladies of the Church of Christ are offering a series on coping with difficult every-day problems. "This series is not designed to change the people around us," says author Katheryn Haddad, a former social worker. "It is also not designed to make women's decisions for them. The series provides spiritual resources from the Bible on which we may call when they are needed."

Pre-registration is being accepted by phone at ___-_____. Registration will also be accepted on the first day. However, since printed materials and cassette tapes must be ordered for each participant, it is urged that everyone pre-register.

This free series will be held at the Church of Christ, [address], every [day] at [time]. Child care will be provided.

END

ABIGAIL (ABUSED)
(mini-article)

According to the *New York Times* in 1992, each year an estimated six million women are beaten by the men they love. Adding verbal beating to this would multiply the figure.

Most women do not knowingly marry an abuser, for they often do not show signs of abuse before the wedding. These men are often confident to the cocky point, cloaking low self-esteem with arrogance and control of others through charm. Then after marriage, their paranoia begins to show up.

There are usually three stages to the cycle of abuse. The first stage is the tension-building phase where he becomes highly critical to the point that nothing she does pleases him.

Stage two is when the physical abuse begins. It is premeditated and occurs at the time and place he selects, and involves whichever parts of her body he decides to attack. He carries it out whether or not there is provocation, and that further confuses his wife. All he can say is that she deserves it for making him unhappy.

The third stage is repentance. He begs her forgiveness, promises never to do it again, and may even offer to go to counseling.

ADD ONLY IF NO OTHER BIBLE WOMEN WILL BE STUDIED

Why do women stay in such marriages? Some hang on because children are involved, for financial reasons, or they hope their husbands will mature and change their behavior. Nearly everyone marries for life, and is willing to work at it.

Topics discussed will be (1) maintaining one's self-esteem, (2) creating patience, (3) keeping one's values sorted out, (4) establishing communication, (5) creating courage, (6) utilizing a support system.

Abigail, on whom this series was based, was an abused wife in the Bible. Her husband's name was Nabal. Her story is in 1 Samuel 25. Nabal was not only abusive of her, but to everyone around him. Abigail made herself a go-between for business dealings, with neighbors, with servants—just about everyone. She had to work to keep her household running as smoothly and as peaceful as possible.

WITCH OF ENDOR (OCCULT)
(mini-article)

Nearly half of Americans believe in ghosts, nearly one third believe some people have magical powers, and one fourth believe in witchcraft, according to researchers James Patterson and Peter Kim learned in a 1990 national survey. Furthermore, one out of every twenty of us has participated in some ritual of satanism or witchcraft.

According to the *Encyclopedia of Witches and Witchcraft*, America has approximately (no one knows for sure) 50,000 witches. That is 1000 in every state, and approximately 10 per county (on average). Witches rule over covens of 13 people. A majority of witches are white middle-class women.

The Witches Anti-Discrimination Lobby led by Dr. Leo Lovis Martello, lobbies for religious freedom for witches such as allowing legal holidays on their sacred days. Among them is Halloween, or the evening (e'en) before the hallowed day of November 1. Witches sometimes claim healing powers.

According to *Books in Print*, there are nearly 3,000 books currently published for the benefit of understanding and pursuing the arts of witchcraft.

ADD ONLY IF NO OTHER BIBLE WOMEN WILL BE STUDIED

Psychology Today reports that about 70 percent of all college students they surveyed resort to some kind of magic such as using lucky pens. Even those who gamble on the stock market or just the lotto rely on "lucky numbers" to obtain significant amounts of money.

Ladies of the Church of Christ will be studying this issue. Topics discussed will be (1) Understanding why we really help others, (2) Understanding why we want to know more than others, (3) Drawing the line in seeking answers to life's mysteries, (4) Stopping before we become a proponent, (5) Knowing that what is not of God is against God, (6) Following God's instructions to reach the spirit world.

ESTHER (BEAUTY & THE BEAST)
(mini-article)

Morally, American women are superior to American men according to a nation-wide survey by James Patterson and Peter Kim in 1990. That makes them better employers and employees. Overall, they are more honest than men, do drugs/alcohol less, and are solid in their relationships.

Women do not lie to their boss or co-workers as much as men do, they are more responsible, and much less likely to goof off at work, leave early, or take home office supplies. Women can be trusted more, are less willing to compromise their values to get a promotion, are less likely to slander their boss or fight with their co-workers, and are more likely to quit their job if they find out their company is doing anything illegal.

Yet, according to *Information Please Almanac*, women are paid overall not quite 72% what men are doing the same job. Furthermore, only 3 out of 50 governors in America are women; there are only 27 female members in the House of Representatives compared with 406 men, and only 3 woman senators compared with 97 men.

ADD ONLY IF NO OTHER BIBLE WOMEN WILL BE STUDIED

One of the most ill-tempered and yet famous world politicians was Xerxes, Emperor of the

Persian Empire about 550 BC. He was known to have beaten the sea with 300 lashes and then branded because it washed away the bridge he had built to cross over into Athens and conquer Greece. His wife was Queen Esther as found in the Bible. She successfully talked him out of some of his craziness such as extermination of the Jews.

Ladies of the Church of Christ will be studying this issue. Topics will be (1) Being an example to others in difficult situations, (2) Making sure we really want what we wish for, (3) Keeping up our health during stress, (4) Understanding the value of nutrition, (5) Understanding the value of tact, (6) Being willing to stand out from the crowd for right.

GOMER (UNFAITHFUL)
(mini-article)

Forty-four percent of Americans believe most marriages will end in divorce. The major problem is communication. But the cost second is adultery. Slightly over half the women and slightly under half the men believe their spouses have committed adultery, according to a recent study by James Patterson and Peter Kim.

Of those committing adultery, 62% don't believe there's anything wrong with it. Although 67% of the men admit to committing adultery, only 17 percent plan to leave their wives. Of the 40% of the men who admit to committing adultery, only 10% of them plan to leave their husbands. Overall, only 28 percent plan to stop committing adultery.

Where are these people coming from? In the same survey, one-fifth of the school children they anonymously interviewed admitted to having lost their virginity before the age of 13. Two-thirds admitted to having sex before they turned 16. Yet only 10 percent said they do it for love. Overall, they don't even like it.

ADD ONLY IF NO OTHER BIBLE WOMEN WILL BE STUDIED

They say they do it because of peer pressure that is not countered by teachers and parents. So where are the peers getting it to pass it on to each other? At least 90% of sexual encounters on television is between couples who are not married to each other. Add to that the lyrical suggestions of many of their popular rock songs, and the gentle nudges of the fashion world, and the stage is set.

Ladies of the Church of Christ will be studying how to survive an adulterous marriage. Topics will be (1) Knowing the foundation of marriage, (2) Working to build a solid marriage, (3) Facing unfaithfulness, (4) Trying to hold it together, (5) Knowing the price we're willing to pay for it, (6) Coping with marriage breakdown.

JOB'S WIFE (UNBEARABLE LOSS)
(mini-article)

One-fourth of America's households are touched by a crime according to the National Crime Survey and Bureau of Justice Statistics. Annual insurance claims average over $43 billion for automobile losses, $15 and a half billion for miscellaneous property losses, $3 and a half billion for losses due to fire, and $28 million for losses due to burglary and theft.

One out of every six funerals in America is for a young person under age 25 down to birth. In general, 71 of these young people die from illnesses, 16 percent die from accidents, 8 percent die from suicide, and 5 percent die from homicide.

Euthanasia, the act of causing someone's death in order to end mental or physical suffering is becoming a big topic in America. People claiming its virtues say they have the right to die with dignity. But when they bring in a second person, it turns from suicide to murder. Murder, not by passively pulling the plug on life-support systems, but by actively providing machines or drugs as weapons of death. Questions surround it. How do we know for sure they'll never get better? How do we know they weren't "brainwashed" into saying they want to die to ease their family's burdens?

ADD ONLY IF NO OTHER BIBLE WOMEN WILL BE STUDIED

Job's wife in the Bible not only faced the loss of the family income to robbers, but she buried all ten of her children, and then watched her husband beg to die.

Ladies of the Church of Christ will be studying facing unbearable loss. Topics discussed will be (1) Helping us face financial setbacks, (2) Helping us face challenges to our faith, (3) Coping with the death of children, (4) Coping with the grieving process, (5) Dealing with shattered faith, (6) trusting that God loves us no matter what.

LOT'S WIFE (HOMOSEXUALITY)
(mini-article)

Remember when there were only two dozen victims of AIDS in all of America? That was just in 1981. Although originally discovered among homosexual men in Africa in the early 1970s, it took just one decade to cross the ocean and implant its deathly seed on our soil and spread to the two dozen homosexual men here.

Three years! It took only 3 years for those 24 cases to grow to 7,000 cases. It took only 7 more years to explode into 180,000 victims in America. Worldwide, in just 22 years, AIDS grew from a couple of cases to an estimated 12 million victims.

In 1985, 75 percent of AIDS victims were homosexual men, 20 percent were drug abusers, and 5 percent were newborn babies. Today, the fastest-growing group of people getting AIDS is women. If this is a homosexual disease, how is it happening?

In the book, *The Day America Told the Truth,* only two-third of those with AIDS tell their spouses/lovers. Although heterosexual men have up to 17 partners in their lifetime, homosexual men have at least 100, or an average of one lover for every month of the year.

ADD ONLY IF NO OTHER BIBLE WOMEN WILL BE STUDIED

Lot and his family of Bible times lived in a highly-homosexual community called Sodom.

Even the community leaders were homosexual. All they wanted to do was be left alone to their own lifestyle.

Ladies of the Church of Christ will be studying this issue. Topics to be discussed are (1) Guiding young people to right decisions, (2) Living among the immoral, (3) Understanding the militancy of homosexuality, (4) Understanding the Creator's hatred for it, (5) Understanding what is wrong with it, (6) Learning when to get out of a bad situation.

MARTHA (TIME MANAGEMENT)
(mini-article)

Attention Deficit Disorder is found only among school children. Right? Wrong. This problem that interferes with people concentrating on any subject effectively causes children to become bad students who feel distracted by the very presence of other people in the classroom. It also causes problems in adults.

We all get it sometimes. We've dialed a phone number, our minds drifted, and when someone said "hello" at the other end of the line, we had to ask with embarrassment, "Who did I call?". We've all driven some distance and arrived at our destination wondering, "How did I get here?". Who hasn't gone into a room to get something, then stood there bewildered asking ourselves, "Now what did I come in here for?". Others have it for a lifetime.

Dr. Gabrielle Weiss and Dr. Lily Hechtman of Montreal followed 100 of these hyperactive children for 15 years into adulthood. Only about half had been able to work around their attention problem and lead productive lives. The National Institute of Mental Health at Bethesda, MD, in late 1990 reported that adults who suffered from ADD since childhood had markedly lower brain activity in the area which controls both mental and physical movements.

ADD ONLY IF NO OTHER BIBLE WOMEN WILL BE STUDIED

Ladies of the Church of Christ will be studying wheel spinning and time management at it relates to Martha in the Bible, a close friend of Jesus who wasn't ready for him when he arrived for dinner. "Adults with this affliction should be list makers," said Katheryn Haddad, author of the series. "If they still cannot function, they should ask someone to help them carry out certain things and not be ashamed."

Topics to be discussed are (1) Learning what gets in the way of hospitality, (2) Understanding impulsive behavior, (3) Getting control of our time, (4) Accepting ourselves without complaint, (5) Setting priorities, (6) Remaining cool, calm and collected.

PRISCILLA (RELIGIOUS UNITY)
(mini-article)

Christianity, started with but one "church." According to *Information Please Almanac,* today there are 39 major Christian denominations in America. But more than 26 million Americans belong to various "other" denominations with less than 4,000 members, taking the number to thousands of denominations.

What happened to the one church? People today erroneously agree it is impossible for everyone to believe the Bible alike. Many of the "founders" of America's denominations sought and begged their followers for Christian unity. As brilliant as they were, how could they ask something that was impossible?

As smart as God is, how could he have caused a book to be written that couldn't be understood? Courts of our nation can come to a large consensus in matters involving thousands of laws in hundreds of volumes bursting at their printed seams. The average person can come to pretty much the same conclusion as even the IRS when working out income taxes, despite their thousands of regulations and exceptions.

So, how hard can the Bible be—a single volume with about 1,000 pages—for us to figure out and come to the same conclusion on?

ADD ONLY IF NO OTHER BIBLE WOMEN WILL BE STUDIED

First-century people faced the same dilemma. Except then they had to decide which religion to follow—Moslem, Jewish, Christian, Pantheism, or that of the many gods which we in our century consider mythological. How did people who ended up being Christians make their decisions?

Ladies of the Church of Christ will study how first-century people became Christians, and what it took for them to remain faithful despite all the pressures to go back to old religious beliefs— or even no belief at all. Topics to be discussed are (1) The Price of the Search, (2) The Price of Sharing, (3) The Price of Salvation.

REBECCA (FIGHTING CHILDREN)
(mini-article)

Over a million minors leave their homes every year. Of those arrested for being runaways, about 80 percent are white and from middle-income families. Two-thirds run away because their parents are physically and/or sexually abusing them One-third leave because they are abusing their parents and were asked to leave. About one-third never return home.

If parents chose sides among siblings, such feuds often carry over long into adulthood. They refuse to talk to each other, and sometimes also refuse to talk to their parents.

Dr. Michael Kahn, professor of clinical psychology at the University of Hartford, reports that about one-third of all adult siblings don't get along. Often there are unresolved feelings of anger, jealousy or disappointment. Parents may have provided examples by not talking to their own brothers and sisters.

Often feuders forget what they're feuding about and it just becomes a matter of pride. Then it is difficult to let go of their righteous indignation and forgive.

ADD ONLY IF NO OTHER BIBLE WOMEN WILL BE STUDIED

According to a study by James Patterson and Peter Kim, 86 percent of children lie to their parents, and 75 percent of parents lie to their children. But 83 percent of the parents are suspicious that their children are lying to them, and 75 percent of the children are suspicious that their parents are lying to them. Trust between parents and children has broken down in America, and so have relationships.

Ladies of the Church of Christ will study problems with children at home and grown children. Topics to be discussed are (1) Identifying problems between siblings, (2) Helping siblings get along, (3) Not being a "controlling" mother, (4) Dealing with deceit, (5) Coping when your children do wrong, (6) Maintaining faith when families fall apart.

RUTH (WIDOWHOOD AND REMARRIAGE)
(mini-article)

What are the chances of becoming widowed in America today? One out of every 400 men ages 25-34 will die this year. One out of every 200 men ages 35-44 will die. One out of every 100 men ages 45-54 will die. One out of every 50 men ages 55 to 64 will die. One out of every 25 men ages 65-75 will die.

The new widow faces emotional turmoil and loss of coupled friends. She faces many possible financial hardship. She faces the decision of whether or ever remarry.

The National Displaced Homemakers Network reports that in 1980 there were nearly 14 million displaced homemakers; in 1990 there were an additional million and a half of them.

Nearly 20 percent of all former homemakers are having major problems being accepted back into the workforce, regardless of their education. At any one time, 41% are forced to work parttime, and 50% have not been hired by anyone. Over one in three live below the federal poverty line. Of these, 76 percent are white, 18 percent are black, and 6 percent are Hispanic.

ADD ONLY IF NO OTHER BIBLE WOMEN WILL BE STUDIED

Wives must make their husbands sit down with them so they can work out the inevitable widowhood of one of them. What needs to be considered? A major topic is finances. Find out about bank accounts, insurance policies, birth certificates, social security numbers, military numbers, former places of employment. Is the wife able to go to work if necessary? Does she know who to call if the furnace breaks down?

Ladies of the Church of Christ will be studying this issue. Topics of discussion are (1) Adjusting to widowhood, (2) Understanding widowhood, (3) Making social adjustments, (4) Making economic adjustments, (5) Choosing a second husband, (6) Blending two lives with habits already formed

SARAH (MOVING AGAIN)

(mini-article)

Between 1980 and 1990, approximately 20 million families moved. If each household averaged four people, that's 80 million people uprooted, or nearly half America's population. It's become the American way of life.

Not only does this uproot adults, but it is often very traumatic on children who are sometimes just told not to be cry babies. Children, with no control over their environment, lose friends forever. They often silently experience the same grief they would with loss by death.

To help children cope with the loss, a scrapbook can be put together of the house they lived in, the old school, the old neighborhood, friends they'll be leaving behind. Parents should also write down the mailing addresses of their children's friends.

The chamber of commerce in a new location can be contacted to send for maps, pictures, brochures on things to do, places to go, schools, churches, etc. This can be done both on the city and state levels.

Parents making house-hunting trips without the children can bring back photographs of the new home, new school, new neighborhood, and possibly other children their age.

ADD ONLY IF NO OTHER BIBLE WOMEN WILL BE STUDIED

Ladies of the Church of Christ will be studying this issue, based on the life of Sarah in the Bible, wife of Abraham, who moved 12 times in her life searching for what may have seemed the elusive dream.

Topics of discussion are (1) Learning how to cope with being uprooted, (2) Learning how to say good-bye, (3) Keeping children content on long trips, (4) Seeing the good side of moving, (5) Adjusting to a new community, (6) Keeping up courage when all seems futile.

TAMAR (RAPED)
(mini-article)

A woman is raped every six minutes in America, according to the FBI. Seventy percent were planned in advance. Two-thirds of all rape victims in America are molested by a close family member or parent.

One out of every 12 male college students admit committing acts which meet the legal definition of rape (MS Foundation Study, 1988). One out of every 7 Americans was raped as a child. One in every nine men and one-third of all women will be sexually assaulted during their lifetime.

Adults molested as children can exhibit any of the following: Physical violence, sexual dysfunctions, obsessive/compulsive behavior, unfounded distrust in others, paranoia, self-destructive behavior, phobias, thoughts of suicide, eating disorders, multiple personalities.

Mothers Against Raping Children (MARC) and Mothers of Sexually Abused Infants and Children (MOSAIC) are two organizations organized to provide moral and physical support to parents with molested children fleeing from rapist relatives.

ADD ONLY IF NO OTHER BIBLE WOMEN WILL BE STUDIED

America has mothers who have proof their children were sexually molested but are being forced to allow visitation rights with the abusive father. Women who are raped debate whether to take their rapists to court, fearing they'll be tagged with the scarlet letter "R". Forgiveness, although necessary for emotional freedom, is nearly impossible.

Ladies of the Church of Christ will study coping with being molested. Topics discussed will include (1) Being a comfort to the victim, (2) Consoling one's self, (3) Avoiding rape situations, (4) Knowing how far to trust, (5) Recovering from Rape, (6) Handling feelings of revenge.

NEWSPAPER ADVERTISEMENT

News is printed free. However, you may not be able to get your article printed. Or the newspaper editor may ask if you were planning to have any paid ads on the series. What they'll be saying is, "If you scratch my back, I'll scratch yours." In that case, you should run a paid ad. Or they may not make this a requirement for printing your news release, but you may wish to supplement the article with ads anyway.

You can request which page you want your ad placed. Consider your topic or topics. Topics such as Rebecca, Jobetta and Tamar might appear on the family page. Topics such as Abigail, Endora, Gomer, Ruth, and Lottie might appear in a section that normally deals with society's problems. Esther might appear on the government news page. Sarah and Martha might appear in the homemaking section. Priscilla would appear in the religious section.

You can also request the part of the page you would like your ad to appear. The top left corner is where people's eyes stop first. Then the top right corner. The middle is next. Try to get your ad off the bottom of the page. They cooperate with you as much as they can.

Ads are charged by column inch. The ad in this manual is 4" by 4", which would make it about 2 column inches wide. In that case, you would be charged for a total of 8 column inches. Some newspapers have a different number of columns on a page than others. There is enough white space around the edge of the ad that you can decrease the width a little if you like, or add a wide border to widen it a little—and also draw attention to it.

This ad is as close to camera ready as possible. Hand deliver it to the newspaper. You may wish to insert the social topics of your lessons in the heart. They will help you do this and also add dates and address.

Free Social Issues Series
Inside the Hearts Of Bible Women

Dates—Time
Church of Christ, Address, Phone

Instead of the heart, you may wish to photocopy the cover of my book. I purchased rights to the photo, and I have the rights to the cover. I give you permission to use it for advertising.

BULLETIN ANNOUNCEMENTS

Turn these in one at a time to the person writing the bulletin a week ahead of time. Make sure you do indeed have a poster and letters ready when it is printed or take that part out of the announcement.

You may wish to have an insert in your bulletin with this announcement. You may shorten it and insert a flyer in the bulletin.

Write a shorter version of it, or talk to the person making announcements at your assemblies to see if they will read it aloud to the congregation. Many people don't read the bulletin.

WEEK ONE:
ATTENTION LADIES: As a result of the recent survey we took of ladies in our congregation, we are offering a special series called "INSIDE THE HEARTS OF BIBLE WOMEN."

This is also an outreach to women in our community. Therefore, letters to your neighbors and friends are sitting on a table near the bulletin board. Take however many you feel you could use. Just address your envelopes to "Lady of the House" or by name if you know them personally.

Study books will be provided to each woman attending. So sign up today. And send out your letters as soon as possible.

WEEK TWO:
ATTENTION LADIES: Have you signed up for "INSIDE THE HEARTS OF BIBLE WOMEN" yet? Do not hesitate. This series could forever change your attitude toward the women in the Bible and what they'd be like if they lived among us today.

Study books will be provided to each woman attending. All those who would like to attend, please sign up on the bulletin board. If you haven't sent letters to your neighbors and friends yet, do so out as soon as possible.

WEEK THREE:
ATTENTION LADIES: Last call for sign-ups to "INSIDE THE HEARTS OF BIBLE WOMEN." This special series will be covering [list title and subtitle of each Bible woman]. If you don't need this series, there will be someone there who does and who needs your courage. Come and share it with us.

We will be meeting in [room] every [day] at [time] for coffee and [time] for the class. Child care will be provided.

SPEECH

Contact your chamber of commerce to locate women's groups to talk to. The program chair ladies of those who meet formally are always looking for interesting topics and volunteers. Others who meet informally may want to get everyone together for a special luncheon just to hear what you have to say. Consider the Garden Club, Women's Golfing or Bowling League, Newcomers Club, Lioness Club, University Women, Women in Construction, National Association of Women Business Owners, and a host of others. There's even your own Ladies Bible Class.

"Current Issues" with respect to the problems experienced by all of the twelve Bible woman are provided. You may tailor your speech to whichever Bible women your class will be studying. Also a "Life Summary" of each Bible woman is provided to help your audience understand who these Bible women are. Insert them in your speech where indicated.

Find out how much time you will be allowed for your presentation. It takes approximately one and a half minutes to read the "Social Issues" part for each Bible woman, and another half minute to read the "Life Summary." If your series will cover four Bible women, that would be a total of six minutes for the "Social Issues" and two minutes for the "Life Summary." Your introduction is about one minute, and your conclusion is about two minutes. Thus, your speech would be about eleven minutes long. (Of course whoever does the speaking will have to read and time it for her own reading speed.)

If you want the speech to be longer, you may add to this time by playing a five-minute segment of one of the Bible women from your MP3 discs. And you can add another five minutes by handing out flyers and answering general questions at the end.

If you do use the tape, before leaving home, find the five-minute segment you want to play and have it wound to that point. Take your own tape recorder. Ask ahead of time if they have a microphone. Arrive early. Test everything before anyone arrives.

In handling questions from your group, some may be opposed to what the series is about. (I think homosexuality would be the only disagreeable topic though.) In that case, just say something like, "Although we understand there are other points of view, this is what we believe, and so this is what the series is about."

Do not argue with her. Just go on and ask for another question. If she persists, just answer again, "I appreciate the fact that you have another point of view," and go on. By now probably one of the other ladies in your audience will elbow her and give her the quiet sign. However, it probably won't happen at all.

Here is What You Can Say

Chairman, program chairman, and ladies of [name of organization]: Thank you for the opportunity you've given me to speak to you a few moments about some critical women's issues in today's world: [List the four topics your class will be studying.]

Insert Current Issue of First Bible Woman to be Studied Here
Insert Current Issue of Second Bible Woman to be Studied Here
Insert Current Issue of Third Bible Woman to be Studied Here

Insert Current Issue of Fourth Bible Woman to be Studied Here

I have brought along an MP3 disc that goes along with this series and would like to play a short excerpt for you at this time. [*Have a player already set up with a microphone. Play a five-minute selection of the disc.*]

And now we come to the reason I am here today. You may be struggling with one of these problems alone, hiding it from your friends to save face. And that's okay. I want you to know that you are not alone. It is statistically probable that there are several women right here in this room who are right now facing problems like this. If you are not one of them, you probably know a woman who is.

The ladies of the Church of Christ at [identify a well-known landmark] are offering a short series on coping with these problems. This series is not designed to change other people. It is designed to help you cope with a bad situation. It is also not designed to make your decisions for you. The series provides friendship and spiritual resources on which you may call when you need them.

It is based real women in the Bible who experienced these same problems.

Insert Life Summary of First Bible Woman Here
Insert Life Summary of the Second Bible Woman Here
Insert Life Summary of the Third Bible Woman Here
Insert Life Summary of Fourth Bible Woman Here

I repeat that this is not a how-to-get even with everyone course, but one to give you inner strength when you believe things can get better.

Topics to be covered are....

> (1) List One Lesson Aim From First Bible Woman
> (2) List One Lesson Aim From Second Bible Woman
> (3) List One Lesson Aim From Third Bible Woman
> (4) List One Lesson Aim From Fourth Bible Woman

Although the material was written by a Christian woman and former social worker, it is set up to provide mutual encouragement and not professional counseling. This series is just to let you know there are people who care about you and want to share specific ways of coping with difficult situations. It will last ____ weeks.

The Church of Christ is located at [give address and landmarks]. I have flyers with me I would like to give everyone. A registration form is inside. Or you may prefer to call in your reservation.

Although it is free, we need to know ahead of time how many are coming because of printed material we are ordering for everyone. Also we are providing the dramatic readings of each Bible woman's story on an MP3 disc for everyone. I played you an excerpt from one a few minutes ago.

Whatever your religious background, or if you do not consider yourself religious, we believe we can be of some help to you as you work through your relationships in life.

I would like to hand out the flyers to each of you now. While we are doing that, I will take questions....

Thank you again for inviting me to spend this time with you.

ABIGAIL (ABUSED)

Current Issues

According to the *New York Times,* each year an estimated six million women are beaten by the men they love. Adding verbal beating to this would multiply the figure.

Most women do not knowingly marry an abuser, for they often do not show signs of abuse before the wedding. These men are often confident to the cocky point, cloaking low self-esteem with arrogance and control of others through charm. Then after marriage, their paranoia begins to show up.

There are usually three stages to the cycle of abuse. The first stage is the tension-building phase where he becomes highly critical to the point that nothing she does pleases him.

Stage two is when the physical abuse begins. It is premeditated and occurs at the time and place he selects, and involves whichever parts of her body he decides to attack. He carries it out whether or not there is provocation, and that further confuses his wife. All he can say is that she deserves it for making him unhappy.

The third stage is repentance. He begs her forgiveness, promises never to do it again, and may even offer to go to counseling.

Why do women stay in such marriages? Some hang on because children are involved, for financial reasons, or they hope their husbands will mature and change their behavior.

Life Summary

Abigail was the wife of a very rich and powerful man who abused everyone around him. He even refused to feed King David and his troops after being protected by them. Abigail became an ambassador of goodwill to keep some semblance of peace in her home.

WITCH OF ENDOR (OCCULT)

Current Issues

Nearly half of Americans believe in ghosts, nearly one third believe some people have magical powers, and one fourth believe in witchcraft, according to researchers James Patterson and Peter Kim learned in a 1990 national survey. Furthermore, one out of every twenty of us has participated in some ritual of satanism or witchcraft.

According to the *Encyclopedia of Witches and Witchcraft*, America has approximately (no one knows for sure) 50,000 witches. That is 1000 in every state, and approximately 10 per county (on average). Witches rule over covens of 13 people. A majority of witches are white middle-class women.

The Witches Anti-Discrimination Lobby led by Dr. Leo Lovis Martello, lobbies for religious freedom for witches such as allowing legal holidays on their sacred days. Among them is Halloween, or the evening (e'en) before the hallowed day of November 1. Witches sometimes claim healing powers.

According to *Books in Print,* there are nearly 3,000 books currently published for the benefit of understanding and pursuing the arts of witchcraft.

Psychology Today reports that about 70 percent of all college students they surveyed resort to some kind of magic such as using lucky pens. Even those who gamble on the stock market or just the lotto rely on "lucky numbers" to obtain significant amounts of money.

Life Summary

The Witch of Endor was a very kind-hearted woman in the Bible who acted as a medium. She brought back Samuel from the dead to talk to King Saul. Or did she?

ESTHER (BEAUTY & THE BEAST)

Current Issues

Morally, American women are superior to American men according to a nation-wide survey by James Patterson and Peter Kim in *The Day American Told the Truth..* That makes them better employers and employees. Overall, they are more honest than men, do drugs/alcohol less, and are solid in their relationships.

Women do not lie to their boss or co-workers as much as men do, they are more responsible, and much less likely to goof off at work, leave early, or take home office supplies. Women can be trusted more, are less willing to compromise their values to get a promotion, are less likely to slander their boss or fight with their co-workers, and are more likely to quit their job if they find out their company is doing anything illegal.

Yet, according to *Information Please Almanac,* women are paid overall not quite 72% what men are doing the same job. Furthermore, only 3 out of 50 governors in America are women; there are only 27 female members in the House of Representatives compared with 406 men, and only 3 woman senators compared with 97 men.

Life Summary

One of the most ill-tempered and yet famous world politicians was Xerxes, Emperor of the Persian Empire about 550 BC. He was known to have beaten the sea with 300 lashes and then branded because it washed away the bridge he had built to cross over into Athens and conquer Greece. His wife was Queen Esther as found in the Bible. She successfully talked him out of some of his craziness such as extermination of the Jews.

GOMER (UNFAITHFUL)

Current Issues

Forty-four percent of Americans believe most marriages will end in divorce. The major problem is communication. But the cost second is adultery. Slightly over half the women and slightly under half the men believe their spouses have committed adultery, according to a study by James Patterson and Peter Kim.

Of those committing adultery, 62% don't believe there's anything wrong with it. Although 67% of the men admit to committing adultery, only 17 percent plan to leave their wives. Of the 40% of the men who admit to committing adultery, only 10% of them plan to leave their husbands. Overall, only 28 percent plan to stop committing adultery.

Where are these people coming from? In the same survey, one-fifth of the school children they anonymously interviewed admitted to having lost their virginity before the age of 13. Two-thirds admitted to having sex before they turned 16. Yet only 10 percent said they do it for love. Overall, they don't even like it.

Life Summary

Hosea was a prophet in the Old Testament who married a woman who continually was unfaithful. When they had their first child, Hosea gave him an acceptable name. When they had their second child, he gave this one a name meaning, "I'll not have mercy on you." When they had their third child, he gave it a name meaning, "Not mine."

Finally he divorced her, but kept sending her support which she thought was coming from her lovers. As she grew older her lovers left her and she became a temple prostitute, and finally an old woman and slave. Then he bought her back to be his wife.

JOB'S WIFE (UNBEARABLE LOSS)

Current Issues

One-fourth of America's households are touched by a crime according to the National Crime Survey and Bureau of Justice Statistics. Annual insurance claims average over $43 billion for automobile losses, $15 and a half billion for miscellaneous property losses, $3 and a half billion for losses due to fire, and $28 million for losses due to burglary and theft.

One out of every six funerals in America is for a young person under age 25 down to birth. In general, 71 of these young people die from illnesses, 16 percent die from accidents, 8 percent die from suicide, and 5 percent die from homicide.

Euthanasia, the act of causing someone's death in order to end mental or physical suffering is becoming a big topic in America. People claiming its virtues say they have the right to die with dignity. But when they bring in a second person, it turns from suicide to murder. Murder, not by passively pulling the plug on life-support systems, but by actively providing machines or drugs as weapons of death. Questions surround it. How do we know for sure they'll never get better? How do we know they weren't "brainwashed" into saying they want to die to ease their family's burdens?

Life Summary

Job's wife in the Bible not only faced the loss of the family income to robbers, but she buried all ten of her children, and then watched her husband beg to die. He was full of a hideous boil-like leprosy and they both believed he could never get well.

LOT'S WIFE (HOMOSEXUALITY)

Current Issues

Remember when there were only two dozen victims of AIDS in all of America? That was just in 1981. Although originally discovered among homosexual men in Africa in the early 1970s, it took just one decade to cross the ocean and implant its deathly seed on our soil and spread to the two dozen homosexual men here.

Three years! It took only 3 years for those 24 cases to grow to 7,000 cases. It took only 7 more years to explode into 180,000 victims in America. Worldwide, in just 22 years, AIDS grew from a couple of cases to an estimated 12 million victims.

In 1985, 75 percent of AIDS victims were homosexual men, 20 percent were drug abusers, and 5 percent were newborn babies. Today, the fastest-growing group of people getting AIDS is women. If this is a homosexual disease, how is it happening?

In the book, *The Day America Told the Truth,* only two-third of those with AIDS tell their spouses/lovers. Although heterosexual men have up to 17 partners in their lifetime, homosexual men have at least 100, or an average of one lover for every month of the year.

Life Summary

Lot and his family of Bible times lived in a highly-homosexual community called Sodom. His three daughters apparently became engaged to heterosexuals. Even the community leaders were homosexual. Although they claimed all they wanted to do was be left alone to their own lifestyle, they became very militant. Sodom was destroyed by fire and sulfur. I wonder if there are a couple of keys in this story to the cure of AIDS? Sulfur and abstinence. Do we love homosexuals? Of course we do. Do we cry for those with AIDS? Of course we do. But AIDS is the only disease we have today that is caused by behavior. That scares us to death!

MARTHA (TIME MANAGEMENT)

Current Issues

Attention Deficit Disorder is found only among school children. Right? Wrong. This problem that interferes with people concentrating on any subject effectively causes bad students who feel distracted by the very presence of other people in the classroom. It also causes problems in adults.

We all get it sometimes. We've dialed a phone number, our minds drifted, and when someone said "hello" at the other end of the line, we had to ask with embarrassment, "Who did I call?". We've all driven some distance and arrived at our destination wondering, "How did I get here?". Who hasn't gone into a room to get something, then stood there bewildered asking ourselves, "Now what did I come in here for?". Others have it for a lifetime.

Dr. Gabrielle Weiss and Dr. Lily Hechtman of Montreal followed 100 of these hyperactive children for 15 years into adulthood. Only about half had been able to work around their attention problem and lead productive lives. The National Institute of Mental Health at Bethesda, MD, in late 1990 reported that adults who suffered from ADD since childhood had markedly lower brain activity in the area which controls both mental and physical movements.

Life Summary

Martha was a lovely and faithful follower of Jesus who lived about six miles from Jerusalem. She and her brother and sister had him in her home many times to eat and spend the night. But she had trouble managing her time. Once, when Jesus arrived, she didn't have dinner on the table yet. She was so upset.

PRISCILLA (RELIGIOUS UNITY)

Current Issues

Christianity, started with but one "church." According to *Information Please Almanac, today* there are 39 major Christian denominations in America and thousands of minor denominations.

What happened to the one church? Someone said it is impossible for everyone to believe the Bible alike. Who is that someone? Many of the "founders" of begged their followers for Christian unity. As brilliant as they were, why would they ask the impossible?

As smart as God is, how could he have caused a book to be written that couldn't be understood? Courts of our nation can come to a consensus in matters involving thousands of laws in hundreds of volumes. The average person can come to pretty much the same conclusion as the IRS when working out income taxes, despite their thousands of regulations and exceptions.

How hard can the Bible be—a single volume with about 1,000 pages? Try a game with your friends. Buy a concordance and get one off the internet. This book lists words alphabetically in the Bible and all the verses where they're found. Pick a word, everyone look up each verse using that word, and write down its meaning. Last, write down the conclusion you made on that topic. Compare it with your friends. Eureka! Christian unity!

Life Summary

Priscilla was apparently from a wealthy family in Rome, but was among the Jews exiled by Caesar. She moved to Corinth for a while, then Ephesus, then back to Rome. The Apostle Paul became a good friend and lived in her home at various times. She figured out Jesus was the promised messiah, probably through her own study. People in the first century had to decide what was truth: The Moslem faith, Jewish faith, Pantheism, or the gods we in this century call mythological.

REBECCA (FIGHTING CHILDREN)

Current Issues

Over a million minors leave their homes every year. Of those arrested for being runaways, about 80 percent are white and from middle-income families. Two-thirds run away because their parents are physically and/or sexually abusing them One-third leave because they are abusing their parents and were asked to leave. About one-third never return home.

If parents chose sides among siblings, such feuds often carry over long into adulthood. They refuse to talk to each other, and sometimes also refuse to talk to their parents.

Dr. Michael Kahn, professor of clinical psychology at the University of Hartford, reports that about one-third of all adult siblings don't get along. Often there are unresolved feelings of anger, jealousy or disappointment. Parents may have provided examples by not talking to their own brothers and sisters.

According to a study by James Patterson and Peter Kim, 86 percent of children lie to their parents, and 75 percent of parents lie to their children. But 83 percent of the parents are suspicious that their children are lying to them, and 75 percent of the children are suspicious that their parents are lying to them. Trust between parents and children has broken down in America, and so have relationships.

Life Summary

Rebecca was the wife of Isaac and daughter-in-law of Abraham. They had twin boys who grew up fighting. Jacob badgered Esau all the time, and at his mother's insistence, even lied to get the family inheritance. Esau threatened to kill his brother, so Jacob ran away from home.

RUTH (WIDOWHOOD AND REMARRIAGE)

Current Issues

What are the chances of becoming widowed in America today? One out of every 400 men ages 25-34 will die this year. One out of every 200 men ages 35-44 will die. One out of every 100 men ages 45-54 will die. One out of every 50 men ages 55 to 64 will die. One out of every 25 men ages 65-75 will die.

The new widow faces emotional turmoil and loss of coupled friends. She faces many possible financial hardship. She faces the decision of whether or ever remarry.

The National Displaced Homemakers Network reports that in 1980 there were nearly 14 million displaced homemakers; in 1990 there were an additional million and a half of them.

Nearly 20 percent of all former homemakers are having major problems being accepted back into the workforce, regardless of their education. At any one time, 41% are forced to work part time, and 50% have not been hired by anyone. Over one in three live below the federal poverty line. Of these, 76 percent are white, 18 percent are black, and 6 percent are Hispanic.

Wives must make their husbands sit down with them so they can work out the inevitable widowhood of one of them. What needs to be considered? A major topic is finances. Find out about bank accounts, insurance policies, birth certificates, social security numbers, military

numbers, former places of employment. Is the wife able to go to work?

Life Summary

Ruth was a foreign girl whose husband and father-in-law both died. She went to work in the fields of a rich man who noticed her and made the foremen give her extra pay. Then she proposed to him! They married and became the ancestors of King David and later Jesus.

SARAH (MOVING AGAIN)

Current Issues

Between 1980 and 1990, approximately 20 million families moved. If each household averaged four people, that's 80 million people uprooted, or nearly half America's population. It's become the American way of life.

Not only does this uproot adults, but it is often very traumatic on children who are sometimes just told not to be cry babies. Children, with no control over their environment, lose friends forever. They often silently experience the same grief they would with loss by death.

To help children cope with the loss, a scrapbook can be put together of the house they lived in, the old school, the old neighborhood, friends they'll be leaving behind. Parents should also write down the mailing addresses of their children's friends.

The chamber of commerce in a new location can be contacted to send for maps, pictures, brochures on things to do, places to go, schools, churches, etc. This can be done both on the city and state levels.

Parents making house-hunting trips without the children can bring back photographs of the new home, new school, new neighborhood, and possibly other children their age.

Life Summary

Sarah in the Bible, was wife of Abraham, and moved 12 times in her life searching for what may have seemed the elusive dream. They were delayed several years getting to their promised land, and when they arrived, it was in the middle of a drought. They moved on to Egypt where she was put in Pharaoh's harem temporarily. They moved somewhere else where the neighbors fought. Her niece was killed when Sodom was burned nearby. Nothing ever went right.

TAMAR (RAPED)

Current Issue

A woman is raped every six minutes in America, according to the FBI. Seventy percent were planned in advance. Two-thirds of all rape victims in America are molested by a close family member or parent.

One out of every 12 male college students admit committing acts which meet the legal definition of rape (MS Foundation Study, 1988). One out of every 7 Americans was raped as a child. One in every nine men and one-third of all women will be sexually assaulted during their lifetime.

Adults molested as children can exhibit any of the following: Physical violence, sexual dysfunctions, obsessive/compulsive behavior, unfounded distrust in others, paranoia, self-destructive behavior, phobias, thoughts of suicide, eating disorders, multiple personalities.

Mothers Against Raping Children (MARC) and Mothers of Sexually Abused Infants and Children (MOSAIC) are two organizations organized to provide moral and physical support to parents with molested children fleeing from rapist relatives.

America has mothers who have proof their children were sexually molested but are being forced to allow visitation rights with the abusive father. Women are debating whether to take their rapists to court but are afraid of being tagged with the scarlet letter "R". Forgiveness, although necessary for emotional freedom, is nearly impossible.

Life Summary

Tamar was the daughter of King David. She was raped by one of her half-brothers, and avenged by a full brother. Her father refused to see the other brother for many years and it tore the family apart. She spent the rest of her life living in the home of her full brother. The family never quite got over her rape.

FLYER

The flyer has been developed to include all twelve women currently being offered in INSIDE THE HEARTS OF BIBLE WOMEN. Just check off with a felt-tip pen the ones you will be studying before photocopying them. Cut out and paste inside the heart the topics you will be studying. (Don't include the names of the Bible women since much of the public has no ideas who many of them are.)

The flyer is made to fold in half. But most word processors have programs for tri-fold There are two blank sides. Before photocopying, print the name and address of your congregation on the opposite side from the registration form. On the other blank side, print your congregation's return address in the upper left corner.

Photocopy them on bright colored paper. Enclose them in letters. Mail them out by themselves to neighborhoods. Hand them out at a public spot if that's legal. Give them to your beauty operator, florist, cleaners, grocery clerk, child's teacher.

Take them door to door and hand to the woman living there. Pre-register her on the spot if you like. Although it is preferable that the women deliver them, perhaps the teen girls would help.

Here is your bi-fold or tri-fold flyer:

Our every-day life seems to be
out of bounds to the Bible.

OR IS IT?

You are invited to attend our

latest Inside the Hearts of Bible Women series.

INSIDE THE HEARTS OF

BIBLE WOMEN

These women will come alive and really speak to you from their hearts.

- ☐ *Abigail: Abused*
- ☐ *Endora: Occult*
- ☐ *Esther: Leadership*
- ☐ *Gomer: Unfaithful*
- ☐ *Jobetta: Unbearable Loss*
- ☐ *Lottie: Homosexual*
- ☐ *Martha: Time Management*
- ☐ *Priscilla: Christian Unity*
- ☐ *Rebecca: Troubled Children*
- ☐ *Ruth: Widowed/Remarried*
- ☐ *Sarah: Constantly Moving*
- ☐ *Tamar: Raped by Incest*

☐ Each year 6 million women are beaten by the men they love.

☐ Most of America's 50,000 witches are white middle-class women.

☐ Morally, women are superior to men but hold few important jobs.

☐About 50% of married couples commit adultery.

☐Lost property/jobs hit every family. A sixth of funerals are for youth.

☐In 1972, we had 24 AIDS victims. Today thousands die of it yearly.

☐Adults have Attention Deficit Disorder almost as much as children.

☐There are thousands of denominations in America, but one Bible.

☐Over a million minors leave home yearly because parents abused them or they abused their parents.

☐Widowhood and divorce hits nearly every family.

☐Nearly half our population moved between 1980 and 1990.

☐A woman is raped every 6 minutes in America.

REGISTRATION

Church of Christ

Address_____

City_____

Phone_____

TIME:_____

DAY:_____

DATES:_____

Free child care provided

I would like to enroll in your series.

Name_____

Address_____

City_____

Return form immediately or call for reservation.

POSTER

You have two alternatives. (1) You may use the sample poster with the general heading "Looking at Women's Problems in Today's Society" and insert your topics of study inside the heart, or use the one with the photo inside the heart. (2) You may use the poster advertising one specific topic. Omit the Bible women's names since many people won't recognize them anyway.

Photocopy your signs on bright colored paper so people in your community will begin to identify them just when they see that color. You may want to color coordinate them with your flyers.

Include your congregation's address and phone number on strips vertically up about an inch along the bottom line of the sign. Cut between them so people can tear the information off and take it with them.

Put posters up two weeks before your class begins. You don't want them to be up so long people get used to seeing them and then just forget about them.

Place your signs in the church lobby, grocery stores, university dorms and student centers, military barracks, beauty shops, restaurants, employee bulletin boards—wherever you can. Get permission.

Take them down when they're no longer current.

YOUR INVITATION TO
LOOKING AT "WOMEN'S PROBLEMS IN TODAY'S SOCIETY"

FREE

Dates of Series _____ **to** _____
Every _____ **at** _____

INSIDE THE HEARTS

OF BIBLE WOMEN

Church of Christ
Address _____
City _____
Phone _____

CHILD CARE PROVIDED

Katheryn Maddox Haddad

INVITATION TO WOMEN "LIVING WITH TROUBLED HUSBANDS"
FREE

Dates of Series _____ to _____
Every _____ at _____

INSIDE THE HEARTS

OF BIBLE WOMEN

Church of Christ
Address _____
City _____
Phone _____
CHILD CARE PROVIDED

~~~~~~~~~~~~~~~

INVITATION TO WOMEN: "Beauty and the Beast"
INVITATION TO WOMEN: "Dealing with the Occult"
INVITATION TO WOMEN: "Coping With Unfaithful Husbands"
INVITATION TO WOMEN "Coping With Family Loss"
INVITATION TO WOMEN: "Time management"
INVITATION TO WOMEN: "Christian Unity"
INVITATION TO WOMEN: "Dealing With Problem Children"
INVITATION TO WOMEN: "Christian unity"

INVITATION TO WOMEN: "Dealing with Problem Children
INVITATION TO WOMEN: "Considering Remarriage"
INVITATION TO WOMEN: "Coping With always Moving"
INVITATION TO WOMEN: "Coping with Rap3e/Incest"

LETTERS

Photocopy as many as you need. Enclose flyers and registration forms if you like. Hand write a personal note in blue ink at the bottom and sign.

So many people don't know their neighbors by name anymore. So ladies wishing to send letters to the neighborhood should drive around and copy their addresses. Then hand address the letters to "The Lady of the House" at each address. Personalize your photocopied letters as much as possible.

Use your home for the return address where appropriate. Hand address the envelope (including return address) to at least get her to open it without thinking it is junk mail.

You may wish to have a letter-signing and -addressing party.

Friend/Neighbor of Member
(Meet at Church Building)

Home Address
City, State, Zip
Phone

Date

Dear Neighbor [or friend's name],

[Although I've never met you,] I wanted to invite you to a short series with the ladies where I attend church. The topics we'll be discussing are _____, _____, _____, and _____. Not everyone attending will be having personal problems with them, but most of us either did in the past or know someone who is. The series is free.

The class starts on _____ at _____ and will last about _____ weeks. We are providing coffee/tea and child care.

Later in the year we will have other current issues pertinent to modern society as the Bible applies to them. We admit there are no easy answers. That's why we need God's help and each other.

If you would RSVP, I would appreciate it.

        Your friend and neighbor,

        Name

Church Name
Church Address

Home Address
City, State, Zip
Phone

Date

Dear Neighbor [or friend's name],

Hi! I'm your neighbor at [your address]. It seems like we never have time for each other. So I wanted to do something about it.

[Although I've never met you,] I wanted to invite you to my home every [day of week] from [time] to [time] for _____ weeks. I thought we could look things up in the Bible together that relate to coping with our everyday lives.

I have located a series of small-group materials that really make the Bible come alive. This material deals specifically with Bible women and issues they faced so much like those of today. Kind of hard to realize they really lived, but they did.

Just come one time and let's see how it goes. Just wear your jeans or whatever you normally do at home. After all, we're neighbors [friends]. If you would RSVP, I would appreciate it.

                    Your friend and neighbor,

                    Name

P.S. If this is a bad day or time for you, what would be more convenient?

Neighbor to Church Bldg

Church Letterhead

To the Ladies in our Neighborhood:

Today we are thinking of you and how we can best serve you. Especially we are thinking of those of you who are hurting inside. Believe it or not, every problem known to us today was experienced by some Bible woman. For this reason, we are beginning a special series called

INSIDE THE HEARTS OF BIBLE WOMEN

The topics we will be discussing are _____, _____, _____, and _____.

The series starts on [day and date] at [time] and will last about ___ weeks. We are providing coffee/tea and free child care. The series is free too.

Since we will be giving everyone printed material and a MP3 audio of the story of ABIGAIL in the Bible, please RSVP as soon as possible. Our phone number is _____.

You no longer have to pass our building and wonder what's going on inside there. Come on in! It's great!

Your sisters,

Name
For the Ladies at the
Church of Christ

Mother of Bible-School Children

Church Letterhead

Dear Bible School Mother,

Your child has come to our Bible classes at various times during the year and we hope learned of God's love, no matter what they do. We have been happy to help in this way.

Today we're thinking of Mom. How are you doing? Many mothers out there are smiling to their friends but hurting inside. Believe it or not, every problem known to us today was experienced by women in the Bible. For this reason we are beginning a special series called

INSIDE THE HEARTS OF BIBLE WOMEN

The topics we will be discussing are _____, _____, _____, and _____.

The series starts on [day and date] at [time] and will last about ___ weeks. We are providing coffee/tea and child care. The series is free.

Since we will be giving everyone printed material an MP3 audio of the Bible stories, please RSVP as soon as possible. Our phone number is _____.

Your sisters,

Name
For the Ladies at the
Church of Christ

Church Visitor

Church Letterhead

Dear [name]:

Since you have visited our worship in the past, our Ladies Bible Class would like to invite you to a short series on _____, _____, _____, and _____. Not everyone attending will be having a personal problems with these things, but most either did in the past or know someone who is.

The class starts on _____ at _____ and will last about _____ weeks. We are providing coffee/tea and child care.

The series starts on [day and date] at [time] and will last about ___ weeks. We are providing coffee/tea and child care. The series is free.

Since we will be giving everyone printed material and an MP3 audio of the Bible stories, we would appreciate an RSVP as soon as possible. Our phone number is _____.

We look forward to seeing you again!

                      Your sister,

                      Name
                    For the Ladies
                at the Church of Christ

Co-Workers

MEMO

Date:
To:
From:
Subject: Lunch

Dear [co-worker's name]:

Funny thing about lunch hours. (1) We get out of the office and see the rest of the world out there passing us by, (2) and/or we just stay here in the building in the same old lunch-hour rut.

I've received permission to use the conference room [lunch room] to have a little support group made up of US women for a little while. (US means everyone who doesn't have a perfect life yet.) We can get together once and see how it goes. If we like it, we continue; if we don't, it was worth a try.

I've run into a series of small-group materials that deal with issues of modern women's every-day lives. I have to say that it includes women who lived during Bible times, but your view of these women will probably change when you see how modern their lives really were. They had the same every-day challenges we do. Even if you're not religious, it's a great way for us to get together and be mutually supportive of each other. That's what it's for.

The material is imaginatively written by a woman with her master's degree in business. It also comes with MP3 audio of dramatic readings which we can order if we like.

So, how 'bout it? Let's get together and try it! Call me at extension ____ if you're interested. Who knows? We may really get to liking it. I know I'll be there. See you in the conference room [cafeteria] at noon tomorrow!

Your co-worker,

SUGGESTED SCHEDULE FOR AD CAMPAIGN

FIVE WEEKS BEFORE:*

1. Form a committee of ladies to work on this outreach together. You might wish to divide up responsibilities according to type of advertising.

2. Take a survey of the ladies in your congregation.

3. Take a random telephone survey of about 35 women in your church neighborhood. Be sure to identify yourselves and what church you're from.

4. Tally and order basic materials for first Bible woman you wish to study.

5. If you currently have a Ladies Bible Class, ask for a temporary weekly collection of pocket change for postage and child care.

6. Call ladies clubs in community to see if someone can give a speech to them about your chosen topics.

7. Pray

*If you decide to go on public-access television, you'll need a good three months—two to take the course, and one month to make the film and get it scheduled for airing.

FOUR WEEKS BEFORE:

1. Prepare your speech the way it will be presented.

2. Prepare your radio spot, and make both written and tape-recorded

copies of it.

3. Prepare your news release and take photographs to enclose with it.

4. Call radio stations to get yourself invited to be on their interview talk show.

5. Pray

THREE WEEKS BEFORE:

1. Put first announcement in your church bulletin. Also ask that it be announced from the pulpit.

2. Place a sign and sign-up sheet in your foyer.

3. Photocopy letters to neighbors and friends and put in foyer by sign-up sheet.

6. Go through list of all non-member children who attend Sunday School or attended your last Vacation Bible School. Photocopy and mail applicable letters.

7. Go through list of all local visitors to your congregation the past year. Photocopy and mail applicable letters.

8. Mail letters to neighbors of members, signed by the Christian neighbor.

9. Pray

TWO WEEKS BEFORE:

1. Call and get names of the city editor and religious editor of a local newspaper. Mail a photograph and news release to each one with a

cover letter asking if they will print it.

2. Make follow-up phone call to see if newspaper(s) will run the article. If not, repeat #1 until you find a newspaper that will.

3. Call and get names of the advertising manager of local radio station(s). Mail one typed and taped radio spot to each one with a cover letter from you asking if they would air it as a community service.

4. Make follow-up phone call to see if radio station(s) will air your spot.

5. Make follow-up telephone calls to visitors and Sunday School/VBS mothers.

6. Pray

ONE WEEK BEFORE:

1. Make speeches

2. Hand deliver paid advertisement to newspaper

3. Hang posters around town

4. Deliver flyers

5. Appear on radio interview talk show or call in to talk show

6. Pray

THE WEEK SERIES BEGINS:

1. Arrange for name tags

2. Arrange for babysitting

3. Arrange for coffee/tea

4. Make outdoor sign directing visitors which door to use. Make indoor sign directing visitors to the room you're using.

5. Set up registration tables

6. Series begins

7. Pray

DARE TO BE THAT STAR

One lone star enlarged with love
led the unknown way
To the Son who'd brought with Him
Hope's redeeming ray.

Compel YOUR eyes to venture high
above what seems so far.
Soar with Mercy's omnipotence
and dare to be that star!

Katheryn Maddox Haddad

Katheryn Maddox Haddad

MOVING AGAIN
Sarah

Lesson One: Packing

Lesson Aim
- ♥ **COPE WITH BEING UPROOTED**
- ♥ **KNOW HOW TO SAY GOODBYE**

Scripture Outline

Genesis 5:32; 7:6; 8:13; 11:10; 9:28,29:
Noah was 500 years old when he began building the ark, 600 when the flood came, 601 when the earth dried up. His son, Shem, was 100 years old two years after the flood, or 98 years old during the flood. That means Noah was 502 when Shem was born. Noah lived 350 years after the flood and died at age 950 when Shem was 448 years old.

Genesis 11:10-26; 12:4:

Noah was	502 years old when Shem was born
Shem was	100 years old when Arphaxad was born
Arphaxad was	35 years old when Selah was born
Selah was	30 years old when Eber was born
Eber was	34 years old when Peleg was born
Peleg was	30 years old when Reu was born
Reu was	32 years old when Serug was born
Serug was	30 years old when Nahor was born
Nahor was	29 years old when Terah was born
Terah was	<u>70</u> years old when Abraham was born

892 years-Noah's age when Abraham is born

Since Noah dies at age 950, Abraham is 58 years old when Noah dies. [I wonder if it was Noah's death that precipitated God telling Abraham it's time to move.]

Genesis 11:27-31: Terah has three sons—Abram, Nahor and Haran. Haran fathers three children—Iscah, Milcah and Lot, then dies.

Genesis 20:12: Sarah is Abraham's half-sister with the same father, Terah.

Genesis 12:31: Terah, Abram, and Lot move to Haran.

Joshua 24:2: Terah is an idol worshiper.

Genesis 22:20; 24:10,15,67: Brother Nahor stays behind in Haran after Terah and Abraham leave, and marries his niece (brother Haraan's daughter, Lot's sister) Milcah. They move to the city of Nahor [after Ur is destroyed?] They have a son, Bethuel, who then has a daughter named Rebekah who someday will marry Abraham's yet-unborn son, Isaac.

Today's World

In 2017, the US had some 325 million people. Every year, approximately twelve percent move—39 million people.

People move for different reasons. The most obvious one we think of is for employment. Other reasons include health, retirement, getting closer to family members, getting farther away from family members, going to a university or into the military, being sent to sea or abroad by the military, or to change environment such as city or country or visa versa, or cold climate to warm climate.

Despite how positive the reason for the move, this still translates into broken relationships with those left behind. To children who must leave behind friends they spent a lot of time with, this can be akin to experiencing loss by death. Many of the problems associated with the death of an extended family member or close friend are experienced to varying degrees by uprooted families—denial, grief, anger.

Some families who have faced moving often have learned to cope by either not allowing themselves to get close to anyone, or by developing superficial friendships that can be severed without too much emotional harm.

Bible World

Ur was also called Hur. It was 12 miles north of the old site of the Garden of Eden, the latter being at the intersection of the Tigris (Hiddekel) and Euphrates Rivers (Genesis 2:13,14). Sixty miles from there archaeologists discovered the first known wheeled vehicle in world history. Writing was also "invented here. The walls of Ur were 70 feet thick and 80 feet high.

For 200 years, it was the capital city of Babylon, also known as Shinar and Chaldea. King Ur-Nammu founded the last great dynasty of this Sumerian territory. He built the towering ziggurat of Ur in the middle of the city, with a temple at the top patterned after what is believed to have been the Tower of Babel. He drew up the oldest code of law yet known to man. In its prologue, Ur-Nammu boasted o removing grafters from office, regulating weights and measures, and protecting widows and orphans. His laws dealt with divorce, runaway slaves, slave girls who tried to be equal to their mistresses, and damage to one's person and property. (Later, Hammurabi based much of his code on this one.)

A man could sell his entire family to pay off his debts. The average adult was sold for less than a donkey. Yet slaves had rights. They could engage in business, borrow money, and buy their freedom.
Thousands of tablets have been discovered here, 90 percent of which were commercial documents—receipts, contracts of sale, deeds, will. The rest were poetry, mythology, and proverbs.

It was a sacred city where the nation buried its dead for 1800 years. In 1922, a huge burial pit was discovered in Ur with women wearing intricate gold jewelry and headdresses inlaid with precious stones. Apparently, they were courtiers buried alive to join fallen royalty in the nether world.

In one chamber, less than 27 feet square, 74 skeletons were found o women with headdresses of carnelian and lapis lazuli, silver and gold. One woman, possibly late for her own funeral, left her silver hair ribbon, still coined, in a pocket. There were also chariots drawn by oxen or donkeys, with the drivers in the cars. It is surmised that, while musicians played, the doomed drank poison. Others came and slew the animals. Then the pit was filled.

The main goddess of the city was Ur-ki, a moon goddess and considered the mother goddess. The name of the moon god there was Sin. One (but not all) ancient writer claimed the priestesses were prostitutes and all women were required to serve as priestesses at someday.

Ur was destroyed around 2000 BC, possibly during Sarah's lifetime, by the Elamites. They carried off the last king, Ibbi-Sin. In an unanswered appeal for help, he wrote, "Lo, in the assembly of the gods the land has been prostrated."

~~~~

In Bible times and even up to the advent of modern travel, it was not unheard of for people to move hundreds or thousands of miles away and never make contact with old friends and relatives again. Mail in some form has always existed, but people usually had to rely on someone they knew traveling to a distant land who might be willing and able to deliver the letter. Only the rich could hire messengers to deliver their mail

King Xerxes went off to fight the Grecians and returned home nine years later. Alexander the Great went off the conquer the world, and died after ten years, still away from home.

Sarah's grandson, Jacob, left home after a serious family quarrel and stayed gone over twenty years with apparently no c0ontact with family members during that time (Genesis 31:41).

Joseph was separated from his family in Egypt from age 17 to 39—22 years—before being reunited with them (Genesis 37:2; 41:46; 45:6).

When the elite of Jerusalem were taken into captivity by Nebuchadnezzar, they stayed gone 70 years (Jeremiah 25:11).

Introducing the lesson

"How many of you have moved?" (If number of times and distance comes up, save until later lessons.)

"Well, you're not alone." Explain the number of movers per year in the US.

"What was it like for you to leave your friends behind and be uprooted?" (If settling in a new community comes up, save until later lesson.)

"Then you know a little of what happened to some of our Bible friends who moved." **Display SOME BIBLE WOMEN WHO MOVED (as a poster, power point, or transparency) and explain.**

- Noah's wife moved from Iraq (Babylon) to Turkey because of natural disaster.

- Hagar moved permanently because she was fired (Genesis 21:9,10).

- Ruth moved permanently after her husband died to start a new life (Ruth 1:4,5,7).

- Mary, Jesus' mother, moved away to Egypt approximately four years (according to the time of the census and Herod's death—Josephus) to escape threats to her baby's life.

- Peter's wife moved around the Middle East and Southern Europe indefinitely as a missionary (I Corinthians 9:5).

- Sarah moved half her life to follow her husband's illusive dream (Genesis 12-23).

"We will be studying Sarah because she must have become an expert at moving. I'm sure she had her share of excitement and discouragement, laughter and tears. Let's share those events with her."

Discussion Questions

1. **In making a major move to another city or even country as Sarah had to do, how did you feel about the necessity of deciding what things to take and what to leave behind?**

    James 1:6-8: Those who doubt are "double minded". They decide one thing and then another.

    POSSIBBLE CLASS RESPONSE: The ladies should tell about things they couldn't decide whether to take or leave behind when they moved. The hard ones could have included drawings or handcrafts of children; or that junky chest they got when first married that carries such fond memories; of the bicycle built for two that just won't fit into the truck.

2. **How did you finally decide what to take and what to leave behind?**

Luke 12:34: Our treasure is where our heart is.

POSSIBLE CLASS RESPONSE: Did they use their heart or logic to make those hard decisions? When they were cleaning out closets, how did they decide? When the moving van was finally full and there were still things left to load, how did they decide? Did they end up giving thigs away to people who'd helped them pack, or their next-door neighbor, or a relative, or a re-sell store?

3. **Sarah had to leave a place where her family had lived for generations. Does God generally consider such uprooting a good experience (Deuteronomy 29:28)? How would such a move affect you?**

Deuteronomy 29:28: Uprooting from one's homeland is "furious".

Possible Class Response: Sarah had to leave a place where her family had lived for generations. She must have walked and re-walked those familiar paths and gone to the places that meant the most of her and just sat and absorbed, trying to etch everything in her memory. She must have met with family and old friends and sat around talking about all the things they had done in years past. They probably did a lot of laughing and a little crying. Today, at least we can take photos of old familiar places and people to ease the transition a little.

4. **People do not normally uproot themselves from where their family has lived for generations except for very important reasons. Sarah's and Abraham's reason was religious. What are some reason today people uproot themselves and move?**

Joshua 24:2: Sarah and Abraham moved for religious reasons.

Possible Class Response: Other common reasons are job promotion, health, military transfer, change of jobs, to live near relatives, to move away from relatives, to escape a bad reputation and start over, to follow that "illusive dream".

5. **Think about Sarah's probable feelings as she listened to her husband tell about his vision. Compare that with your or a friend's dream.**

2nd Corinthians 9:8: In all things and at all times [and places], God is able to show you grace.

Possible Class Response: In Sarah's society, it was usually the husband's decision to make such a drastic move. A great deal of empathy would be necessary. There must have been times in your class's past when the decision was difficult. Would they be uprooting their children from a good school system and good friends?? Would they be leaving behind a good congregation for a smaller one. Or a small one for one that would be too big? Would they be able to afford a house in the new area? Would the move be worth it?

6. **During the days of sorting and packing and getting tired and continual good-byes, how can 2 Timothy 1:7 help?**

   2 Timothy 1:7: God does not give us fear. Satan does that. God gives us a sense of power and love.

   Possible Class Response: If we love the person who made the decision to move, we will have a sense of peace. If we trust in God to go with us, we will be strong when we say goodbye to loved ones, even in the midst of our tears. No matter how far apart, we will be looking into the same stars and into the same smile of God.

7. **In order to replace the grief of leaving, we must find some exciting things about where we're moving to. How can this be done?**

   Matthew 12:43-45: When a person loses something out of her life and doesn't try to fill the void with something else, almost anything can come into her life.

   Possible Class Response: We can go to the library and look up books about the new place. We can try to find a video on the new place. We can write the Chamber of Commerce to find out what there is to do there, as well as to get information on special interests (church, club, etc.). We can ask our preacher to look up the address of the church there, then ask to be added to their bulletin mailing list in order to get a sense of the activities there.

Good Work

Write a note to someone who has just learned they must move. Tell them you will miss them but wish them luck. Send one note a day from each person in your discussion group if you only have one family to write.

BEFORE CLASS:

A1. FOR LARGE AND MEDIUM CONGREGATIONS:

Obtain names of members who are relocating to another city in the next few months. Or obtain the new addresses of members who have recently moved away from your city.

A2. FOR SMALL CONGREGATIONS:

Alternative One: If members of your congregation have relatives away at college or military service, obtain their names and addresses.

Alternative Two: Contact the administrator of a nearby nursing home or juvenile home and ask that your notes be passed on to new residents there.

B. Pre-address envelopes with names obtained.

C. Obtain stationary. It can be white or colored bond cut in half.

D. Write on black board or poster board suggested things to write for those who have trouble wording what they feel.

<u>For Members Moving Away</u>: "Even though we did not get to know each other as much as we would have liked, you will certainly be missed. Your smile and words of encouragement will always be remembered. There will be an emptiness here when you leave. But wherever you go, you will fill an emptiness people have there and they will be blessed by you."

<u>For Residents of Group Homes</u>: "We just wanted to let you know that we realize this is a difficult time for you being away from home. If you would like to talk with any of us, please let us know. God bless you during this time."

<u>For College and Military People</u>: "This is a time of excitement with new adventures ahead of you while you are away from home. Sometimes it can be scary too—moving to a new community. We just want to wish you good luck. Even though old friends cannot be with you there, God can and is.

DURING CLASS:

"We've been talking about moving. We've all experienced it and know how difficult it can be. There are others around us going through the same thing. In order to apply what we learned in class today, we now have the opportunity to reach out to these people."

Hand out pre-addressed envelopes and stationary. "If you aren't sure what to say, I have written some suggestions for you on the board. Feel free to copy them if you like."

"You will have about eight minutes to write your note. Let's all be quiet now and allow each other to think and write. When you are done, give your note to me, then offer a silent prayer for the one you wrote while the others finish."

Concluding Remarks

When time is up and while the slower writers complete their notes, sing one verse of a song, possibly one of the following:

1. *God be With You Till We Meet Again*
2. *Blest be the Tie that Binds*
3. *Take the Name of Jesus With You*
4. *If We Never Meet Again*

In a few moments, your students will be going back out into the hustle and bustle of their own lives, so end the class rather up beat. Smile!

(Wait for one or two quick replies to each of the following.) "In a few words, what advice would you give people who are....

    1.   Making packing decisions?
    2.   Being uprooted from their community or church?
    3.   Weighing the importance of the move?
    4.   Saying good-bye?

Give a list of those the class wrote to the person leading the closing prayer. Hold them up before God.

Some Bible Women Who Moved

NOAH'S WIFE

HAGAR

RUTH

MARY

PETER'S WIFE

SARAH

Inside the Hearts of Bible Women: Teacher's & Advertising Manual

Moving Again

Lesson Two: Traveling

Lesson Aim

- ♥ **KEEPING CHILDREN CONTENT ON LONG TRIPS**
- ♥ **SEEING THE GOOD SIDE OF MOVING**

Scripture Outline

Genesis 11:31: Terah takes Abram and his grandson, Lot, to Haran, a city named after Lot's father.

Genesis 11:32: They are on their way to Canaan, but never get there. Terah dies in Haran.

Genesis 12:1-3: God appears to Abram, tells him to leave Haran, and promises to bless the whole world through his family. Abraham is now 75 and Sarah is 65.

Genesis 12:4-7: When they arrive at last in Canaan, they settle in Shechem. God appears to Abram there to say he will give this land to his descendants. There is a famine in the land at the time.

Genesis 12:8: Abram moves on to Bethel, possibly hoping things will get better, but the famine continues. So they pull up stakes again.

Genesis 12:9: The term "south" is also translated "Negev."

Today's World

Every year over 40 million Americans move. Many of those who move have children. Children's feelings are often overlooked during a move, and this can leave them emotionally empty. Child psychologist Mitchell Baris said "Parents need to acknowledge that, no matter how positive a move it is, there probably will be an element of loss for children."

Parents should at least acknowledge with their children the painful side of moving, the losses. Further, they need encourage their children to talk about it, rather than make them be quiet and quit being cry babies.

Ryder Truck Rental suggests families should hold meetings to talk about everyone's feelings. Parents could ask children to identify what they'll miss most, and discuss how these aspects can be recreated in their new home.

A scrapbook could be put together of pictures of the old house, the old school, the old neighborhood, and the old friends being left behind. This sometimes helps children cope, knowing those things will still be there even when left behind. Sympathetic parents should also write down the mailing addresses of their children's friends.

Some moves are easier on children than others. A move due to a divorce or loss of job is extremely difficult. A move across country is harder than a move to a bigger house in the same city. Preschoolers will find moving easier than teenagers who must leave their high school and close friends.

Children will ask specific questions about their new neighborhood, new house, new school, new church, new friends. These should be provided to them as soon as possible after the move is announced.

Parents making advance house-hunting trips without the children can bring back photographs of the new home, new school, new neighborhood, new church, and possibly other children their age. The Chamber of Commerce can be contacted, and they'll be happy to send back maps, pictures, brochures on things to do, places to go, schools, churches, etc.

Once at their new home, parents should take time with their children to go on exploratory drives through the new neighborhood pointing out landmarks they should remember so they don't get lost on their way to school, stores, parks, and so on.

(*Moving is Hard on Kids,* by Karen Abbott, Scripps Howard News Service)

Bible World

SARAH'S FIRST MOVE FROM UR WAS TO HARAN. Haran was about 600 miles northwest of Ur between the Tigris and Euphrates Rivers. If the caravan traveled 10 miles per day (some people walked), it would have taken them six months to make the trip.

Haran was probably named after Sarah's half-brother Haran. It would have been solace to old Terah to move to where his deceased son had once lived. People worshipped the moon god of Ur here. It was located in southern Turkey near its border with Syria and not too far from where the Tigris and Euphrates Rivers once again draw close to each other at their northern source.

Their travels would have taken them within view of Mount Ararat to the east. Sarah and Abram could see where the ark rested with their beloved Noah's family years before. The people around Ararat even today have stories of Noah living for a while in this area, and possibly dying here. (There are other stories that he moved back to the area of the Garden of Eden and died there.) Remembrances of Noah must have been strong while living here.

SARAH'S SECOND MOVE WAS TO SHECHEM. She was about 65 years old when they headed out for Shechem, and her husband was 75. Shechem was about 450 miles southwest, which would have been about a four-month journey. They passed Damascus on the way, and hired her husband's foreman here (Genesis 15:2).

Shechem was located in Mount Ephriam (1 Kings 12:25). Huge oaks grew here; Shechem means "place of the great tree" (Genesis 35:4). Shechem's valley normally had very green pastures (Genesis 37:12-14 and Psalm 60:6), and this would be a good place for Abraham's and Lot's herds.

SARAH'S THIRD MOVE WAS TO THE OUTSKIRTS OF BETHEL, which is about 20 miles farther south. It was still in the mountains and normally had evergreen trees, bears (2 Kings 2:23-25), deer, lions, etc. But the famine continued. What a promised land!

So they left to move even farther south and even farther from her beloved home back in Ur. Just ten miles south was a town where Melchezedic lived. It was sometimes called Jebus (Judges 19:10) and sometimes Salem (Genesis 14:18, Psalm 76:2), hence Jeru-Salem as it was later called. Melchezedic was called the king of Salem. Genesis 10:21,32 say that Shem was the father of all the children of Eber, also translated Hebrew. Many believe Melchezekic was Shem.

Noah was 502 years old when Shem was born and 892 years old when Abraham was born. That would make Shem 390 years old when Abraham was born and 490 years old when Abraham was 100. Shem lived to be 600 years old. Melchezedik was the priest of the most high God (Genesis 14:18-20). Hebrews 7:1-4 says he had no beginning of days; at that time, no one had any memory of Shem's birth because he was born before the flood and lived to be so much older than everyone else born after the flood. This is just a theory. But Abraham and Sarah may have stopped to see him on their way south at this time. He would have certainly strengthened their faith.

The Canaanites lived here then, and were known for their sexual sins (Leviticus 18:24-28).

SARAH'S FOURTH MOVE WAS TO "THE SOUTH" ALSO TRANSLATED THE NEGEV and found labeled that way on maps. Later part of this is given to Judah (Genesis 13:1; Joshua 15:1). It is about 100 miles south of Bethel. It would have taken about a month to get there. Normal rain fall is 5" per year. It is at the bottom of the mountain range that began in Shechem. It has rough terrain, hard traveling, and is dangerous. Sarah was now about 68.

Introducing the Lesson

"In our first lesson on Sarah, we talked about the number of people in the US who have moved, and all of you who have moved raised your hand. Today we'd like you to share the distances you have moved."

"How many of you have moved within the same city?"

"What is the farthest you have moved at one time?"

"Totaling all the places you have lived, farthest point to farthest point, about how many miles away were those farthest points from each other?"

"Let's invite Sarah to join our ranks." ***Display 1000 Miles Abraham Traveled*** "and with no car!" Point out Ur where he started, then follow up the Euphrates River to Haran (which is in today's southern Turkey) where he moved first, then Damascus, then Shechem, then Jerusalem, then Bethel, and Egypt.

"Our study continues today about many of the problems we can encounter on the road, especially with family, and also the difficulties of getting settled in a new city."

Discussion Questions

8. Read Psalm 78:72 and discuss how proper nutrition helps and how to maintain it on a long trip. Also read and discuss Proverbs 17:22 in this light.

Psalm 78:72: God's integrity of heart led him to not only lead the Israelites as they traveled, but also make sure they were fed.

Possible Class Response: The strength and alertness of the traveling family needs to be kept up. God provided meat (quails), bread (manna), and good water—fairly balanced meals. A regular meal might do better than a greasy hamburger, greasy fries, and zilch nutrition soft drinks.

Proverbs 17:22: A lot of sweets and junk food on a long trip could make people cranky by the next day.

Possible Class Response: Do everything possible to keep everyone in a good mood such as take along fruit for snacks instead of sweets that sometimes make people hyperactive and then depressed. Such could also avoid upset stomachs, inability to sleep at night, and other physical ailments associated with travel.

9. What can be done in preparation to make each day of the trip exciting rather than a drudgery? Use your imagination. See also Psalm 24:1

Sarah experienced a very long transition. The move to Haran must have taken two or three months at least (10 miles per day maximum). A long move today is considered a week.

Psalm 24:1: If what's in the car is boring, look outside as you drive by God's fascinating world.

Possible Class Response: Have a contest between the left window and right window counting for perhaps 100 miles such things as clumps of flowers, advertising billboards, dead trees, stalled cars. Inside the car, you may bring along small inexpensive toys wrapped like presents and allow each child to open one gift every hour or so.

10. **Suggest some things that should be done to begin a mutual feeling of acceptance as soon as possible in a new community.**

    Sarah's family moved to a town established by her deceased half-brother. Your family arriving in a new town of complete strangers faces a greater difficulty.

    Acts 17:1,2: Paul looked up the local synagogue as soon as he arrived in each town.

    Possible Class Response: Stop by the church you think you'd like to attend. Meet the minister, secretary, youth director, or whoever is in the church office on weekdays. Attend church as soon as possible, even if you're tired and not settled in yet. There will always be people there who can give you tips on things you need to know. Some might even think to bring by sandwiches while you're setting up your kitchen, or babysit for your children while you sort through boxes. Buy a newspaper. Watch the local news on TV.

11. **While away from family "back home" whether just a few years or permanently, what today must you do to remain in touch and maintain ties? One of these is mentioned in Acts 1:1.**

    Acts 1:1: Luke wrote his friend, Theo, twice. Paul wrote a lot of letters back to churches he had recently established and then moved away from.

    Possible Class Response: Sarah must have wondered many times what was happening to loved ones left behind, but probably couldn't send them letters. In modern times we can not only send letters, but we can make phone calls. Those less close, we can send Christmas cards or birthday cards to. We could send a note to the church we left behind and ask that it be printed in the bulletin. We could send postcards to people we left behind where we used to work, or volunteer groups we used to be part of.

12. **What should be in the company of faith to make it effective (1 Corinthians 13:13)?**

    1 Corinthians 13:13: We must also love God and trust him.

    Possible Class Response: Faith affects our attitude toward difficult times. We must not only love and trust God, but also the person responsible for the move whether it be a husband seeking a promotion, or whoever it is. If we ever become bitter, it will demoralize everyone in the family.

13. **How can a personal benefit to moving make a difference to family members?**

    Genesis 12:1,2: Their father Terah died, and Abraham told Sarah they would have to move a second time. Once they got to the new country, God would make Sarah a mother.

    Possible Class Response: A larger church with more programs, a smaller church where you would be used more, a better school system, better forms of entertainment, a better house to live in, lower taxes, less smog, better volunteer opportunities, better job opportunities, closer to the water.

14. **Have you or a friend ever moved and found upon arrival that things weren't as bright as they had been pictured? Tell about it and how you or they coped. What scriptures would help in a time like this?**

Sarah must have been extremely disappointed arriving in the promised land just in time for a draught.

Philippians 4:11: Paul was in prison when he said he was content. Content does not necessarily mean overjoyed, but it means readily accepted and at peace with the situation.

Job 1:21: We came into this world with nothing, so whatever we have over nothing is a blessing, and we should praise God for it.

Romans 8:28: The promise is not that things will work out for the best, but they will work out for some good elusive.

Possible Class Response: The job wasn't available after all; they found a lesser job, but a better house/congregation/neighborhood/friends. Her daughter/son was caught up in his own life and didn't have time for her; but she found a great senior group to join/senior housing to move into.

15. **What things did you do differently on your second move?**

Proverbs 24:3-5: The more knowledge we have of the ins and outs of moving, the more short cuts and fewer mistakes we make the second time.

Possible Class Response: Sarah probably had an easier time settling down after her second move, which was to Shechem in Canaan. Perhaps some of us learned to have our credit bureau reports and school and doctor records forwarded ahead of time. We learned to write a list of contents on the side of each box so they could be identified even when stacked. We learned to write the name of the room where each box should be placed. Perhaps we taped pieces of paper on walls telling where to place items of furniture.

Good Work

Write suggestions on how to keep children happy on a long trip.

BEFORE CLASS:

A1.   FOR LARGE AND MEDIUM CONGREGATIONS:

Alternative One: Send a sign-up sheet around a class of young parents. Ask for the names and ages of children in families who will be moving in the next few months. Also find out their mode of travel and how long it will take them to arrive at their new home.

Alternative Two: Send a sign-up sheet around a class of young parents. Ask for the names and ages of children in families who will be going on vacation in the next few months. Also find out their mode of travel and how long they will be traveling during each segment.

A2.   FOR SMALL CONGREGATIONS:

Alternative One: Obtain a list of children's first (not last) names and ages from a scout troop. Have them list where they're moving to or where they're going on vacation and how they will travel.

Alternative Two: Obtain a list of children by age and first name (not last) who will be moving out of the school district along with about how many miles away their new home will be.

B.   Pre-address envelopes with names and destinations.

C.   Obtain 3x5 cards.

DURING CLASS:

"We've been talking about many of the difficulties encountered on the road, especially with small children. Some of us are old pros and have learned by experience; others of us have thought of some good entertainment ideas we've been anxious to try on real people. There are some parents out there who would love to receive your ideas for their next trip. Let's share with them."

Hand out the name of at least one child per class member along with a supply of 3x5 cards. "Please write the child's name at the top of each card, then one suggestion on what this child could do for entertainment while in the car.

"You will have about three minutes to write your suggestion. Let's all be quiet now and allow each other to think and write. When you're done, give place the card(s) in the envelope I gave you and hand it in. Then offer a silent prayer of safety for this child's family while they travel."

Concluding Remarks

When time is up and while the slower writers complete their notes, sing one verse of a song, possibly one of the following:

1. *Jesus Loves Me*
2. *This Little Light of Mine*
3. *Jesus at the Morning, Jesus at the Noon Time*
4. *Love is the Flag that Flies O'er the Castle of My Heart*

In a few moments, your students will be going back to whatever they've got planned for the rest of the day or evening.

(Wait for one or two quick replies to each of the following.) "In a few words, what advice would you give people...

    1.   Planning meals for a trip?
    2.   With children?
    3.   As soon as they arrive to make new friends?
    4.   Who become discouraged after their arrival in their new home?

Have a brief closing prayer for the safety of people who will be moving or going on extended vacations. Give a list of the children's first names to the person leading the class in prayer.

1000 Miles Abraham Travelled

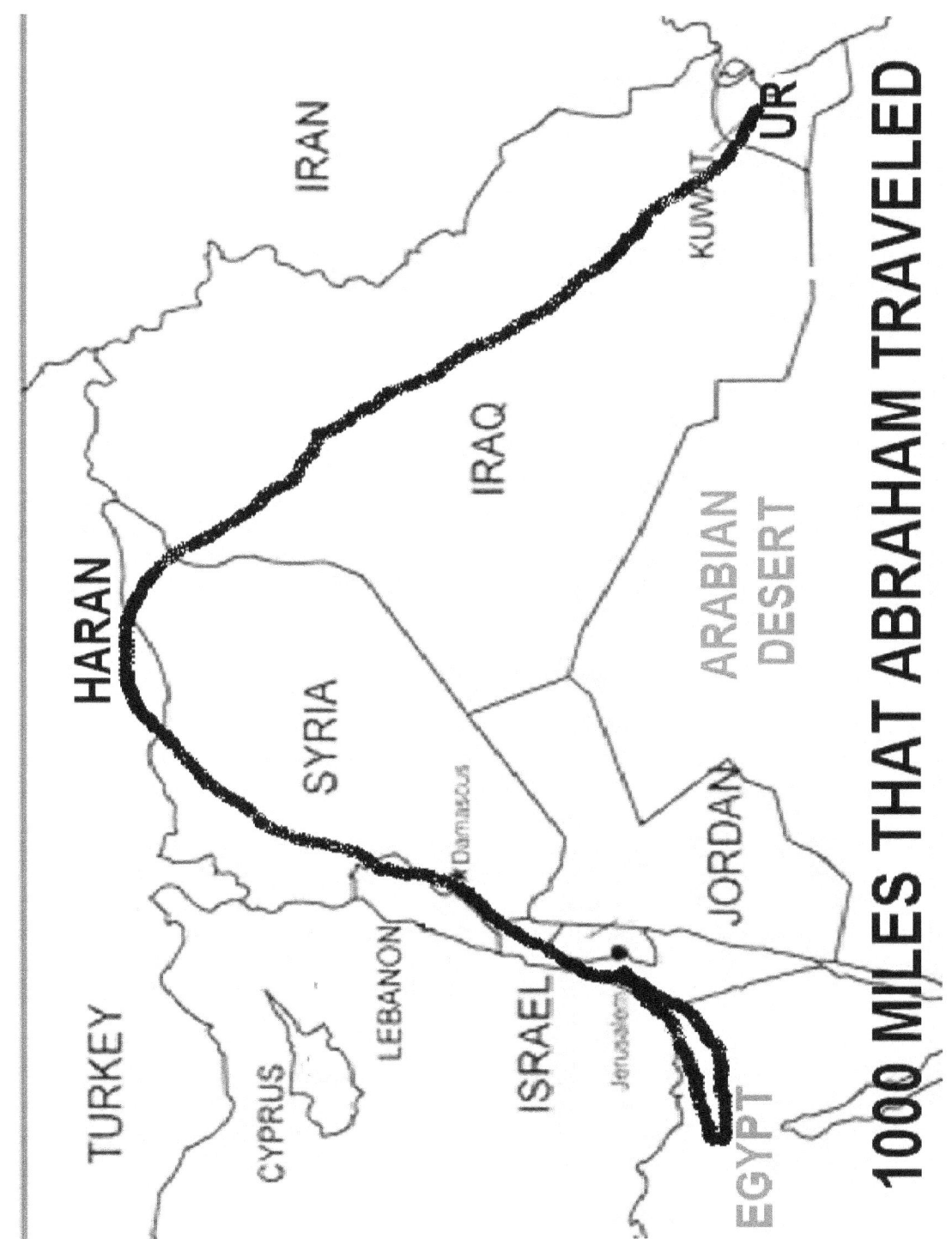

Katheryn Maddox Haddad

Moving Again

Lesson Three: Settling In

Lesson Aim

- ♥ **ADJUSTING TO A NEW COMMUNITY**
- ♥ **KEEPING UP COURAGE WHEN ALL SEEMS FUTILE**

Scripture Outline

Genesis 12:10-20: Sarah and Abram arrive in Egypt. He is a powerful sheik from the East. He knows the Pharaoh will want to meet him since he could be a threat to Egypt. He's afraid when Pharaoh meets Sarah he will want to marry her because of her beauty, even though she is now about 70 years old. He tells Sarah to say she's Abram's sister, a half-truth. At his lowest, Abraham willingly gives her up to save his own life. Pharaoh does take her to his palace, but learns of the deception and banishes Abram and Sarah from his kingdom in disgrace.

Genesis 13:1-3a: They travel again through the Negev.

Genesis 13:3b-17: Sarah and Abram settle in the area of Beth-el. Abram's and Lot's herds are getting mixed up, Lot decides to stay in the area, so to keep peace, Abram moves again.

Genesis 13:18-19:38: They move to Hebron. Abram is now so powerful that his army single handedly conquers five powerful kings from the East who have captured four local kings and the citizens of their cities including Lot. Melchizedek blesses him. God reaffirms the promise of a nation made up of their descendants. They don't see how, so Abram takes an Egyptian girl, Hagar, to be his mistress and bear him a son. Sarah is now 76 years old (Genesis 16:16). Then Sodom and Gomorrah are burned and Lot is left homeless.

Genesis 20:1-14: Possibly for fear of retaliation for being related to the only survivor of the destroyed cities, they move again, this time toward the Negev, but stop in Gerar. Again Abraham claims Sarah is his sister, this time to the King of Gerar. But when he learns of the deception, he just tells Abram to settle somewhere else in the area.

Genesis 20:15-21:14: They move farther to the "south" (Negev) where they started to go in the first place (20:1). At last Sarah bears Isaac at age 90. At 92 Sarah weans Isaac, and smart-alek 15-year-old Ishmael (Genesis 16:16; 21:5) gets himself and his mother kicked out by Sarah. Hagar and Ishmael wander in the wilderness of Beersheba.

Genesis 21:15-22:24: Abram digs a well, plants trees, creates an oasis and names it Beersheba. Abram and King Abimelech have a dispute over it; Abimelech leaves him alone. Abraham sacrifices Isaac nearby.

Genesis 23:1,2: Finally they move to Hebron. When her long-promised baby is 37 years old and she is 127, Sarah dies.

Today's World

Fifteen years ago, a startling book came out called *The Day America Told The Truth*. They used Joel Garreau's "moral/cultural regions" as follows:

NEW ENGLAND:	**METROPOLIS:**	**NEW SOUTH:**	**OLD DIXIE:**
E. Connecticut	N. Delaware	Florida	Alabama
Maine	N. Maryland	Georgia	Arkansas
Massachusetts	New Jersey	N. Carolina	E. Texas
New Hampshire	New York City	S. Carolina	Kentucky
Rhode Island	W. Connecticut	S. Virginia	Louisiana
Vermont	Philadelphia	S. West Virginia	Mississippi
		S. Delaware	S.Oklahoma S.Maryland
		S. Missouri	
		Tennessee	

RUST BELT:	**GRANARY:**	**L.A.—MEX:**	**MARLBORO CTRY**
Illinois	E. Colorado	S. Arizona	E. California
Indiana	E. N. Mexico	S. California	Idaho
Michigan	Iowa	S. Colorado	Montana
Ohio	Kansas	S. Texas	Nevada
W. New York	Minnesota	W. New Mexico	N. Arizona
W. Pennsylvania	Nebraska		N.W. N. Mexico
	N. Missouri		Wyoming
	N. C. Texas		W. Colorado
	N. E. Michigan		W. Oregon
	South Dakota	**PACIFIC RIM:**	W. Washington
	W. Wisconsin	N. W. California	Utah
	W. C. Illinois	W. Oregon	
	W. C. Oklahoma	W. Washington	

Overall, the following areas ranked <u>higher than the national average</u> in these traits:

POSITIVE

GIVING TO CHARITY:
- New South
- Pacific Rim
- Metropolitan
- Granary
- New England

NEGATIVE

NUMBER OF SOCIOPATHS:
- New South
- Pacific Rim
- Marlboro Country

BELIEVING IN GOD:
    Rust Belt
    Old Dixie
    Granary
    LA-Mex

DRUNK DRIVING:
    Rust Belt
    Marlboro Country

KEEPING VIRGINITY UNTIL MARRIAGE:
    Metropolis
    Old Dixie
    Granary

CHEATING ON SPOUSE:
    Metropolis
    Old Dixie

GIVING TOTAL EFFORT AT WORK:
    New South
    Granary
    Marlboro Country

CARRYING A WEAPON:
    New South
    LA-Mex
    Marlboro Country

TRUE TO SELF AND OTHERS:
    Pacific Rim
    New South

CONSIDERING SUICIDE:
    Pacific Rim
    Granary
    LA-Mex
    Marlboro Country

So, it seems that none of us has anything to brag about. We all have both good and bad. As Paul said in Romans 3:23 after telling the Jews and Gentiles that neither was superior to the other, "ALL have sinned and come short of the glory of God."

Bible World

SARAH'S FIFTH MOVE WAS TO EGYPT. Egypt was founded by Noah's son Ham. It was another 250 miles through wilderness. She was now 1,200 miles from her homeland. They'd abandoned their promised land. Then her husband betrayed her by allowing her to be put in Pharaoh's harem to await his call some night. He was given a rich dowry for her (Genesis 16:1), possibly including Hagar. When sickness hit the palace, Sarah may have sent word to Pharaoh explaining why. What courage! If they spent a year traveling to Egypt and she spent another year in the harem, that would make her now about 70, some 20 years after the promise of a son. Luckily, Pharaoh apparently feared retaliation possibly by Lot or Shem, so banished them rather than execute them.

SARAH'S SIXTH MOVE WAS BACK TO THE NEGEV. Travel was always slow. She was probably 71 by the time they camped there to rest a few months. Then they moved on.

SARAH'S SEVENTH MOVE WAS TO BACK TO BETHEL. Perhaps they felt safer near the King of Jeru-Salem (Shem?) just ten miles away. God had appeared to Abram there. The famine was over and she saw it was truly a good land. Perhaps now they could settle down. But they had problems with Lot's herds intermingling with theirs. Sarah was perhaps 73 years old now.

SARAH'S EIGHTH MOVE WAS TO HEBRON. It was also named after Arba, the ancestor of Anak (Joshua 15:13) and the giants (Numbers 13:33). This is where the Israelites later spied out the land and saw the giants and giant grapes. Today there is a huge oak 23 feet in girth that bears Abraham's name. It is 20 miles south of Jeru-Salem. Ishmael was born here to Hagar when Sarah was 76 years old. She spent the next 13 years wondering. Then, when she was 89 (Genesis 17:1) she was told she would soon become pregnant. Abraham laughed in disbelief and even tried to back out by suggesting to God that they just settle on Ishmael being the heir (Genesis 17:15-19). On the other hand, Sarah laughed so hard, she was afraid she'd offended God and he'd change his mind (Genesis 18:9-15). Her name had been SARAI, "Jehovah is Prince," but was now changed to SARAH, "Princess." Later God would name their grandson after her, I-SRA-EL, "Prince of God" (Genesis 32:28). Then Sodom and Gomorrah were destroyed by God. Lot was the only survivor. Perhaps they thought they'd better leave before the surrounding cities attacked them.

SARAH'S NINTH MOVE WAS TO GERAR. This was a city in the Negev, 50 miles southwest of Hebron. It was near the southern tip of the promised land, but still inside it. Again her husband betrayed her and said, "If you really love me, you'll say you're my sister," and she ended up in the king's harem again. She had to stay there several months to make sure she wasn't pregnant when she arrived. When the king's wives become barren, perhaps Sarah sent word to him that it was God's curse, for he let her out and sent Abraham away. They could stay in the area, but not in the same city (Abraham was too powerful to make him mad).

SARAH'S TENTH MOVE WAS BACK TO THE NEGEV. Now she was 90 years old, and 40 years from the original promise. Here at long last she had the promised son, Isaac. Two years later, smart-alek Ishmael made fun of the baby, and Sarah kicked him and his mother out of the house.

SARAH'S ELEVENTH MOVE WAS TO BEERSHEBA. It is 25 miles southeast of Gerar and almost out of the promised land. Perhaps they wanted to raise Isaac away from so many people. They dug a well, planted trees, and created an oasis; this took considerable time to develop, of course. During this time, her husband took a week trip and offered to sacrifice their only son, Isaac, to God. He was at least a teenager by now. Sarah would be around 105. But Abraham got restless again.

SARAH'S TWELFTH MOVE WAS BACK TO HEBRON. Perhaps they thought it would be better for Isaac to grow into manhood in the middle of their promised land. She settled down there for probably 20 years. Then, 80 years after receiving the original promise that she would have a baby and be the mother of a great nation, and when she was 127 years old, Sarah died.

Introducing

the Lesson

Sarah moved 12 times as her husband followed his elusive dream. ***Display SARAH'S MOVES.*** "How many times have you moved? Let's find out who has moved the most." Allow class to respond.

"It's hard getting settled and accepted in different parts of the country. Some places don't want newcomers and some do. Are some easier to adjust to than others?" Allow class to respond to this for a couple minutes.

In a startling book called *The Day America Told the Truth,* a survey team covered every region in the United States with numerous questions answered anonymously by thousands of people. This book divided up summaries of their findings by the "nine moral regions of America" developed by Joel Garreau.

As a result of their survey, they found that there is unique good and bad in each region. In comparing the best and worst, they found that areas were kind of like the little girl with the curl in the middle of her forehead. If, in some traits, they were very, very good, in other traits they were horrid. On the other hand, the areas that had only a few traits best in America also had only a few traits worst in America.

Display the chart, THE BEST AND WORST IN AMERICA. Read through the highlights, noting especially your own area. Possibly also discuss prejudices we have toward certain areas and how they really are morally compared with our own area.

Discussion Questions

16. **Acts 16:12-14 tells of two such temporaries who met each other. How did they handle this problem?**

    <u>Acts 16:12-14</u>: When Paul and his friends arrived at Philippi, they found a traveling merchant from Thyatira, Lydia, to worship with.

    Sarah settled her family several places temporarily. Some people are required to move every year or two for their job.

    <u>Possible Class Response</u>: Making a few friends quickly at each location rather than trying to make many friends is one key to surviving this period. Rather than try to break barriers of social circles who have known each other many years, find out who the newcomers are. Making friends with them is easier since they don't have a long-established circle of friends.

17. **Have you ever known anyone to move with their husband when they knew the move was wrong? How did they handle it?**

    <u>Psalm 23</u>: Even when David had to go through a death-defying valley, he trusted God to get him through it and find greener pastures on the other side.

    <u>Possible Class Response</u>: There is both good and bad in everyone and every situation. We can spend our time concentrating on the bad or concentrating on the good. That

is our choice, and ours alone. We can become self-destructive or self-constructive.

18. In what ways do we feel culture shock moving from north to south and east to west? How about facing prejudices? How do you think Sarah coped?

1 Corinthians 9:22: We need to pick out whatever things we are comfortable with that the people in our new community do, and do those things also.

Possible Class Response: If the local people say ya'll, start saying ya'll. If the locals admire pickup trucks, start admiring pickup trucks. If they never wear sleeveless dresses, don't wear sleeveless dresses. If someone says you're from a part of the country that isn't friendly, ask them if you pass the friendly test. If the local people laugh at your accent, get a sense of humor until it fades some.

19. Through the ups and downs, the elation and doubts of all the moves chasing the elusive dream, what do you think helped Sarah keep going?

Hebrews 11:8-10: Abraham searched for the city and land God had prepared for him. The more he searched, the less he took for granted.

Possible Class Response: It doesn't matter where we live. Paul was content to live in prison even. The important thing is to "shine where you are." The more moves we make, the more friends we can make, invite to church, and show God's love to.

20. Have you ever or do you know of anyone who moved from an area to get away from a bad experience? Do you know anyone who made such a move successfully? How?

Philippians 3:14: All of us equally are doing the same thing—trying to get to heaven the best we can.

Possible Class Response: No matter where we live, there will be bad experiences. If one has gone through an exceptionally bad experience, perhaps a move might work. But usually, if a person continues to live as good a life as possible, smile, and remain positive, people will forget the experience. Most people are too busy with their own lives to spend very long concerned with what other people did.

21. Tell of a thread that kept the hope and courage going for you or someone you know under similar circumstances?

Genesis 37:6-8: Joseph, too, had a dream. He was in prison 12 years. But he believed that dream from God, and apparently it got him through those dark hours.

Through all the moving, one thread wove through Sarah's life that kept her going: The divinely promised child.

Possible Class Response: Encourage the class to share the life-long dreams that have kept them going through difficult times.

22. How do you think Sarah applied Psalm 6 to her life?

Psalm 6: David prayed all night with tears (v.6), then said in confidence that God heard him and would receive his request (v.9).

There are times when we have to hand everything over to God because we do not believe we can go on.

Possible Class Response: After so many moves, a class member may have set aside the exhaustion and excitement and worry of earlier times. She may have cried all night, then got up the next day, brushed her hair, and rolled up her sleeves. Then, using the same energy she would have to repaper a room or plant flowers in her garden had she been able to stay home, she got to work packing to leave.

23. **How can we obtain strength and courage from an older**
    person we admire (Titus 2:2,3)?

    Titus 2:2-4: Older men and women are to be good examples for younger people, and should be aware that they are being observed.

    Possible Class Response: Let's pay attention when an older woman is patient and see how she does it; we can even ask her how. We should encourage the older women to teach classes of younger women—even if they're in their seventies or eighties. We could ask them to talk about the Christian graces. They're not perfect, but they've seen what works and what doesn't work.

24. **Give some personal examples of when you resorted to a sense of humor to get through a bad situation.**

    Matthew 7:3,4: Jesus got a kick out of people going around with telephone poles in their eyes and trying to get little slivers out of other people's eyes.

    Possible Class Response: Jesus used humor to get points across to others. We can use it on ourselves. We can feel sorry for ourselves which is destructive emotionally and physically, or we can see the humor and even tell a story on ourselves to release the emotion resulting from the occurrence. Encourage your class to tell on themselves.

25. **Give instances where a marriage was made stronger as a result of similar struggles.**

    Ecclesiastes 4:9-12: Often it is only when problems occur and the other marriage partner chooses to suffer and struggle too, that we see how much we are loved.

    Proverbs 17:17: We know who our true friends are when bad times come along and they don't desert us.

    Possible Class Response: Going through the stress of moving as many times as this couple did must have made them feel closer. Abraham dearly loved Sarah. Encourage the class to tell of times their spouse stood by them or their parents stood by each other during bad times.

Good Work

Write a welcome note to a newcomer.

BEFORE CLASS:

A1. FOR LARGE AND MEDIUM CONGREGATIONS:

<u>Alternative One</u>: Obtain names of visitors to your congregation. If your congregation has cards for visitors to fill out, obtain your names from them.

<u>Alternative Two</u>: If you do not have visitor cards, a week or two before this lesson, make a point to meet the visitors and ask for their address so you can send them something.

A2. FOR SMALL CONGREGATIONS:

<u>Alternative One</u>: If your congregation seldom has visitors, locate names of people who have just moved to your area. Public utility companies can give you names. Children of class members would know who new students are and often know where they live. Or you could obtain a few names from a local realtor.

<u>Alternative Two</u>: Obtain the names and addresses of some missionaries who live away from home.

- B. Pre-address envelopes with names obtained.
- C. Obtain stationary. It can be white or colored bond cut in half.
- D. Write on the blackboard or poster board suggested things to write for those who have trouble wording what they feel.

<u>For Congregational Visitors</u>: "We are so glad you visited our congregation recently to worship with us. We hope you will return and give more of us an opportunity to meet you. God bless you in your search for a closer walk with God."

<u>For New People in Community</u>: "We are so glad you have moved to our community. We would like to invite you to worship with us. We want to meet you and make you feel at home. God bless you in your new home."

DURING CLASS:

"We've been talking about the difficulties of moving into a new community and trying to adjust to their ways and make new friends. I have a list of people who right now are a little lonely. They have not yet made many friends in their new home if any at all. Let's be a friend to them."

Hand out pre-addressed envelopes and stationery. "If you aren't sure what to say, I have written some suggestions for you on the board. Feel free to copy."

You will have about eight minutes to write your note. Let's all be quiet now and allow each other to think and write. When you are done, give your note to me, then offer a silent prayer for the one you wrote while the others finish."

Concluding Remarks

When time is up and while the slower writers complete their notes, sing one verse of a song, possibly one of the following:

1. *Anywhere with Jesus I Can Safely Go*
2. *He Leadeth Me*
3. *Where He Leads Me I Will Follow*
4. *Take My Life and Let it Be*

In a few minutes your students will be leaving and possibly setting aside today's discussion. Leave them with some upbeat quick summaries.

(Wait for one or two quick replies to each of the following.) "In a few words, what advice would you give people who ....

1. Are new to your congregation and want to make friends?
2. Should know a local custom to help them fit in with the customs of your area?
3. Are constantly moving?
4. Need to overcome something bad happening to them?

Have a brief closing prayer for people who have moved to your area. Give a list of people class members wrote to the person leading the class in prayer and ask her to name them by name before God.

Sarah's Moves

DESTINATION	Estimated Miles	Estimated Age	Estimated Yrs There
HARAN	600 miles	age 50	15 years
SHECHEM	450 miles	age 65	2 years
BETHEL	20 miles	age 67	1 year
NEGEV	100 miles	age 68	2 years
EGYPT	150 miles	age 70	2 years
NEGEV	250 miles	age 72	1 year
BETHEL	75 miles	age 73	3 years
HEBRON	30 miles	age 76	3 years
GERAR	50 miles	age 79	1 year
NEGEV	25 miles	age 80	15 years
BEERSHEBA	25 miles	age 95	15 years
HEBRON	25 miles	age 110	17 years

Katheryn Maddox Haddad

The Best and Worst in America

Positive Traits	Negative Traits

New England

*Fewest drunk drivers
*Give to charities
*Fewest homosexuals
*Most ethical employees

*Cheat on spouse
*Don't help the poor
*Violent sexual urges

Metropolis

*Keep virginity until married
*Never considered killing someone

*Unethical employees

Rust Belt

*Believe in America right or wrong
*Believe America still has heroes

*Don't support civil liberties

Old Dixie

*Believe in God
*Fewest use drugs
*Willing to die for what they believe

*Racists

New South

*Give to charities
*Don't spy on their neighbors

Granary

*Willing to go to war and drivers
 die for what they believe in

*Most drunk
*Violent sex urges

LA—Mex

*True to one's self and others

Pacific Rim

*Least hardcore racists
*Support civil liberties
*Willing to die for what they
 believe

*Most homosexuals
*Consider suicide
*Don't believe in God
*Don't give to charity
*Use drugs the most
*Don't keep virginity
   until married

Marlboro Country

*Help the poor
*Don't consider suicide
*Don't cheat on spouse
*Give their best at work

*Carry weapons
*Considered killing
*Keep virginity until
   married

Peter Kim, pages 14-22

Katheryn Maddox Haddad

HOMOSEXUAL BUT NOT SO GAY
Lot's Wife

Lesson One: Protecting our Morals

Lesson Aim
- ♥ GUIDE YOUNG PEOPLE TO RIGHT DECISIONS
- ♥ LIVE UNTAINTED AMONG THE IMMORAL

Scripture Outline

Genesis 11:27-32: Terah has three sons. One is Abram who will later father Isaac. One is Haran who fathers a son Lot, but dies soon thereafter. One is Nahor who eventually has a granddaughter, Rachael, whom Isaac will someday marry. Terah moves Abram's and Haran's family to the city of Haran far north of Babylon near Turkey. Terah dies in Haran.

Genesis 12: God tells Abram to move on to Canaan; he takes Lot's family along also.

Genesis 13:1-8: Abram is very rich; Lot's riches are great also. Their cattle intermingle too much and causes arguments between the herdsmen. To nip the problem in the bud, Abram tells Lot they should separate their herds completely to keep peace in the family.

Genesis 13:9-18: Lot selects the fertile plain of Jordan and pitches his tent near the great city of Sodom, even though the people there are extremely immoral. Abram moves to Hebron and God promises to eventually give all the land to his descendants.

<u>Genesis 14:1-12</u>: Four great kings from around Babylon attack the cities of five kings in the plain of Jordan, including Sodom. Lot has moved into Sodom by now, so his family is captured too.

<u>Genesis 14:13-16</u>: Abram leads his personal army of 318 men to chase off the four kings, and rescues those taken captive, including Lot's family.

<u>Genesis 14:17-24</u>: The king of Sodom tells Abram to keep the spoils of war against the marauding kings as his reward for rescuing the people. Abram diplomatically refuses the reward lest anyone say they made Abram rich.

Today's World

Most universities in Europe and the United States, including Harvard and Yale, were started as institutions of higher learning to teach primarily the Bible, and other subjects with a Biblical foundation. Of the first 119 universities in America, 104 were built specifically to train ministers. Harvard University was 100 years old before it had any professors who were not ministers. Harvard's founding charter includes this statement: *Let every student be plainly instructed, and earnestly pressed to consider well, the main end of his life and studies is to know God and Jesus Christ which is eternal life.*

But the pendulum has swung to the other side in a majority of these universities today. The National Sexual Violence Resource Center gives the follow statistics:

One in 5 women and one in 16 men are sexually assaulted while in college. More than 90% of sexual assault victims on college campuses do not report the assault. 63.3% of men at one university who self-reported acts qualifying as rape or attempted rape admitted to committing repeat rapes

The LGBT Student Movement has been active on university campuses since the 1950s. By 2012, the top twenty universities in the United States had an LGBT (Lesbian Gay Bisexual Transgender) organization.

According to Campus Pride, twenty-five universities in the United States have sexual orientation as one of their questions on acceptance applications. Thirty of our universities have gay-lesbian centers and or studies. Great Value Colleges reports fifty as gay-friendly.

The Taskforce for Gays and Lesbians goes to college and university campuses and takes surveys of how badly gays and lesbians are treated, then evaluate how fast the administration acted on behalf of those discriminated again. Upon these bases, they then demand policy changes to "protect" them.

If a Christian university does not offer the types of courses our children want for their future careers, we need to carefully investigate the alternatives of other universities, and allow plenty of time (at least a year) to do this. Libraries carry books listing all accredited religious and secular colleges and universities in the country along with their addresses. We should order their catalogs and carefully read their course descriptions and their rules of behavior. Perhaps we can make up a list of questions about issues not listed in the catalog, and send those to the Dean of Admissions for answering. The souls of our children are too important to leave to chance.

* * *

The Lambda Literary Awards are given out yearly in Anaheim, California, recognizing the best gay and lesbian literature in America. Blanche McCrary Boyd explains that "gay literature, once a separate, almost ghettoized niche of the U.S. publishing industry, is edging into the mainstream."

Of the 17 Lambda Awards, seven went to books produced by such well-known publishers as Columbia University Press, University of New Mexico Press, Norton, Viking, Dutton and Knopf. "By now, most mainstream publishers have some lesbian and gay books on their lists....But the real change is that now it's desirable for them to be there," explained Matthew Lore of Harper San Francisco.

Today, specialty and mainstream publishers produce an estimated 1,000 new titles a year aimed directly at gay and lesbian readers. "We're trying to publish the best books in these areas that we can," said Arnold Dolin of Penguin. "For quite a while now, I've been telling people that gay and lesbian writing is what's going to be happening in the '90s in serious American literature," said Michael Denneny of St. Martin's Press. He predicts that a diversified group of gay men and lesbians will lead the new century's next literary wave.

* * *

Who has the right to determine whether homosexuality is wrong? According to research published in *The Day America Told the Truth,* only 52% of Americans believe the Bible has the right to tell us what is right or wrong, 50% believe religion has that right, and 42% believe the church has that right. (Note how they differentiate the Bible, religion, and the church.)

Bible World

Who were the four kings who around 2000 BC plundered Canaan (including Sodom and Lot's family), and were chased out single-handedly by Abraham's personal troops?

AMRAPHEL was the most prominent of them all as he is believed to have been Hammurabi, king of Babylon. This campaign to Canaan occurred apparently early in his reign when he with other kings were still subject to the king of Elam (see below). However, since his name is listed first in verse 1, but not in the other two verses, it may have been obvious to the writer he was about to overpower Elam's king and should be kept happy for political reasons. He was Babylon's most famous warrior king. He emphasized education, books, law and order. One of the first ancient kings to collect and categorize his laws into one code, his "Code of Hammurabi" still exists today, a stone 8' high, with 4,000 lines and 300 laws. At the top of the stone is Hammurabi receiving authority from the sun god. These laws cover false accusations, witchcraft, military service, land and business regulations, family relations, tariffs, maximum, prices, minimum wages, trade, loans, debts. The code set up a social order based on the rights of the individual and that "the strong shall not injure the weak." He gradually enlarged his kingdom by careful administration and planned conquest of other cities. As he did so, he named his growing empire after his city, Babylon.

KINGDOM OF SHINAR. When Amraphel (Hammurabi) came to power, it covered only 50 miles in radius. He began his reign by becoming friends with other city-state kings, and then overpowering them when he got strong enough. He probably planned to take over Canaan after he helped the other kings conquer it. He did this to the king of Larsa after 31 years of friendship. Then he went all out to expand his kingdom. Eventually Shinar, also called Chaldea and Babylon, extended 400 miles north between the Tigris and Euphrates Rivers.

ARIOCH means "lion-like." Nothing else is known about this king.

KINGDOM OF ELLASAR was also called Larsa after the primary city where King Arioch lived. The city of Larsa was a primitive capital city of the area even before the Tower of Babel (Babylon) was built. When Amruphel (Hammurabi) became king of Babylon, the city of Larsa had expanded its domain to the cities of the south region known as Chaldea; up into Mari an area northwest of Babylon; and Eshnuma, a region north of Babylon; and Assur, about 200 miles northeast of Babylon. Thus, Ellasar nearly surrounded Amraphel's Babylonian territory.

CHEDOR-LAOMER is listed first in verses 5 and 9 as leading the "kings that were with him." This king could have been Kudor (Chedor)-Mabuk (Laomer) who conquered Babylon about 2000 BC. "Laomer" is an Elamite goddess whose name was "Mabuk" in a nearby language. Babylonian documents around this time tell of an interruption in their local kingship by a king from Elam. An Elamite prince is said to have held court in Ur. He made himself lord over the kings of Shinar and Ellasar. The inscriptions give Kuidor (Chedor)-Mabuk (Laomer) the label of "Apda Martu" meaning "ravager of the West." He did not establish a lasting empire in these areas, but was noted primarily as a conqueror. This agrees with his activities in Genesis 14.

KINGDOM OF ELAM is known today as the region Khuzistan in Iran. Its capital has always been Susa or Shusha and is where Daniel, Nehemiah and Esther lived. The Elam empire ruled over Babylon for a while, but was not powerful enough to maintain it. Babylon in turn took over Elam. About the time of the Greeks, Elam began to be called Persia. It did not become really great until it joined with the Medes to the North and conquered the Babylonian Empire about BC 500, and then freed the captive Jews to return to Jerusalem.

TIDAL means "reverence." King Tidal was also called Thurgah meaning "the great chief." The Arabians still today have chieftains over several nomadic tribes, much as existed in most of the Mid-East then.

KINGDOM OF NATIONS refers to either city-states or nomadic tribes. During early civilization, unless one king was powerful enough to control several cities or tribes near it, every city and tribe was independent with its own king or chief. The "nations" mentioned here are likely to be cities or tribes in the Media area since its people were related to Elam (Persia) and eventually formed an alliance and kingdom of the Medes and Persians. Another possibility for the "Nations" of Genesis 14 is that they were in Syria north of Canaan, which would be anxious to enlarge its borders. But due to its close relationship with the nations farther east, it is most likely he ruled miscellaneous scattered cities and tribes in Media.

NOTE. A stone tablet found in the region of Mari, northwest of Babylon in eastern Syria, reads that all city-kings were equal. *There is no king who is mighty of himself. Ten or fifteen kings follow Hammurabi, the man of Babylon, a like number to the king of Larsa, a like number the king of Eshunna, and twenty follow the king of Yamkhad in Syria.*

Introducing the Lesson

Lot and his wife and children were captured by foreign kings and taken away with the troops. The things that woman must have thought of during that time must have been devastating. Then here came Uncle Abraham to the rescue!

Display map **of nations listed in GENESIS 14.** This map shows Ur where Abraham's and Lot's families started out. At the top of the map is Haran, named after Lot's father, where they lived until Grandfather Terah died. And of course, you know where Canaan is. At the bottom of the Dead Sea is Sodom where Lot moved his family. Then five kings from the east descended on Canaan to plunder and capture, including Lot's family. Explain where each king came from and show the size of his territory.

During those early years, Lot and his wife had to make hard decisions that would influence their daughters' upbringing and adult lives. Perhaps they thought of that and perhaps they didn't. But they ended up in Sodom, possibly for the educational opportunities, possibly for the cultural exposure. What they ran into in the city eventually killed Lot's wife, and destroyed the morals of her daughters.

Display **DETERMINERS OF RIGHT AND WRONG.** These statistics were published in the book *The Day America Told the Truth*. Notice only 52% of Americans believe the Bible has the right to tell us what is right and wrong. Only 50% believe religion has that right, and only 42% believe the church has that right. It was also interesting how people separated these entities rather than seeing them as one.

Discussion Questions

1. **Tell of a time you had to make a decision for your children to stay away from bad influences and later they thanked you for it.**

   Joshua 24:15: "As for me and my house, we will serve the Lord."

Possible Class Response: We make more decisions for our children the younger they are. Some mothers may have told their children not to play/associate with certain people who later got in trouble. Or mothers told them they had to return something they stole, or made them pay for something of someone else's they broke. Some parents have to force their children to attend church until the children begin to develop a faith of their own. Sometimes, when children don't know how to go against peer pressure even when they want to, they will privately ask their parents to tell them in front of their peers they can't do that particular thing.

2. **Tell of a time you were discouraged from standing up for something right because you weren't getting along with someone you loved.**

   One thing for sure we don't need if we are going to stand firm for right in the world: Bickering from within—family bickering, church bickering, close friends bickering.

   John 13:35: People will know we are followers of Christ if we love each other.

   Possible Class Response: Sometimes teenagers go along with the crowd, even when they know the activity might lead to trouble, because they're arguing with their family and "just don't care." Some women may have been arguing with a committee at church over something and just decided not to go to church for a while. Some people, when they aren't getting along with those they love, binge on food or shopping, etc. to turn their anger inward.

3. **Under what circumstances might higher education and better culture be left well enough alone?**

   There are many things in the world that are good of themselves, but surrounding circumstances make them too costly.

   Matthew 16:26: What good will it do in eternity if we lose our souls but were considered a success back on earth?

   Possible Class Response: We should look through the catalog of a university being considered to see what type courses are being taught and what the student regulations are. They may be teaching humanism, extra-marital sexuality, evolution without equal time for creationism, situational ethics, etc. Affluence attracts the criminal element wanting to take for themselves part of that affluence, so some families just move to small country towns to get away from it.

4. **If you decided to live and do missionary work among people who were rich and given to drugs openly, for instances, what could you do to keep your moral standards above theirs?**

   In some cultures of the past, such as the Chinese, certain drugs such as opium were considered relaxing. In the U.S. when soft drinks first came out, some had cocaine in them. Some cultures today have a high incidence of alcoholism, among them France and Russia.

Matthew 28:19: Go to every type of culture and peoples in the world and teach those people how to become Christians.

Possible Class Response: I would have to learn the reasoning people used for using the drugs and prepare my reasons ahead of time for not indulging with them. These reasons should be self-protective as well as educational, and should be an encouragement to them to stop rather than full of condemnation because they do. I would select as my close friends those who either do not partake of drugs at all, or do not force their habits on others. I would want to take written material with me against these drugs so I could reread them whenever I became weak. I would write to my friends back in my homeland about the problems and ask them to send me letters of encouragement. I would invite some of my friends back home to come visit me sometimes. I would return to my homeland sometimes to get restored spiritually and my sense of values reinforced.

5. **How can we guard against flattery (Psalm 37:11)? Give some specific examples of such flattery.**

   Psalm 5:9: Certain flatterers feel no obligation toward other people's welfare, their words lead to death and they don't even care as long as the flatterers get what they want.

   Psalm 37:11: The meek who seek what is good for others and for God instead of themselves will end up with everything that evil people desire but will eventually lose.

   Possible Class Response: People might tell us "Everyone is doing it," "It will make us richer/more popular/more beautiful," "It will help us understand things better," "We will be able to get what's only due us." The meek remember God's commandments, regardless of our own welfare, and think of others we may be hurting directly (those we take advantage of) and indirectly (family who will be hurt by our hurt).

6. **Try to think of as many types of sin as possible and determine whether you believe people on earth would continue to be born and live if these sins were committed by everyone.**

   Romans 1:22,24,26-28: Those who claim to be wise, but are actually fools, degrade their own bodies and call God a liar. Eventually God backs away from them to let them wallow in their sexual perversions of homosexuality and reap the results.

   1 Corinthians 6:18-20: We must flee sexual sins which are sins against our own bodies. The Holy Spirit dwells in our bodies to do his good works.

   Possible Class Response: Homosexuality and abortion practiced by everyone would bring about the fast extinction of the human race.

7. **Specifically, how can we get control of anybody function that we are abusing (Romans 12:1,2)?**

Leviticus 20:13-16: Several sexual sins are linked with homosexuality—all called sodomy—and the participants are condemned to death because they are abominable.

Ab means away as in abhor and abuse, and *omin* comes from omen referring to a sign of the future. God is telling us that homosexuality is a sign of an abhorrent future.

Such people who do not obey God's commands in this *abomination* are not likely to take other self-respect and self-control commands of God seriously, thus leading to a bad future.

Romans 12:1,2: Because God has given us mercy and forgiven the sins of our mind and body, we should sacrifice our bodies to him by doing good works in his name. His mercy bought us, so we are now his.

Possible Class Response: We can transfer the center of our attention and activities from self-pleasure to others-pleasure. If we exhaust ourselves in service to God, we will have little or no time/opportunity to abuse our bodies.

8. **Read 2 Timothy 2:22 and discuss how such a person can accomplish this.**

The *Encyclopedia Britannica* states that sexual inversion "rarely appears by itself, and is frequently associated with other...abnormal immature ways of obtaining sexual pleasure." The key here seems to be immaturity.

2 Timothy 2:22: Run away from youthful lusts. Instead, make friends with other followers of God and do whatever is right, good, and peaceful.

Possible Class Response: Immature people don't know how to say "no" or "not now" to things they want. We should seek out people who seem to be strong where we have weaknesses. In return, we can help them in areas we are strong and they are weak. Associations seem to be the key.

Good Work

Send a note to a Christian you know working or associating with people who make little pretense of following God.

BEFORE CLASS:

A. Gather up church directories and phone books.

B. Gather up stationary (colored bond paper cut in half) and envelopes.

On poster board or the blackboard, write the following:

"I just wanted to write this note to tell you I know things can be difficult for you at work/school. People who are not Christians don't understand God loves them and means for his commandments to help them and not hurt them. I know you have always worked hard to be a good example before them and it hasn't always been easy. I am proud of you, and so is God. You are in my prayers that God will remain with you and continue to give you strength."

DURING CLASS:

"We've been studying about standing up for God's ways when people around us don't like God or insist that God didn't really mean that a particular act was a sin. We all know people who associate with godless people every day. Many of us are among them."

"Today, let's send a note of encouragement to someone we know who works or goes to school with some godless people. You may select your husband, a teenager in school somewhere, or a business person in the church who has a good reputation in the community for standing for what is right."

Hand out stationery and envelopes. "You will have about eight minutes to address your envelope and write your note. I have written on the board an example in case you are unsure how to express yourself. Feel free to use it if you like."

"Let's all be quiet now and allow each other time to think and write. When you are done, give your letter to me to mail and offer a silent prayer for the person you wrote."

Concluding Remarks

When time is up and while the slower writers complete their notes, sing one verse of a song, possibly one of the following:

1. *Stand Up, Stand Up for Jesus*
2. *Yield Not to Temptation*
3. *In the Hour of Trial*
4. *Trust and Obey*

In a few minutes, your class will be returning home, some possibly to face problems with homosexual members of their family or even their own background. End the class by giving everyone courage to overcome.

(Wait for one or two quick replies to each of the following.) "In just a few words,

1. Are there times we must make moral decisions for our children?
2. Common sense tells us that if homosexuality were practiced by everyone, what would go out of existence?
3. What is one way to encourage ourselves if we live among people who are ungodly?
4. We can guard against flattery by putting who first?

Have a closing prayer, especially remembering those with the "gay life style".

Map-Kings Abraham Conquered

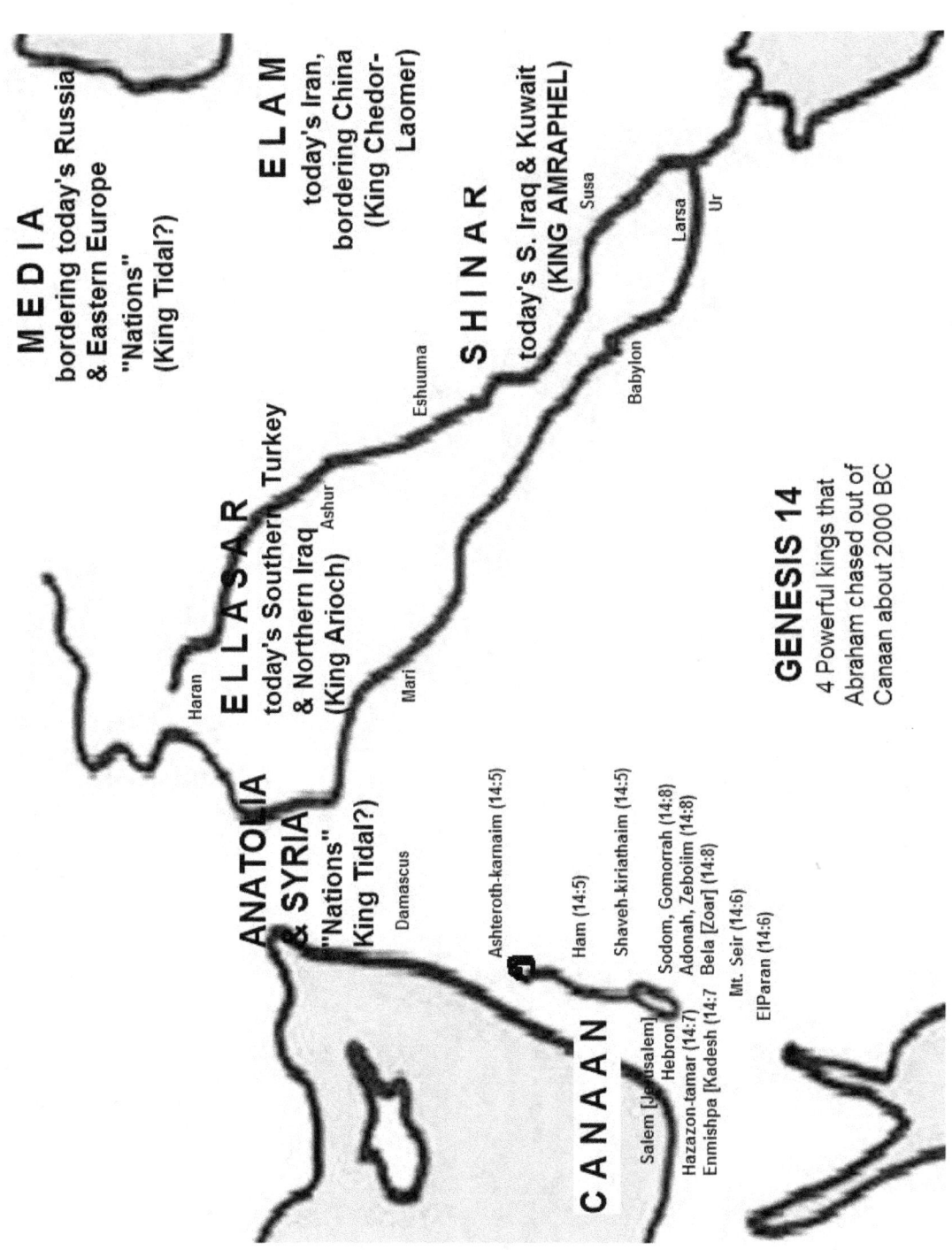

Determiners of Right and Wrong in the US

Spouse	77%	55%	Spouse
Parent	71%	46%	Parent
Bible	52%	37%	Bible
Religion	52%	34%	Religion
Local Police	50%	33%	Local Police
Church	44%	25%	Church
Supreme Court	42%	25%	Supreme Crt

Katheryn Maddox Haddad

Homosexual But Not So Gay

Lesson Two: Compromising Our Morals

Lesson Aim
- ♥ UNDERSTAND THE MILITANCY OF HOMOSEXUALITY
- ♥ UNDERSTAND OUR CREATOR'S HATRED FOR IT

Scripture Outline

Genesis 18:1-3: The Lord and two other "men" [angels] appear at Abraham's home.

Genesis 18:16-22: The Lord tells Abraham he is about to destroy Sodom and Gomorrah because of their great wickedness. Then the two "men" head toward Sodom while the Lord remains back with Abraham.

Genesis 18:23-33: Abraham convinces the Lord to not destroy Sodom if he can only find five or ten righteous people in it.

Genesis 19:1-3: The two "men" now called angels, arrive at Sodom

and are met by Lot. They say they'll spend the night out in the street, but Lot convinces them it's too dangerous and to come to his house instead.

Genesis 19:4,5: Just before bedtime, men from every part of Sodom and of every age and status, come to Lot's house. They call in to him to bring his two guests out so they can have sex with them.

Genesis 19:6,7: Lot goes outside to talk sense into them, and is careful to shut his door behind him. He tells them how terrible their request is.

Genesis 19:8: Lot then, tainted by some of the morals of Sodom, offers to bring his daughters out to the men to have sex with instead. Perhaps he hopes that, since they are homosexual, he can call their bluff, for they wouldn't want to have sex with females.

Genesis 19:9: They turn on the man who used to sit as judge at their gates and whose uncle saved the entire city from slavery or death. They call him an outsider who wasn't from Sodom in the first place, and begin to storm his house and break down his door.

Today's

World

Anita Bryant is a former Miss America and singer. She was one of the first people in America to stand publicly against homosexuality. It cost her her career. Although her ordeal took place in the late 1970s, it is still relevant. In January 1977 she publicly spoke against an ordinance proposed in Dade County, Miami, Florida which would give homosexuals special privileges in housing, public accommodation, and employment. She was made chairman of SAVE OUR CHILDREN.

She endured death threats, distortions of statements by the media, and job discrimination. Those who stood against homosexuals were considered bigots, haters, discriminators, and deniers of basic human rights. The Orlando *Sentinel-Star* interviewed Anita and she quoted I Corinthians 6:9 which lists those who will not inherit the kingdom of God such as murderers, drunkards, thieves, and homosexuals. The headline in the paper read: ANITA BRYANT CALLS HOMOSEXUALS MURDERERS! There were other distortions, including a bumper sticker which read KILL A QUEER FOR CHRIST.

Not too long after the proposition was passed in Dade County, a national homosexual bill (HR2998) was introduced which would make it mandatory nationwide to hire known practicing homosexuals in public schools and other public sectors.

Day after day Anita received letters that she called "filth—just filth" and with them pictures of such things as two nude men committing an act of homosexuality. She had to work to cast them out of her mind, and wondered how children exposed to pornography are molested in their minds because they cannot cast these images out.

When poet Rod McKuen came to Miami, he said, "I intend to call upon every comedian friend I know to have so many jokes go forth about her throughout the land that she will be a laughingstock such as this country has never seen before."

When Anita appeared on the "Good Morning, America" show with David Hartman, she began quoting the Bible, and was "accidentally" cut off. Immediately following her was Gore Vidal who claimed he'd never heard such expounding of hatred since Hitler.

House Representative Elaine Noble of Massachusetts was the first legislator to admit publicly to being homosexual. She was an outspoken advocate of "gay rights" with speaking engagements all over the country espousing gay doctrine and urging homosexuals to run for political offices on all levels. She said it would be more effective to get states to pass anti-discrimination laws than rely on the Supreme Court.

An Associated Press report datelined Washington said: "The Federal Communication Commission was petitioned to require radio and television stations to pay more attention to the problems, needs and interests of homosexuals. Jean O'Leary, co-director of the National Gay Task Force, told a news conference, 'We are asking FCC to add leaders of the gay community to the checklist that broadcast licensees.'"

The Los Angeles *Times* critic, Cecil Smith, interviewed TV producer James Komack who said: "Do you know the most powerful lobby in the entertainment business? Bigger than blacks or women's lib or any nationalist or racial group? It's the gays. If you don't have the approval of the Gay Media Task Force, you don't go on the air." He went on to say that their number one priority was passage of the National Gay Rights Bill in Congress.

Various denominations are now studying gay rights, and have already stated they would accept homosexual ministers. Many have come to see homosexuality not as a sin or even a sexual deviation, but an "alternate lifestyle."

Dr. Shirley Van Ferney, a member of the psychiatric staff at New Jersey's Medical Center in Princeton warned: "Constant media coverage of the gays has made their lifestyle appear to be commonplace and acceptable rather than unusual and deviant....This is particularly disturbing to those who are concerned that their children could easily be misled into thinking that homosexuality is an attractive kind of lifestyle to adopt. Parents are absolutely correct to be fearful of the effects all of this is having on their kids. <u>Homosexuals are so active on high school and college campuses that there is hardly a child in America who has not been exposed to their influence.</u>...If parents capitulate to the homosexual influences which surround them, society as we know it will be destroyed."

A Gables [Florida] Youth Resource Officer reported: "A lot of regular people have the general attitude of 'live-and-let-live' about homosexuality. People generally presume that in the homosexual world, it's a case of a couple of guys living together and not bothering anybody. That simply is not the case. A couple of guys might live together for a while, but eventually one of them is going to get tired of it and go out looking for new kicks. He will go looking for a boy; he will start occupying bus station [and mall] restrooms or whatever.

The Washington *Star* reported April 11, 1977 that child porn peddlers are aided by such groups as the American Civil Liberties Union which believes censorship of such material violates the First Amendment protecting free speech.

Reacting to a photo he saw of a man performing sex with an 8-year-old boy, Lloyd Martin, head of a special unit with the Los Angeles Police Department dealing with sexual exploitation of children said: "What put me to work was one picture....The look on that boy's face....No amount of words can describe it....In order for pornography to survive, there must be a new product. They'll do anything to make that almighty buck. Authorities say that perhaps 70 percent of the child porn market now involves young boys—'chickens' in the vernacular—and adult male homosexuals....children will suffer lasting harmful effects and...probably grow up and become sexual abusers themselves."

Despite all this, A federal appeals court ruled in 2017 that Title VII of the 1964 Civil Rights Act, which bans discrimination on the basis of race, color, religion, sex, and national origin, also covers homosexuality. The U.S. Court of Appeals for the 7th Circuit, which handles cases in Indiana, Illinois, and Wisconsin, decided 8-3 that discrimination on the basis of "sex" also means discrimination on the basis of "sexual orientation."

Bible

World

Traditionally, sodomy is the word used for male homosexuals, however it can also include females. It has ever been with us. C. S. Ford and F. A. Beach, who studied primitive societies, state that 65% accepted homosexuality as being normal. Some were allowed to wear the clothing of females and "marry." In some cases, sodomy was found among shamans, priests who people believed had the only influence over evil spirits, and found in ancient religions of northeast Asia and the American Indians.

In his book *Man and His Gods*, Homer W. Smith says that *pederasty* (the love of boys) so permeated the early culture of Greece that anthropologists of our century referred to it as "Greek love." It was the custom of every Spartan youth of good character to have his lover, or "inspirator," and for every well-educated man to be the lover of some carefully chosen youth. Plato condemned the practice only insofar as it turned men from marriage and the begetting of children; if they did marry, Plato said, it was only in obedience to the law.

One factor promoting *pederasty* (homosexuality) in Greece was the wide cultural gulf between men and women. The wife lived in retirement and ignorance, almost in seclusion and excluded from both education and public cultural activities. Hence the intellectual Greeks regarded love of women as the offspring of the vulgar goddess Aphrodite. Homosexual companionship was regarded not only as permissible, but was praised as the highest and purest form of love, as a path leading to virtue, and a source of national greatness and glory.

Sodomy was a problem, not only in the time of Abraham and Lot, but continued as a scourge to later generations. Job, who lived about the time of Esau, Abraham's grandson, condemned it (Job 36:13f). God commanded that anyone committing sodomy was to be put to death (Leviticus 20:13). Many began the practice in worship to Ashtoreth, the goddess of fertility and given other names in other languages including Venus, and was worshipped with male prostitutes. Her counterpart was Baal, the male god of fertility, with female prostitutes.

Although the Hebrews were to kill the people of Canaan for their sexual idol worship (Genesis 15:16; Leviticus 18:22,27), soon after the Hebrews settled in the new land, they began serving Baal and Ashtoreth (Judges 2:13). It got as bad as it had in Lot's Sodom.

Judges 19 tells the gruesome story of sodomites (homosexuals), much like those in Lot's time. A man and his concubine were traveling and stood in the city square of Gibeah hoping someone would take them in for the night. An old man saw them, warned them not to stay in the square, and took them home. While they were eating, the homosexual men of the city surrounded the house. "Pounding on the door, they shouted...'Bring out the man who came to your house so we can have sex with him'" (19:22). The old man went out, just as Lot had, begged them not to because the man was his guest. Instead, he offered them the man's concubine and his virgin daughter. "I will bring them out to you now, and you can use them and do to them whatever you wish. But to this man, don't do such a disgraceful thing" (19:24). When the men persisted, the concubine was forced to go outside to them, "and they raped her and abused her throughout the night, and at dawn they let her go." Soon thereafter she died. The man cut her into twelve parts and sent them to each of the Twelve Tribes of Israel. Then Israelites from everywhere went to the tribe of Benjamin and nearly obliviated it.

Homosexuality continued in the time of Samuel, the last judge (1 Samuel 7:3,4). During the reign of Solomon, he built places of worship to fertility gods and worshipped with male prostitution, sodomy (1 King 11:4-8; 2 Kings 23:13f). Rehoboam, Solomon's son, continued the practice, with male prostitutes (sodomites) at shrines dedicated to Ashtoreth.

When Solomon's grandson, Asa, came to power, he exiled the male prostitutes (sodomites) from the land (1 Kings 15:12). His son, Jehoshaphat, found a few who'd escaped, and exiled them too (1 Kings 22:45f). Sodomy gradually found its way back into the Hebrew culture for 250 years until King Josiah again destroyed the sodomites. By then, they had taken over the Temple (2 Kings 23:7). He also broke down Solomon's "high places" which were still in the hills on which he erected the customary pillars (poles) as well as buildings or tents for the priests and priestesses. (Read all of 2 Kings 23 to see just how much it had taken over the Temple and the life of the Jews.)

Introducing the Lesson

Besides, AIDS, to what extent is homosexuality affecting our society today? **Display AND GAYS SAY THEY WANT LEFT ALONE TO THEIR OWN LIFESTYLE.** Discuss the gay movement in America to whichever degree you wish.

This is a problem that has plagued mankind since the beginning. **Display GOD SAID HOMOSEXUALITY IS A SIN.** Discuss homosexuality (sodomy) in the Bible to whichever degree you desire.

Discussion Questions

9. **Tell about an unmarried Christian you know of (never married or widowed) and the opportunities for Christian service they have taken advantage of.**

   <u>1 Corinthians 7:34,35</u>: Women who are married must spend time pleasing their husbands as well as God's work. Women who are unmarried don't have divided interests like this.

   <u>Possible Class Response</u>: Even if the unmarried woman has to support herself, she still has evenings to either go home to an empty house, or reach out to others. Some spend time with other widows. Some visit hospitals or nursing homes regularly. Some get involved in volunteer work such as for abused women, abused children, the homeless. Some teach World Bible School correspondence courses. Some go on campaigns to communities with small churches. Some teach classes and spend a great deal of time preparing for them. The author knew one widow in her eighties who taught the fourth grade at Sunday school and required her students call her every day at home; they loved her!

10. **Compare the price of a non-Christian marriage to the price of a Christian marriage.**

   Often there are benefits to a Christian young person going off to a Christian college during the normal time of dating and seeking a marriage partner.

   2 Corinthians 6:14: Christians should not be equally bound to non-Christians. What they don't have in common is too important.

   Possible Class Response: A higher price is usually paid if a Christian marries a non-Christian. The Christian has to get up alone early enough on Sunday morning to go to worship, sometimes while her husband is pressuring her to just stay in bed and rest or go with him somewhere else. Unless he becomes a Christian later, they will not be together in eternity. When they have children, the children become confused as to whether God is worth fighting over; so her children's souls are put in jeopardy. She is held back in getting to know the other Christians on a personal and social basis; she and her husband have different friends.

11. **Share a time when you associated with a group of people who did not act Christian, and your own resistance was worn down.**

   Lot and his wife had been trying to live a good life under the circumstances condemned in many parts of the Bible.

   Psalm 1:1: We're not to walk among evil advisors, stand by them, or sit with them to make our decisions.

   Possible Class Response: It will take some confessing. The teacher should be the first to confess. Some may have allowed their children to go to an R-rated movie because it was so rated for violence and not sex, and their children kept saying it was "no big deal." Some may have not gone to worship because they had company that was leaving late Sunday morning. Some may have left a lonely person off a guest list because they had behavior no one else could handle. This will sometimes involve times when the ladies were young.

12. **What can we do to protect ourselves from their influence?**

   Gays say they want to be left alone to their own "lifestyle" and that they do not bother anyone. However, one of the characteristics of most gays is that their relationships do not last. So, what actually develops is the nose-in-the-tent or foot-in-the-door syndrome.

   2 Timothy 3:13: People who do wrong will continue to seduce others to participate with them more and more.

   2 Peter 2:17-19: Because of their lusts, they enslave themselves and then try to convince others that it is okay to participate with them.

   Possible Class Response: We must spend our time thinking about good things. There is a fine line between learning about their philosophies, and allowing our minds to be overcome by their philosophies. We may watch a TV talk show about homosexuals, but don't have to watch the whole thing, or don't have to watch every such show that is broadcast. It is easy to let personalities influence us when we see a wholesome-looking person endorsing an evil way of life.

13. **Tell how you could help a homosexual overcome these two problems.**

    It is believed that some homosexuals learned to identify with the opposite gender as a child, and therefore try to carry this pattern out in every area of life. It is also believed that some homosexuals have grown to fear or resent the opposite gender from one or more very bad experiences. Their homosexuality in both cases is apparently just a symptom. What are the real problems in these cases, and how can they be solved?

    Philippians 4:11: We must learn that whatever state we're in, whether male or female, we are to be content.

    Proverbs 29:25: When we resent or fear something/someone, we can overcome by trusting in the Lord.

    Possible Class Response: If a person has a gender-identification problem, perhaps they missed a close relationship with a person of their own gender while growing up and don't know how to treat the opposite sex. If they grew to resent or fear the opposite sex, perhaps it would help if someone of that gender became a good but non-threatening friend to them. Either way, a simple and trusting friendship with a homosexual (but making it clear you disagree with their sexual leanings) might help.

14. **What can we do to help our family over such burden if it happens to them?**

    When homosexuality hits a family, most relatives go in to shock. They think it happens to other people.
    John 5:39: Search the scriptures for answers.

    2 Timothy 3:16,17: The scriptures were given to us to instruct us in the right way of living before God and man.

    Colossians 4:5,6: We should use the scriptures to learn God's wisdom, then learn how to explain God's way with firmness but gentleness.

    Possible Class Response: We can continue to love the person who is homosexual, but let them know we disapprove of their choice. We could write out or photocopy the scriptures about homosexuality, and at the top tell the person these scriptures are shared with love. We can try to help them learn to accept without fear or resentment the opposite sex. We can let other family members know our love for them has not changed, and promise not to gossip about them.

15. **When we close our eyes to sin in our community, we often find it has become a sleeping giant just awakening. If we feel it is too late to control the giant, what must we do? Tell about someone you know who did this. Do you think Lot and Lottie should have?**

Joshua 24:2,3: When faithful Abraham became surrounded by idol worshippers in Ur of Babylon, God took him away from his home and led him to live somewhere else.

Possible Class Response: When things get too bad and we feel we can't change society around us, we should just leave them to their evil ways, just like God does. We should just move away. Many people know of young couples who moved out of large cities to rural communities to get them away from as many bad influences as possible. Definitely Lot should have moved out of Sodom. Eventually did, when there was no more Sodom to live in. We can't stay and let ourselves be destroyed.

16. **When all the justifying and excuses are cleared away, what puts us in such no-win situation (James 1:13,14)? How can we get out of such situations?**

Sometimes we put ourselves in such a bad situation we come to the conclusion we must weigh and choose the lesser of two evils.

James 1:13,14: God allows us to go through trials, but he does not tempt us to do bad things. We allow ourselves to be exposed to temptations and then stay around them long enough to give in to them.

Possible Class Response: We are the ones who place ourselves in bad situations, whether they be at work, or our neighborhood, or our children's school systems, or the radio stations we listen to, or the TV shows we watch. We must not let ourselves be drawn into something that is wrong, just because it is not nearly as wrong as something else we are tempted with. We can begin justifying our wrong actions if we don't reinforce ourselves with the scriptures and Christian associates.

17. **When by our own doing we place ourselves in circumstances where only bad can be the outcome, what is our only recourse as Christians?**

Romans 12:19: We must surround ourselves with peace.

Possible Class Response: When there is one bad social problem, there are usually others with them. We hurt ourselves by not taking ourselves out of bad situations. If the church does not surround us with enough people who are not tempted, we should just move away. We must run from them all as hard as we can.

Good Work

Send a letter to various congressmen (state and national) from your state. Explain that you are opposed to homosexual marriage or unisex bathrooms.

BEFORE CLASS:

A. Gather up a list of the congressmen from your state and your district.

B. Write the name and address of these congressmen on individual envelopes.

C. Gather up enough stationery for your class.

D. On poster board or the blackboard, write the following:

"I want to make my voice heard. What I believe may or may not be popular, but it is valuable. I am opposed to homosexual marriage because...."
or
"I want to make my voice heard. What I believe may or may not be popular, but it is valuable. I am opposed to unisex bathrooms because...."

DURING CLASS:

"We are beginning to lose the battle against the sin of sexuality. Homosexuals have a large lobby and strong organizations backed by a lot of money. We must make our voices known. The value of one is great.

"I have located the names and addresses of our congressmen—enough for each of us to write to a different one."

Pass out stationary. "You will have about five minutes to write your message. If you are unsure what to says, I have written on the board an example for those unsure how to express yourself. Feel free to use it if you like."

"Let's all be quiet now and allow each other time to think and write. When you are done, give your envelope to me to send to the counselor. Then offer a silent prayer that our nation will return to the Bible."

Concluding Remarks

When time is up and while the slower writers complete their notes, sing one verse of a song, possibly one of the following:

1. *Jesus Will Give You Rest*
2. *Softly and Tenderly Jesus is Calling*
3. *Whiter Than Snow*
4. *I Heard the Voice of Jesus Say*

In a few minutes your class will be returning home, some possibly to face problems with homosexual family members or even their own background. End the class by giving everyone courage to overcome.

(Wait for one or two quick replies to each of the following.) "In just a few words,

1. Do unmarried or married people have more time to serve the Lord?

2. What could happen to children produced in a marriage of one Christian and one non-Christian?

3. What is one way we can help a homosexual overcome their resentment of the opposite sex?

4. If temptation stays around us and we can't control us, what should we do?

Have a closing prayer, remembering those with homosexual problems as well as their families.

Childhood of Gays

And Gays Say They Want Left Alone to their Own LifeStyle

☞ **One-fifth of Americans anonymously confessed to having homosexual fantasies.**

☞ **Although heterosexual men have a maximum of 17 sexual partners in their lifetime, homosexual men have at least 100.**

☞ **Homosexual men average nearly one "lover" for every month in the year.**

*The Day America Told the Truth by James Patterson and Peter Kim

God Said Homosexuality is a Sin

Leviticus 18:22,27 ~ God had the people of Canaan killed because of their idolatrous sodomy.

Leviticus 20:13 ~ God said anyone caught committing sodomy was to be put to death.

Romans 1:27,32 ~ God said homosexuals and those who approve of them are worthy of death.

1 Corinthians 6:9 ~ God said homosexuals, thieves, covetous, drunkards will not inherit the kingdom of God.

1 Timothy 1:10 ~ God said murderers and liars and homosexuals are ungodly.

Katheryn Maddox Haddad

Homosexual But Not So Gay

Lesson Three: Losing Our Morals

Lesson Aim
- ♥ KNOW WHAT IS WRONG WITH HOMOSEXUALITY
- ♥ LEARN WHEN TO GET OUT OF A BAD SITUATION

Scripture Outline

Genesis 19:10,11: Lot escapes by the skin of his teeth when the angels open the door, pull him inside, close it after him, then make the would-be attackers blind. Even then they continue to look for Lot's door so they can break it down. Eventually they stop.

Genesis 19:12-14: The angels announce the Lord is going to destroy Sodom because of everyone's evil. They give Lot a chance to warn relatives and friends to escape with them. With the little bit of time left, Lot chooses to go to his betrothed soon-to-be sons-in-law. They just make fun of Lot.

Genesis 19:15,16: All night the family holds back, possibly packing everything they can carry. Finally, one angel takes the hands of Lot and his wife, the other angel takes the hands of the two daughters, and they literally pull them out of the city. Then they tell the family to "run for your life" for the fire is just moments away, and not to look back lest the fire catch up with them.

Genesis 19:17-23: Lot still argues. He doesn't want to move his family to a cave. He begs the Lord to save one of the five cities of the plain, the smallest one. They arrive just as the sun slips up to the horizon.

Genesis 19:24-26: The moment Lot steps inside Zoar, the fire comes down upon the whole plain destroying all the cities, and coming just a few feet from Zoar. Lot's wife is behind him, and stops for one last glance just before entering the gate herself, and is caught by the brimstone which encases and kills her instantly.

Genesis 19:27-30: For Abraham's sake God has saved Lot's family. Apparently, the people of Zoar are suspicious of Lot because his was the only family to escape. So, Lot ends up going to the mountain cave where he was supposed to go in the first place.

Genesis 19:31-36: Lot is so heartbroken by the tragic loss of his wife and friends, he drowns his sorrows in alcohol. The still immature daughters decide they are so unpopular that no one will ever want to marry them. So, still inflicted with the influence of Sodom even from its fiery grave, while their father is drunk, they apparently pretend they are their mother, and get pregnant by him.

Genesis 19:37,38: They both bear sons. One is named Moab and becomes the nation out of which Ruth is born, the ancestress of David and eventually of Jesus. The other is named Ammon and is the enemy of God's people for centuries to come.

Today's World

In 1981, the first cases of AIDS (Acquired Immuno-Deficiency Syndrome) in the United States were discovered in a group of homosexual men. From about 25 cases discovered at that time, within three years over 7,000 cases were discovered. Within ten years, 180,000 were reported in the U.S. with 115,000 deaths caused by it.

Worldwide, the first cases were discovered in the early 1970s in Africa. The World Health Organization estimated in 1992 that 10 to 12 million people worldwide, including one million children, had been infected with the AIDS virus in less than twenty years.

Since the beginning of the epidemic, more than 70 million people have been infected with the HIV virus and about **35 million people** have died of HIV. Globally, **36.7 million** [34.0–39.8 million] people were living with HIV at the end of 2015.

The World Health Organization is concerned that deaths of these adults who include members of social, economic, and political elites, could weaken the economic and even political stabilization of the world.

In 1985, some 75 percent of AIDS cases were homosexual men, 20 percent drug abusers, and 5 percent newborn babies who usually die within a month of birth. Today, by far the fastest-growing group to get AIDS is WOMEN, and the upward trend of women will snowball, because bisexual men with AIDS are not telling their female partners.

AIDS involves a virus which affects the lymph system and lowers the body's resistance to any infection. The most common fatal infection is pneumonia. Chronic herpes ulcers/ rashes attacking the esophagus is the next most common. It also lowers resistance to mononucleosis, encephalitis, colitis, TB, salmonella. Initial symptoms are vague—fever, malaise, swollen lymph glands, anorexia, periodic herpes episodes, dry cough, diarrhea, sudden weight loss, night sweats.

* * *

Dr. Laura Allen and Dr. Roger Gorski of the University of California at Los Angeles released a report in 1992 resulting from a study to see if homosexual men were physically different from heterosexual men. They concluded that a bundle of nerves called the anterior commissure is larger in gay men than in straight men. This nerve bundle is not thought to influence sexual behavior directly, but relates to how the two sides of the brain communicate with each other.

Many scientists are saying this new research is likely to prove as questionable as past studies trying to prove neuro-anatomical difference between blacks and whites. Dr. William Byne, Columbia University College of Physicians and Surgeons, commented, "I just don't think sexual orientation is going to be represented in any particular brain structure. It's like looking in the brain for your political party affiliation."

* * *

Cal Thomas, Los Angeles Times syndicated columnist, said that "AIDS is one price we pay for a society without rules." He explained that those who acquire AIDS do so because of behavior they could avoid if they wanted to.

Thomas said he thought men who use drugs and commit adultery, then pass on AIDS and other venereal diseases to each other and unsuspecting wives should be cornered and told to straighten up their lives. Gays and lesbians declare that people should be able to do whatever they want. That's precisely how AIDS is spread, so what do those who condone homosexuality expect?

He went on to say that America has failed to set boundaries for acceptable behavior. Without such rules declaring what is "right and honorable and decent," people can indeed do anything they want. He suggested that since the gays are organized, we should look for adulterers and incest practicers to get organized too. Then, as soon as they get as big as the gay rights movement, they too can appeal to Americans for "tolerance."

Thomas concluded his column by saying, "Woe to those who call evil good, and good, evil," which he explained was a quote from "America's most banned and least consulted book."

Bible

World

THE SALT SEA AND THE CITIES OF THE PLAIN THAT WERE BURNED AND DESTROYED. Sodom means "Place of Salt" and was also called Usdom, which has the same meaning. Above the five cities of the plain is Mount Usdom surrounded at its base by many steep cliffs. It has a layer 150 feet thick of salt, and above it a thick layer of sulfur, also called brimstone. Sulfur is extremely flammable and is used to make matches and explosives.

Earthquakes still in modern times throw up large quantities of bitumen (oil) detached from the bottom of the southern lagoon of the Salt Sea. The Salt Sea lies on the deepest fault in the earth's crust. Its northern tip is 1,300 feet deep and still sinking. It is known as the DEEPEST DEPRESSION ON EARTH. At the southern tip in the lagoon, it is only 3 to 12 feet deep, leading many to believe Sodom literally turned over into that end of the sea.

If God sent lightening down on to the mountain to strike the sulfur, or if he caused it to erupt from the fire in the belly of the earth, or if he used his own finger to light the sulfur, it could have touched off a stupendous explosion in the salt and brimstone of the volcanic mountain, shooting up into the heavens, and then falling down on the surrounding countryside as if raining fire down from heaven. God could have used any method he chose.

Genesis 14:10 refers to the "slime pits" in the area, and this phrase is the same Hebrew word as "bitumen," a chief element in tar, coal, or oil. When this salty brimstone and fire came down from the heavens, it would hit the slime pits, and cause further explosions.

The word *overthrew* in Genesis 19:25 means to literally *turn over*. If the fire out of heaven was caused by a volcanic eruption, and considering how deep the earth's fault is there, the cities of the plain could have burned, and then turned over into the earth's opening and closed up again, thus causing that end of the Dead Sea to nearly fill up. God used this method at other times for destroying people (Number 26:10).

The Salt Sea or Sea of the Plain (Deuteronomy 3:17) is fed from the north by the fresh waters of the Jordan River. But these waters quickly turn salty because of the salt-sulfur mountain at the southwest tip. Scientists agree that the southern bay or lagoon was once the Plain of Jordan, and today abounds with salt, bitumen (oil), sulfur (brimstone), and niter (used to make gunpowder). Anything that flows into it from the Jordan dies due to the salt. At the southern tip it is marshy and has only small outlets that go a little way and stop. It is as though the Jordan once flowed through it and emptied into the Red Sea, but was DAMMED UP. The cities of the plains could have easily caused the damming.

Archaeologists in 1924 found 5 oases with freshwater streams on a plain above the southern tip of the Dead Sea. There were great quantities of pottery and flints, etc., indicating a place for religious festivals, all originating about 2500 BC. It was very fertile there "like the Garden of God" (Genesis 13:10). The population ceased abruptly about 2000 BC, the time of the overthrow of the cities of the plain. The region has been one of complete desolation since.

The Dead Sea today is a glassy blue, and is transparent, reflecting the beautiful colors of mountains surrounding the southern end. But all this beauty is belied by the sterile look of the shores, the stifling heat, the sulfur smell of the gases rising out of it, and the salt marsh at the southern tip which make it too unpleasant to even go near. It truly justifies the most common name for this body of water today –the Dead Sea.

Introducing the Lesson

Today we're going to talk about a problem most of us don't think involves us. Let's start at the beginning. *Display US AIDS CASES.* Although originally this was a homosexual man's disease, today the fastest-growing group to get AIDS is women. Why? *Display chart HOMOSEXUAL MEN and discuss.*

Man hasn't known about germs for very many years, but in the Law of Moses, God ordered people to wash their hands before eating, ordered quarantines, etc. God knew something about homosexuality we didn't until recently either. How did he handle it? He burned and then apparently turned four homosexual cities upside down into the Dead Sea. *Display map used in Lesson One showing the four cities at the southern end of the Dead Sea.* Discuss.

Discussion Questions

18. **Give some examples of how we describe the "all American girl" or "all American boy." How can we train ourselves to not do this without becoming suspicious of every "limp-wristed" man and low-voiced woman?**

    1 Samuel 16:7: God told Samuel not to look at outward appearance and height in anointing the next king, but what is in his heart.

    Matthew 10:16: We must be harmless as doves, but wise as serpents when we are around worldly people.

    Possible Class Response: We think of the wholesome person as being fairly attractive, clean, a nice dresser, healthy, easy to get along with, friendly, and having a ready smile. We think of homosexual women as being large, tall, wearing no makeup, having short straight hair and a husky voice, and walking with a long gait. We think of a homosexual man as being small, short, having delicate facial features, using feminine gestures, and walking with short steps. These prejudices are far from true. We must not snicker behind anyone's back, make them the brunt of unfair jokes, and we must assume they are innocent unless proven guilty. We must judge them by their works.

19. **Tell about a time when something unusual happened and caught you off guard because it had "just never happened before." What lessons did you learn?**

    Luke 17:28-30: During the days of Lot, everyone was having a good time, and building homes, and going to work every day. Then suddenly, in just moments, the whole city of Sodom was wiped out.

Possible Class Response: Many have experienced an automobile accident, some ending in permanent disability or death. Some may have worked for the same company for many years, and one day were told everyone was laid off permanently. Some may have had a house burn down or flooded. Some may have had spouses who walked in one day and said they wanted a divorce. Quickly we learn to reevaluate our priorities. We learn not to take a peaceful life for granted. We learn just how reliable our relationship with God is.

20. **Without giving names, tell of a time you tried to warn someone of anything, and the feelings you had when you finally left them alone.**

Even with warnings, some people persist and even enjoy doing the opposite of God's will for their lives.

Isaiah 5:20-24: God pronounces a "woe" on those who call good evil, and evil good, and think they're so liberal-minded. He pronounces a "woe" on those whose heroes are great wine connoisseurs or big beer guzzlers. He pronounces a "woe" on those who don't call a spade a spade, and let the guilty keep doing wrong, and say that it is the good people who are bad. They have rejected God, and he will burn them up like straw.

Possible Class Response: The author once went to a new Christian lady she'd heard had gotten drunk at a party, had gone out into the street and was finally warned by the police to stop. Although patiently realizing the other lady may not have meant to let things get carried away, her neighbors did know she'd become a Christian; so perhaps she should stay away from her party friends. The new Christian ran into her bathroom, locked it, and refused to come out until left alone.

21. **Have you ever had to destroy part of something so the rest could grow and be healthy? How does this compare with rejecting evil people (John 15:2)? Who actually does the condemning (Isaiah 3:9)?**

John 15:2: Every branch in Jesus that does not bear fruit for him will be cut off.

Isaiah 3:9: The look on their faces is arrogance and pride that they are so "liberal-minded" as to accept all sins as just "alternative lifestyles." They're just foolishly bringing disaster upon themselves and have blinded themselves to it.

Possible Class Response: We cut dead leaves off of plants so the healthy ones can grow and flourish. We amputate parts of our body (both inside and out) so the rest of the body can live. We take impurities out of fabric by washing it, so it does not fade and eventually rot. To keep ourselves pure, we must disassociate ourselves from self-destructive people who refuse to heed God's will for their lives and actively try to get others to join them.

22. **How would following their bad example hurt them even more?**

Have you ever heard anyone say, "If I believe that part of the Bible, I'll be condemning my _____ [loved one]"?

Luke 16:23,27,28: When the rich man who wouldn't feed the poor died, he went to hell. Even while he was in torment, he begged Abraham whom he saw far off, to send someone to his father's house to warn his five brothers so they wouldn't go there too.

Possible Class Response: If we continue to do something wrong that a loved one did and has since died, we only cause them further torment. Somehow they apparently know whether their loved ones are saved. Perhaps we ease their torment by following God's way now.

23. **When we get ourselves into a mess and can't seem to get out, what should we rely on (2 Peter 2:6-9)? Give an example of this in your life.**

2 Peter 2:6-9: God rescued Lot because the sins by people all around him distressed him every day. So too, he will rescue us if we continue to follow him instead of those evil influences around us.

Possible Class Response: We should rely on God to help us out of bad situations. God will always offer us a way out. Sometimes God puts barriers in our way and forces us out of bad situations for our own good. Some may have been unable to get the tuition to go to a university that would have been a bad influence. Some may have been married to a man who caused havoc on the entire family, and the man left them. Some may have associated with the wrong people as a youth and suddenly moved. Some may have been working with unethical people in a job and suddenly got fired.

24. **Something that can help us cope is directing our anger at what source? Another aid is increasing our love and dedication to the one trying to eradicate sin in the world. Talk about this.**

The most terrible thing in the world is living with the knowledge someone you love has refused to follow God. Coping with the heartache is extremely difficult.

Romans 14:12: Eventually, every one of us must give account of our own actions before God. We won't stand before him as a group.

I Peter 5:8: Our permanent adversary is Satan, and he walks around trying to devour as many people as he can with sin and spiritual death.

2 Peter 3:9b; John 3:16: God does not want anyone to be lost eternally. He wants everyone to acknowledge their sins so he can forgive us. He wants this so much, he sacrificed his own son to a torturous death to make it possible for us.

Possible Class Response: First, we must let go of full responsibility for the souls of people we love. We cannot be saved for them, and they cannot be saved against their will. Second, we must direct our anger at Satan whoever puts temptation in front of us and makes it look so good. Finally, we must put our faith and all our energies into the work of God who doesn't want anyone to perish and is giving everyone as much time as they need to repent.

25. How can we encourage our teenage girls to associate with other teenagers busy doing good works today?

Despite everything, Lottie's daughters had not learned their lesson much better than their mother. They only grew more bitter and grew to assume only the worst. Instead of going into hiding, might Lot have been better off taking his daughters far away such as back to Haran?

Ezekiel 16:49: Sodom was destroyed because it was arrogant about how liberal they were to condone its sins. Her people spent all their spare-time pursuing those sins, and neglected the poor and needy.

Possible Class Response: If we belong to a large congregation, there is automatically a group of Christian young people to associate with. But if the congregation is small, other things need to be done for the few young people. We can have youth activities involving other small congregations in the area. We can take our youth to Christian college senior days. We can send them to Christian camps. We can encourage them to be involved in the work of the church in a special way such as assisting in teaching younger classes (especially if they would be the only one in a teen class).

26. What can we do to help people love God so they will then believe and respect his laws?

1 Corinthians 5:2: People are often considered narrow-minded if they do not approve of popular sins; right now it's homosexuality.

Jude 7: People of Sodom and Gomorrah spent their spare time in sexual perversion, polluting their bodies, and slandering God's followers.

Hebrews 10:31: It is fearful to fall into the hands of the living God.

2 Corinthians 5:14,15: Since Jesus died to save our lives, we should believe and dedicate our lives to the one who saved us.

Possible Class Response: We should try to convert homosexuals, keeping in mind that all have sinned and come short of the glory of God (Romans 3:23). We should never deny Christianity to someone who sins, whether it be alcoholism, white-collar crime, or whatever. Once, then, they accept how much God loves them and how much he sacrificed for them (his Son), they will be more likely to accept what God considers sin. We can show them medical truths in the Bible such as quarantines, washing before eating, resting one day a week, not eating fat, and other rules in the law of Moses. Then we can explain that our creator has named certain things sin because they hurt us. The only reason God gets angry at our sins is because we are hurting ourselves. We are just now learning of the terrible result of homosexuality which none of us knew about until the early 1970s. We must take God's word for some things rather than demanding to understand why on everything and rejecting what our logic rejects. God just wants the best for us.

Good Work

Write a combined letter to the editor from your discussion group regarding homosexuality using any of the scriptures used in these lessons, and express your concern. Keep in mind you may be criticized by the general public if/when it is published.

BEFORE CLASS:

A. Look in your telephone book or a nearby library for the names of some nearby newspapers.

B. Call the newspapers and ask what their letter-to-the-editor policies are (they may be length, subject, grammar, space available, etc.).

C. Review the scriptures brought up in class against homosexuality and make a list of them with very brief summaries of each.

D. Review dictionary definitions mentioned in the teacher's manual and write them down.

E. Ask your elders if the letter to the editor can be signed by your ladies Bible class. If not, it should come from some volunteer in class, along with her home address (policy with most newspapers).

F. Write the scriptures and definitions on poster board or the blackboard.

DURING CLASS:

"We have been studying about teaching homosexuals in order to try to save their souls and our community. People read in the newspaper only those articles which interest them. A sensitively- and intelligently-written letter to the editor could attract the attention of those on both sides of the gay issue."

"I have written on the board the scriptures we have covered that specifically condemn homosexuality, and the dictionary definitions related to them."

"Let us collectively write a letter to the editor of [name of newspaper]. If they do not print it, we will try the [name of another newspaper]. First, we need a secretary to write on the board as we decide what to say." Get a volunteer.

"Let's start out with 'WE BELIEVE HOMOSEXUALITY IS NOT GOOD FOR US BECAUSE....'"

Allow class members to list them.

"Let's continue with 'IF WE BELIEVE GOD CREATED US, WE MUST BELIEVE HE GAVE HIS LAWS TO HELP US HAVE BETTER LIVES, EVEN THOUGH WE DON'T UNDERSTAND THEM. HOMOSEXUALITY IS THE MAIN CAUSE OF AIDS.

"In closing, let's invite them to worship God with us. For we are all sinners trying to do the best we can with each other's encouragement and God's love."

"I will send the letter to our newspaper editor.

Concluding Remarks

While the class secretary is finishing writing on the board, sing one verse of a song, possibly one of the following:

1. *I'm Not Ashamed to Own My Lord*
2. *Will You Not Tell It Today*
3. *Jesus, and Shall It Ever Be*
4. *Take the Name of Jesus with You*

Have a closing prayer, especially for the homosexuals we might be able to reach out to with help and with salvation.

Homosexual Men are More Likely to...

*2 times more likely than heterosexual men to have sex more than once a day

*4 times more likely than heterosexual men to have had a MINIMUM of 10 lovers in a year's time

*4 times more likely than heterosexual men to have had 100 or more lovers in their lifetime

ONLY 2/3 OF THOSE INFECTED WITH AIDS TELL THEIR SPOUSES or LOVERS

(The Day America Told the Truth, James Patterson and Peter Kim)

Inside the Hearts of Bible Women: Teacher's & Advertising Manual

NOT MY CHILDREN
Rebecca

Lesson One: Family Confrontations

Lesson Aim

- ♥ IDENTIFY PROBLEMS BETWEEN SIBLINGS
- ♥ HELP SIBLINGS GET ALONG

Scripture Outline

Genesis 24:1-28: Abraham's servant travels to Mesopotamia to find a wife for Isaac among Abraham's relatives, and meets Rebecca at a well.

Genesis 24:29-49: Rebecca takes the servant to her home to meet the head of her family, big brother Laban.

Genesis 24:50-67: Laban consents, Rebecca travels back to Canaan, and is married to Isaac.

Genesis 25:19-26: Rebecca is barren, but finally gives birth to twins when Isaac is 60; Jacob comes out holding on to Esau's heel.

Genesis 25:27-28: Isaac's favorite is Esau a hunter. Rebecca's favorite is Jacob a farmer.

Genesis 25:29-30: Out away from home and very hungry, Esau spots Jacob with a campfire cooking beans. Esau tells Jacob he'll die if he doesn't get something to eat.

Genesis 25:31-34: Selfish Jacob says he'll sell part of his beans for Esau's inheritance as the firstborn, their father's fortune. Impetuous Esau agrees.

Genesis 26:34-35: When Esau is 40, he marries two Hittite (Turkish) girls; this makes his parents bitter toward him.

Today's World

Tattling means different things to different age children. When a preschooler tells parents what a sibling is doing, it is actually a non-judgmental report of what's going on.

Dr. Eugene Urban, a clinical psychologist at the Wilder Child Guidance Center in St. Paul, Minneapolis, says tattling in older children is a power play, a way for one child to look better than the other by making them look bad. It has nothing to do with solving a problem such as getting the other child to stop their behavior. Too, tattling can position the child as an ally of the parent resulting in more love and attention.

Parents should be cautious about making their children's problems their own by trying to solve the children's problems for them. Parents need to give the problems back to the children to solve as long as they're not physically aggressive. They can be put in a room together to stay until they have worked out their problem. Of course, if they get loud or destructive, they need to be put in separate rooms until they individually decide to get along. This helps children learn conflict resolution.

Some children are just unable to solve these day-to-day problems. In that case, they have underlying difficulties with normal social skills. In school, Dr. Jan N. Hughes, professor of educational psychology at Texas A & M University, explains these children tend to be "unpopular, neglected or rejected." They need help from adults learning how to make and keep friends, things to say and do, perhaps by roll playing.

Sometimes children experiment with certain social behaviors on their family where they feel safer. Or perhaps one child is trying to get across to the other child that they are their own person; they do not want to be a carbon copy of the other and don't want the other to try to carbon copy them. Still another reason for the fighting is displaced anger for the parents whom they don't dare show anger toward.

Canadian clinical psychologist, Dr. Catherine Gildiner, reported in Chatelaine Magazine that childhood competition for parental love can persist into adult jealousy. Often the root of the problem is in the role they were assigned by their family—the pretty/ugly one, the smart/dumb one, the rebel/squeaky clean one.

The best way to get rid of adult sibling jealousy is to focus on one's own feelings during typical childhood rivalries, then sharing it with that brother or sister who probably also feels constricting roles assigned by family to him/her. "I felt excluded because...." "I felt unimportant because...." and so on.

Bible World

The Law of Moses made "law" some customs people had already been practicing in the Patriarchal Age just prior. Among them were privileges of the first-born son. Even though having more than one wife was tolerated during the Old Testament times, it was forever put to rest in the New Testament era.

God slew the first born of both humans and animals in Egypt except for the Israelites' firstborn (Exodus 13:2,12); therefore, they were required to be dedicated to God's service (Numbers 3:13). However, God set aside the Tribe of Levi to take the place of these firstborn (Numbers 3:40,41) and allowed families to redeem their first-born son from full-time service when a month old by taking money to the priests at the temple (Numbers 18:16; 3:42-51). Even the first-born of "clean" animals was to be sacrificed to God (Numbers 18:17,18) and the first-born of "unclean" animals was to be redeemed with money or a lamb (Numbers 18:15; Exodus 13:13; 34:20).

The first-born son of the legal wife, as opposed to concubines, inherited his father's personal property, a double portion over the younger sons of the legal wife; and he was responsible for supporting his sisters until they were married (Deuteronomy 21:15-17). Real estate, however, was never completely inherited by an individual, for it belonged to an entire family. It could be sold, but only within one tribe, so that the land given to each tribe when they first entered Canaan remained with them (Leviticus 25:23,24). At the year of Jubilee (49th year), all land returned to the original owner (Leviticus 25:25-27).

There was a distinction made between the firstborn of the father and the firstborn of the mother. The father's firstborn was the one who received the honors because it was "the beginning of his strength" (Genesis 49:3; Deuteronomy 21:17). Therefore, the firstborn of a favored wife could not be skipped over to if he was born later among the children (Genesis 21:9-13).

In the absence of the father, the first-born son had authority over his brothers and sisters (Genesis 24:55,60). This position was greatly envied by those who did not have it (Genesis 25:29-34; 27). However, in cases where the firstborn did something strictly against the father's standards, the father felt free to transfer the privilege to the next-born son (Genesis 49:3,4). Sometimes in a father's weakened state, the more favored son of a father got by with deposing the rightful firstborn such as David did with Solomon over his older son Adonijah (1 Kings 1:1-34); Jacob did with Joseph's sons, Manasseh over his older grandson Ephraim (Genesis 48:8-21); and with Joseph himself over his older brothers (Genesis 48:22); and Rebecca deceived Isaac into doing with Jacob over his older son Esau (Genesis 27:1-29).

In the New Testament, Jesus was the firstborn (Matthew 1:25), so his parents took him to the temple to redeem him from a lifetime of service to God "after the custom of the law" (Luke 2:27). Jesus was also the firstborn of his heavenly Father with complete authority over God's adopted children (Romans 8:29; Hebrews 1:6). By his resurrection, he was the "firstborn from the dead" (Colossians 1:18; Revelation 1:5). The title "firstborn of every creature" (Colossians 1:15) refers only to his authority over all creation, and not that he was created (Colossians 1:15). Christians are called "firstborn" because we are privileged above all other people on earth (Hebrews 22:23).

Introducing
the Lesson

Being a first-born son in Bible Times was extremely important. The firstborn always inherited twice as much as the other children, and had authority over the family in the father's absence. The son receiving this privilege had to be the son of the man's first wife, not successive wives or concubines. Sometimes this caused trouble. Remember when Joseph, the first-born of Jacob's second wife, showed up with clothes much nicer than his brothers'? They wanted to kill him for it. Remember when Sarah became upset with Ishmael, the first-born son of her husband by a concubine? She had him and his mother kicked out of the house.

No family in the world has ever existed without problems getting along with each other, even when its members obviously loved each other. Arguing comes as a result of two or more people wanting to do different things or the same thing in a setting not agreed with by one. Often personalities get involved and take away from the issue trying to be resolved. Tattling is an age-old problem of younger children, and some never outgrow it and become gossips. (Discuss further to whichever degree you like.)

One of the major things to help them is to try not to let their emotions take over their logic. We have been taught to varying degrees that, if we're angry, we have to yell and hit and be emotional. We've been taught that others will not believe how strongly we feel about something unless we become aggressive.
Is it possible to tell someone we're angry without emphasizing the point with aggressive emotions? It is if we explain to the people we disagree with that we feel as strongly about it as if we were yelling or hitting, but we don't choose to confuse the issue with that.

If we are to raise children who understand how to deal with conflict, we need to know how to help them deal with it as children. **Display SUGGESTIONS TO HELP CHILDREN GET ALONG BETTER.** Read through them to whatever detail you desire.

Questions
Discussion

1. **What can a mother do to get such childish attitudes as labeling and I'm-better-than-you under control?**

   1 Corinthians 4:7: It is God who makes us different from one another. So, who are we to brag?

   Possible Class Response: People label others when they're trying to make themselves look better. A mother can refrain from using labels herself, such as calling her child "brat," even in fun. When a mother sees someone on the street who looks different, she can comment about their courage in getting out among people, and add that their minds are as good as anyone else's. When someone is seen who acts different from others, she can say that if we had gone through what they had, we might have the same problems. Sometimes saying "there, but by the grace of God, go I" is effective.

2. **Discuss the good and bad ways laughter is used as a mask.**

   Job 9:23: Disease [personified here] attacks anyone it wants, no matter how innocent, then laughs at the sufferer.

   Possible Class Response: When people tease, they are blunt to tell the truth about someone's problem, possibly blowing it out of proportion, then laugh to cover up the fact that they are hurting that other person. Teasers usually get angry if the other person doesn't laugh too, and then call them names such as "spoilsport." One- or two-sentence teasing -controlled and limited—can, however, be used beneficially to address a serious problem that the other person always gets angry about if discussed.

In this case, the smile says, "You have a problem, but I love you anyway;" it opens up the subject for possible discussion. Teasing should be used sparingly and briefly.

3. **All children argue, usually over what they want. Is it possible with careful teaching to make the arguing stop?**

    Proverbs 27:4: Anger and temper are bad, but it is nearly impossible to stand up to envy.

    1 Corinthians 13:4: People who love others are not jealous of them.

    Possible Class Response: We can teach a child to be happy when someone else has something special. We can start with things the child doesn't want personally, and then move to things the child would want too. We can teach, "We are happy for them." It's okay to want something, but not at the expense of taking it from someone else.

4. **What does teasing usually accomplish in families?**

    Proverbs 21:24: People who are proud in an egotistic way and who look down on other people are really showing "proud wrath."

    Possible Class Response: Teasing occurs in all families. But it must be used with extreme care and with the right person. Teasing usually turns to tears if carried on long enough. Teasing is usually a form of saying, "Look at the baby!" or "Just can't control yourself!" People who have been teased a great deal in their life get so they cannot take even the slightest hint of teasing, and are considered having a "chip on their shoulder." Is it worth it?

5. **How long should a parent stay out of an argument before putting it to a stop? Give some examples of how she can pacify both children in a dispute**

    Proverbs 11:17: People who are cruel bring trouble upon themselves.

    Possible Class Response: Arguing should be nipped in the bud. It is very difficult to tell who started it. Sometimes the perpetrator starts it in another room, then moves the argument near the parents just before the other child defends itself with a shout or kick. We could send them to their rooms to not come out until they work it out themselves. If they come out and don't agree with the result, send them back. In a dispute such as who gets the biggest piece of food, one child can cut it and the other make the first choice. Sometimes arguing is just pent-up energy, and the children can be told to run around the house five times. That can also make them forget what they were arguing about.

6. **What are some methods parents should use to teach their children?**

    Genesis 25:21-22: Isaac and Rebecca were godly parents who truly tried to do God's will and teach their sons to do the same.

    Possible Class Response: They can be an example by the way they talk and do things with family and strangers and also alone. When a teachable situation comes along, the parent can explain why they made the decision they did; e.g., "I told the clerk he gave me the wrong change because it would have been stealing to have kept it."

7. **What can we do as they grow up to influence our children to marry Christians?**

   Deuteronomy 7:3,4: The non-believer usually has stronger influence and pulls the believer away from God.

   Possible Class Response: The non-believer usually actively tries to convince the believer to stop attending worship and classes, etc. On the other hand, the believer usually doesn't say much to the non-believer about becoming a Christian for fear of "chasing them away." The person on the pedestal can be easily pulled down by someone below. But it is nearly impossible for the person on the pedestal to pull someone up to their level. Converting a spouse is extremely difficult and often takes many years.

8. **When a child chooses to marry a non-Christian despite their upbringing, what can a parent do to challenge the choice in a way that it does not make the child even more rebellious?**

   Proverbs 26:1-12: Verse four says that if we argue about the answers the fool gives us, we are foolish too. Verse five says if we do anyway, the fool might recognize his own foolishness, possibly by our willingness to make ourselves look foolish over and over to prove we love them. However, arguing is a difficult way to go.

   Possible Class Response: The family can be hospitable and invite the other person to participate in family activities, including devotionals and attending worship. If the non-Christian is uncomfortable, s/he is likely to break off the engagement. If the non-Christian is comfortable, they are teachable and you may be able to convert them.

9. **How can "losing a battle but winning the war" help a parent tempted to disown their child?**

   Proverbs 17:24,25: The parents are overcome with grief and bitterness when their child goes against the standards by which s/he was raised.

   Possible Class Response: Parents must, more than ever, think of the child above their own feelings of shame and disgrace. They must keep the door open. Time calms people down. Time allows people to regroup and look at their options more clearly. Time allows people to see things in their proper perspective. Time allows a foolish child to see that things can only get worse if they continue on their path. The father of the N.T. prodigal son knew this. Always keep the path back home open for the child.

10. **What are some ways you've thought of for strengthening yourself during family turmoil but have not yet done? How could you get started doing them?**

    Psalm 33:18: God is watching over everyone in the family. God loves everyone in the family.

    Possible Class Response: Nerves are on edge during family turmoil. Parents must find some quiet time, time to hand things over to God, time to absorb peace—prayer, reading Jesus' life of outreach to hurting people. Complete quiet in the home with all radios, TVs, and stereos turned off helps. Going for walks helps. Peace in the heart helps us think more clearly.

Good Work

Send a note to someone you know who has a constant struggle with a strong-willed child.

BEFORE CLASS:

    A. Gather up telephone books and church directories.

    B. Gather up stationary (colored bond paper cut in half?) and envelopes.

    C. Write on blackboard or poster board this suggested note:

"I just wanted to drop you this note to tell you how much I appreciate what you do for your children. Raising children is not easy. But I see you sometimes with them, and can tell you are really working hard at being a good mother to them. I pray that God will continue to be with your family, keep you healthy, and bless you with his continual love."

DURING CLASS:

"We've been studying about the problems of raising children, especially those who are strong-willed and seem to argue all the time. Rebecca certainly had her hands full.

"Everyone knows a mother with a strong-willed child that she is continually struggling with and trying to shape without breaking their spirit. Certainly, all children are strong-willed sometimes. Take a moment now to send a note of encouragement to one of these mothers."

Hand out stationery and envelopes. "If you aren't sure what to say, I have written a suggestion for you on the board. Feel free to copy it if you like. You may wish to keep the person you write confidential and mail the letter yourself. If not, I will mail them for you."

"You will have about eight minutes to address their envelope and write your note. Let's all be quiet now and allow each other to think and write. When you are done, offer a silent prayer for the one you wrote while the others finish."

Concluding Remarks

When time is up and while the slower writers complete their notes, sing one verse of a song, possibly one of the following:

1. *Angry Words, Oh Let them Never*
2. *I've Got the Joy, Joy, Joy, Joy*
3. *We Have an Anchor*
4. *A Charge to Keep I Have*

In a few moments, your students will be going back home, so end the class rather up beat. Smile!

(Wait for one or two quick replies to each of the following.) "In a few words, what advice would you give a mother to ….

1. Teach her children not to do name calling?
2. Keep her children from arguing?
3. Influence the non-Christian fiancé of a child?
4. Keep inner peace during family turmoil?

Have a brief closing prayer for the families of your congregation.

Suggestions to Help Children Get Along Better

(1) Respect each other's stuff. If one of them wants to play with the other's toy, they should ask. If they want to wear their shirt, they should ask.

(2) Respect each other's turf. If they have separate rooms, they should ask if they can come in. If they just have separate beds, they should not sit on the other's bed or go through the other's dresser drawers.

(3) Hitting is just not allowed. It just makes things worse. If a child wants to hit, that person should go off alone for a while.

(4) When an argument gets out of hand, take time out away from each other. Then come back to try talking again.

(5) Don't run to parents to solve differences. While alone, give each other uninterrupted time to explain their side, perhaps with a kitchen timer.

(6) Ask parents to plan special times with each child individually.

(Source: "Brothers & Sisters: Friends or Rivals?" Washington Post)

Katheryn Maddox Haddad

Not My Children

Lesson Two: The Irrevocable Act

Lesson Aim
- **DON'T BE A "CONTROLLING" MOTHER**
- **DEAL WITH DECEIT**

Scripture Outline

Genesis 27:1-4: Old Isaac sends for his first born, Esau, to prepare a feast of venison so he can then officially pass on the birthright to him.

Genesis 27:4-10: Rebecca overhears her husband, and hurriedly sends for Jacob to pose as Esau and be given the first-born's special birthright instead.

Genesis 27:11-13: Jacob objects, saying he will be discovered and cursed instead, but Rebecca says she'll take the curse onto herself if that happens.

Genesis 27:14-25: Rebecca and Jacob carry out their deceit.

Genesis 27:26-29: Jacob is given the rights of the first-born son by blind Isaac.

Today's World

A 13-year-old failed in becoming a cheerleader, so the mother went to the school board to object to a competitor because she lived in the wrong school district. When this failed, she tried to hire someone for $2,500 to kill her daughter's competitor.

This woman was in her mid-thirties, was active in her church, and lived in a trim brick home just two blocks from her intended victim. Both her daughter and her competition were inducted into the Junior Honor Society and given the award on the stage at graduation at the same time. (Source: *The Washington Post*)

* * *

In research done by the team of James Patterson and Peter Kim and published in their book, The Day America Told the Truth, interviewed people around the U.S. anonymously and in a setting in which they felt comfortable to tell the truth. About 91 percent of them said they lie regularly. Most find it hard to get through a week without lying, and 20 percent lie every day. These lies are premeditated lies.

People divided lies into white/trivial fibs, and dark/serious lies. They defined serious lies as those that (a) hurt other people, (b) violate a trust, (3) involve crime, (4) mask what and who we really are. Over 35 percent confessed they'd told serious lies.

Eighty-six percent of Americans lie to their parents, 69 percent lie to their spouses, and 59 percent lie to their children. But Americans believe other people are lying to them even more than they do. They suspiciously believe that 83 percent of their children lie to them, 78 percent of their spouses, and 75 percent of their parents lie to them.

Interestingly, most of the world thinks Americans are too open. But the survey team came to the conclusion that lying had become an American cultural trait. They decided that Americans lie about everything, and not for any particular reason - they just do.

Those who refrain from a lie do so simply because it is wrong 45 percent of the time; the rest refrain when they think they'll get caught. Less than one-third of Americans believe it's wrong to lie.

Comparing it with quitting smoking, many wanted to stop, but didn't know how. The survey teams felt there were honest people inside most liars that didn't know how to get out. Often the interviewers gave permission or empowered interviewees to stop lying, at least for a day.
According to a 1997 study by Psychology professor Kang Lee of Queen's University in Ottawa, Ontario, children have started lying by the age of three, know they are wrong by age five, and understand that false intention is the same as lying. They also know when their parents are lying, but do not tell them they know.

Dr. Charles Schwarzbeck of the University of British Columbia in Canada followed up on an Ohio study and learned that most of today's teens make decisions based more on getting caught than a personal moral code. One example was a 15-year-old honor student who admitted stealing from mall booths, adding, "I don't lie." Her only concern was the school would find out and ruin her chances for college, and she'd hurt her parents.

Habitual delinquents who steal consider it a reaction to circumstances and not a crime. "If they're stupid enough to leave that stuff out, it deserves to disappear." When two delinquents beat up on someone who caught them, they said it wasn't a crime because "he was stupid to try to stop two guys." Such delinquents, after explaining their actions, often add, "I don't lie," but the circumstance called for their action.

Dr. Schwarzbeck has talked to some 100 families about teaching children not to steal and most parents react as one father did: "Stealing's got nothing to do with our kids. We don't have to talk about that."

Whatever happened to the days when telling the truth was one of the most strictly held morals? What happened to us between the '50s and '90s? Do we not take ourselves seriously any more?

Bible World

The first liar in the world was Satan, the father of liars (John 8:44). He lied to Eve and told her God just didn't want her to be as smart as him and that's why he was keeping the fruit from the forbidden tree from her (Genesis 3:4). When Abraham, Jacob's grandfather, was in Egypt, he feared Pharaoh would kill him to take Sarah away from him, so said she was his sister (Genesis 12:13; 20:2). His son, Isaac, was afraid King Abimelech or other Philistines would kill him for his wife, Rebecca, so said she was his sister (Genesis 26:7).

After Jacob fled from Esau to Haran, Laban, Jacob's father-in-law, lied to him and said he could marry Rachael when he actually gave him Leah (Genesis 29:21-25). Still later, Jacob's sons lied to him and said their brother, Joseph, had been killed by a wild animal when really they'd sold him as a slave (Genesis 37:29-35).

Those who are free from lying and deceit will receive the blessing of God, and salvation (Psalm 24:5). God calls liars hypocrites (1 Timothy 4:2), and says they will have their part in the lake of fire (Revelation 21:8). Do we really believe this? Or do we believe this is God's lie?

God places mercy and truth together numerous times in his word (Psalm 85:10,11). The Word of God is truth (John 1:14). Jesus said THE TRUTH SHALL MAKE YOU FREE (John 8:32). Jesus was the way, THE TRUTH, and the life (John 14:6) and the SPIRIT OF TRUTH (John 14:17).

***

The word *supplanter* can also be translated *heeler*. It is from the Hebrew word *Aqab* meaning *footstep, lier in wait, at the last*. It is used in the following scriptures:

Genesis 3:15: "You shall bruise/crush his heel" (see also Romans 16:20).
Genesis 25:26: Jacob was born holding Esau's heel.
Genesis 27:36: Jacob supplanted Esau twice.
Genesis 49:17: Dan shall judge the people as a snake bites a horse's heels and then throws off its rider.
Job 18:8,9: The wicked person is cast into a net by his own heel.
Psalm 41:9: "Mine own familiar friend in whom I trusted, which did eat of my bread, has lifted up his heel against me."
Psalm 49:5: The iniquity of my heels
Jeremiah 9:4: Trust not your brother who will supplant you.
Jeremiah 13:22: Your heels are made bare, you shall fall over.
Hosea 12:3: "He took his brother by the heel in the womb, and by his strength he had power with God."
John 13:18: "He that eats bread with me has lifted up his heel against me."

In *Webster's New World Dictionary*, *supplant* is said to come from the words *sub* meaning *under*, and *planta* meaning *sole of the foot* or *what comes under the foot*. It means "to put something under the sole of the foot, trip up; to take the place of;

supersede, especially through force, scheming, or treachery; to remove or uproot in order to replace with something else."

Introducing the Lesson

What would we be willing to do for our children? I think we'd all be willing to die for our children. We've all sacrificed important things in our lives for our children because we love them so much.

We all go to a different extreme. A few years ago, you may have read the story of a woman who tried to have her daughter's cheerleading competition killed. (Recall the story briefly.)

Sometimes we just lie for our children. ***Display WHO LIES MOST and discuss.*** Lying is a real problem in America. According to a recent anonymous survey, about 91 percent of Americans say they lie regularly. Most find it hard to get through a week without lying, and 20 percent lie every day. These lies are premeditated lies. Discuss further to whichever degree you wish.

Display chart WHAT IS WRONG WITH LYING. Discuss Bible background on this to whichever degree you wish.

Discussion Questions

11. **If a family dwells on a bad choice made by one member and lets it taint everything else from then on, what can happen to that person? The whole family? What is the alternative?**

    Proverbs 19:11: A person with discretion postpones her anger, and it is to her glory to not dwell on a fault.

    Possible Class Response: Jacob was named a "supplanter" and his brother was made aware of that every time anyone said Jacob's name. It may have influenced Esau not taking his first-born birthright very seriously and selling it to Jacob for beans. It may have influenced Jacob to rub it in, that he would someday take Esau's place. That in turn may have influenced Esau to marry non-believing girls even though he knew it would hurt his parents. Families should learn not to label each other. It can damage a child for life.

12. **Did you ever try to "set things up" for your child so (s)he would come out ahead in something? Share it, and tell how you felt about it later.**

    Genesis 16:2: God didn't need Sarah to help him out by giving her handmaid to Abraham by which to father the promised child.

    Possible Class Response: A mother might create a story plot so her child can turn in a good story to the teacher. She might look up and dictate the answers for a homework assignment. She might do most of the work on a craft project so her child can earn a scouting badge or science fair award.

13. **Did you ever make a mistake in judgment with a child who later got in trouble with someone else over it? If you contacted the other person involved to explain everything, what did you say? How did the way you tried to reconcile affect your child?**

   Psalm 73:22: I did such a foolish thing. I really embarrassed myself.

   Possible Class Response: When you make a mistake, tell the child you did, and ask the child's forgiveness. Then explain that you would like to go to the other person affected by your child's actions, and ask their forgiveness also. This could be a good lesson for your own family as well as someone else's.

14. **What might Rebecca have done differently?**

   1 Samuel 15:22: Saul disobeyed God by not destroying all the enemy's herds, and then tried to smooth it over by sacrificing one of the animals to God. God said that was rebellion and he didn't want the sacrifice.

   Possible Class Response: She might have tried to explain to Isaac that Esau had an unbelieving family; therefore, the birthright to pass on for the coming new nation (Jews) should come through Jacob. She might have told Jacob that even though he would not inherit the family's wealth, God would still be with him and bless him.

15. **What can parents do to help a child keep its conscience?**

   John 8:9: Jesus appealed to the inner consciences of the men trying to stone the adulterous woman to death.

   Possible Class Response: With deceit comes guilt and fear. As long as the wrong act is being done, either the guilt continues because of a tender conscience, or it ceases because of lost conscience. Getting by with things too long, such as threatening a child and never following through, can destroy a conscience. Being punished too often and too strong for the crime can give a child a constant feeling of guilt and no mercy. As long as this child hurts with too much guilt, s/he may try to make others hurt too so they do not have to hurt alone.

16. **When a parent justifies deceit, is the child able to see through it? What is the alternative (Proverbs 30:5)?**

   Deceit ran in the family. Jacob's grandfather and father both used it (Genesis 12:13; 26:7). Rebecca taught her son to use it. Her niece used it to marry Jacob later (Genesis 29:25). Jacob's sons used it to cover up Joseph's enslavement.

   Proverbs 30:5: We should put our trust in the Truth. For the Truth will shield us.

   Possible Class Response: At first the child sees the deceit. "Tell them I'm not home."

"They gave me too much change, so it's their fault." Often the child asks the parent why the deceit, and the parent replies it's someone else's fault—justifies. Instead, the parent should trust that the truth will ultimately be best for everyone, and provide a sense of inner peace and joy.

17. When a child is trapped by something irrevocable s/he has done that cannot be undone (Proverbs 29:6), what is there left for the parent to do?

Proverbs 29:6: Sin creates a trap sinners have to watch out for. Righteous people have peace.

Possible Class Response: The parent should stand by that child and let them know, "What you did is wrong, but my love for you will never cease."

Good Work

Send a note to the mother of a teenager who has difficulty doing right.

BEFORE CLASS:

A1. Gather up telephone books and church directories.

A2. Obtain the address of a Christian home for troubled children. Send letters to administrator to mail on to parents.

A3. Obtain the address of a nearby juvenile home. Send letters to administrator to mail on to parents.

B   Gather up stationary (colored bond paper cut in half?) and letter-size envelopes.

C   Write on blackboard or poster board suggested things to write for those who have trouble wording what they feel:

For Someone Who Conceals her Child's Difficulties from Friends: "I just wanted to send you this note to let you know that I appreciate all the hard work you must be putting into being the mother of a teenager. It's never easy. It seems teenagers challenge nearly everything we ever taught them that was important. But God's love is always there. Through it all, your love will shine through, and your teen will come through these years just fine. So keep up the good work, Mom."

For Someone Whose Teenager is in Trouble of a Public Nature: "I wanted to send you this note to let you know that I love you. No matter what problems your teenager has—and they all do—God will see you through. God's love is stubborn. Do not be hard on yourself, for you are doing the best you can. Teenagers seem to have a mind of their own. But God will always be near them. Your courage is a strong example to other parents. Some day things will return to normal, and you will have peace. God bless you all."

<u>For Someone Whose Teenager is in a Home for Troubled Teens</u>: "I wanted to send you this note to let you know that you are not alone. You have stuck by your teenager all these years and done the very best you could. That is all any of us can do. Teens have a mind of their own. But they see your example of loving them no matter what happens. May God continue to be with your family while you are separated, and bring you back together again someday.

DURING CLASS:

"We've been studying about the turmoil often brought into a family by a child's behavior. These are extremely difficult times, and often last several years."

"You may know someone who's teenager is bringing turmoil into her family. I have brought phone books and directories for you to look up their addresses. If you do not, I have brought the address of the _____ Home for Juveniles. You can write the parents of the teens there and the administrator will forward them on."

Hand out stationery and envelopes. "If you aren't sure what to say, I have written suggestions for you on the board. Feel free to copy one if you like. You may wish to keep the name of the person you write confidential, in which case you should mail it yourself. Otherwise, I will mail your letters."

"You will have about eight minutes to address their envelope and write your note. Let's all be quiet now and allow each other to think and write. When you are done, offer a silent prayer for the one you wrote while the others finish."

Concluding Remarks

When time is up and while the slower writers complete their notes, sing one verse of a song, possibly one of the following:

1. *Amazing Grace*
2. *Trust and Obey*
3. *Victory in Jesus*
4. *Sunlight and Shadows*

In a few moments your students will be going back home, possibly to a great deal of untold disharmony. So end the class with assurance. Smile!

(Wait for one or two quick replies to each of the following.) "In a few words, what advice would you give a mother who....

1. Got her child into trouble because of her wrong advice?
2. Wants to teach her child to have a conscience?
3. Wants to teach her child to be honest?
4. Has a child who got into serious trouble?

Have a brief closing prayer for the teenagers and parents of your community.

Who Lies the Most?

Men	40%
Women	31%
Catholics	36%
Protestants	34%
Jews	25%
Ages 18-24	50%
Ages 25-44	34%
Ages 45-64	29%
Ages 65 +	9%

(Source: THE DAY AMERICA TOLD THE TRUTH)

What is Wrong with Lying?

- ☹ It keeps us in confusion and away from the knowledge of God (Jeremiah 9:6).
- ☹ It keeps us away from God (Jeremiah 8:5).
- ☹ It leads to pride and oppression (Jeremiah 5:27,28).
- ☹ It often is accompanied by fraud and injustice (Psalm 10:7; 43:1).
- ☹ It is the folly of fools (Proverbs 14:8).

*The TRUTH will make you
free!
(John 8:32)*

Katheryn Maddox Haddad

Not My Children

Lesson Three: Falling Apart

Lesson Aim
- ♥ COPE WHEN YOUR CHILDREN DO WRONG
- ♥ MAINTAIN FAITH WHEN YOUR FAMILY FALLS APART

Scripture Outline

Genesis 27:30-33: Esau brings Isaac his feast and they both discover Jacob's deceit.

Genesis 27:34-40: Esau cries out bitterly, asks his father if there is even one blessing left, and begs for it. Isaac tells his son he doesn't have to wear Jacob's yoke, for he can break it off if he tries.

Genesis 27:41: Esau vows to kill his brother as soon as his father dies.

Genesis 27:42-45: Rebecca continues to decide Jacob's fate and decides to send him back to Mesopotamia to stay with her brother a few days until Esau cools down. She has apparently lost Esau that day (perhaps he disowned her as his mother), and she doesn't want to lose Jacob too.

Genesis 27:46: Rebecca, without mentioning Esau's death threat, reminds Isaac how Esau's marriages to unbelievers is killing her, and if Jacob does the same thing, she'll just die.

Genesis 28:1-5: Isaac stands by his word and reiterates his blessing on Jacob, then sends him to Abraham's homeland to find a wife.

Genesis 28:6-9: When Esau sees how pleased his parents are that Jacob is obeying them to marry a God-fearing girl, he goes out and purposely marries more unbelieving women.

Genesis 32, 33: Esau stays home and inherits the family fortune after all. Jacob stays gone 20 years, gets rich on his own, and decides to try to make up with his twin brother.

Genesis 35:27-29: Although Jacob (now named Israel) goes back to live with his father, Isaac, and later the twins bury him, there is no mention of him ever seeing his mother again.

Genesis 36:15,28,31,33: Esau settles in the land of Edom (a variation of his name), one of his descendants builds Uz, and a farther descendant becomes king of Uz—Job. (See also Job 2:11)

Genesis 49:1-22: Jacob/Israel dies, having had twelve sons whose families eventually became the twelve tribes of Israel, one tribe from which will come the Savior of the World.

Today's World

A school in Massachusetts carried a student-written article in 1992 entitled "15 Ways to Kill Your Sister." Among the suggestions were to chop one's sister with an ax, squish her head in a clamp, tie her to the front bumper of a car with no brakes. Among indirect methods suggested was to tell her a boy in school likes her, and when she finds out he really hates her she will commit suicide. *(Insight, "Hall of Shame," July 13, 1992)*

In the book, *The Day America Told the Truth*, it was alarming what people said they would do for money. For just $2,000,000, people would abandon their families, abandon their church, or kill a stranger.

According to the National Runaway Safeline, between 1.6 and 2.8 million youth run away each year in the United States. Children can begin running as young as ages 10-14. The youngest are the most at-risk for the dangers of street life. According to the U.S. Department of Health and Human Services, two-thirds run away because of physical or sexual abuse, and one-third are abusive toward their families and are told to leave. Perhaps there is a correlation with the one-third who return home; perhaps there is forgiveness.

Sometimes parents who ask teenage children to leave are just seeking peace within the home. Almost always many reconciliation efforts have first been made, even with professional counseling, but to no avail. Parents are full of guilt when they tell their children to leave, wondering where they went wrong. Teenagers go out the door to all the freedom they ever wanted, and then decide it wasn't as exciting as they thought it would be. Gradually most work out compromises with parents and return home. *(The New York Times, June 15, 1989)*

Miles McPherson, president of Miles Ahead Ministries, recommends that, regardless of how unsuccessful parents have been in helping their children pull out of serious problems, they must believe in Matthew 19:26 that says "With man this is impossible, but with God all things are possible." Parents also need to remember that "Man looks at the outward appearance, but the Lord looks at the heart" (1 Samuel 16:7).

In helping such children, parents should ask their child what their dreams are so they can encourage them in those dreams. They should also notice what comes naturally to their child and what others say their child's talents are so they can be nurtured.

Keeping in mind that people give in to peer pressure if peers are the most important in their lives. Parents should become so involved in their child's life that they become the one children most desire to please. Finally, parents should pray for an outside mentor for their child. *(Source: Focus on the Family)*

Sometimes feuds result from sibling rivalry and are carried into adulthood. Dr. Michael Kahn, a professor of clinical psychology at the University of Hartford, reports that his surveys show about one-third of all adult siblings don't get along. Children learn early that the way to deal with relationship problems is to quit talking.

Often the feuders forget what the original problem was. They just claim they never got along. Their original feelings of anger and jealousy are replaced by pride and righteous indignation. They view reconciliation as a sign of weakness. They feel like martyrs, and it is sometimes tough to give up the nobility one feels with such a title. *(Detroit Free Press)*

Bible World

Esau was not the only one in the Bible who had thoughts of killing his own brother. Cain killed his brother, Abel, out of jealousy because God accepted Abel's sacrifices and not Cain's (Genesis 4:8).

Gideon was a supreme judge to the Israelites. God told him he'd give him victory over their enemies. Gideon's army of 300 men conquered 120,000 of the enemy (Judges 7:16,22; 8:10). He had 70 sons by his wives, and one son by a mistress. That one son, Abimelech, killed all his half-brothers so he could reign as king (Judges 9:1-6).

Absalom, the son of David, killed his half-brother Amnon for committing incest with their sister, Tamar (2 Samuel 13:28,29).

Solomon, Absalom's brother, murdered his older brother, Adonijah, for trying to marry their father's youngest wife after his death and making himself king. He was probably in his twenties when he did this, being a younger son of David (1 Kings 1 and 2).

Jehoram became king when he was 32. He had six brothers, all of whom he killed to protect his position (2 Chronicles 21:4).

* * *

Edom was the surname of Esau and means "red." Esau was born red-headed (Genesis 25:25), and sold his birthright for red beans (Genesis 36:1,8).

The territory of Edom which eventually was the place settled by Esau's family, is very mountainous and its barren rocks have a reddish hue. Much of it is forest-covered, but it also has many rocky cliffs and caves. For many years people lived in these caves in the mountains of Seir.

Edom was 100 miles long and 20 miles wide, and located at the southern border of

Canaan (Jacob's territory). Its capital was Petra ("Rock"), a city was literally carved out of steep cliffs on each side of a deep canyon, its main street.

Esau first married two Hittite women from the area today known as Turkey (Genesis 26:34), but saw how angry it made his parents. So, when Jacob went to his mother's brother's people in Haran to find a wife, Esau went to his father's brother's people in Arabia to find a third wife. There he married Ishmael's daughter, Esau's aunt (Genesis 28:8,9). Ishmael was the oldest son of Abraham. Esau lived in Mount Seir, the heart of Edom, after his marriage (Genesis 32:3-6), this territory was possibly a dowry from Ishmael.

Esau continued to have a home also in Canaan, because he did not permanently leave that area until Jacob returned to Canaan with his own family/tribe (Genesis 36:6-8), and their father Isaac died (Genesis 35:29). Esau couldn't have been far away at his father's death, for burial then was within hours of death.

Years after Edom was established as a kingdom, a new nation rebelled and came out of Egypt—the Israelites, descendants of Jacob. Edom allowed them passage through their land (Deuteronomy 2:2-8,28f) on their way back to Canaan. However, they later became enemies of Israel, and King Saul conquered them (1 Samuel 14:47), and later King David reconquered them (2 Samuel 8:14). Finally, Jehoshaphat dethroned Edom's king (1 Kings 11:14).

However, the Edomites were able to eventually throw off Israel's yoke as predicted by Isaac when he blessed Esau centuries earlier (Genesis 27:40). This was in the days of King Joram (2 Kings 8:20-22). At that time, they invaded Southern Israel (2 Chronicles 28:17). Still later they joined the Babylonians in destroying Jerusalem (Psalm 137:7).

King Herod who slew the babies in Bethlehem was from Edom, also called Idumea. Finally, just before Titus of Rome destroyed Jerusalem in the early Christian times, 20,000 Edomites were allowed to go in to Jerusalem and kill whoever they desired. Then Titus turned against Edom, and it too was destroyed. Its people were obliterated.

Introducing the Lesson

Today we're going to talk about coping when families fall apart under stress, and keeping faith that someday all will be well.

Esau was willing to kill his brother over the family inheritance. In a survey, people anonymously confessed they would leave families if paid enough. *Display WHAT WOULD YOU DO FOR $2,000,000?* Discuss.

There are things parents can try to do to help delinquent children. *Display WHAT CAN PARENTS DO?* Here are some suggestions of what parents can doing to try to avoid their children leaving home too soon, or to aid in a reconciliation and return to home.

Another reason Esau wanted to kill his brother was because his mother always took his brother's side. Such family feuds often continue into adulthood. Rebecca suggested that her son leave home to keep the peace. *Display 1.1 MILLION MINORS LEAVE HOME.*

Rebecca must have gone to bed crying and praying for her twin boys to be able to make up someday, praying for the reuniting of their family. Her beloved Jacob was gone 20 years. We have no indication that Rebecca ever saw him again. She may have died believing her prayers were never answered and her sons would never love each other again.

Discussion Questions

18. What are different types of results that may come from a strong show of emotions with children, both good and bad?

Mark 15:34: When God turned his face away from his son bearing the sins of the world on the cross, Jesus shouted at him, "Why have you forsaken me?".

Possible Class Response: When a parent first sees the signs of irrevocable rifts in the family, s/he may shout, cry, plead, or something similar in a desperate attempt to make its reality go away, or mourn its occurrence, or let the child know how important the problem is. Shouting "You ungrateful child," or something like that is damaging. But shouting, "Don't you know I love you? Don't you know I want the best for you? Don't you know what you're doing to our relationship?" can sometimes drill home a point. It says, "My love will never let go of you."

19. Under what conditions can a parent help a child see that something bad can be used for good (Romans 8:28)? Give some examples.

Romans 8:28: All things—no matter how bad—can be turned into something good. It may not be the best, but it can be good.

Possible Class Response: Salvaging a mistake takes much perception, wisdom, and love. There may be a permanent physical injury. There may be someone who leaves home and never returns. There may be hurtful words said that can never be taken back. A mother can look back on bad things that happened to her, and tell how they ended up being good after all. Or she can tell about people who decided to start organizations to avert such disaster in others such as MADD, started by a mother whose daughter was killed by a drunk driver.

20. Tell about a time you helped your child overcome a past mistake.

Genesis 27:40: Isaac told Esau he did not have to wear the yoke put on him by his brother; he could break it off.

Psalm 3:2-4: There were people telling David there was no hope for him. But God believed in him, and that's all he needed.

Possible Class Response: We may have explained to our child how to apologize, even rehearsing the words together. We may have helped them write a note. We may have built them up and told them to go back (to school or wherever), hold their head up, and show a positive attitude. We may have told them they lost one battle, but they could still win the war. We may have told them it is better to run the race and lose than to have never run at all.

21. **If you had a child who got in a lot of trouble, but at least was truthful about it and admitted it, how could you use this positive trait to help him or her?**

    Proverbs 14:8: The fool runs away from the truth. The wise and prudent are willing to talk about their ways to make them better.

    Possible Class Response: Like Esau, despite some young people's many shortcomings, they may still seem to tell the truth, whether about good or bad. Perhaps they have a greater sense of fair play (Esau at least warned his enemy, Jacob, rather than deceiving), and this positive trait can be brought out. Also, a child who readily confesses shortcomings is anxious to talk about them, and usually wants to stop doing them, but does not know how. Such a child might be receptive to counseling.

22. **Are there instances when we should hold back information from a family member (John 16:12)? If so, what are these occasions?**

    John 16:12: Even Jesus told his apostles there were other things he wanted to tell them, but they couldn't handle them yet.

    Possible Class Response: If a family member is going through a great deal of stress personally, perhaps it might be better to wait to tell them about it. The age of the person might determine how much and how simple it should be explained. In the "Sound of Music," the widower's children rebelled against each nanny because she wasn't their deceased mother they couldn't have. When the nanny played by Julie Andrews came to them, she covered for them and did not tell their father the trouble they were getting into; this made them see she truly cared for them and was the first step to them acting better and loving her.

23. **What can parents do to guard against becoming bitter and not forgiving their child when a family breaks up because of that child's actions?**

    2 Samuel 14:24: When David's son committed incest against his daughter, Absalom killed his brother in revenge. So David sent him into exile, and when he finally returned years later, David refused to see him ever again.

    After years of this, David's bitterness finally swept over Absalom, and he gave up on his father. He then tried to take over his father's kingship. What terrible remorse must have swept over David when Absalom was finally killed without this father and son ever having made up!

    All families break up eventually. But when it occurs because of things that should not have been done, a tie within that family is broken, and the parents especially are left heartbroken. Nothing will ever be the same again.

Possible Class Response: Keep the lines of communication open. We should call them or send them notes occasionally, filled with small talk, not rehashing the old problem. We should patiently wait for the child to mature and emotionally return to us; that could be ten years. We can invite them over for a meal, still staying clear of the old hurt. Talking it out—"clearing the air"—isn't always the answer; that was unsuccessfully tried while the child was still at home. With little things, let the child know you still love them, no matter how bad the wrong.

24. **If a child does something strictly against the parents' teachings just to see if it is true, how should the parents react (Ephesians 4:32)?**

    Children blindly believe their parents' teachings while young, but later challenge them when they develop some analyzing skills. These teen years are very difficult for all.

    Ephesians 4:30-32: Don't grieve one another and the Holy Spirit by being bitter. Remember, as God's children, we continually challenge his word and continually need forgiving day after day.

    Possible Class Response: We can ask the child if they learned anything from their experience. Some children will admit they did, others will not admit it but will know inside their hearts they did. We should tell them we will stand by them no matter what they do, even though the wrongdoing will break your heart. We can remember the story of the prodigal son Jesus told.

25. **Parents must learn once their children are grown to let go of their children's guilt (Ezekiel 18:4). How can this be done?**

    2 Kings 11:1,2; 12:2: When a certain king was killed, his mother had all her grandchildren killed so she could be queen. One grandson was hidden until old enough to become king. He did not let the evil of his father and grandmother influence him; he was a good king.

    Ezekiel 18:20: The father should not have to account for his son's sins.

    Possible Class Response: We all know children of bad parents who grew up to be good citizens, of worldly parents who grew up to be dedicated Christians. Some may be in the class today. We cannot blame or give credit to the parents for every way their children turn out. There are very few godly parents in the Bible who did not have children who did things the parents were ashamed of. There are other influences besides parents: School teachers, popular song lyrics, peers, economic and social trends. We can ask our children to forgive us for anything we might have said or done to lead them to do the wrong (they will likely tell the parent it had nothing to do with them.) We can comfort ourselves that we did the best we could under the circumstances. We can believe and pray that someday our children will pull out of their problem—always believe this.

26. **Give some examples of someone returning to religious and moral teachings of childhood late in their adult years.**

Proverbs 22:6: Eventually after learning the hard way, s/he will return to the teachings of the parents, maybe even after the parents' death.

Ecclesiastes: Solomon tried riches, women, and adventure, and found the only thing that could really make him happy was following God.

Possible Class Response: The class may remember parents being worldly most of their lives, but mellowing when they got older. Class members may have been worldly in their own earlier lives, but now have learned what really brings happiness.

27. **Since Christians have a kind of "guardian" or ministering angel (Hebrews 1:13,14), could it be that our prayers strengthen these angels who fight Satan? Perhaps this explains why we must often pray for things so long. Would this give hope to parents if this is the case? Tell how it would encourage you. Do you think it would help to explain this theory to your troubled child?**

Hebrews 1:13,14: The angels are ministering spirits to Christians.

Daniel 10: Note that Daniel prayed 24 days (verse 4) and the angel who came to him said he was heard on the first day (verse 12). The angels of God and of Satan were fighting for the past 21 days over the issue Daniel was praying about. After the reassurance, the angel asked Daniel to go back to his praying, for he must return to his fighting (verse 20,21).

Possible Class Response: Parents of troubled children grasp at nearly anything that gives them hope. They do not want to have troubled children. It is music to their ears to hear there is hope for their children. We must never quit encouraging them. Children who get in trouble a great deal don't know the root cause and don't want to be without friends, but they do not know how to change. We can tell our children to be patient with themselves and believe that "God ain't finished with me yet."

Good Work

Send a note of encouragement to the parents of some young person in your community who has gotten into serious trouble.

BEFORE CLASS:

A. Read the newspaper for several days and clip out articles about automobile accidents with teenagers involved, possibly gunfights involving teenagers, perhaps a local athlete caught cheating, a young person who robbed a store, a young person arrested for immoral or disorderly conduct. Clip those articles.

B.   Try to locate the parents' names and addresses in the phone book.

C.   Write the parents' names and addresses on envelopes. On the glue part of the envelope flap, write the name and crime of the child.

D.   Transfer the articles onto a transparency for use on an opaque projector.

E.   Gather up stationary (bond paper cut in half).

F.   Write on blackboard or poster board suggested things for class members to write who won't be sure what to say to a family in such turmoil:

"I wanted to write and tell you how sorry I am about the trouble your child is involved in. Being in the newspaper must be very embarrassing to you. But you are not alone. Every parent has had a child do things they were not taught to do. No matter what happens, God loves you and God loves your child. My prayers are with you during this most difficult time."

DURING CLASS:

"We've been studying about a family that was broken up because of terrible things that happened between them—lying, cheating, stealing, and even threat of murder.

> "It's hard for us to think of such terrible things happening to us. I doubt Isaac and Rebecca ever thought when their twin sons were young that this could possibly ever happen to their family, BUT IT DID. No one plans for such things to happen to their families.

> "There are families in our community right now hurting because their children have brought terrible burdens to their parents. Here are some that have been going through this lately."

Scan the articles you clipped out of the newspaper.

"There but by the grace of God go us! The parents of these children didn't mean for this to happen. They need our encouragement." Hand out stationary and pre-addressed envelopes. "I have looked up and written the addresses of the parents on the envelopes going around. Their child's name is on the glue part of the envelope flap. Please select one."

"If you aren't sure what to say, I have written a suggestion for you on the board. Feel free to copy it if you like. You will have about five minutes to write your note. Let's all be quiet now and allow each other to think and write. When you are done, give the letter to me, and offer a silent prayer for the parents you wrote while the others finish."

Concluding

Remarks

When time is up and while the slower writers complete their notes, sing one verse of a song, possibly one of the following:

1. *God is Calling the Prodigal*
2. *In the Hour of Trial*
3. *We Have an Anchor*
4. *Give Me the Bible*

In a few moments, your students will be going back home, possibly to their own home of turmoil. So, end the class by giving everyone hope and encouragement. Smile!

(Wait for one or two quick replies to each of the following.) "In a few words, what advice would you give a mother who

1. Doesn't know whether to keep yelling at her child over doing the same things wrong over and over?

2. Has a child in a rut of doing wrong all the time?

3. Whose child left home in a huff?

4. Whose child has turned against religion?

Have a brief closing prayer for the families you wrote notes to.

What Would You Do For $2,000,000?

One out of every 4 people would

☹ Abandon their family
☹ Abandon their church

One out of every 14 people would

☹ Kill a stranger

(Source: The Day America Told the Truth)

What Can Parents Do?

☺ **Believe Matthew 19:26—"With man this is impossible, but with God all things are possible."**

☺ **Ask child what their dreams are and encourage them.**

☺ **Take note of what others say your child's talents are.**

☺ **Become so involved in your child's life that you are the "peer" they most want to please.**

☺ **Pray for an outside mentor**

2 Million Minors Leave Home Every Year

2/3 run away

1/3 are told to leave

2/3 never return home

1/3 return home

(Source: National Runaway Safeline and The Wall Street Journal)

Inside the Hearts of Bible Women: Teacher's & Advertising Manual

UNBEARABLE LOSS

Job's Wife

Lesson One: Loss of Possessions

Lesson Aim
- ♥ FACE FINANCIAL SETBACKS
- ♥ FACE CHALLENGES TO FAITH

Scripture Outline

Job 1:1-3: In a land called Uz is a man named Job who loves God, has ten children, and is richer than anyone around.

Job 1:4,5: His children get along well, taking turns having parties at each other's houses. Job offers a sacrifice for each one of them every day.

Job 1:6-12: Satan (translated from the word adversary or accuser) approaches God and accuses Job of following God just because he's rich. Furthermore, if he is able to take all that away from Job, Satan believes Job will blame God for it.

Job 1:13-15: One day the Sabeans from the kingdom of Sheba near Ethiopia rustle Job's 500 oxen and 500 donkeys, and kill all the herdsmen but one.

Job 1:16: The same day, lightning catches Job's fields on fire and burns to death his 7,000 sheep and all the shepherds but one.

Job 1:17: The same day, Chaldeans from Babylon divide into three raiding parties, surround them, rustle Job's 3,000 camels, and kill all the herdsmen but one.

Today's World

Annually, one-fourth of households are touched by a crime, according to the US National Crime Survey, US Bureau of Justice Statistics, and Gallop. Nearly one-fifth of people were personally victimized. Theft and vandalization were the most common crimes. These percentages have not significantly changed over the past ten years.

Households with combined incomes of at least $25,000 are more than one and one-half times as likely to experience a personal theft than those with incomes below $7,500. However, households at all income levels are equally susceptible to breaking and entry to their homes.

Households with higher incomes and households in urban areas are more vulnerable than those in rural areas (suburbs come between).

The more people in a household, the greater its vulnerability to burglary. A house with six or more people is one-third again more likely to be broken into than a house with one person.

* * *

Facing the loss of one's income, as Job and his wife did, is also terrible. Everyone has faced directly or indirectly such catastrophe some time in their lives. We have heard stories of suicides at the time of the stock market crash in 1929; many have parents and grandparents who suffered hardships during the following depression (severe recession). Many southerners flooded to the industrial north to find jobs in factories.

During the recession of 1981 many lost their jobs, people flooded from the industrialized north to western and southern oil-producing states, Many lost both jobs and homes, so loaded their clothing and families in their cars and headed to their last place of hope. At first welcomed in these better-off areas, eventually there were more people than jobs. Some breadwinners just walked off from their families in disgrace, others committed suicide. Another severe recession hit in 1991 with critical results.

Those lucky enough to find jobs elsewhere around the country often sold their homes at less than what they paid for them and had to start all over again in another town. In 2007 there was another recession. It lasted nearly two years, longer than any other recession since World War II. Incomes dropped significantly. People lost their homes. Some banks collapsed.

When the stock market crash occurred in 1987, more severe than the one in 1929, people lost all their assets, some of which represented people's entire life savings. Sam Walton, one of the richest men in the world, lost millions of dollars on that "Black Monday" in the October 1987 crash. Philosophically he replied that he started with nothing long ago and he could always rebuild.

Bible
World

Where was Uz? There are two people by the name of Uz in the early scriptures. Genesis 10:23 lists Uz, the son of Aram (who settled Persia), the grandson of Shem. Genesis 36:20f,28 lists Seir, who was the father of Dishon, who was the father of Uz. Seir is where Esau dwelt, which was called Edom (Genesis 36:8) by the Horites who lived there before he did. It is located in the lower end of what one day would be southern Jordan on the east side of the Dead Sea. Seir's and Esau's descendants are listed side by side in the same chronology.

So, we have one Uz settling around Persia to the east which does not seem to be where Job lived, and one fairly near the Red Sea to the west. To determine which Uz Job was from, we can consider where his four friends were from who came to see him during his illness.

1. Eliphaz was from Teman (Job 2:11). Teman was one of the grandsons of Esau (Genesis 36:9-11). Tema and Buz were condemned by Jeremiah, both being in the "utmost corners" of Arabia (Jeremiah 25:23f). Arabia touched Edom on both the south and east.

2. Zophar was from Naamath (Job 2:11). Naamath was in the area of what Joshua gave the Tribe of Judah. Naamath was in an area of southern Hittites (not the ones up in Turkey) and were descendants of Noah's grandson, Canaan, Ham's son. (Job and all the others were descendants of Noah's son, Shem.)

3. Bildad was from Shuah (Job 2:11). Shuah was a son of Abraham by Keturah whom he married after Sarah died and sent to the east (became a tribe of northern Arabia) away from Isaac (Genesis 25:2).

4. Elihu was from Buz (Job 32:6). Buz was a nephew of Abraham. Tema and Buz were condemned by Jeremiah, both being in the "utmost corners" of Arabia (Jeremiah 25:23f). Arabia touched Edom on both the south and east.

All is drawn together with a final scripture, Lamentations 4:21, which calls the land of Uz the daughter of Edom.

* * *

So now, who was Job? Look back in Genesis 36 with the genealogies of both Esau (aka Edom) who took over the land of Seir (the original Edom). One of Seir's sons was Dishon. Dishan had a son named Uz (36:20f,28). Then following are the names of the dukes and kings of Edom. One of those kings was named Jobab (36:33). Job himself said he was a respected king (Job 29:8-11, 16-25). Furthermore, he was very rich.

* * *

The Sabeans who attacked and carried off Job's cattle (Job 1:14f) were from Sheba near Ethiopia to the south (Isaiah 43:3). These people were giants (Isaiah 45:14). Sabeans merchandised spices, precious stones, silver and gold (Ezekiel 27:22f). Kings of Sheba visited Solomon (Psalm 72:10) as well as did one of their queens (1 Kings 10:1-13).

The Chaldeans who rustled Job's camels were from the area where Abraham had been born, Ur of Chaldea.

* * *

It is evident that the fields were caught fire by lightning (Job 1:16) which subsequently killed Job's sheep.

Introducing the Lesson

Job and his wife suffered devastating financial losses. Job was probably king of Edom at the time they lost the source of their income. ***Display pedigree chart and map showing* HOMETOWN RELATIONSHIP OF JOB AND HIS FRIENDS.** Discuss to whatever degree you wish.

How many of you have ever made an insurance claim for property losses? (Allow class a couple minutes to share this.) ***Display* US 2015 INSURANCE CLAIMS.** Did you ever lose a house because of a job loss or recession?

Today, we are going to talk about facing major financial setbacks and challenges to our faith. Job's wife has been given a fictitious name just for the convenience of not calling her Mrs. Job.

Discussion Questions

1. **Recall times in your life when you lost something precious and then found out it wasn't as important as you had thought.**

   Job 29:25: Considering the population, Jobetta [name the author made up] could today be compared with the wife of a mayor; Job was king of a small kingdom. She must have felt successful and happy in every way.

   Possible Class Response: We reevaluate our priorities usually when a larger loss follows a smaller loss. Some may have been frustrated over warts on their feet until they ended up in the hospital with a more serious problem. Some may have been angry over a shopping cart running into their car in a parking lot; then their car was totaled in a traffic accident. They may have gotten angry that a precious family photo was accidentally thrown away; then they had a house fire and all mementos were burned up.

2. **Do you think that most tragedies of this magnitude have warnings or not? Which could you cope with easiest, and how?**

   Luke 17:27,28: On the last day, people will be eating their meals, getting married, going to work, and building houses like they always did.

Possible Class Response: As far as we can tell, the day of Job's and Jobetta's tragedy was apparently just as ordinary as any other. Some in the class will say they would prefer a warning so they could get ready. Others will say they wouldn't want a warning, because they would worry all the time and be so full of dread, they wouldn't be able to function sanely.

3. **When we hear of relative strangers facing loss of property or loved ones, do we normally run to their aid or do we stay away to keep such thoughts out of our lives? Why?**

   Considering the size of the fires that destroyed their property that day, it is doubtful Jobetta could have missed the first sign of something wrong—smoke in the sky. There is no indication she made any inquiries about it. Possibly she felt annoyance that people could allow themselves to get into such predicaments, and also pity for them from afar.

   Luke 10:30-32: When the man was robbed, beaten up, and left by the road for dead, the priest hurried on his way (to make his hospital rounds?) and the Levite didn't slow down (so he wouldn't be late for church?).

   Possible Class Response: When we read of natural disasters in the newspaper, some people will send money to help the victims. Very few will go to their aid personally. If people are killed and we read about it in the newspaper, we certainly want to stay away from the neighborhood; we don't want such things to hardly even be talked about in our lives. We work hard to keep things on an even keel and we don't want anyone rocking the boat.

4. **Tell of some difficult times you have faced or could face because of people challenging you or your husband's leadership. What things about yourself did you discover that you hadn't realized before?**

   As a political leader, Job faced the daily possibility of being assassinated or destroyed by an enemy, and Jobetta faced being a widow and/or left destitute.

   1 Samuel 18:8,9; 20:22-24,31: King Saul's son, Jonathan, the heir-apparent to the throne, knew David was a greater leader than he could ever be. He recognized this, loved David for his strong goodness, and sacrificed his throne for him.

   Possible Class Response: Lead the discussion toward INVALID challenges such as character assassination, revolt, doing away with the organization being led altogether. In such times, we see how much faith we have in ourselves and the rightness we are doing. We have to decide if it is worth fighting for. We have to decide if we are fighting because of our egos or the cause. Anita Bryant fought nearly alone in Miami, Florida, against homosexuals and lost her entire career.

5. **Do you think if someone loses their faith because of tragedy as Jobetta did, it is more likely to occur if we think the possibility through ahead of time or avoid the thought? (Remember, Job and his wife responded differently to their tragedy.) What is the difference in worrying and thinking through something ahead of time?**

Job 3:25: The thing Job most greatly feared was losing his wealth, his family, and his health.

Possible Class Response: We should read the Bible enough that we feel we could stand up against any atheist or any personal tragedy. This means we need to research the scientific truths listed in the Bible centuries before man discovered them, as well as the many prophecies of every part of Jesus' life made centuries before he lived (see the lesson on the Witch of Endor for this). We need to be prepared and continually renew our faith by continually studying. Only then can we feel confident to face anything and not worry.

6. **Tell about children who did well despite poor home lives (don't name names). In what percent of cases in the church do you think all of the children in a family turn out relatively good with no "black sheep"? Why?**

Jobetta's children seemed to have gotten along with each other quite well, taking turns hosting get-togethers. Yet Job seemed a little concerned over their spiritual maturity and prayed for them in case of moments of weakness.

Possible Class Response: Some members of your class will have been brought up in homes where their parents did not attend worship, and may have even abused them. Some of your class members may be willing to talk about children who got into trouble. You as the teacher should be the first one to admit your children weren't perfect and why. Certainly Abraham, Isaac, Jacob, Eli, Samuel, and others all had "black sheep" among their children.

7. **Have you ever helped someone not ever dreaming someday you would be in the same circumstance? Did your helping such people beforehand help you when you went through the same thing? How?**

Job 31:16-22: Job and his wife helped the needy at every opportunity.

Possible Class Response: Some may have gone to visit the sick, and one day were in the hospital themselves. Some may have tried to help a divorced woman have the courage to hold her family together, and one day were divorced themselves. Some may have given food or furniture or loaned money to someone who went through a fire, flood, etc., and one day they lost everything themselves.

8. **What are some bad approaches and good approaches to revealing bad news to someone?**

Rulers of old sometimes executed people who brought them bad news. We don't do that, but are still upset when it happens.

Proverbs 31:26: She expresses herself with wisdom and not foolishness, and her voice is full of kindness.

Possible Class Response: We can blurt it out. We can say "I told you so," or "You should have known better," or "What did you waste your time getting all that stuff for anyway?" or "It wasn't any good to start with." We can say we know how much those things/that person meant to them. We can touch their hand when we tell them, and then put our arms around them as they absorb the tragedy. We can tell them how very sorry we are.

9. **Tell of a time when several tragedies of a financial nature occurred to you or a friend. Compare the perspective you felt about that first loss when it occurred and later after several other losses had occurred.**

   1 Timothy 6:6-8: We must be content no matter what happens. We brought nothing into the world and for sure we're not going to take anything with us. If we have enough food to eat and enough clothing to protect us from the elements, that is really and truly all we need.

   Possible Class Response: Someone may have become angry when she was short-changed in the store; then a personal check bounced. Someone may have been frustrated when some peaches in her refrigerator spoiled, then her freezer went out. Someone may have found out too late that a service station across town was selling gas for five cents less than any other, then got into a car accident.

Good Work

Read the newspaper and send letters of encouragement to people who have been burned out or suffered some other financial loss.

BEFORE CLASS:

Obtain a few recent issues of a local newspaper with articles about natural disasters. Underline highlights.

Look up in the phone book the addresses of several of them and write them on poster board or the blackboard.
Circle in red the articles mentioning families for whom you found addresses. Leave the newspaper pages intact.

Obtain line (loose-leaf) paper to use for stationary. Now is not the time to flaunt how much more we have than them. Also obtain envelopes.

Write on poster board or the blackboard the following:

"I read about your tragedy in the newspaper and was so sorry for what you went through. I have [have not] gone through a similar

tragedy. We know it is Satan and not God who causes such things. It seems the love of God shines through from people around us the most when Satan tries to hurt us. My prayers are with you. Although I cannot help with much at this time, please accept what is enclosed. May God give you strength and stand by you as you overcome this."

DURING CLASS:

"We have been talking about losing our possessions. We have all lost material things that were very important to us. Some of us even lost jobs that led to losing nearly everything else. There are people all around us suffering losses."

Get out your newspapers and scan the articles of people whose addresses you located.

"Let's reach out to these people today and not just forget their problems even exist. I have addresses for them all. Who would you like to write to?"

The class should decide whether they want to (a) go together to send a check to one family, (b) each write a separate check, or (c) some write separate checks and some go together. If several go together, they should collect their money now and give it to the person writing the check. Even $5 would help.

Hand out paper to write on and explain why it's not nice stationery. "If you aren't sure what to say, I have written a suggestion for you on the board. Feel free to copy it if you like."

"You will now have about five minutes to write your note. While you write it, I will address the envelopes. Let's all be quiet now and allow each other to think and write. When you are done, give your note and check to me to put in the envelope and mail, then offer a silent prayer while the others finish."

Concluding Remarks

When time is up and while the slower writers complete their notes, sing one verse of a song, possibly one of the following:

1. *Count Your Blessings*
2. *He is My Everything*
3. *All to Jesus I Surrender*
4. *Take the World, But Give Me Jesus*

In a few moments, everyone will be returning to their homes, possibly still thinking about their own financial losses. Leave them with courage.

(Wait for one or two quick replies to each of the following.) "In a few words....

1. Who causes tragedies to come on us?
2. What kind of facts in the Bible can help prove it is true?
3. Does every family have perfect children?
4. Even if we lose everything, we still have what?

Give your list of families in the newspaper to the person leading the closing prayer and lift them up before God.

Insurance Claims for Losses in the US 2015

EVENT	LOSSES
Storms	$2,800,000,000
Drought	2,200,000,000
Floods	1,700,000,000
Burglary & Theft	28,000,000
Fire	3,422,000,000
Miscellaneous	5,670,000,000
Automobiles	43,313,000,000

*National Underwriter Company

Hometown Relationship of Job and His Friends

GENESIS 22, 25, 36

NOAH				
SHEM				HAM
Arphaxad			Joktan	Canaan
Abraham the EBERS		Nahor	HORITES	S. HITTITES (Later Judah)
(Keturah) | **SHUAH** **(Bildad)**	(Sarah) | Jacob | Esau (Edom) | Eliphaz | **TEMAN** **(Eliphaz)**	| Uz | **BUZ** **(Elihu)**	| EDOM Seir | Anah | Dishon | **UZ** | Bela | **JOBAB** **(JOB)**	| | **NAMATH** **(Zophar)**

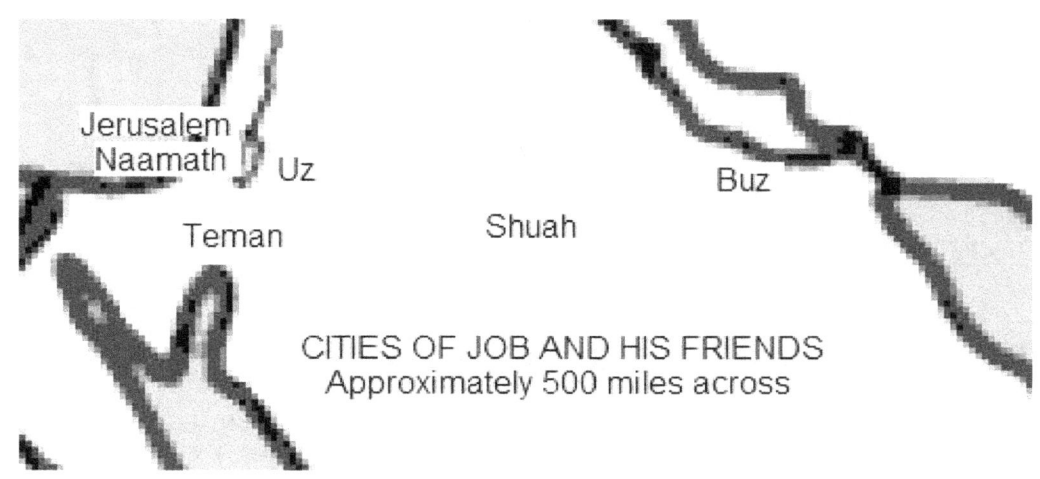

CITIES OF JOB AND HIS FRIENDS
Approximately 500 miles across

Katheryn Maddox Haddad

Unbearable Loss

Lesson Two: Loss of Loved Ones

Lesson Aim
- COPE WITH DEATH OF CHILDREN
- COPE WITH THE GRIEVING PROCESS

Scripture Outline

Job 1:18: As usual, Job's and Jobetta's grown children are having a party in one of their houses.

Job 1:19: A cyclone from the desert comes in and flattens the house killing all their children and all the servants but one.

Job 1:20-22: Job turns to God and says he does not blame him, and loves him anyway. (Job spends most of the rest of the book bemoaning his losses. Never, ever does he blame God.)

Job 3:25: But the very thing Job feared finally has happened to him.

Job 2:10; 7:20: Job has not sinned with his lips, but he has sinned with his attitude. (More later at end of book.)

Job 29:12; 30:25: Job had always helped the poor. Now he is poor himself.

Job 31:1: Job makes sure he doesn't look on other women lustfully.

Job 31:21-22: Job self-righteously says that if he hasn't helped the poor, let his arm fall off.

Job 31:23: Job is good because he is afraid of God, not because he loves him.

Job 32:1; 37:24: God does not respect those who are self-righteous.

Today's World

Of the total deaths both in the US annually, sixteen percent are young people under age 25 and down to birth. That means that four out of every 100 young people you know will die before they reach their 25th birthday. That also means that one out of every six funerals is a young person's.

In the US, 71 percent of these young people die from illnesses, 16 percent from accidents, 8 percent by suicide and 5 percent by homicide

Breaking cause of death down by age adds a little more information, however. Those less than a year old almost always die from perinatal conditions or congenital animalities. Those from one to 14 years of age usually die from accidents and malignant neoplasms. Those from 15 to 24 years of age usually die from accidents and suicide or homicide.

Automobile accidents is one of the leading causes of death among young people. In the US, there is one automobile-caused injury every 19 seconds, and there is one automobile-caused death every 11 minutes.

Organizations in Canada which hold memorial services for lost children and even stillborn babies include Bereaved Families of Ontario and Perinatal Bereavement Services. Some religious groups have started annual memorials in which they invite the public to mourn with them.

*** * * ***

The house that collapsed on Job's children was hit by a cyclone (Job 1:18f). Cyclones are rotating wind systems similar to tornadoes but much larger. In more tropical areas, they are also called typhoons or hurricanes. There are several relatively permanent cyclonic areas over warm continental regions of the earth, among them the one that extends from the Sahara Desert through the Red Sea and across the southern Arabian Desert to the Persian Gulf. Edom was in this area.

Bible World

Job's calamities became known far and wide, and were the subject of public conversation everywhere (Job 7:3) for months. There were apparently letters sent to Job by friends possibly begging him to repent so his calamities would go away (Job 13:26).

Deep emotions quite often bring out eloquent writing, an effort to express and possibly release the deepest groanings of our soul. Job did want very much, if he ever got well enough to do so, to write down his words in a "book." He described the book as "graven with an iron pen and lead in the rock" which partially describes the antiquated form of writing still in existence in his day (Job 19:23). The writings in this book contain some of the things that Job, his friends, and God said. They must have been brilliant men. Some of the original language is grand, though in places a little obscure.

Jewish tradition has it that what Job wrote may have been shared with Moses while he spent his 40 years in the territory nearby, and that Moses inserted his own prologue and epilogue in order to help the reader understand the larger purpose of God's will in Job's experience. It would help us all to go through calamity with grace, if we could see that we are part of the BIG PICTURE.

It has to do with Satan. Satan apparently entered the hearts of sons of God who had come before God in worship. This worrisome term, "sons of God" also appeared in Genesis 6:2, when they married the daughters of men. Since angels are never married (Mark 12:25), the sons of God couldn't have been angels as some believe.

On the other hand, sons of God are described as God's followers in Hosea 1:10. Both sons and daughters of God are referred to in 2 Corinthians 6:18. Satan is the accuser of the brethren (Revelation 12:10). So, it may have been that Satan entered the hearts of some worshippers who began to accuse Job of following God just because God continually blessed him. Certainly, Job was accused of this by his so-called friends after he got sick. At the same time, a duplication of this and more direct contact may have been going on in the spirit world with Satan directly speaking to God.

Why would God allow Job to be put through this? For God's own pride? No! More for proving to Satan the superiority of good over evil, the superiority of love and trust over hate and suspicion. Ephesians 3:3f,9 tells us that the explanation of this mystery was the purpose for creating the world in the first place. Satan and his angels do not understand this mystery; even God's own angels don't. God must be vindicated. God must judge rightly. The source of good (God) must prove to the source of evil (Satan) the superiority of good over evil. Job and his wife had the privilege of being used by God to make an incredible and stupendous point to Satan. WHAT A PRIVILEGE!

Introducing the Lesson

Today's subject is going to be very difficult. We will treat it as sensitively as possible, and try to keep you from feeling more pain than you feel comfortable with. However, it does need to be talked about. Why? *Display and discuss charts ANNUAL DEATHS OF YOUNG PEOPLE IN AMERICA, CAUSES OF DEATH AMONG YOUNG PEOPLE, LEADING CAUSES OF DEATH BY AGE, AUTOMOBILE-CAUSED DEATHS.*

Why do we have to suffer such pain? When people have suffered the loss of loved ones, especially those which were untimely, this has caused many people's faith to waiver and even die along with their loved ones. It has to do with the reason the world was created.

Ephesians 3:8-12 says "I am...to preach...Christ, and to make plain to everyone the administration of this mystery, which for ages past was kept hidden in God, who created all things. HIS INTENT was that now THROUGH THE CHURCH, the manifold WISDOM OF GOD should be made known to the RULERS AND AUTHORITIES [principalities and powers] IN HEAVENLY REALMS, according to his ETERNAL PURPOSE, which he accomplished in Christ Jesus our Lord. In him and through faith in him we may approach God with FREEDOM and confidence." *Display MYSTERY chart.*

Column 2:   You will notice that those who understand the mystery are everyone but the angels.

Column 3:   The mystery originated from the wisdom of God. One exception is when Satan is involved and his interpretation is a lie.

Column 4:   The mystery originated at the beginning of the world

Column 5:   The mystery is that we can be saved from Satan's evil power through Jesus and his church!

Column 6:   The explanation of the mystery will be completed at the end of the world, at the "fullness of time."

When will the church be able to quit standing up to Satan? When the "fullness comes." When will the fullness come?

FULLNESS OF EVIL: The Israelites were left as slaves in Egypt to build up their numbers and strength and to wait for the fullness of the Amorites' iniquity (Genesis 15:16).

FULLNESS OF RIGHTEOUSNESS: When all the Jews and Gentiles possible follow Christ (Romans 11:11,25f and 2 Peter 3:9). Satan will continue to spread hatred and death. But Christians will continue to love. And just as the early church won over paganism by submitting
to evil and death, the church will ultimately win "the war of the worlds."

THEN GOD WILL BE ABLE TO DO THE ULTIMATE: He will forgive us eternally (Romans 11:32). By his forgiveness, he will prove Love ("God is love" 1 John 4:8) is superior to all things. Satan's way, being accuser and unforgiver of the brethren, will fail. When Jesus returns and raises us from death, he will overcome Satan (2 Thessalonians 2:8).

Discussion Questions

10. How can you gently help such a person during this time to prepare for the reality?

Some people refuse to allow anyone to reveal a death to other people for hours or even days in a desperate effort to keep that person alive in their minds a little longer.

Psalm 85:10: Truth should be combined with mercy. What is right should be combined with what is peaceful.

Possible Class Response: We can talk to them about the good times they had together. Later, we can talk about how much we wish they were still here. Later we can try to give them something to hold (even if just a photo) that belonged to the person. Finally, we can tell them there's going to be a funeral and they'll want to be there to say good-bye, for it will be their only chance. At each step, we can pray for them aloud for strength to accept those things. Always we must acknowledge God's love. Satan, not

God, causes death. God conquers death. We can talk about living on in heaven.

11. **Is there any right or wrong way to express indescribable grief? Who sets the standards?**

    2 Samuel 18:33; 19:4: When David's son Absalom died, he went walking through the halls to his room with his hands up to his face sobbing and calling aloud for him.

    Possible Class Response: Only if it is self-destructive. We must grieve in the same fashion as the person who suffered the greatest loss such as parent or spouse. If they want to laugh and talk about good times, do that. If they want to pace, pace with them. If they want to cry, cry with them. If they want to sit in silence, sit in silence with them. If they want to be angry, be angry with them.

12. **When several people go through the same grief at the same time, what is communication among them like? Give some examples.**

    1 Samuel 30:4: David and his men had left their wives and children in a town that was captured by the enemy while the men were gone. When they found out, David and all his men cried together until they couldn't cry anymore.

    2 Samuel 15:30: When Absalom took over his father's throne, David escaped by foot out of Jerusalem crying as he walked, and everyone with him cried too.

    Possible Class Response: Often not as much is said trying to explain their grief. They just show their emotions with no explanation and no excuses. Some class members may have seen someone expressing great anger or refusing to talk, etc. and wanted them to stop acting like this. But they become more patient when they learned there was just a recent death in the family.

13. **What are different ways people cope with the loss of a close loved one?**

    Job 21:1-3a: Job wanted to just talk without anyone judging him. He

    had things to get off his chest, and he didn't want anyone trying to "talk sense" into him, as three of his four so-called friends kept trying to do.

    Possible Class Response: They may cry, mow the lawn, refuse to admit it, talk about the good times, hit the wall, go completely silent with numbness while they get used to it.

14. **What are some ways to lend strength to someone going to the funeral home to select a casket and return later to see a loved one in it?**

    Psalm 16:5: We should hold up the faltering who may hardly be able to see where they're walking for their tears.

    1 Corinthians 15:54: These bodies that are left behind are only empty shells now; for their souls now have new and wonderful bodies in heaven.

Possible Class Response: The reality of the death hits home like a hammer when they have to pick out the casket. The funeral home director will be very sensitive and allow time for crying between what s/he has to explain. We can continually tell them we know how hard it is. We can encourage them to take their time. If they run out of the room with the caskets in it a few times, go out into the hall and wait for them, or even follow them into the restroom and hold them tight. Offer them a glass of cold water and perhaps put a cold paper towel on their head. Remain calm yourself if possible and talk about the options. Ask them if they want the cheapest or most expensive casket. Ask if they have insurance to cover it. Ask if they want a color the same as the color of the deceased hair. Ask what their favorite flowers and colors were so they don't clash with the casket and lining. Ask what color tie or blouse they are going to have the deceased wear. In the end it doesn't matter what color anything is anyway. Help them make a quick decision and leave.

When they return later to see their loved one in the casket, let them walk alone and at their own pace but be close behind them. Don't bother them, no matter how much they cry, unless they turn around to look for you or start to be faint. They need to be completely alone with the deceased at times. Ask them when they want to.

15. **Share personal experiences of comforting funerals. What songs and scriptures would you prefer yourself and why?**

    Matthew 4:16: To those who are in the valley of the shadow of death, light is sprung up!

    Possible Class Response: The above scripture might be more comforting than the usual 23rd Psalm. Songs sung may include the deceased's favorite, or a song about seeing God and the joys of heaven. Some people prefer all happy songs at a funeral. Some people don't like the symbolism of certain funeral songs such as "I'll Fly Away." Read a list of funeral songs in the index of a hymnal and ask people to tell what their favorites are.

16. **Have you ever gone through periods of doubting God after a tragedy? Did "If God is so good...." enter your thoughts? Tell about it.**

    Psalm 115:2,3: People who have trouble with their faith will be thrown off balance by tragedy and say such things as, "Where is God now?".

    Possible Class Response: You as the teacher should be the first to disclose any times of doubt you may have had. Encourage your class to share theirs also. We need to be careful not to blame God for things Satan does. We need to remember that God hurts as much when he sees one of our loved ones suffer and die as he did when he watched his own son suffer and die on the cross.

17. **What drives people to rise up and rebuild? What about those who do not? Which are you?**

    Nehemiah 1:3; 4:6: The huge wall of Jerusalem had been broken down three-fourths of a century earlier. But a remnant of the captives returned, and with strong wills, they rebuilt it.

<u>James 5:11</u>: People who patiently endure hardship like Job did are ultimately the happiest.

<u>Job 42:11b,12</u>: Job's brothers and sisters and friends all rallied to him and each gave him one piece of money and one earring.

<u>Possible Class Response</u>: The last book of Job says he rebuilt and had twice as much wealth as before. This must have taken hard work, rebuilding from scratch. But he had family and friends to encourage him. Some people enjoy the work of building much more than when it is finally built. Some people just sit back and feel sorry for themselves because they don't like work in the first place. We all react differently to different losses. If destroyed by a flood, we might work hard to rebuild a garage, but not our favorite flower garden. We might not try to rebuild if we don't have the same time and energy we had before. We might try to rebuild even bigger and better.

18. What does it take to get over such stress diseases?

When we are under emotional stress, our natural body defenses are also stressed and broken down. Ulcers, strokes, high blood pressure, respiratory problems, skin rashes, or boils can result. Often it is because our mind cannot take any more stress and our body won't stop and listen.

<u>Psalm 46:1-3,10</u>: No matter how terrible our disaster, God will be our refuge and strength. We must be still and relax. With God, we can do anything.

<u>Possible Class Response</u>: We must stop fretting. That may mean having long sessions of quiet time with all radios and TVs off, leaning back, and letting our minds wander. If our mind is still racing, we can read portions of the Bible where God gives us strength and is in control of everything. We could possibly read a short book or chapter in an inspirational book on waiting for God. We need to refocus from our loss to God and his great love for us. Once we have done that, we can gradually begin thinking again of our problem from our new perspective. We might then begin making a list of what can be done to rebuild. If physical stress comes back, we need to back up and start all over again with our quiet time.

Good
Work

Read the newspaper and/or church bulletin. Send notes of sympathy to people who have lost loved ones; share in one or two sentences a similar loss you experienced. Give them hope.

BEFORE CLASS:

A1.   FOR LARGE CONGREGATIONS: You could read the church bulletin back one year for those who have lost loved ones. Write down their names, their addresses, and the names of their loved one.

A2. FOR SMALL CONGREGATIONS: Read the obituary section of your local newspaper. Look up the families' names in the telephone book and write them down.

B. Write addresses on enough envelopes to give each lady in your class one. On the glue of the flaps, write the name and age of the deceased person and their relation to the person to whom you addressed the envelope.

C. Gather up stationary, possibly colored bond paper cut in half.

D. On poster board or the blackboard, write the following:

"I am so sorry about the loss of your _____. I know there's a large empty spot in your heart for them that no one can ever fill. I hope you'll let the love of God in there so he can comfort you. He doesn't want anyone to die, and hurts as much when that happens as when his own son died. May God walk close to you as you heal a little at a time, and may he give you a special amount of strength and peace. My prayers are with you."

DURING CLASS:

"We have been talking about something very difficult, but it needs to be talked about. Many of us have gone through losses and they hurt very much. Let's reach out to others now to share with them the comfort we feel."

Hand out stationery and envelopes. "I have obtained the names of families whose loved ones have died during the past year. The inside flap of each envelope gives their loved one's name and relationship. If you're not sure what to say to them, I have written a suggestion on the board. Feel free to copy it if you like."

"You will have about five minutes to write your note. Let's all be quiet now and allow each other to think and write. When you are done, give your note to me to mail, then offer a silent prayer while the others finish."

Concluding Remarks

When time is up and while the slower writers complete their notes, sing one verse of a cheerful song, possibly one of the following:

       1.   *Faith is the Victory*
       2.   *We Shall See the King Some Day*
       3.   *Where the Soul Never Dies*
       4.   *On Jordan's Stormy Banks*

In a few moments, everyone will be returning to everyday lives with

everyday responsibilities. Help them further put away their tears and laugh again. Smile!

(Wait for one or two quick replies to each of the following.) "In a few words....

1. If a grieving person wants to mow the lawn, what should you do?

2. How should we make sure we know our loved ones' favorite songs?

3. Do you prefer to go to a sad or happy funeral?

4. What's your favorite heaven song?

Have a closing prayer, asking God to give joy to those of us left behind when our loved ones are able to go ahead of us to live with him in heaven. Pray with a smile!

Overall Causes of Death Among Young People

Illness—71%

Accident—16%

Suicide—8%

Homicide—5%

Leading Causes of Death in Young People by Age

Under 1	**Perinatal Conditions and Congenital Anomalies**
Ages 1-14	**Accidents and Malignant Neoplasms**
Ages 15-24	**Accidents and Suicide/Homicide**

Katheryn Maddox Haddad

Numbers of Deaths of Young People

ANNUAL DEATHS OF YOUNG PEOPLE IN AMERICA			
AGE GROUPS	TOTAL POPULATION	DEATHS PER 1000 POPULATION	ACTUAL DEATHS
Birth to 5	18,753,000	16.2	303,799
5-14	35,161,000	.2	7,032
15-24	36,514,000	.6	21.908
TOTALS	90,428,000		342,73909

Department of Health and Human Services National Center for Health Statistics

There are about 2,150,000 deaths a year in all age groups

16% are young people

About 1 out of every 6 deaths is a young person

About 4 of every 100 young people will die before age 25

What Is the Mystery?

SCRIPTURE	WHO UNDER-STANDS	PERSON ORIGIN	WHAT IT IS	TIME ORIGIN	WHEN COMPLETED
Matthew 13:10,11,34,35	Disciples	Jesus	Kingdom of heaven	From foundation of world	
Romans 10:1; 11:11, 12,19,25,27,35	Jews and Gentiles	Wisdom/Knowledge of God	Complete forgiveness of sins		When fullness of Jews and Gentiles complete
Romans 16:24-27	All Nations	Power/Wisdom of God	Grace of Lord Jesus Christ	When world began	
*1 Corinthians 1:2,17; 2:7,9	Church of God	Wisdom of God	The cross of Christ	Before the world	
1 Corinthians 1:2; 3:19-4:1,5	Church of God	Foolishness of God (Greater than Wisdom of Man)	World, life, death, past, present, and Christ all belong to Christians		When the Lord comes
1 Corinthians 15:50-57	Brethren		Christ'ns will raise from death to immortality		At the last trumpet
Ephesians 1:1-4,9,10	Faithful in Christ	God's Wisdom and Prudence	Christians will be without blame	Before the foundation of world	Fullness of times when all gathered to Christ
Ephesians 3:3,4,9	Jews and Gentiles	Wisdom of God	Christians have access to riches of Christ	From beginning of world	
Ephesians 5:30,32	Members of Jesus' Body		Christians are one with Christ		
Colossians 1:23,26-28	The Church/Saints	Word of God/Wisdom	Christ, the hope of glory, is in Christians	Before all ages and generations	When Christians are presented to God
Colossians	Saints/Faithfu	Wisdom of	Christ'ns		

1:1; 2:2,3	I	God	risen w/Christ		
Colossians 3:24; 4:3-6	Saints/Faithful Servants of the Lord	Wisdom	Christians will receive the reward of Christ		When inheritance given
2Thessalonians 2:2-10	The Church		Wicked destroyed		The day of Christ
1 Timothy 3:15,16	House of God	Godliness	Jesus was resurrected		
Revelation 10:6,7		God the Creator of the World	The mystery will be completed		At the seventh (last) trumpet
Revelation 17:7-9,14,17	Those both in and not in the Book of Life	Wisdom	Lamb of God shall overcome the beast	From foundation of world	When Word of God fulfilled

SCRIPTURES ON MYSTERY: Show similarities that lent themselves to charting

WHO UNDERSTANDS THE MYSTERY? Christians

WHO DOESN'T UNDERSTAND THE MYSTERY? Principalities and powers (dominions) in heavenly places (Ephesians 3:8-12)

The World Was Created to Explain the Mystery to Principalities and Powers

Ephesians 3:8-12 "I am...to preach...Christ, and to make plain to everyone the administration of this mystery, which for ages past was kept hidden in God, who created all things. HIS INTENT was that now THROUGH THE CHURCH, the manifold WISDOM OF GOD should be made known to the RULERS AND AUTHORITES [principalities and powers] IN HEAVENLY REALMS, according to his ETERNAL PURPOSE, which he accomplished in Christ Jesus our Lord. In him and through faith in him we may approach God with FREEDOM and confidence."

WHO ARE THESE PRINCIPALITIES AND POWERS?

Evil:	Can separate the ungodly from God's love (Romans 8:37-39)
Evil:	Christians wrestle against them (Ephesians 6:11,12)
Evil:	Jesus showed his superiority over them when he was resurrected from death (Colossians 2:10,12-15)
Good & Evil:	Christ raised from death to be above all Ps & Ps and head of Church (Ephesians 1:20-22)
Good & Evil:	Do not understand God's wisdom; it will be explained through the church (Ephesians 3:10)
Good:	Jesus created all Ps and Ps. (They were good to start with. See below)

CONCLUSION: They are good and bad angels (angels can sin and have choice?)

WHY DID GOD NEED TO PROVE HIS WISDOM?
ANGELS DON'T UNDERSTAND EVERYTHING

>When they watch us, they are sometimes amazed: "We are made a spectacle to...angels" (1 Corinthians 4:9)
>They are inferior to Christians: "...we shall judge angels" (1 Corinthians 6:3)
>God's wisdom, God's love, is a mystery to them: "...unto the Ps & Ps...might be known...wisdom of God" (Ephesians 3:10)

They don't understand Christ giving us glory: "...with the Holy Spirit sent down from heaven; which things the angels desire to look into."

GOOD ANGELS

Good angels do not have their own kingdom. They follow God's will and do his bidding (Jude 9).
1. They guide us (Phillip-Acts 8:26,29; Cornelius-Acts 10:2,3)
2. They rescue us (Elijah-1 Kings 19:5,7; Jesus-Matthew 4:11; Sick-John 5:4; Jesus-Luke 22:43; Paul-Acts 27:21-35)

3. They defend us (Jacob before Esau; Daniel before Lions; Jesus-Matthew 4:6; Children-Matthew 18:10; Peter from prison-Acts 5:19; 12:7)
4. They watch the church (1 Timothy 5:21, 1 Corinthians 4:9)
5. They're in charge of the dead (Lazarus-Mark 13:27; Jesus-John 20:12)
6. They will accompany Jesus at His return (Zechariah 14:5; Matthew 25:31; Luke 9:26; 2 Thessalonians 1:7,9; Jude 14,15)
*7. They will carry out God's sentences (Matthew 13:41,42, and most of Revelation)

*This is a key to why God needs to prove His justice and love's superiority (God is Love)

We are to respect the angels and not speak evil of them (Jude 8), but we are not to bow down to them (Revelation 19:10)

BAD ANGELS

*Satan was evil from the beginning (I John 3:8)
*He was a murderer from the beginning (John 8:44)
He is the father of liars (John 8:44)
He has access to heaven sometimes (Job 1:6-7)
Jesus saw him falling from heaven [present tense] while the 72 preached
    (Luke 10:18)
God sends bad angels to be with Satan (2 Peter 2:4, Jude 6)
Satan his his own kingdom of darkness (2 Samuel 23:6,7; Matthew 12:24-30;
    Luke 11:21,22; 1 John 3:8)
Jesus did not die to save angels (Hebrews 2:16)
*John 1:1 says Jesus was the Word in the beginning

*Beginning is defined in John 1:1 – "In the beginning was the Word. The
    Word was with God and the Word was God.

SATAN'S OTHER TITLES

Abaddon-Destroyer (Revelation 9:11)
Accuser (Revelation 12:10)
Adversary (1 Peter 5:8)
Beelzebub-Lord of the Fly (Matthew 12:24)
Beliel-Worthless, Lawless (2 Corinthians 6:15)
The Devil (Matthew 4:1)
Dragon (Revelation 12:3)
The Enemy (Matthew 13:39)
Evil Spirit (1 Samuel 16:14)
Father of Lies (John 8:44)
Gates of Hell (Matthew 16:18)
God of this World (2 Corinthians 4:4)
Lying Spirit (1 Kings 22:22)
Murderer (John 8:44)
Power of Darkness (Colossians 1:13)
Prince of this World (John 12:31; 14:30; 16:11)
Prince of Devils (Matthew 12:24)
Power of the Air (Ephesians 2:2)

Ruler of Darkness of this World (Ephesians 6:12)
Satan (Romans 16:20)
Serpent (Genesis 3:4,14)
Spirit that Works in Disobedience (Ephesians 2:2)
Tempter (Matthew 4:3)
Unclean Spirit (Matthew 12:43)
Wicked One (Matthew 13:19,38)

SATAN HAS ACCESS TO GOD AND TO MAN

Eve (Genesis 3:1-4)
David (1 Chronicles 21:1)
Job (Job 1:6-12)
Joshua the High Priest (Zechariah 3:1-2)
Jesus (Matthew 4:1-11)
Hearers of the Word (Matthew 13:19,38,39)
Sick (Mark 3:22-26, Luke 13:16)
Peter (22:31)
Judas (John 13:2,27)
Ananias (Acts 5:3)
Elymas (Acts 13:9,10)
Church at Corinth (2 Corinthians 2:11; 4:4; 11:3; 12:7)
Church at Ephesus (Ephesians 2:2; 4:27; 6:11-16)
Church at Collosae (Colossians 1:13; 2:15)
Paul (1 Thessalonians 2:18; 3:5)
Hymenaeus and Alexander (1 Timothy 1:20)
Elders (1 Timothy 3:6,7; 5:15)

GOD'S ANGELS ARE FIGHTING SATAN'S ANGELS RIGHT NOW
OUR PRAYERS FOR THE KINGDOM SEEM TO GIVE THEM STRENGTH
OR PERHAPS THEIR BATTLES GIVE US STRENGTH

1. Daniel prayed for 3 weeks—21 days (Daniel 10:2)
2. On the 24th day, Gabriel appeared to Daniel as he had on previous occasions (Daniel 8:16, 9:21, 10:4-11)
3. Gabriel said Daniel's prayers had been heard from the 1st day (Daniel 10:12)
4. During those 21 days, Gabriel was fighting the Angel of Persia. Gabriel wanted to explain to Daniel what was going on, but had to send for the angel Michael to hold him off while he was gone (Daniel 10:13; 12:1)
5. Gabriel then explained the earthly kingdoms that would rule the world until Jesus came (Daniel 11:1-12:7)
6. Daniel said he didn't understand, but Gabriel said he would at the end of time when he received his inheritance (Daniel 12:8-13)
7. Then Gabriel returned to fight the angel of Persia, and later the angel of Greece.

**SO HOW DOES THE CHURCH REVEAL THE MYSTERY
TO PRINCIPALITIES & POWERS?**

The church will bruise Satan (Romans 16:20) in fulfillment of the promise at the Beginning (Genesis 3:15, John 13:18, Romans 16:20).

Satan wants to prove all are ultimately evil (Job 1). Satan does not believe in forgiveness and mercy. If he is going to have to suffer in hell and not be in heaven, he wants to make sure no one else gets to heaven either. Therefore, he continually accuses and condemns. Satan wants to convince us that stuff like mercy and love are weak and ridiculous. He wants to prove his way will bring us glory. He wants people to follow his "wisdom" that is "from below". He wants us to be "wise in our own conceits" our own pride.

Worldly people accuse (find fault and refuse to forgive) each other, for Satan
     is the accuser of the brethren (Revelation 12:10)
Worldly people lie, for Satan is the Father of Lies (John 8:44)
Worldly people disobey God, for Satan is the spirit that works in disobedience
     (Ephesians 2:2)
Worldly people have pride, for that is what made Satan fall (Isaiah 14:12-14)

This type of thinking is considered wise in the world (1 Corinthians 1 and 2). But they are "wise in their own conceits (pride) (Romans 11:25; 12:16).

Proud wisdom from below is:
>Bitter
>Envious
>Striving

Wisdom from God is:
>Pure
>Peaceable
>Gentle
>Easy to be Entreated
>Merciful
>Full of Good Works

HOW LONG DOES THE CHURCH HAVE TO STAND UP TO SATAN?
Until the "fullness"

FULLNESS OF EVIL: The Israelites were left as slaves in Egypt to build up their numbers and strength and to wait for the fullness of the Amorites' iniquity (Genesis 15:16). God warned the Israelites that if they did the sins of the Canaanites, the land would spew them out too (Leviticus 18:27-29). God helped the Israelites destroy them "for the wickedness of these nations" and not because they were so good themselves (Deuteronomy 9:4-6).

FULLNESS OF RIGHTEOUSNESS: When all the Jews and Gentiles possible follow Christ (Romans 11:11,25,26) (2 Peter 3:9). Satan will continue to spread hatred and death. But Christians will continue to love. And just like the early church won over paganism by submitting to evil and death, the church will ultimately win "the war of the worlds."

THEN GOD WILL BE ABLE TO DO THE ULTIMATE: He will forgive us (Romans 11:32). By his forgiveness, he will prove Love ("God is love" 1 John 4:8) is superior to all thing. Satan's way, being accuser of the brethren, will fail. When Jesus returns and raises us from the dead, he will overcome Satan (2 Thessalonians 2:8).

According to Ephesians 3, God will prove to the angels by the church that his wisdom is the most powerful. If we love God, we will remain loyal to him, and prove every way we can that LOVE is the strongest force in the universe. Hence,

COLOSSIANS 2:2b,3

UNITED IN LOVE,
SO THAT YOU MAY HAVE THE FULL RICHES
OF COMPLETE UNDERSTANDING,
IN ORDER THAT YOU MAY KNOW
THE MYSTERY OF GOD,
NAMELY CHRIST, IN WHOM ARE
HIDDEN ALL THE TREASURES OF WISDOM.

Katheryn Maddox Haddad

Unbearable Loss

Lesson Three: Loss of a Personal God

Lesson
AIM
- ♥ **UNDERSTANDING EUTHANASIA**
- ♥ **DEAL WITH SHATTERED FAITH**

Scripture Outline

Job 2:1-6: God brags on Job. Satan says Job will blame God if his life is threatened. God tells Satan he can do anything to fool Job into thinking he's dying, but he can't kill him.

Job 2:7-9: Satan makes Job sick with boils from the bottom of his feet to the top of his head. Job tends his wounds and becomes deathly ill. Job's wife finally tells him to give in to God's will, give up the fight, and die. At least he won't suffer anymore.

Job 2:10: Job says she is being foolish, and we should accept good and evil both from God. He does not sin with his lips, but during most of the rest of this book he complains he's not appreciated enough, and also begs God to quit torturing him and go ahead and kill him.

Job 2:11-13: Three close friends of Job hear about his illness and travel some distance to go to his side. When they see him, they don't recognize him. Then they sit down with him and wait for him to break the silence. Job does after one week.

Job 3-7: Job wants to die, for that which he most feared happened to him. Eliphaz reminds him of all the people Job has helped, but he doesn't like it when the shoe is on the other foot (v.5). He should be glad God is correcting him. Job continues to beg God to kill him and get his suffering over with (6:8) and to forgive his sins (7:20f).

Job 8-10: Bildad wonders if Job has been a hypocrite. Job replies that he doesn't claim to be perfect (9:20). But he's confused, not knowing why he's going through this (10:15).

Job 11-14: Zophar tells Job God should hurry up and tell him how he sinned bad enough to deserve this. Job sarcastically asks if he is the source of all wisdom and if God needs him to do his talking for him (13:7). Even if God does kill him, Job will still trust him (13:15). Job believes after death, he'll raise alive again (14:12,14).

Job 15-19: Eliphaz sarcastically asks Job if he was the first man ever born (15:7). Job complains they're all miserable comforters (16:2). Bildad warns Job of the punishment of sinners. Job begs them to stop breaking him in pieces, for he's sick enough already.

Job 20,21: Zophar warns Job what happens to the wicked. Job interrupts that even the wicked get rich. Eliphaz accuses Job of getting rich by taking from the poor, but Job denies it and says God knows his life and heart.

Job 25-31: Bildad says all men are sinners. Job replies that God, who created the world, doesn't need their help accusing him. God knows how good Job has been in judging, helping the poor and sick, remaining faithful to his wife, and taking in the homeless.

Job 32-37: Young Elihu can no longer keep silent. Perhaps he arrived late, having traveled the farthest, since there were only three "friends" to begin with. He says God talks to people in different ways and chastens in different ways for different reasons. Job has continually said how good he is (35:2). God isn't affected by Job's goodness or
sins either one; sin only hurts the man doing it (35:6-8). We can't question God about our lives any more than we can how and why he created the earth the way he did.

Job 38-41: God picks up on the same subject and asks Job if he understands all the workings of the earth and sky. "Do you dare argue with God to instruct God?" (40:2). Job replies that he spoke rashly and wouldn't anymore. God continues questioning whether Job understands many scientific truths and he doesn't.

Job 42:1-6: Finally, Job confesses that he knew God before, but now he feels his presence in his heart, then asks God's forgiveness.

Job 42:7-10: Then God commands Job's three friends to repent for thinking they understood any more than Job did. (Never did God tell Job's wife to repent though!)

Job 42:11,12: Then Job's brothers and sisters and friends who had originally deserted him (Job 19:13-16) come to him each with a piece of money and an earring of gold, and help nurse him back to health.

Job 42:13-15: Job rebuilds his estate so that he is twice as rich as he had been before. He has seven more sons, unnamed. He has three more daughters which the Bible names, tells how beautiful they are, and how they inherit as much as their brothers. Job lives another 140 years and dies an old man.

Today's World

According to early 1990s research published in the book, *The Day America Told the Truth,* 90 percent of all Americans say they truly believe in God. In Canada 85 percent do. But six out of every seven of these "believers" believe it is okay not to believe in God.

Less than two-fifths of these believers believe that "sin" is going against God's will and/or the Bible. Forty percent believe in five or less of the Ten Commandments. Over three-fifths define sin by their own consciences. Although 82 percent believe in both heaven and hell, only fifty-five percent believe in Satan.

One-third of these "believers" have not been to a religious service of any kind for over a year. Yet 46 percent of them expect to go to heaven someday and 4 percent expect to go to hell.

How many truly religious people do we have in North America? About 15 percent. Who are these people likely to be? On the average, one out of every four is a college graduate, the rest have some college or have never been to college. What do people today lean on when loss of property and life and health comes face to face with them?

* * *

Euthanasia, according to Webster, means an *act or method of causing death painlessly, so as to end suffering.* In the past twenty years, a related practice has emerged called "assisted suicide."

Although assisted suicide was illegal in the Netherlands until 1993 and punishable by 12 years in prison, this law had not been enforced in about 20 years. Dutch doctors estimated 2,300 died annually in this way, but critics place the number closer to 10,000 annually.

In 1991, the Dutch government made a survey among doctors, promising them immunity, and found over 1,000 cases just in one year where lethal injections were administered without explicit patient requests. They all said they believed it was the patient's unspoken wish.

Dr. Pieter Admiraal has assisted about 100 suicides because "you cannot imagine the longing for death." Yet he admits it depresses him because it's actually murder. He uses a lethal injection such as is used for criminal executions.

The Dutch Anti-Euthanasia Society says the practice promotes hopelessness. There's growing fear and distrust among the elderly and handicapped that they'll be targeted for misplaced "mercy killing." One such disabled person said, "We feel our lives threatened....We realize that we cost the community a lot....Many people think we are useless
....Often we notice that we are being talked into desiring death....We find it extremely dangerous and frightening." Tens of thousands of frightened Dutch now carry "life declaration" cards in their wallets saying under no circumstances are they to be put to death with mercy killing/assisted suicide.

In September 1999 it was announced that the Netherlands is now set to become the first country to legalize "mercy killings."

Switzerland allows non-doctors to assist with suicides in incurable cases. But a Basel University study questions the whole system, citing a man supposedly having terminal lung cancer but reported by the coroner as having bronchitis. Another questionable case was a 30-year-old woman chronically depressed.

IN THE U.S. in June 1990 Janet Adkins, 54, a victim of Alzheimer's disease, pushed a button on a "suicide machine" and ended her life with the assistance of Jack Kevorkian, AKA "Dr. Death." He went on to personally assist in over 120 such suicides before being stopped.

A report was found written by Kevorkian after assisting one man stating that the man apparently changed his mind at the last minute and requested twice, "Take the mask off! Take the mask off!" No one took the gas mask off. He was dead a minute later.

In 1993 the State of Michigan (where Kevorkian lived) enacted a law against assisted suicide, but it was in effect only until the end of 1994. In 1994 and twice in 1996, Kevorkian was tried in Michigan and found not guilty by a jury because of his claim, "What I do is relieve suffering. That is the whole point. Unfortunately, death is the result."

In June 1996, the U.S. Supreme Court ruled that the terminally ill have no constitutional right to doctor-assisted suicide. In October 1997, Kevorkian announced that he planned to donate organs from his victims. The ultimate aim of assisted suicide, he said, should be organ donation and human research.

In December 1997 Kevorkian assisted in the suicide of a man who had a history of major mental illness. In March 1998 Kevorkian assisted a young paralyzed college student in dying by lethal injection in his shoulder, thus overstepping his own bounds of relieving pain and suffering in the terminally ill, and also of having the patient push the button on the suicide machine.

Not Dead Yet, a disabled-rights group contended that Kevorkian was slowly conditioning people to view death as the alternative to living with a disability. "People are so indoctrinated into considering a disability as a fate worse than death. In the disabled community, there are many who consider Kevorkian a serial killer."

Kevorkian forswears all religion. "I hate dishonesty and hypocrisy. Religion is founded on the fear of death." Is he happy? "No." When asked what happens when we die, he replied, "You rot."

 In September 1998, another law went into effect in Michigan making assisted suicide a felony punishable by up to five years in prison and a $10,000 fine. Despite this, On September 7, Kevorkian gave a lethal injection to a disabled man, videotaped it, and succeeded in having it aired over CBS's 60 Minutes. Early the following year, Kevorkian was found guilty of second-degree murder and sentenced to 10-25 years in prison.

Gonzales v. Oregon was brought to the **United States** Supreme Court in 2006. The court ruled that the **United States** Attorney General could not enforce the federal Controlled Substances Act against physicians who prescribed drugs, in compliance with Oregon state **law**, for the **assisted suicide** of the terminally ill. Most states have ruled assisted suicide illegal, but not all.

Bible World

Job 2:7,8,12—And smote Job with sore boils from the sole of his foot unto his crown. And he took him a potsherd to scrape himself withal; and he sat down among the ashes. And when they lifted up their eyes afar off, and knew him not, they lifted up their voice and wept. **7:4,5** -When I lie down, I say, "When shall I arise, and the night be gone?" And I am full of tossings to and fro unto the dawning of the day. My flesh is clothed with worms and clods of dust; my skin is broken, and become loathsome. **17:1**—My breath is corrupt, my days are extinct, the graves are ready for me. **19:17-20**—My breath is strange to my wife....children....my inward friends. My bone cleaves to my skin and to my flesh, and I am escaped with the skin of my teeth. **30:17,18,27-31**—My bones are pierced in me in the night season; and my sinews take no rest. By the great force of my disease is my garment changed: it binds me about as the collar of my coat. My bowels boiled, and rested now; the days of affliction prevented me. I went mourning without the sun: I stood up, and I cried in the congregation. I am a brother to dragons, and a companion to owls. My skin is black upon me, and my bones are burned with heat. My harp also is turned in mourning, and my organ into the voice of them that weep.

"Boils" comes from a Hebrew word meaning a malignant inflammation. It has been generally concluded from the above verses that the disease Job had was **elephantiasis**, a marked and strongly developed form of **leprosy**. This disease creates an intense heat, a burning and ulcerous swelling. It is leprosy in its most terrible form, taking its name from the appearance of the body, which is covered with a knotty, cancerous bark like the hide of an elephant. The whole frame is in a stage of progressive dissolution, ending slowly, surely in death.

Elephantiasis is generally local, attacking some part of the body, especially the arms, legs, or genital organs. But in the worst forms, the entire body suffers. The ulcers are often much inflamed, and sometimes discharge a white fluid which is burning and irritating with an offensive odor. And they attract maggots in some conditions. As the fluid drained and dried on his skin, Job apparently scraped it off with his potsherd.

He was so deformed by his disease, his friends didn't recognize him. His disagreeable breath was another indication of elephantiasis. Job's wife, mother's children, and friends apparently found it so offensive, they would not get close to him. His foul breath was also a sign that death was near.

The voice ("harp/organ") is also affected by the disease, and it becomes low, melancholy and unrecognizable. Job's bowels which boiled refer to his "entrails," tormented and thrown into confusion. A better translation of "I went mourning without the sun" is "I go about blackened, but not by the sun." Grief and suffering both blacken the face, and the body where the disease destroys the flesh is blackened. Job stood up and cried in the assembly of people, literally, he cried for help in his agony, desperation, and depression. He felt like a brother to animals which cry and wail in the night. Indeed, deep within his bones are deep-seated burning pains caused by the disease. These pains are greatest at night. They prevent sleep and give rise to restlessness and nightmares.

Introducing the Lesson

Watching a loved one suffer nearly tears us apart, whether we observe it over a few minutes or many years. Those who have watched a loved one suffer for a long period of time spend a great deal of time trying to figure out how to end their suffering, whether it be taking them to a different doctor or discontinuing medical treatment. Some of these patients beg to die as Job did. There are people today who beg to die, and there are several doctors willing to help, including one with his "suicide machine" called, "Dr. Death" by his opponents. It is legal in the Netherlands, but being promised immunity, 1,000 doctors confessed that in one year they practiced assisted suicide without the consent of the patient.

Job was suffering terribly and thought he was going to die and wanted to hurry and get it over with. Job's wife did the same thing. She told him to give in to God's will and just die. How they must have agonized. They both thought he would never get well, that he was incurable. But he DID get well.

Job probably had the disease called "elephantiasis," a horrible form of leprosy that makes a person's skin become thick and scaly like an elephant's, and full of infected nodules. They have terrible pain through their bones, and have nightmares. Even their voice changes so that it is low and melancholy, and even their breath is foul. He was hard to look at, hard to listen to, and hard to be close to. *Display JOB'S DISEASE.*

Discussion Questions

19. If God does not intercede and the tragedy occurs after many prayers, how can people begin to doubt either themselves or God?

2 Samuel 12:15-23: David's and Bathsheba's baby fell sick, and David fell prostrate on the ground crying and begging God to save its life. It died anyway, so David got up, washed his face, and ate. He'd accepted God's decision. His son would never return, but he could go to his son someday.

Job 13:15: Job said that even if God killed him, he would trust him.

Possible Class Response: They can lose their trust in God. They can think God doesn't really care about them. Or they can think they sinned too much for God to hear them. Or they can think God is punishing them for being so bad. They can wonder, "If God is so good, why did he let this happen?"

20. Job's friends sat in silence with him for a long time. What are some benefits of this type comfort?

Ecclesiastes 3:7: There is a time to speak and a time to keep silence.

Possible Class Response: We should not force a sick or grieving person to talk if they don't want to. They may be too sick to talk and hold a conversation. Nor should we force them to talk about things they don't want to talk about, for that could make them sicker. Sometimes all the sick need is to know we are there. We could pray for them aloud, we could read the Bible or sing quietly to them. But we need to be sensitive to whether this is the time for that too. What they may need most is rest.

21. **What benefit is there in allowing a person with their faith being tested to first explain which parts of the trial are bothering them the most?**

    Acts 7:22-28: Moses was just trying to defend his Israeli brothers when he killed the taskmaster. His brothers never gave him a chance to explain, and they accused him of wanting to kill them too.

    Job 16:1-4: Job said his friends were miserable comforters full of foolish talk, and they didn't even know when to shut up.

    Job 19:1-4: Job accused his friends of breaking him in pieces, and not even being ashamed. They were like strangers to him, not friends. Besides, if he did sin, he certainly wouldn't admit it to them.

    Possible Class Response: We can waste a lot of time and talking and take the chance of hard feelings for nothing. We cannot outguess other people. We must ask them. Furthermore, we need to give them enough respect for their opinions that we will listen to them, right or wrong. Sometimes they just need to hear themselves explain things out loud, to think things through out loud. By remaining silent, we give them a chance to do this, and we may never need to tell the other side after all; they will figure it out themselves. Or, if we listen carefully to them, they are more likely to listen carefully to us.

22. **Discuss people living out a self-fulfilling prophecy. What benefit can occur by being forced to face and overcome one's fears?**

    Numbers 13:25,30f; 14:40,45: The Israeli spies returned from Canaan saying they could never conquer the Canaanites. Then when God said they could just wander in the wilderness for a generation, they changed their minds, attacked the Canaanites anyway, and were killed.

    Job 3:25: Job said that what he had greatly feared had come about.

    Possible Class Response: If we complain no one likes us and we go around telling people so, people won't want to be around us for fear we'll condemn them too; so we end up with no one liking us. If we go job hunting and complain no one will hire us, sure enough this employer won't want to be any different and won't hire us either. People are afraid of complainers and don't want to be around them for fear they will be accused of things by the complainer too. If we see a trend in what we're complaining about, we can try to work out a way to see the good side instead. The poet said, "Cry and we cry alone. Laugh and the world laughs with us."

23. **Tell of times when you or a friend stubbornly held on to a cause you believed in despite evidence to the contrary.**

As miserable as Job was, he still refused to blame God, even though Satan had said he would.

1 Corinthians 1:18-2:16: Over and over man's wisdom is compared with God's wisdom. Man's wisdom is foolishness to God who knows so much more than we. On the other hand, man thinks God's ways are foolish and don't work.

Possible Class Response: Some may have participated in a race no one thought they could run. Those who invented the automobile were laughed at and told to get a horse. Some may have marched alone or written against abortion. A single woman against drunk driving started MADD and eventually got laws changed.

24. **How can arguing with someone whose faith is being tried make things worse? How can we discover the thread that keeps their faith going so we can reinforce it?**

Hebrews 11:1: Faith is unseen but is based on evidence that is seen.

Possible Class Response: They need first of all to know we understand what they are going through. Sometimes just talking about their doubts helps them reason through them. Sometimes when they're done explaining why they don't believe, they ask for help because they do want to believe. Further, the reason they give at first for not believing may not be the root reason. We need to give them time to filter through all their "reasons" one at a time, for each one will likely be a deeper reason than the one before. Once we find that inner thread that makes them want to believe, we can start building on it.

25. **Have you ever wished you could suffer and/or die in the place of a loved one? Tell about it.**

2 Samuel 18:33: When David's son, Absalom, was killed by David's troops, David cried and said too late he wished he had died for him.

Possible Class Response: More are willing to suffer for someone else, so encourage the class to discuss this first. When we see our children suffer, we want to take the pain away and put it on ourselves. If anyone was ever extremely close to someone who had a full and productive life ahead of them, they may have truly wished they'd died to give this person a chance to fulfill their own destiny in life.

26. **Tell of times in your life when your view of God became distorted or you thought he wanted bad to happen to you (Exodus 16:3; Number 14:3).**

The word translated curse comes from a Hebrew word *barak*. This word was translated in the Bible 326 times as *bless* or *kneel down* and only four times as curse. It indicates a kind of submission to a superior will. So why did Job call her foolish for saying he should submit to the will of God and die?

Job admitted he was willing to accept both bad and good from God. Job called more than his wife foolish in this book; he called his friends fools on many occasions and argued with them constantly. Furthermore, Job said more than once that he wanted to just die and get it over with.

We can only speculate why Job was upset by his wife saying what he himself had said—I want to die. It may be perhaps that his wife said it fairly early in his illness but after he'd had a particularly bad night. Or perhaps she said it during one of his more courageous moments, during a time when he wasn't quite so discouraged. Job called more than his wife foolish in this book; his called his friends who came to console him fools several times.

Exodus 16:3; Numbers 14:3: When the Israelites got into the wilderness with nothing much to eat, they complained to Moses they wished they were slaves again back in Egypt.

Possible Class Response: We become confused with God when a lot of bad things happen in our lives and don't seem to have any end to them. Does God want us to submit to them or fight them? We can't see the big picture and don't understand why these things are happening to us. Perhaps we were engaged to someone once, then he broke it off and we thought the world would end; then we met our husband and know it was all for the best after all. Other things bad have happened to us, and in the end they turned out to be for the better.

27. **Have you ever wished a suffering loved one could go ahead and die and get it over with? (1 Samuel 31:4) Compare your feelings with Job's wife.**

1 Samuel 31:34: Saul begged his armor-bearer to go ahead and kill him so he wouldn't be tortured by his enemies.

Possible Class Response: Those who have watched loved ones with painful diseases have wished they would no longer suffer. You don't need to get into a long discussion about it in class. Some in your class may have had to decide when to stop the medication and go ahead and let someone die whose brain had already died. There is a difference in that and Euthanasia which can be in the form of helping people commit suicide.

28. **When things challenge our faith in a loved one (such as gossip), what is it that keeps us having faith in that person when you don't know all the facts?**

After searching his soul during his terrible illness, Job began to face the fact that he obeyed God out of fear of God destroying him if he didn't (Job 31:21-23). Intellectually Job knew God had to exist and even had a lot of pride in this knowledge (41:34). But he had never really seen God—the God who is love.

1 Corinthians 13:7: Love never stops believing in others.

Possible Class Response: Job did believe in God no matter what happened because he was afraid of him. By the end of his illness, he had learned to truly love God. Love makes the difference. Encourage your class to tell about times people believed in them or when they believed in friends when the crowd didn't.

29. **Do you know of people who knew the Bible well, but dropped from the church? How can it be dangerous to brag how much we know about the Bible? Is it safe to think we can know all the answers?**

   Job thought he had God all figured out, but finally realized He was much too awesome to make that possible (42:5, 6). At this point Job went on to the next level of faith - faith out of love instead of fear, and knowledge of the Word of God with humility instead of pride.

   Possible Class Response: Preachers have dropped out of the church. Some have even decided they didn't believe in God after all. We can become arrogant and indirectly think we know nearly as much as God when we become "experts" on the Bible. We can then indirectly begin demanding to know more than what is in the Bible, and possibly go elsewhere for those answers such as the occult, extra-sensory experiences, etc.

30. **How do you think Job was able to help restore his wife's faith? Did you ever have such an experience? Share it.**

   Proverbs 17:17: People close to us love us at all times, even in the bad.

   Job 19:25: Job knew beyond the shadow of a doubt that after he died, he would live again in another realm.

   1 John 4:7,8: He that loves is from God, for God is love.

   Possible Class Response: Job was undoubtedly patient with his wife. He certainly loved her or he would not have been careful not to allow himself to be tempted by other women. He set an example before her, praying often, and probably praying for her as much as for himself. People often don't believe God, not because they need proof, but because they need to feel God's love. Some in the class may have tried to reason with an atheist and got nowhere. Then they may have said they were praying for them, and the shell began to soften. Alexander Campbell, who was often invited to speak at atheist gatherings, converted many of them, not because of reason but because of love.

Good Work

Write a note to someone who does not normally attend worship.

BEFORE CLASS:

A1. FOR LARGE CONGREGATIONS. Contact your church secretary and ask for the names of members who have not attended in many months. Write down their names and addresses on envelopes.

A2. FOR SMALL CONGREGATIONS. Contact neighborhood friends or relatives.

B. Gather up church directories or telephone books.

Gather up envelopes and stationery (colored bond paper cut in half).

On poster board or the blackboard, write the following:

"I just wanted to drop you this note to let you know I wish you would come back to church [with me]. None of us is perfect, but we're trying the best we can. We have a loving God who wants to make life easier for us, and for you. We want to encourage you and receive encouragement from you. There are many reasons why we drift away from the church, but things just seem to be better when we return. Satan causes bad to happen, not God. God still loves you. If you can't decide to come just yet, you can call [phone number] any time and we can just talk. Whatever is going on in your life, my prayers are with you. God does care for you and so do I."

DURING CLASS:

"We have been talking about things that cause people to lose their faith in God. Job and his wife faced the same thing. Job's wife decided God wanted Job to die. Sometimes people today think God just doesn't care. Let's reach out to some of them."

Hand out envelopes and stationery (pre-addressed if members, blank if they choose friends out of the phone book). "If you are unsure what to say, I have written a suggestion on the board. Feel free to copy it if you like."

"You will now have about eight minutes to write your note. When you are done, give it to me to mail, then offer a silent prayer for the one you wrote while the others finish."

Concluding Remarks

When time is up and while the slower writers complete their notes, sing one verse of a song, possibly one of the following:

1. *God Moves in a Mysterious Way*
2. *God is Love*
3. *Oh Love That Wilt Not Let Me Go*
4. *There is Beyond the Azure Blue a God*

In a few moments, everyone will be returning to busy lives and responsibilities. Let your last few moments be upbeat and positive. Smile!

(Wait for one or two quick replies to each of the following.) "In a few words....

1. God wants what kind of things to happen to us?

2. What makes people keep believing in someone, even when they're accused of doing wrong?

3. Hebrews 11:1 says that invisible faith has visible what?

4. God is what?

Have a closing prayer, mentioning by name the ones the class wrote to, that God will give them some extra love this week.

Job's Disease

Boils—2:7
Wrinkled—16:8
Lean—16:8
Gaped at—16:10
Breath corrupt—17:1
Skin cleaving to bones—19:20
Bones burn him at night—30:17
Sinews take no rest (hurt)—30:17
Garment binds him—30:18
Skin is black—30:30
Bones burn—30:30
Voice weeps—30:31

Inside the Hearts of Bible Women: Teacher's & Advertising Manual

SECOND TIME AROUND
Ruth

Lesson One: Letting Go

Lesson Aim
- ♥ ADJUST TO WIDOWHOOD
- ♥ UNDERSTAND WIDOWHOOD

Scripture Outline

Ruth 1:1,2: During a famine in Bethlehem, Naomi and her husband and two sons move to Moab.

Ruth 1:3-5: They live there about ten years and the boys marry Moabite women. Then Naomi's husband and both sons die.

Ruth 1:6-15: Naomi hears the famine is finally over in Bethlehem so decides to return. Her daughters-in-law start to go with her, but she urges them to go back and remarry and rebuild their lives. Finally she convinces one of them to return home.

Ruth 1:16-18: But Ruth stays and tells Naomi she wants to adopt her ways and her religion and her home for the rest of her life, for she loves her so much. So Naomi allows her to go to Bethlehem with her.

Ruth 1:19-21: Ten years after she has left Bethlehem, Naomi returns, now probably grayer and more stooped from age, and grief showing in her eyes and demeanor. Further, everyone expects her to return with her entire family. At first no one recognizes her. When the word spreads and everyone greets her, tired and worn from her trip and earlier trials, she bitterly tells them to call her Mara, which means bitter.
Ruth 1:22: Naomi has carefully chosen the time to return to Bethlehem, for it is harvest time.

Today's World

Are we prepared for widowhood? Regardless of your age, you must sit down with your husband and work through it. If you don't want to talk about it for very long at a time, make a list of things that need to be covered and bring up one topic at a time, perhaps once a week for several weeks. Why? What are your chances of being widowed?

About one out of every 400 men ages 25-34 will die this year.
About one out of every 200 men ages 35-44 will die this year.
About one out of every 100 men ages 45-54 will die this year.
About one out of every 50 men ages 55 to 64 will die this year.
About one out of every 25 men ages 65-74 will die this year.

So, estimate the number of men you know—from the congregation, your neighborhood, at work, relatives and so on—and you can estimate the number of funerals for men you will hear about. One of them could be your husband. How do you prepare?

FINANCIAL:

A. Find out where all bank accounts are. Have your name put on them if possible if they aren't already.
b. Get the names and addresses of all life insurance companies, including accidental death policies which are sometimes automatically tacked on to credit card coverage, bank accounts, organizational memberships, etc. To Get a copy of your husband's birth certificate so his death certificate can be made out correctly.
d. Get your husband's social security number, union number, armed service number, civil service number, etc.
e. Make an updated list of places your husband has worked in case they had insurance policies or pension plans you didn't know about.
f. Keep a list of all subscriptions, memberships, etc. your husband uses so they can be canceled immediately.
g. Put as many things as possible in both of your names.
h. Have a will made up by an attorney. Ask your husband to make a video tape reading and explaining his own will to everyone involved.
i. Decide what cemetery you want to use—a local one or a family burial plot in another state.

DAILY LIVING:

a. If you don't know how to drive, learn now.
b. Ask your husband to find someone who will come in and help when things break down such as the furnace, a faucet, the lawnmower, the car. Repeat this every time you move.
c. Find out where the electric box, gas turn-off, and water turn-off meters are and how to turn things on and off.
d. Ask him to put good locks on the doors and windows and spotlights in the front and back of the house.

SPIRITUAL/EMOTIONAL:

a. Talk about heaven and how you'll wait for each other with open arms. If he is a spiritual-minded person, ask him to make a short and very positive recording of all the things he's going to do in heaven such as "Walk those golden streets!" and "Sing with all those angels!" and "Ask God all those questions I always wondered about!" and "Have long walks and talks with Abraham!" This will help you when you cry.

b. Ask him what he wants for his funeral—songs, preacher, etc.
c. Ask him if he'd want you to remarry (of course he wouldn't mind). Hearing him say it will help you let go of him emotionally if the time ever comes.
d. Since you'll seldom be invited by your coupled friends to do things with them after you're single, decide what you'll do for entertainment and pastimes, and who you'd like to make new/closer friends with.
e. About once a year, ask him to write a letter to each of your children telling them he loves them, exhorting them to obey and help their mother, and encouraging them to carry on his name in this world with dignity and pride.

Bible World

Moab, the land of Ruth's birth, was started by Lot's son whom he fathered through his daughter after his wife's death (Genesis 19:37). It was located at the east and bottom of the Dead Sea near where Sodom had been, and their country was 40 miles long by 12 miles wide—480 square miles (Deuteronomy 2:10,11). Their capital was originally Zoar where Lot had run to escape the fire on Sodom and Gomorrah.

When the Children of Israel were freed from Egypt and came to their promised land, God forbade them to bother the Moabites because of their blood ties (Judges 11:9,19). Balaam, their prophet, said they could not conquer the Israelites, but could seduce them. So the Moabites seduced the Israelites into worshipping their Baal gods by going to their temple prostitutes, resulting in the men being executed (Numbers 25:1-9). Further, God excluded them from his congregation to the tenth generation (Deuteronomy 23:3,4), which would have been far beyond Ruth's lifetime.

When the Israelites requested to buy bread and water and have safe passage through Moab to get to their promised land, Moab refused (Numbers 20:14-21). However, as the Israelites marched around Moab, they finally gave in and did sell them bread and water (Deuteronomy 23:3,4). Just prior to their entry into the promised land, Moses climbed Mt. Pisgah in Moab, viewed the land, and died.

After the Israelites settled in their land, they were ruled by a supreme-court judge. After a 40-year period of peace while Othniel judged, the Israelites went after idols again, so God allowed Edom's King Eglon to conquer the Israelites, a hold which he had for 18 years. Their next judge, Ehud, sneaked into the palace in Moab and stabbed Eglon, a very fat man. The Israelites took courage, slew 10,000 Moabites in battle, and won back their freedom (Judges 3:10-30).

Ruth moved to Israel about 120 years before David was made king (David being born some time during Samuel's long judgeship). That would mean she arrived in Israel possibly late in Jair's peaceful 22-year judgeship. Since David's father was Ruth's grandson, David still had ties with Moab. So, when Saul sought his life, David took his parents to Moab for asylum (1 Samuel 22:3,4).

We hear little about Moab after that until the time of Ahab long after David's death. King Mesha of Moab rendered heavy taxes on King Ahab (2 Kings 3:4). Ahab's successor son, King Jehoram, attacked Moab and broke it down to a weak country. Both Isaiah and Amos predicted it would be eventually destroyed, and a century and a half later, Ezekiel and Jeremiah said its destruction was imminent as an independent country.

About 600 years later, John the Baptist was imprisoned in a palace in Machaerus of Moab, and beheaded there.

Introducing the Lesson

Widowhood is not something we like talking about. If we're not widowed yet, it puts a sense of panic in us. But it is something we need to talk about. **Display DEATH RATES OF MEN IN THE U.S.**
About one out of every 400 men ages 25-34 will die this year.
About one out of every 200 men ages 35-44 will die this year.
About one out of every 100 men ages 45-54 will die this year.
About one out of every 50 men ages 55 to 64 will die this year.
About one out of every 25 men ages 65-74 will die this year.

(Source: 1992 Information Please Almanac)

I would like to encourage each of you who are married to begin now to prepare for living without him should he become a victim of an automobile accident, disease, or whatever. Force yourself to talk to him about things you need to know and do. Write them down. There are about three categories of things you need to talk about right now and not put it off. **Display PREPARE FOR YOUR HUSBAND'S DEATH.** They are: (1) Financial Matters; (2) Everyday Matters; (3) Spiritual and Emotional Matters. (Pick up a few highlights, but don't go into detail unless you have time.)

In our lesson, Naomi moved back to the town where her relatives lived because she needed them as a new widow. Ruth, in turn, moved with her mother-in-law, again needing moral support from the one who was closest to her at this difficult time.

Discussion Questions

1. **After 50 years of marriage, what is the letting go process like for the widow? Tell about some widows you know (be careful about names).**

When we marry, we plan to live and grow old together. What we don't plan for is the inevitability of letting go.

1 Corinthians 7:39: A wife is bound by her marriage vows to her husband as long as he lives. If he dies, she may remarry, but only a Christian.

Possible Class Response: The husband and wife have grown in maturity together, grown old together, had thousands of meals together, fought hundreds of times forgiven hundreds of times, had children and grandchildren together, experienced ecstatic happiness and deep sadness together, and gone just about everywhere together. Their lives were so enmeshed, they couldn't imagine life without the other. Now half of the couple is dead and she feels lost, not sure how to function alone. The person she confided in most is gone. Confiding in her grown children just isn't the same. No one to talk to, no one to go places with, no one to eat with, no one to snuggle up to at night. The house is suddenly so very quiet.

2. **Explain how shattered dreams affect younger women differently than older ones.**

Job 7:6-10: Time went by so fast, and our hopes for the future now rush from my grasp like the wind. He that I loved will never see me again. He'll never come through the door and kiss me hello, he'll never sit at his place at the dinner table or his favorite chair or anywhere else. He's gone forever.

Possible Class Response: Those who lose husbands by death in their youth suffer a greater shock. Plans intended for a lifetime are suddenly shattered and no sense can be made of it. Perhaps they hadn't had children yet; or if they did, he'll never see them grow up. There was that dream house he was planning to build. He was just being recognized for his talents at work. He was just getting involved with the church. They were just getting so they didn't live paycheck to paycheck and could do a few recreational things together.

3. **Tell about someone you know who sacrificed a more secure future for the sake of a younger person. How could such a person guard against the sacrifice leading to bitterness in the future?**

Naomi had to face the double burden of losing husband and sons, and she felt she would probably never remarry. She did not want this for her daughters-in-law. She wanted them to heal, remarry someday, and not be lonely anymore. Apparently, she felt their chances of remarrying were too slim if they tended to her loneliness and postponed the letting go process.

John 15:12-15: The greatest love we can show for another is to give up our life for someone else.

Possible Class Response: Some have put a second mortgage on their home so they could send their children to college. Some have delayed retirement to raise a grandchild. Some have given up promotions at work involving relocation so their children could stay in the same school. We must make the decision completely on our own without others begging us to. We could write ourselves a long letter explaining the situation which led to us making this decision, telling all the hardship we may go through as a result but which will be done willingly, and reminding ourselves that it was our decision and ours only. Then we could save the letter and get it out any time we began resenting the outcome of our decision.

4. **How important in adjusting to a husband's death is finding a close friend? How can the close friend help?**

    Ecclesiastes 4:9,10: Two are better than one, for if one falls, the other one can help her up.

    Possible Class Response: We all need someone to let our hair down with and who will love us even when our feet are dirty and we have no makeup on. We need someone who will laugh with us when we laugh and cry with us when we cry. We need someone who has shared in some of the same experiences we have. We can't live in a vacuum. We need someone to talk to and go places with. Someone who's been widowed for a while might best be able to help through this transition.

5. **Discuss the different attitudes people tend to have toward a newly widowed person and the awkwardness they feel toward her. How can she develop her own identity without her husband?**

    People were used to seeing Naomi with her husband for decades. There briefly when she returned home they did not recognize her. She did not seem to be the same person.

    Jeremiah 32:19: One who can counsel us wisely understands why people do what they do, and can help us according to our situation in life.

    Possible Class Response: They are afraid she'll start crying. They don't know whether to bring up her deceased husband in a conversation. They leave her out of gatherings that she and her husband used to be part of perhaps for many, many years. They think that, if she's with a group of couples, she will feel even more lonely. They don't know what to talk to her about because in the past her conversation always included her husband in some way. She can develop her own identity by enlarging on or taking up a new hobby. She can go to adult education classes or college. She can offer to do things at church that she didn't while her husband was still with her.

6. **What can friends do to help such a woman out of this phase of grief?**

    With all we know of Naomi, she was a gracious loving and giving woman. But when she returned to the emptiness of her home town and her home, it overwhelmed her, and she became bitter

    Ruth 1:20,22: Naomi sharply told everyone to just call her Mara which means bitter, because that's how she felt.

    Possible Class Response: She has a right to be angry. Satan causes sickness and death, not God. She doesn't want to be alone or to take over the responsibilities he used to handle. She didn't want to see him suffer. Her friends are going on with their husbands, but she is not. They didn't do anything to deserve this. Yes, she knows they can be reunited in heaven, but that's so far away. We can allow the widow to express these things and agree with her. Once she recognizes that we understand why she is bitter, she can move on to resigning herself to it, and starting to build a new and different kind of life without him.

7. **Where does it cease to serve a good purpose? About how long does it take most women to let go of these memories and make them secondary factors in their daily lives?**

   In early stages of widowhood, a woman lives in the past. While it is good to look around and store in one's heart precious life memories, where is the limit?

   Psalm 112:6: Those we love will live in our memories forever.

   Possible Class Response: Spending time with one's memories is healing at first. We filter out the bad and remember primarily the good, and it is a soothing ointment to our broken hearts. But we can't neglect certain responsibilities just because he used to always take care of them. We can't just sit home and do nothing because he's not there to do things with. It takes about a year for the memories to lose their vividness and to get used to doing things without him. The second year, especially after the second "goodbye" at the first anniversary of his death, she can let go better and begin to look to the kind of future she can make for herself by herself.

8. **What are some good remedies for sorrow? List as many ideas as possible.**

   Ecclesiastes 3:22: The best thing in the world for a person's self-esteem is to accomplish something on her own.

   Possible Class Response: Keeping busy is a good remedy. Immediately after a husband dies, the new widow may do housework non-stop for hours, or the ironing, or something that she doesn't have to concentrate on but will keep her moving until she can absorb mentally what has happened. Music helps some people, complete silence helps some, being in a crowded mall helps some. After the initial grieving, she can start inviting company over, and hopefully the company will accept. She can spend more time with children. She can start doing things she didn't have time to do before but wanted to; perhaps things she used to do when she was young.

9. **Give some specific and practical suggestions of what can be done alone during the night to help this terrible feeling go away and bring peace.**

   Psalm 6:6: I am so tired. All night I groan and cry.

   Possible Class Response: She can drink warm milk just before going to bed, and make sure her room is dark enough. On the other hand, if part of her staying awake is from fear, she could have a night light in her room or even keep all the lights on in the house; or she could put an extra lock on her bedroom door. She can get a dog or put in an alarm system. She can have a book beside her bed to read, or some hobby to work on. She can have some telephone numbers by her bed that she can call such as "Dial-a-Prayer," or a local Hot Line that is available 24 hours a day for people to just call and talk if that is what they need. If she does get up and do something during the night, she should be sure to take naps during the day.

Good

Work

Send a note of encouragement to a widow.

BEFORE CLASS:

A1.   FOR LARGE CONGREGATIONS: Go through your church directory for the names of widows. Make a list of them and their addresses.

A2.   FOR SMALL CONGREGATIONS: Contact a nearby senior center and ask for the first names of widows who attend their functions. Make a list of them and the address of the center.

B.   Write down the names and addresses of these widows on envelopes.

C.   Bring blank envelopes and a telephone book for those who wish to write a note to a widow friend you may not know.

D.   Gather up stationary, possibly colored bond paper cut in half.

E.   On poster board or the blackboard, write the following:

"I just wanted to write and tell you that I know it hasn't been easy since you lost your husband. He was a part of you and losing him was like an amputation. No matter how long ago he passed away, you will always miss him. You've had great courage in going on with your life. Though at the time you thought you could never laugh again, you have been able to return laughter to your life. May God walk beside you in whatever you do. Today I am saying a special prayer for you. [Let's get together some time for coffee.]"

DURING CLASS:

"We've been talking about widowhood and facing life without someone that we were one with for just a few years or for many years. We all know people who have been widowed. Some of you in this class have been widowed, and you know firsthand what it's like. Today we are going to reach out to some widows with our love and friendship."

Hand out envelopes and stationery. "These envelopes have been pre-addressed with the widows who attend the [church/senior center]. If you have a widow friend not included, I have some blank envelopes and telephone books."

"If you're not sure what to say, I have written something on the board you may copy. It doesn't mean it will be less from your heart than if you worded it yourself. The important thing is that you thought of this person."

"You will have about five minutes. When you are done, hand your envelope to me for mailing, and say a silent prayer for your widow while the others finish writing. Let's all be quiet now so we can think and write."

Concluding

Remarks

When time is up and while the slower writers complete their notes, sing one verse of a song, possibly one of the following:

1. *Walking Alone at Eve*
2. *God Will Take Care of You*
3. *It is Well with My [His] Soul*
4. *Count Your Many Blessings*

In a few minutes, part of your class will be returning to a busy home full of children and things going on, and it will be easy to forget the widow she wrote. And part of your class will be returning to an empty home and memories of a husband gone on before her. End the class with reminders of those alone, and encouragement to those alone.

(Wait for one or two quick replies to each of the following.) "In just a few words....

1. When inviting company over to our house, we should not leave out who?

2. What can we do when a widow gets mad that her husband died and left her?

3. What can a widow do to develop her own identity?

4. Think of a widow you can become a special friend to.

Give the list of widows everyone wrote to the person leading the closing prayer, and bring them by name before the throne of God.

Death Rates of Men in the U.S.

Age Group	Percent Who Die	Number Who Die
15-24	.17%	31,380
25-34	.27%	59,246
35-44	.41%	73,903
45-54	.81%	98,091
55-64	1.8%	183,600
65-74	3.7%	296,277
75-84	8.0%	294,173
85 +	16.0%	136,935

Source: Department of Health and Human Services, National Center for Health Statistics

Inside the Hearts of Bible Women: Teacher's & Advertising Manual

Prepare For Your Husband's Death Now

FINANCIAL:

a. Find out where all bank accounts are. Have your name put on them if possible if they aren't already.
b. Get the names and addresses of all life insurance companies, including accidental death policies which are sometimes automatically tacked on to credit card coverage, bank accounts, organizational memberships, etc.
c. Get a copy of your husband's birth certificate so his death certificate can be made out correctly.
d. Get your husband's social security number, union number, armed service number, civil service number, etc.
e. Make an updated list of places your husband has worked in case they had insurance policies or pension plans you didn't know about.
f. Keep a list of all subscriptions, memberships, etc. your husband uses so they can be canceled immediately.
g. Put as many things as possible in both of your names.
h. Have a will made up by an attorney. Ask your husband to make a videotape reading and explaining his own will to everyone involved.
i. Decide what cemetery you want to use—a local one or a family burial plot in another state.

DAILY LIVING:

a. If you don't know how to drive, learn now.
b. Ask your husband to find someone who will come in and help when things break down such as the furnace, a faucet, the lawnmower, the car. Repeat this every time you move.
c. Find out where the electric box, gas turn-off, and water turn-off meters are and how to turn things on and off.
d. Ask him to put good locks on the doors and windows and spotlights in the front and back of the house.

SPIRITUAL/EMOTIONAL:

a. Talk about heaven and how you'll wait for each other with open arms. If he is a spiritual-minded person, ask him to make a short and very positive recording of all the things he's going to do in heaven such as "Walk those golden streets!" and "Sing with all those angels!" and "Ask God all those questions I always wondered about!" and "Have long walks and talks with Abraham!" This will help you when you cry.
b. Ask him what he wants for his funeral—songs, preacher, etc.
c. Ask him if he'd want you to remarry (of course he wouldn't mind). Hearing him say it will help you let go of him emotionally if the time ever comes.
d. Since you'll seldom be invited by your coupled friends to do things with them after you're single, decide what you'll do for entertainment and pastimes, and who you'd like to make new/closer friends with.
e. About once a year, ask him to write a letter to each of your children telling them he loves them, exhorting them to obey and help their mother, and encouraging them to carry on his name in this world with dignity and pride.

Katheryn Maddox Haddad

Second Time Around

Lesson Two: Single Again

Lesson Aim
- ♥ MAKE SOCIAL ADJUSTMENTS
- ♥ MAKE ECONOMIC ADJUSTMENTS

Scripture Outline

Ruth 2:2: Naomi explains to Ruth that, according to the Law of Moses, she can pick up for herself whatever of the crops the harvesters drop, and whatever is left in the unharvested corners of the fields.

Ruth 2:1,3: Coincidentally, Ruth chooses a field of Boaz, a rich relative of Naomi's husband, possibly a cousin.

Ruth 2:4-7: Boaz rides out to see how his servants are doing in the field, and spots Ruth. His foreman says she asked permission to reap there and has been at it all morning except for a short rest in the shelter.

Ruth 2:8: Boaz goes up to Ruth and tells her not to go to anyone else's field, but to stay with his servant girls to reap.

Ruth 2:9: Boaz orders his men-servants to not bother Ruth in any way, and to allow her to get a drink any time she wants from the water jugs regularly filled by the men.

Ruth 2:10-13: Ruth doesn't understand why Boaz is giving her extra favors, but he says it is because of her kindness to Naomi and her conversion to the Jewish faith.

Ruth 2:14-18: Boaz stays around until noon, then gives Ruth some of his lunch which was so much she takes some of it home to Naomi. When she goes back to work, Boaz orders his servants to pull out a little extra grain for her and pretend they dropped it by accident.

Ruth 2:19-23: When Naomi finds out where Ruth has received all this special treatment, she tells her to stay in Boaz's field, both for the extras he is giving her and also to keep from being harmed by men in some other field. [Could it be she was very beautiful?]

Ruth 3:1-4: Finally, realizing Boaz has fallen in love with Ruth, Naomi explains to her how to follow the Jewish custom of proposing to him. She tells Ruth to get cleaned up and put perfume on, slip out of town just before the gates close, and go back to his field. Boaz will be there guarding his harvest and spending the night. When he goes to sleep, Ruth is to quietly lay down at his feet. Naomi trusts Boaz to not hurt Ruth because of his love for her.

Today's World

The National Displaced Homemakers Network headquartered in Washington, D.C., reported a few years ago that one out of every five widowed or divorced women was living with unrelated people, that is, doubling up with another household, in order to make ends meet.

A "displaced homemaker" is a woman, regardless of education, who stayed out of the workforce (usually to raise children), lost her primary source of income (husband), and is having trouble getting accepted back in the workforce. Nearly 20 percent of all former homemakers are having major problems being accepted back in the workforce. Regardless of education, they are viewed with no valuable skills. Americans have devalued homemaking to the point that many women are "just a man away from poverty."

At any one time, 41% of displaced homemakers work parttime to at least have some kind of work, while 50% have not been hired by anyone. Of these, 76 percent are white, 18 percent are black, and 6 percent are Hispanic.

One in three of these displaced homemakers is in her prime productive years—between 35 and 64 years of age. About one-third of them have young children at home. About one in ten are under age 35, most with young children at home. Over half are over 65.

These are the women who become den mothers and scout leaders, are made PTA officers, volunteer for charitable fund drives, visit the sick at hospitals. They are the ones who get heavily involved in church work teaching VBS, visiting the sick, having home Bible studies, babysitting while someone is hospitalized, taking food to families after a funeral, sending notes of encouragement. They are at the center of what the community sees of the church. Then the world of work penalizes them for it. Cheryl Brown Henderson, President of the displaced homemakers' organization said, "Our study paints a picture of displaced homemakers' lives that is unrelentingly grim." Over one in three live below the federal poverty line.

* * *

According to the Bureau of Census, fifteen percent of all second marriages are by widows. However, only 23 percent of all widows remarry. Of those who do, 45 percent of widows with children under 18 remarry, while 12 percent with no children remarry. The average age of widows remarrying with children is 38, and those without children is 62.

Bible World

The Law of Moses made provisions for widows and their fatherless children. Every three years, the Israelites were to bring one-tenth of their "increase" (meaning crops and livestock) to the gates of the city. There everything was divided between the Levites, the travelers, the widows and the fatherless (Deuteronomy 14:28,29).

When Israelites harvested their fields, they were not to harvest the corners, nor were they to go back and pick up what they dropped; that was to be left to travelers and widows and their children (Leviticus 19:9). In their fields at harvest time, if someone forgot to bring in a sheaf, they were not to go get it; it was to be left for travelers or widows and their children. When they beat the fruit trees to get the fruit down, they were not to do it twice; the rest was to be left for the travelers or widows and their children. When they gathered grapes in the vineyard, they were not to go back and get what they missed; that too was for the travelers or widows and their children (Deuteronomy 24:17-21).

During religious feasts in each home, they were to make sure all widows and their children were invited to join them (Deuteronomy 16:10,11).

The Israelites were not to charge interest if they loaned money to the poor, or to take their clothing as collateral (Exodus 22:25-27). Every seventh year, they were not to cultivate their fields; whatever grew up on its own was to be left for the poor (Exodus 23:11). When a person sold her fields to support herself or any other reason, in the year of jubilee (every 49 years) she was to receive the property back as the original owner without charge (Leviticus 25:25-28).

If a person sold herself into slavery to pay bills and support herself, she was not to be treated as a slave but rather as a paid servant. In the seventh year, she was to be freed, and given part of the household herds, harvest, and things around the house. In the year of jubilee (every 49 years), she and any children she had while in that household were all to be freed. (Leviticus 25:39-41 and Deuteronomy 15:12-14). When the poor went to work for someone, she was to be paid every day (Deuteronomy 24:14-16).

In the New Testament, Jesus said we are to feed the hungry, give water to the thirsty, take in the homeless, clothe the cold, and visit prisoners (Matthew 25:35,36), even if they are our enemies (Romans 12:20). Anyone with two coats is to give one to a poor person (Luke 3:11). We are to invite poor people to our home for dinner (Luke 14:12-14). The church collection is to be set aside partially to help the poor even before they come to the church for help (1 Corinthians 16:1,2).

Christians widows were cared for by the early church on an everyday basis, even to the point of appointing several people within a congregation to be in charge and make sure it got carried out. Seven men were chosen in the congregation in Jerusalem, possibly each one taking charge of one day of the week (Acts 6:1-6).

Widows were sometimes fully supported by congregations. Paul said they could be if they were over 60, had been the wife of one man, had been charitable to others while younger, and continued to devote themselves to Christian works (1 Timothy 5:3-16).

Introducing the Lesson

We're going to be discussing the difficulties of living as a widow today. ***Display HOUSEHOLDS IN AMERICA HEADED BY WOMEN.*** A household means there is more than one person in a home and one of those people is in charge. Of the households in America, 24% are headed by women with no husband, up from 12% twenty years earlier. 31% have incomes under $15,000. $27% have incomes between $15,000 up to $29,999. Discuss the plight of the displaced homemaker to whichever degree you desire.

Display WOMEN STILL EARN LESS THAN MEN. This chart deals with all women whether single or married.

The Bible made provisions for widows. (Discuss this to whichever degree you like.) When things get rough, some women wish they were married.

The Census Bureau reports that 45 percent of widows with children under 18 remarry, while 12 percent with no children remarry. The average age of widows remarrying with children is 38. However, overall, only 15% of all remarriages are by widows. So a widow is faced with the problems of keeping her household together financially and deciding whether or not to remarry.

Ruth and Naomi faced similar problems.

Discussion Questions

10. **In your own community or congregation, do you believe things can get desperate for some widows? How can you find out?**

    1 Kings 17:12: Widows often have financial difficulties without the income (job or social security) of their husbands.

    Possible Class Response: It is surprising how many widows are having a difficult time financially, but will not tell anyone because they don't want to burden others. To find out, we can ask the elders if they know, since sometimes they are helping a widow and are keeping it confidential. We can ask them directly, or ask relatives or close friends. Otherwise, we probably need to go to their home for coffee sometime and see what's in their cupboards and refrigerator when they open them. However, even then it may not be an indication, since some widows don't eat much just because they don't like eating alone. If we are very concerned, we might also try calling their utility companies to see if payments are up to date, and the tax office to see if taxes are up to date, since many of these are public records. But we should do this discretely and not tell other people we did so she can save face. Then we could possibly help her anonymously as a "Christian friend."

11. **Do you think advice she has given to young women in the past would now apply to her? In which ways? How would reading the Proverbs help her?**

Proverbs 1:1,8: Proverbs was written by Solomon for his son, and possibly part of it by his mother too.

Possible Class Response: Although previously at ease with both men and women while married, a single-again woman find traits returning to her she never expected to feel again. If she was shy and awkward around men before she ever married, this often returns. If she struggled with temptation then, she likely will now. Or however she was, this usually returns to some degree. Proverbs is full of advice on many things, and was written especially to young people.

12. **So that she is not neglected (Acts 6:1), who could a widow go to for such help?**

    Ruth found a male relative who could take care of things she couldn't. Today it is important to have some man available to help with things -- advice on the car, moving something heavy, etc.

    Acts 6:1: Widows in the early church were assisted on a daily basis.

    Possible Class Response: She should go to her relatives first. If she doesn't have any nearby, or they will not help her, she should go to the church. Women with husbands should be willing to let them go over and help with things around the widow's house. If there is concern about being faced with moral problems while there, the wife can always go along and hold the ladder or tools, or have coffee and a nice visit with the widow. Sometimes young people's groups set aside a Saturday each spring and fall to go to widows' homes to help them out.

13. **What should a widow do to make sure she is respected and safe?**

    Isaiah 10:2: Some people prey on lonely widows to get their money from them by coercion or even take from the little they own by outright theft.

    Possible Class Response: She more easily is a target for assault, whether bodily or just being taken advantage of by men at a business such as service station. A widow can ask if a man from the church could go with her when she takes her car in for servicing, or be there when a plumber comes to her home. She can also ask the man to put deadbolt locks on her doors, make sure her windows are safe from entrance from outside, and possibly install exterior lights around her house.

14. **If a woman just is not interested in a future relationship with a man, how can she firmly explain it to her friends?**

    1 Corinthians 7:8,34: It is good if a widow can stay single, for she can then spend more time doing things for the Lord.

    Possible Class Response: There are well-meaning matchmakers everywhere. She can explain to them that they may not understand how someone could go through life alone, but she doesn't feel alone anymore. All the people she's doing things for are now her family. If she were to marry, she would have to give up some of her church work, and she is not willing to do that.

15. **If she is to marry a Christian (1 Corinthians 7:39), where should she go to associate with Christian single men, and how should she conduct herself to reassure them she is a Christian?**

    1 Corinthians 7:39: If a widow chooses to remarry, she must marry only a Christian.

    Possible Class Response: Much depends on her age. If she is young and has children at home and/or job, she might join a single-again organization sponsored by a church. Even then, she should check into the reputation of the group. If there is none nearby, she could ask her elders to allow someone to start one and promise to help. If she is older and independent, she could join a group of senior Christians who goes around the country helping knock on doors, pass out pamphlets and do other outreach things for smaller congregations. She could start attending a Christian college (some students have widowed fathers). She could attend Christian college or metropolitan lectureships. She should conduct herself in a modest way, and talk of things which reflect Jesus in her life. Worldly people are uncomfortable around such talk, and this would filter out the non-Christians or non-Christian "Christians."

16. **If a woman desires to marry a Christian man, should she spend her time trying to meet such a person, or working to make a good life for herself?**

    Proverbs 31:31: Her own works praise her throughout the city.

    Possible Class Response: She should spend her time doing Christian works among people around her, and this will build her reputation. At the same time, she could meet widowers trying to do the same thing. If she spends all her time trying to meet a Christian man, she will probably find herself frustrated and unable to concentrate on reaching out to others.

17. **How can she go about finding out about him?**

    When a woman believes there might be a man in her life who could fill the emptiness with love again, how can she judge whether he would be good to her after marriage?

    Proverbs 22:1: A good name is the most valuable thing a person can have - far above all the wealth she could possibly have.

    Possible Class Response: She can find out what his marriage was like before. In conversing with him and talking about personal things, she could ask how his parents' marriage was. She can try to find out how he treated his children and if they feel close to him. If all seems well, she could have a long-enough engagement that he will begin treating her as if she "belongs" to him. She can tell him what her negative points are and then ask him what his are. If she's been open about herself, he might admit to having a temper, being jealous, etc. She could tell him things she expects to continue doing after their marriage and see how he reacts.

18. **How can Proverbs 3:15-18 help her guard her future happiness?**

    In choosing a future mate, what about emotions being stronger than logic? Is that still a possibility at her age?

Proverbs 3:13-18: A relative stranger can flatter someone into forsaking what they know to be right and ruining her life.

Possible Class Response: Bluntly, she can be as tempted sexually as young people are. Yes, it is possible at any age. She should be just as careful about when and where they visit. She should not allow him to say the old lines young men say, "If you love me...." She could write down some reminders to herself about guarding herself morally, and get them out to reread whenever she feels a need to.

Good Work

Send a note to a young or older widow you suspect is having a hard time financially. Invite her to have dinner with you, either one time or once a week indefinitely.

BEFORE CLASS:

    A. Get out your list of widows who your class wrote to last class period. Be sure to include those you don't know who class members wrote as long-time friends.

    B. Purchase some small invitation cards.

    A. On poster board or blackboard, copy the inside of the invitation cards. Then fill in the blanks with an example such as your address, day, time, and "to have dinner with me." Then on the blank page, write, "[Although I don't really know you,] I really do want you to come. If this time is not good for you, please call and tell me at _____ when you can come. Do you need someone to pick you up?"

    B. Also on the board, write a list of the women written last week along with their addresses. Ask before class if you can include the widows who are in your class.

DURING CLASS:

"We have been talking about the loneliness and hardships of ongoing widowhood. We all need to reach out to them, just like the early church did. Most widows have a hard time financially. We should have them over for a meal occasionally, or even once a week on the same day. This would help with their meals; or if that's not a problem, it would still give them friendships and get them out of their house."

Hand out invitations. "On the board is a list of the people you wrote last week. I've included the widows who attend our class also. They said they wouldn't mind you all fighting over who will invite them over at all. As I read them off, raise your hand if you'd like to have this person over for dinner."

You will have about five minutes to fill in the blanks of your invitation and write a sentence or two on the blank page. I have written an example of what you might say. Feel free to copy it if you like."

"You will have about five minutes. When you are done, hand your invitation to me for mailing. Then say a silent prayer for your widow while the others finish writing. Let's all be quiet now so we can think and write."

Concluding Remarks

When time is up and while the slower writers complete their notes, sing one verse of a song, possibly one of the following:

1. Walking in Sunlight
2. What a Friend We Have in Jesus
3. Brighten the Corner Where You Are
4. Make Me a Channel of Blessing

In a few minutes, part of your class will be returning to a busy home full of children and things going on, and they might be wondering where they're going to find the time to have company over. Others in your class will be returning to an empty, quiet house. End the class with reminders of those alone, and encouragement to reach out to each other.

(Wait for one or two quick replies to each of the following.) "In just a few words....

1. Should we take our own advice to young people when we are older?

2. Who should a widow go to for help around her house or with her car?

3. What kind of widows often do not wish to remarry?

4. Where can a widow go who wants to remarry a Christian?

Have a closing prayer, especially remembering the widows listed on the board.

Households in America Headed by Women 2012

TOTAL HOUSEHOLDS   73,817,000

24% HEADED BY WOMEN   17,990,000

        31%   income less than $15,000
        27%   income less than $30,000

The Average poverty line (household of 4) is $24,000

Women Still Earn Less Than Men

Katheryn Maddox Haddad

Second Time Around

Lesson Three: Readjusting

Lesson Aim
- **CHOOSE A GODLY SECOND HUSBAND**
- **BLEND TWO LIVES WITH HABITS ALREADY FORMED**

Scripture Outline

Ruth 3:5-9: Ruth goes to Boaz's field, waits for him to fall asleep, then lies down at his feet. In the middle of the night he stirs and discovers a woman there in the dark. Startled, he asks who she is, and she replies that he is her husband's next closest relative, and she wants him to carry on her husband's name by marrying her, according to Moses' law.

Ruth 3:10-13: Boaz is ecstatic. He is quite a bit older than her. He reassures her he will not hurt her, and he realizes she is not there to seduce him because everyone knows how moral she is. He admits there is one other man—a closer relative to her than he is—but he can take care of that.

Ruth 3:14-18: In the morning just before dawn, Boaz wakes her, tells her to keep what she did a secret. He then fills her apron with more grain and sends her back to town just as the gates are unlocked but while it's still too shadowy to be identified. Naomi had known it would work, and tells Ruth to stay home from work that day and wait for Boaz to make the next move.

Ruth 4:1-6: Boaz meets the man who is a closer relative to Ruth than he, and tells her Ruth and Naomi are selling their family's land, but if he buys it, he has to marry Ruth as part of the deal. The closer relative says it would interfere with his own inheritance, [possibly by dividing it up among more children than he wanted to?]. So he tells Boaz he can have both the land and Ruth.

Ruth 4:7-10: To seal the deal, the closer relative removes his sandal and gives it to Boaz as a sign of telling him he can "walk in his shoes." Then Boaz announces his engagement to Ruth to everyone around who will listen. He has made sure he did this at the city gate where there are a lot of people so the relative couldn't back out of the arrangement.

Ruth 4:11-13: Everyone congratulates Boaz and wishes him a happy marriage with lots of children. Their first child is a son.

Ruth 4:14-22: All the women gather around Naomi and tell her that her new grandson will now give her new life and give her something to live for. Naomi carries the little baby around so much her friends say "Naomi has a son." Ruth, the Moabitess, becomes the great grandmother of David, and ancestress of Jesus, the Messiah.

Today's World

Thirty-four percent of all marriages today are among couples who have been married before. Alarmingly, 40 percent of them fail in the first four years, according to Kenneth Forest Davis, author of *Kids & Cash*. Two primary reasons for these failures are children and finances. He says the couple needs to discuss how much allowance the children will get. If they must do chores for their allowance, what will the parents pay for? What must the children do with any earned income? What will the parents do with their earned income? How much child support will go out to or come in from former spouses?

Barbara Page, financial planner for Price Waterhouse in Chicago, said people come into marriages sometimes with different philosophies of money handling. They should discuss before their marriage what they consider mutual-decision money matters, and personal-decision money matters. If they are set in their spending ways, they may even consider two bank accounts with each responsible for certain bills, and the rest as they desire such as spend, spend, spend, or save, save, save.

As for general finances, the couple needs to decide the following:

INSURANCE: Do your policies cover all current assets and have assets sold been removed from policies? Do beneficiaries need changed?

TAXES: Will you file separately or jointly? If the husband owns a business, will her name be filed with the business taxes? If one has a pension plan at work, will that make ineligible the other partner for an IRA if taxes are filed jointly? If both homes are sold at a profit and it is more than you plan to put into a home owned by both of you, will you be able to claim the exemption of $125,000 if only one of you is 55 or over?

INVESTMENTS: Should they be merged into one portfolio or kept separate? Should they liquefy their assets? Does one partner prefer to invest highly while the other one likes a lot of cash around?

ESTATE PLANNING: Get new wills made. How much will go to the surviving spouse, and how much to the natural children and the stepchildren? You can leave an unlimited amount of assets to your spouse without her having to pay estate tax. A Qualified Terminable Interest Property trust fund (QTIP) can do the same thing for the children. The wife gets lifetime income from the assets, but they pass on to the children at her death. As long as they are in the trust, you can do anything with them you wish.

Another possibility if there are no children born to this marriage, is to evaluate the assets and liabilities of each spouse upon entering the marriage, and set up wills so the couple's respective children inherit the percent of value their mother or father had at that time. For instance, if at the beginning of their marriage, the wife brought 30% of their total assets to the marriage and the husband brought 70% of their total assets to it, their children would inherit 30% and 70% respectively; this occurs only after both spouses die. They may wish to add 1% for each year married to the lower-asset spouse's side not to exceed 50%.

* * *

Half of the women who remarry while still in their childbearing years give birth in that second marriage, according to research by Howard Wineberg of Portland State University in Oregon. Most of the births occur within two years of the remarriage. The younger she is, the more likely she is to have more children. Women with two or more children by a previous marriage are significantly less likely to have any more children. Interestingly, poor white women and college-graduate black women are considerably more likely to give birth in a second marriage.

* * *

According to Ruth B. Weg of the University of Southern California, estimates that the number of older people getting married has increased 25 percent in just the past ten years. "What's exciting about it is that it's a renewal, not to go back to the same old things but to create something new at a time when you're thinking that is all over."

Among the widowed, they often meet during a time when they are still depressed about losing their first mate. One such couple signed up as phone partners at a bereavement support group sponsored by their local senior center. At first they sympathized with each other. Then one day when he was having a particularly bad time, she offered to take him out for a brunch. They sat and talked for three hours, with their conversation moving quickly from their losses to each other.

When they married, they sold both homes and bought one together. She took along a collection of toy bears, he took along plaques from his long career, and they both brought pictures from their past. They also had to adjust to each other's habits and eccentricities, and said it was difficult. After a lifetime with a partner from one's youth, they'd learned all their strengths and weaknesses; now they had to start that learning process all over again with each other.

They still never expect to put their earlier marriages and losses behind them. When he sometimes thinks of his first wife, he stares off into space, and when she talks of her first husband, she blinks away tears with a faint smile. They were both happily married before. They both kept photographs of their "former" mates and sometimes they talk of experiences they shared in the past, and even visit the graves together. "We do our little housekeeping around the graves, and that's part of our experience together. We experience our loss together." Marrying late in their years was something not taken lightly. They both talked about the likelihood of one becoming chronically ill.

They also had to consider grown children. They told their children of their growing fondness and love for each other. They also assured them that they would not suffer financially in their wills because of the marriage. At the wedding reception, they made separate toasts to each of their children and grandchildren in an effort to bring them all closer together. *(Source: Washington Post)*

Bible World

In the Law of Moses, if a man died leaving a wife and no son, but had daughters, his inheritance was to go to the daughters. If, however, he died with no children at all, his inheritance was to go to his brothers. If he had no brothers, his inheritance was to go to his uncles. If he had no uncles either, his inheritance was to go to the nearest relative they could find, possibly a cousin. (Numbers 27:8-11)

If a man died and had no children, such as with Ruth, she had to marry the nearest male relative of her husband's. Their first-born child was to be named after her first husband so his name would not disappear.

If, however, the nearest relative did not want to marry her, she could go to the city gate where the elders were and tell them about it. The elders in turn were to send for this nearest relative to ask if it were true. If he stuck by his decision, she was to take his shoe off, spit in his face, and say, *So shall it be done unto that man that will not build up his brother's house.* After that, he was to be called by the people in the town The Man Whose Shoe Was Loosened." (Deuteronomy 25:5-10) This was called a Levirate marriage.

During the days of Judah, the son of Jacob, and before the Law of Moses, there was a similar custom, wherein the widow was to marry the next nearest male to keep her deceased husband's name going. Judah's son married Tamar and died; so she married Judah's oldest son, but he let his sperm fall to the ground because he didn't want to carry on his brother's name. So she remained a widow until his youngest son was grown, but Judah did not let Tamar marry him.

In the meantime, Judah's wife died. So Tamar dressed up like a prostitute and made sure Judah saw her. He went to bed with her and she conceived a son. When he found out later she was pregnant, he wanted to have her stoned, but she showed him his cane which he'd left behind, and he realized he was the father. He felt ashamed for not marrying her to his son. Tamar bore twins. One of them, Perez, became the ancestor of Jesus who was of the Tribe of Judah.

By the time Boaz did the above, he apparently took care of the matter instead of Ruth. Further, he apparently did not spit in the relative's face. The relative removed his own shoe completely rather than just loosening it, and gave it [temporarily?] to Boaz.

In the Christian era, a widow is allowed to marry, but only a Christian (1 Corinthians 7:39); however, Paul thought widows would be happier remaining single so they could devote their lives to the church. He believed younger widows, however, should remarry and have a family (1 Timothy 5:13,14).

Introducing the Lesson

Thirty-four percent of all marriages today are among couples who have been married before. Alarmingly, 40 percent of them fail in the first four years. ***Display 40% OF ALL SECOND MARRIAGES FAIL and discuss.***

Display FINANCIAL MATTERS THAT NEED TO BE DISCUSSED before marriage. Discuss to whichever degree fits your class.

Widows are only to marry Christians. That means they must marry someone who is already a Christian or convert someone. We will be talking about this in our lesson.

Discussion Questions

19. **Name some situations that can be good under one circumstance but not in another.**

    What Ruth did in going to see Boaz at night could have led to disaster had she done this with a dishonorable man.

    Proverbs 6:27: People can't take fire into their bosom and not burn.

    Possible Class Response: A widow might think she heard someone outside her window in the middle of the night and call her male friend to come check rather than calling the police. If one of them is lonely during the night so calls the other one to meet them for coffee just to talk, they should meet in an all-night restaurant not associated with a motel. If he takes her home late at night after a long and full day, she shouldn't let him sleep on her couch. If one of them is sick and needs someone to sit up with them, other friends should be called to help with this.

20. **How can a woman know she has no more doubting? When she is ready to do what? If that determination is not there, should she marry him?**

    An older woman is now more aware of deceit in the world, of the pain of losing (again?), of having to adjust long-established life patterns, etc. Someone once said, "If in doubt, don't."

    Ephesians 5:22-24: Wives, be prepared to submit yourselves to your husbands' judgments in everything, just like the church submits itself to Jesus in everything.

    Possible Class Response: Before a woman says, "I do," she'd better be sure this is who she wants to be submissive to, and that he will not abuse her. She needs to be around him enough and in enough situations that she sees how he handles problems, and how he reasons through them. She also needs to know what types of relationships he has with others whether it be at work, with neighbors, with family members, with Christian friends. Also she needs to know whether she can live with his odd habits, and he's willing to live with hers. Does he spend lavishly and she saves every penny?

She's been on her own a long time and made decisions on her own; he may be expecting her to be awkward at deciding certain things like they both were as young newlyweds; and she may feel a need to continue making her own decisions on things she is capable of doing. There is a lot of flattery before a marriage; she needs to know if it is sincere. Second marriages are not easy.

21. **In the process of discussing or experiencing differences, if tempers flare, might some find out they were not suited to each other after all and should not marry? Would that be bad?**

    2 Corinthians 6:14: Don't be unequally bound to a husband or wife.

    Possible Class Response: If tempers flare, it means someone feels very threatened about changing their attitudes. It is better to find this out before marriage than after. They may both have completely different expectations of each other after marriage; they should discuss this. If they find they cannot reconcile these differences, they should back off from each other, break off the marriage plans, and just see each other as friends. Marriage for the wrong reasons and with the wrong people has made a lot of lives much more difficult than the single life would have been.

22. **Do you think it would be better to pick and choose whose furniture, linens, china, and house to keep or try to sell everything and start over together?**

    Amos 3:3: Two can't walk together unless they agree with each other.

    Possible Class Response: Almost always they should sell everything and start over together. People, though they don't intend to, are possessive of what they purchased in the past. This may create confusion in their wills if they have them. However, they could list the financial assets they each brought into the marriage, subtract the debts each brought into the marriage, and leave that percentage to their respective children.

23. **What can a woman say and do to avoid such a situation?**

    Sometimes older single-again men have good-paying jobs and are tempted to spend a lot on a woman he wishes to marry in an attempt to "buy" her love. And sometimes an older single-again woman is having a hard time supporting herself, thus leaving her vulnerable.

    Exodus 23:8: Gifts blind even the wisest of us.

    Possible Class Response: She could confide in a close friend or even her elders that she has a special man in her life and he has offered to give her money to help pay her bills. In some cases, the people she tells realize her financial problems they didn't know about before, and can then step in and help. This would release her of feeling she owes anything to her man friend.

24. **How is this type person likely to treat a wife after marriage?**

    Boaz had to do certain legal things to make it possible to marry Ruth - among them, eliminating the "competition". This he did graciously. If a woman today is being "wooed" for marriage by a man and finds he is using deceit to get her to quit looking at any other men, what conclusion can she draw?

1 Corinthians 3:13: Eventually, the truth behind everything a person does is laid open, for all our deeds are tested in some way.

Possible Class Response: If a woman suddenly finds certain of her friends not coming around anymore, she may call them and ask if there is a particular reason. It may be her male friend has talked to them and told them to leave her alone. He can also try to beat the competition by appearing richer, holier, healthier, more patient than he really is. If she hasn't known him in the past, she should get him to introduce her to some of his friends and relatives, then spend some time alone with them getting to know them. If his friends have doubts, they'll slip it into their conversation in subtle ways. She shouldn't wait until after their marriage to find out how truthful he was.

25. **Older people marrying should be able to watch for signs of wisdom easier. What are the signs of wisdom?**

Boaz had done much to make Ruth's life easier in the new town, but not too much. He had fought for her with another possible suitor, but not too much. He was honored in the gates for his wisdom.

James 3:17: Wisdom from God is pure, peaceful, gentle, easy to approach, merciful, full of good works, and not hypocritical.

Possible Class Response: The couple should talk about difficult times in their lives and how they handled them. They should talk about difficult situations they will face such as acceptance by step-children, separating themselves from life-time treasures they plan to sell, health problems they have or probably will begin having as they age, who their coupled friends will be, what they'll do for entertainment. They should try to put themselves in stressful situations just to find out how each other responds, such as driving in heavy traffic, being around little grandchildren, spending time doing a good work.

26. **How can the "forgetting" of the past be accomplished and the emptiness filled in?**

A vital part of remarrying is putting the deceased mate in the back of one's mind and walking into the future, not with a replacement, but with someone loved for who and what they are.

Philippians 3:13: I forget what I've accomplished in the past, leave it behind for good, and spend my thoughts and energies on the now and the future.

Possible Class Response: The widow needs to give her pictures and mementos of her deceased husband to her grown children or some other close relative to keep for her. If he ever made anything special for her, she needs to give those to relatives for keeping also. She needs to quit going to the cemetery. Who she is marrying should do the same thing. They should keep pictures of the past only of themselves and their children/friends, but not those with the former mate in them. They can take a lot of pictures of them as a newlywed couple - their honeymoon, their new home, having company over. They can start a guest book for their new home. They can begin routines that are special just to them in order to develop a past, a sense of "we always do this."

27. What can such relatives do to jeopardize a remarriage? What can they do to encourage it? What benefits are there to a remarriage?

There are in-laws and children of the former marriage to consider.

Ecclesiastes 9:9: Live joyfully with your mate all the days of your life, for this person is a gift from God.

Possible Class Response: Children can jeopardize a marriage by talking to them in private about what they don't like about the new mate, or comparing them to the old mate in public. To encourage the new marriage, they can invite the new couple to their homes for special occasions, send greeting cards, be friendly to them. There are benefits to a remarriage to everyone. Sometimes grown children didn't have the time needed to devote to their widowed mother. Younger children need two parents. No one is lonely anymore.

Good Work

Send a note to a widow and widower who married each other, whether it was recent or a few years ago.

BEFORE CLASS:

A1.   FOR LARGER CONGREGATIONS: Look through your church directory and write down the names of married-again widowed couples.

A2.   FOR SMALLER CONGREGATIONS:

Alternative 1: Ask your minister who he has married in the last few years who had been widowed.

Alternative 2: Ask a nearby senior center for the first names of married-again widowed couples.

B.   Make a list of their names and addresses.

C.   Address envelopes to these couples. Leave a few blank.

D.   Obtain a telephone book for people who know a widowed couple they'd like to write not on your list.

E.   Obtain stationary such as colored bond paper cut in half.

F.   On poster board or blackboard, write the following:

"I just wanted to drop you a note to tell you that I am so happy you found each other. Having been widowed before, you know what loneliness is, and I'm sure you never take each other for granted. May God continue to bless you, and may your marriage be a blessing to him."

DURING CLASS:

"We have been studying about second marriages after widowhood. Some of us know people who have remarried and are very happy. Let's share in their joy."

Hand out stationery and envelopes. "I have written the names and addresses of remarried widows which I obtained from _____. Or you may know a couple you'd prefer writing to. If you're not sure what to say, I have written a suggestion on the board; feel free to copy it if you prefer."

"You will have about five minutes. When you are done, hand your envelope to me for mailing and say a silent prayer for the couple while the others finish writing. Let's all be quiet now so we can think and write."

Concluding Remarks

When time is up and while the slower writers complete their notes, sing one verse of a song, possibly one of the following:

1. *Oh Thou Fount of Every Blessing*
2. *Let the Beauty of Jesus Be Seen in Me*
3. *Standing on the Promises*
4. *I Choose Jesus*

In a few moments, part of your class may be returning to a quiet and lonely home with no marriage. Leave with them feeling good about their own lot in life.

(Wait for one or two quick replies to each of the following.) "In just a few words....

1. How can a woman know for sure she is willing to submit herself to a new husband?

2. What should the woman do who is used to making all her own decisions and doesn't want to give up that freedom to a man who can tell her to do just the opposite?

3. If a woman is single and doesn't have to work all the time to support herself, what can she spend more time doing than if she were married?

4. What is God's type of wisdom like?

Give a list of the widowed remarried couples your class wrote to the person leading the closing prayer and mention them by name, asking God's blessings on them.

Second Marriages

*40 %
OF ALL SECOND
MARRIAGES
FAIL*

THE REASONS ARE DIFFERING....

Child-raising philosophies

Money-spending philosophies

Time-spending philosophies

Financial Matters that Need to be Worked Out Before a Second Marriage

*** INVESTMENTS**

*** INSURANCE**

*** TAXES**

*** WILLS**

Katheryn Maddox Haddad

ABUSED
Abigail

Lesson One: Enduring Abuse

Lesson Aim
- ♥ **MAINTAIN ONE'S SELF-ESTEEM**
- ♥ **HAVE PATIENCE IN TRIALS**

Scripture Outline

1 Samuel 25:2: There is a very rich man who has 3,000 sheep and 1,000 goats up at his other residence, a ranch at Mt. Carmel. It is now shearing time, a time of festivities.

1 Samuel 25:3: His name is Nabal which means hard-hearted, selfish, harsh with others, and sharp-tongued, and he lives down to his name. He has a beautiful wife, Abigail, who is also very understanding.

1 Samuel 25:15,16: All summer when Nabal's shepherds were out in the pastures, David and his soldiers have protected them like a wall day and night from being harmed by man or beast, and never took anything from them.

Today's World

Social churchgoing men are among the most likely men to abuse their wives, according to the *Journals for the Scientific Study of Religion*. Although men who attend services weekly abuse their wives the least, those who attend about once a month are twice as likely to be abusers. Further, the latter are much more likely to be violent abusers than those who never attended services at all.

"Those that attend a moderate amount are the most abusive," according to Merlin B. Brinkerhoff, one of the researchers at the University of Calgary in Canada.

Originally the study was set up to determine whether fundamentalist men were more likely to abuse their wives since they more often believe in the literal Biblical interpretation that man is the head of the house and Eve was created to serve Adam. However, 17.2% Catholic, 19.3% mainline Protestant, 18.8% fundamentalist, and 23.2% non-religious men abuse their wives.

When all church-goers were rated against non-church goers, one-third of all men surveyed who attend church once a month abuse their wives.

* * *

The *Huffington Post* carried warning signs of a man while dating that he will abuse her after marriage:

1. He will romance you with flowers, sing to you, and be too good to be true.
2. He will want you to commit to him quickly.
3. He will want you all to himself and easily becomes jealous.
4. He will be so "concerned" for you, he will check on you several times a day.
5. When he is not sweet to you, he says he would be if you loved him more.
6. He is always the victim, accusing others of not treating him right.

There are three stages in his cycle of violence if he both verbally and physically abuses his wife. If he only verbally abuses her, he has a two-stage cycle.

Stage one is the tension-building phase. He becomes highly critical of everything she does to the point he is angry whether she doesn't please him or does please him. He is filled with verbal abuse.

Stage two is when the physical abuse comes in. It is premeditated and occurs at the time and place he selects, and involves whichever parts of her body he decides to attack. He carries it through whether or not there is provocation, thus confusing his wife even more. All he can say is that she deserves it and it is her fault for making him unhappy.

Stage three is the repentance stage. He begs her forgiveness, promises never to do it again, and may even offer to get counseling. This is also sometimes called the honeymoon stage.

Early in the marriage, the cycle may take a full year to complete itself. Later it takes months, then weeks, and then days. As it gets worse, the wife begins to bury her feelings so he can't hurt them.

Bible World

Women lived in separate quarters from their husbands, such as did Sarah (Genesis 24:67) and Esther (2:9,11). They veiled their faces in public (Genesis 24:65). Later when the tabernacle and temple were built, they worshipped in a separate courtyard (Exodus 38:8; 1 Samuel 2:22).

Wives entertained the women in a separate location from where their husbands entertained the men (Esther 1).

Women took part in ancient worship (Exodus 15:20; 1 Samuel 2:22) and sang in choirs (1 Chronicles 25:5,6); Ezra 2:65; Nehemiah 7:67). They were invited to attend the reading of the law (Deuteronomy 31:12; Joshua 8:35).

Young women were given in marriage by their parents (Genesis 24:3,4; Exodus 22:17). Sometimes they were sold for their husband's debts (Matthew 18:25).

The societies of the great river valleys of the east and the Mediterranean gave similar roles to women. Women of the lower classes labored in the fields close to home. Women of wealth in the upper classes were more restricted. They lived in seclusion and subjection and with no significant work at home or in public. Such women had little education. Being uneducated, they seemed to men to have inferior minds.

When man began to philosophize, he explained the inferiority of woman. "A woman without ability is normal," said one Chinese philosopher. Hindus considered "infidelity, violence, deceit, envy, extreme avarice, a total want of good qualities, with impurity" the natural faults of woman. Aristotle saw women's virtue in obeying, being less complete, less courageous, weaker, more impulsive than men.

Christianity credited women with souls equal in the sight of God. The full benefit of this moral status was long deferred, however.

The Greek philosopher, Plato, asserted in the REPUBLIC that there should be complete equality between the sexes. China, India, and Rome boasted small groups of highly cultivated women. The restricted education of girls was described by Jerome in the late 300's AD.

Although limited, and though she had to leave normal life to get it, nunneries opened for women a path to education and administrative positions as abbesses. England had about 140 nunneries in the late middle ages. But nuns were only a small fraction of the female population, and came chiefly from the upper classes. Lower-class women carried on the world's work with men. High social status kept women from the world of labor. Cathedral school and university, the highest institutions of the middle ages, led to the supreme profession, theology—closed to women.

In the late 1400s, Erasmus of Rotterdam ridiculed an ignorant abbot who declared that "books destroy women's brains...it is not safe for a woman to know Latin." In the 16th century, certain philosophers defended women's rights to education. But it stopped there. Literature defending women's rights to education increased in the 17th, 18th, and 19th centuries.

Only since the middle 1800s has there been any substantial progress toward equality in education, voting, property rights, industry, the professions, and politics.

Introducing the Lesson

In public, we all like everyone to think we have the perfect marriage. And that's great—to a point. Some of you may be wondering why we are discussing a problem like wife abuse. Those of you who may now be or in the past have been victims of abuse perhaps have thought you were alone and people in the church just didn't understand.

Before I present to you some startling facts, I'd like to assure you that no one is going to pry into your personal life. No one is going to point fingers at anyone and say, "Oh, he or she fits the profile!" We must make this clear from the very beginning. NO ONE, ABSOLUTELY NO ONE in our class is to leave today and start pointing fingers.

If we suspect there is an abusive relationship among us, we MUST HELP THE WOMAN KEEP HER SELF-RESPECT, HER DIGNITY. Therefore, we will say nothing to her or anyone else about any suspicions. We must just keep on loving each other, and that's it.

Now, I'd like you to look at this chart. ***Display and explain WIFE ABUSERS BY RELIGIOUS AFFILIATION chart. Next I have some even more interesting news. Display and explain WIFE ABUSERS BY CHURCH ATTENDANCE HABITS chart.*** Go over the percentages of each, and end with emphasis that one-third of men who attend church once a month are most likely to be wife abusers.

Young ladies need to watch for these signs the young man they are dating will be an abusive husband. ***Display EARLY WARNING SIGNS OF AN ABUSER.***

There is a common three-stage cycle men go through with their wives. ***Display THREE-STAGE CYCLE and discuss.***

Discussion Questions

1. **How does a man assuming his wife is always against him make it look like she is a bad person?**

   Genesis 3:1-5: Satan tried to make God look bad in order to take trust and friendships away.

   Possible Class Response: There are two ways to look at everything—the good or the bad. It is possible to make an ordinary occurrence look very good or very bad, depending on the self-image of the person observing it. A man could come to the conclusion he had a bad wife because she put his tools away for him and now he doesn't "know where anything is."

2. **If a husband motivates out of fear (his own self-image), how can the wife determine just what he is afraid of and then help him overcome it?**

   1 John 4:18: If we fear someone, we can get rid of that fear by loving them and being concerned for their welfare.

   Possible Class Response: He may be afraid others will think he's a wimp if he treats women equally, he will lose his wife to a more handsome man, or she will think he is inferior because he can't make a good living. She could bring up the subject by saying, "Sometimes I'm afraid of ....[whatever she thinks he's afraid of]...." Then she could ask his advice on how to overcome the fear and they could talk about options.

3. **Contrast Nabal's attitude with Song of Solomon 1:15,16.**

Song of Solomon 1:15,16: The wife tells her husband in verse 15 how wonderful he is. The husband tells his wife in verse 16 how wonderful she is. Then they want to make love.

Possible Class Response: Nabal's personality indicates he also demanded physical attention and probably made Abigail feel used. Some insecure men view sex as a power experience, therefore they see no reason for love to be involved.

4. **Find some verses in Proverbs which condemn an abuser's sins.**

A woman patiently enduring abuse for the sake of love needs to learn to condemn his sin because it is against God's laws, and not because it makes her feel bad. This way her ego is protected (1 Samuel 8:7; Exodus 16:8). One way to make the distinction is to consider his actions logically: Just what is a sin in God's eyes?

1 Samuel 8:7: God told Samuel the people were not rejecting him as their Supreme Court Judge by wanting a king, but were rejecting God's command.

Exodus 16:8: The Israelites complained to Moses they didn't have very good food to eat in the wilderness and wanted to return to Egypt. God comforted Moses by telling him it was God they were really complaining about.

Possible Class Response:

Proverbs 4:24: Don't talk negatively.
Proverbs 6:16-19: God hates arrogance, liars, those who hurt innocent people, and those who keep people stirred up.
Proverbs 11:9: A hypocrite can destroy people with his mouth.
Proverbs 11:13: A person who tells others how bad their wife is does not have a faithful spirit.
Proverbs 11:29: He who troubles his family will inherit the wind.
Proverbs 14:17: He who loses his temper easily is a fool.
Proverbs 23:29: Those who drink a great deal can only have sorrow for themselves.
Proverbs 28:1: A bad man continually fights people, even when they love him.

5. **How can a wife respond to verbal abuse as Christ would who is the one living in her?**

Galatians 2:20: If a Christian no longer lives, but Christ lives in them, their ego cannot be attacked. We cannot insult dead people; they do not hear or respond. To humble people, it is easier to defend another than themselves.

Abusers tend to manipulate and control people's emotions much like a cat and mouse. If a wife is in a good mood, he will try to make her cry. If she is depressed, he will laugh at her and tease a little, tell a joke, and finally get her to smile. Once her mood improves, he inserts a little thorn just under the emotional fingernail to pull her back down.

Possible Class Response: Abusers are insulting Christ, not their wives. If she, being a Christian, is dead, she does not hear his insults and does not respond to them. This spiritual stability leaves her emotional stability intact.

6. **What can friends of an abused wife do to encourage her? What can they do to help him?**

   <u>1 Corinthians 13:4-7</u>: Those who love continue to be patient, kind, humble, fail to lose their temper, and are able to believe the best in others and endure whatever happens.

   An abusive marriage has two sides. He thinks he is strongest because of his ability to over talk and overpower her. She thinks he is weak because of his inability to control himself. She believes only a strong person like her could endure his abuse long enough to help him learn he can accept love through her example.

   <u>Possible Class Response</u>: They can compliment both of them. They can tell both they are worthwhile people and single out particular things they do. They can provide examples for the dysfunctional couple by allowing themselves to be observed during times that normally trigger abuse.

7. **How can a young woman tell before marriage if a man's heart is hard?**

   Abigail was a very beautiful, intelligent, and practical woman. Sometimes a young lady like this dates a man known to abuse others but not her. She attributes this to his response to her true love. But after the marriage, he begins to abuse her too, for he had wooed her as a challenge from a hard heart and not out of love.

   <u>Isaiah 32:7</u> "Nabal" means churlish. The churl (KJV) are evil people who lie and destroy the poor just to make themselves rich. Nabal may have been a sociopath and had no conscience.

   <u>Possible Class Response</u>: She can visit with his family to see how his father treats his mother. She can compare the way he talks to her to the way he talks to everyone else. She can compare his charming speech with his actions.

Good Work

Write a love note to a woman you think is being abused at home. Don't talk about the suspected abuse, but tell her how precious she is, appreciated, admired, and loved.

BEFORE CLASS:

    A1.   Gather up a small supply of church directories and local phone books.

    A2.   Obtain first names from a nearby shelter for abused women. If they cannot give out names, ask how many women usually live there at one time.

    B.   Obtain enough letter-size envelopes that each class member can have one.

    C.   Obtain stationary. Use colored bond paper cut in half.

    D.   Write on blackboard or poster board suggested things to write for those who have trouble wording what they feel.

<u>For Women You Know</u>: "I just wanted to drop you this note to let you know how special you are to those who know you. You always have a sweet smile of encouragement for everyone. You are a source of strength and a Christian example to us all. May God continue to walk close to you and give you peace. I love you."

<u>For Women You Do Not Know</u>: "Even though I do not know you by name, I just want you to know that God cares for you and loves you. It is taking a great deal of courage for you to leave a marriage you once had so much hope for. Even when you think you don't have the strength to go on, remember, you can have God's strength. I would like to personally invite you to attend church with us soon. Ask for me by name so we can meet each other. My prayers are with you."

DURING CLASS:

"We've been talking about what it is like to live with an abusive husband, and what coping methods the wife can use. We've also said she needs a great deal of encouragement from outside her home. That's us! You may know someone you think is being abused by her husband perhaps because of the way you've seen him talk to her in public, or perhaps because of bruises that she cannot logically explain. I have brought some church directories and phone books so you can write a confidential note to your friend."

"If you do not know anyone who may be abused at home, I have brought a list from a woman's shelter nearby, along with the shelter's address. Just address her by her first name, or 'Dear Special Friend.' Having just left the husband she once loved and had so much hope for, she needs to know she is loved by God and by you."

Hand out envelopes and stationery. "If you aren't sure what to say, I have written some suggestions for you on the board. Feel free to copy them if you like."

"You will have about eight minutes to write your note. When you are done, address the envelope. If it is to a friend, you should keep it confidential and mail it yourself. If it is to a shelter, I can mail it for you."

"Let's all be quiet now and allow each other to think and write. When you are done, offer a silent prayer for the one you wrote while the others finish."

Concluding Remarks

When time is up and while the slower writers complete their notes, sing one verse of a song, possibly one of the following:

1. *Oh Love That Will Not Let Me Go*
2. *The Love of God*
3. *Christ's Love is All I Need*
4. *Leaning on the Everlasting Arms*

In a few minutes, your class will be returning to their day-to-day lives. Some may be returning to an abusive home. End the class with fast-paced words of encouragement.

(Wait for one or two quick replies to each of the following.) "In just a few words, what advice would you give a woman when....

1. Her husband doesn't show much love to her?
2. She seems too humble to condemn his sin toward her?
3. She wants to avoid a hurt ego when he insults her?
4. She seems discouraged.

Have a brief prayer for women in abusive marriages.

Wife Abusers By Religious Affiliation

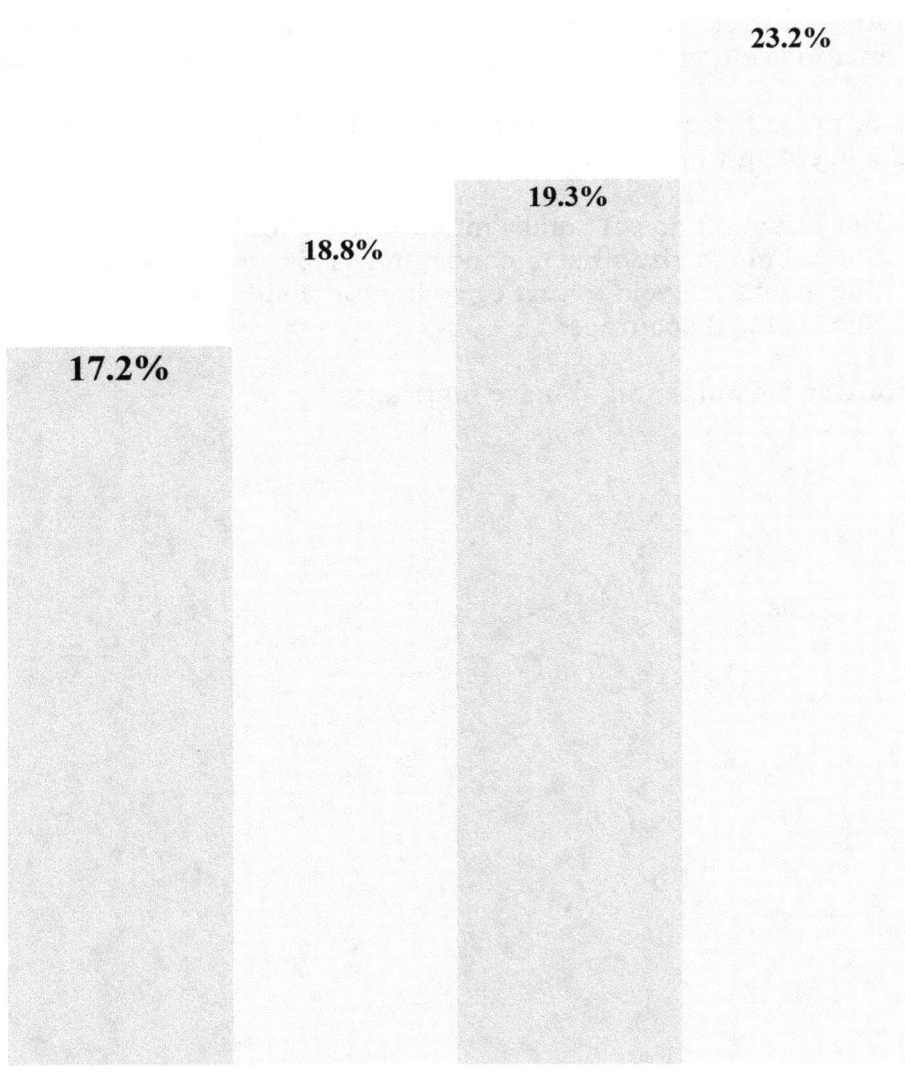

17.2%   Catholic
18.8%   Conservative
19.3%   Mainline Protestant
23.2%   No Religion

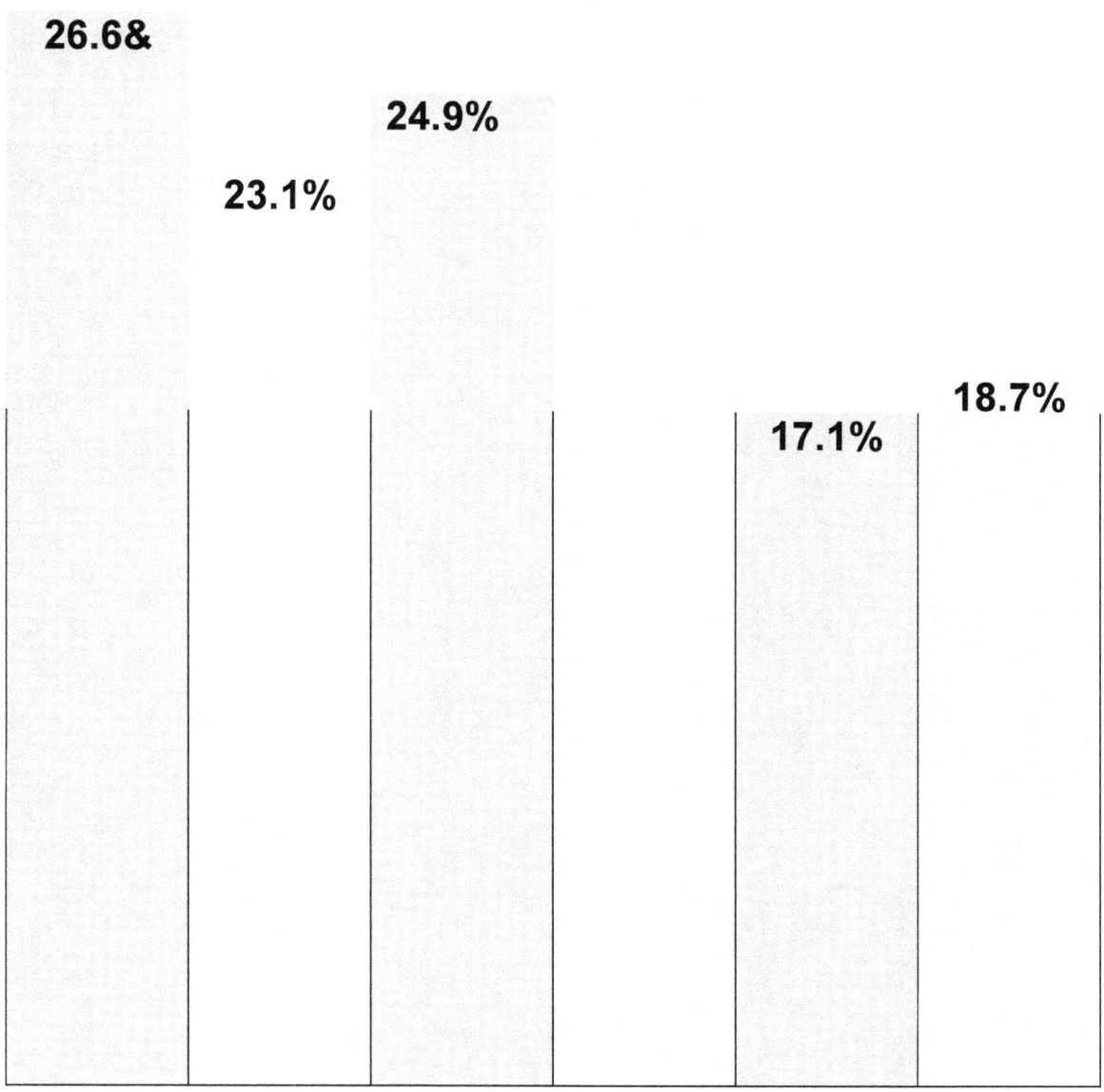

Wife Abusers by Attendance Habits

Never Attended	**26.6%**
Attended Special Occasions	**23.1%**
Attended Less than Monthly	**24.9%**
Attended 1 to 3 Times a Month	**32.2%**
Never Attended	**32.2%**
Attended Weekly	**17.1%**
Attended More than Weekly	**18.7%**

Early Warning Signs of an Abuser

He will overly romance you with flowers, sing to you, and be too good to be true.

He will want you to commit to him quickly.

He will want you all to himself and call it being protectively jealous.

He will be so "concerned" for you, he will check on you several times a day to see where you are and who you are with.

When he is not sweet to you for a while, he says he would be if you loved him more in ways he specifies.

He is always the victim, accusing others of not treating him good enough.

Three-Stage Cycle of Abuse

**State One:
Tension Buildup**

**Stage Two:
Physical
Abuse**

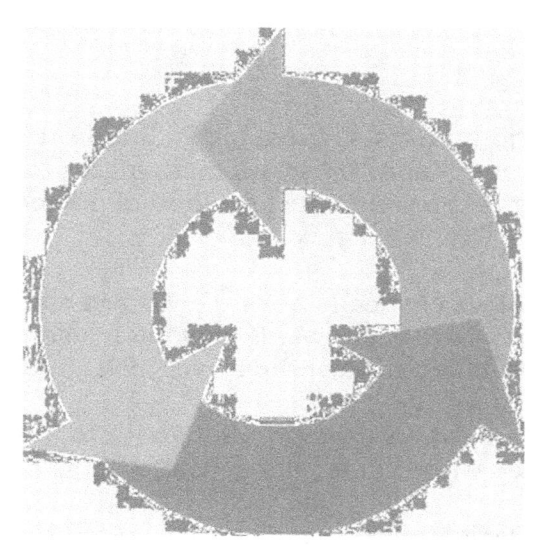

**Stage Three:
Repentance**

Abused

Lesson Two: A World of Abuse

Lesson Aim
- ♥ **KEEP OUR OWN VALUES SORTED OUT**
- ♥ **ESTABLISH COMMUNICATION**

Scripture Outline

<u>1 Samuel 25:4-9</u>: David and his soldiers are hiding from Saul in the wilderness of Paran near Mount Carmel and Maon. He sends messengers to Nabal asking if he would share some of his bounty at this festive time as a kind of payment for protecting Nabal's possessions all summer.

<u>1 Samuel 25:10</u>: Nabal sarcastically asks who David thinks he is anyway. He could just be a runaway slave for all he knows. (Everyone in Israel knows David by now, the slayer of Goliath, the king's son-in-law, the slayer of 10,000s.)

<u>1 Samuel 25:11</u>: Further, Nabal says he's not about to take HIS bread, and HIS water, and HIS meat that he has with him for his servants, to give to strangers from who-knows-where.

<u>1 Samuel 25:12-17</u>: David's messengers return to tell him, and David takes two-thirds of his soldiers, 400 men, to go after Nabal. But one of the messengers runs ahead to Abigail and tells her how Nabal spoke abusively to them, and no one can talk sense into him.

<u>1 Samuel 25:18,19</u>: So Abigail quickly starts preparing 200 loaves of bread, two jugs of wine, five sheep ready to cook, corn, a hundred clusters of grapes, and 200 fig cakes to take to David. She sends a messenger on ahead to tell David she's on her way.

<u>1 Samuel 25:20-22</u>: She meets David and his men on the road. He is hot under the collar against Nabal's returning evil for David's good, and is determined to kill all the men in his household.

<u>1 Samuel 25:23-26</u>: Abigail jumps off her mount, and bows herself to David. She begs him to place the sin of her husband onto her, for she hadn't known about his request. She acknowledges that her husband lives down to his name's reputation as a foolish wicked person. Then she subtly suggests that David would be as foolish to go after him and stain his own hands with a fool's blood, especially after he has received the food he wanted.

<u>1 Samuel 25:27-29</u>: Again she begs David's forgiveness for "her sin" and to accept her gifts of food. She acknowledges that the Lord loves David and will protect him.

<u>1 Samuel 25:30,31</u>: She knows he will be king someday, and he wouldn't want the reputation of killing people needlessly following him. And finally, she asks David that when he becomes king, to remember her.

Today's World

According to *The New York Times*, American women, if they fear anyone, are more likely to fear their own husbands whom they once loved. Domestic violence is the leading cause of injury and death to American women, far ahead of all vehicular accidents, rapes and muggings put together. Each year 6,000,000 women are beaten by the men they love.

Dr. Samuel C. Klagsbrun, medical director of Four Winds Hospital in Katonah, N.Y., reports that most abusive relationships start out normally as loving, romantic, and exciting. When abuse begins, women have trouble believing that something initially so wonderful is turning sour. There is a lot of apologizing and making up, and the woman thinks everything will go back to the way it once was. He asks forgiveness each time, and she forgives seventy times seven. Slowly, barraged by repeated abuse, she becomes dehumanized, helpless, and unable to see herself as a separate person and to distinguish right from wrong.

Dr. Klagsbrun says that to survive, these women react as slaves, trying to behave well, being accommodating, and living from day to day. Well-educated, economically stable professional men do it as much as anyone else; they just are more creative at making her look like a liar and he the victim.

Why do women stay? According to Sarah Buel, assistant district attorney for Norfolk County, Massachusetts, a woman who gets the courage to leave may be thrust into poverty with what is typically a woman's salary range. She is afraid her children will be taken from her by her husband who has the higher salary for lawyers and a better house. She is also afraid he'll take revenge on her in other ways.

The law still fails to protect abused women. Often the abuser is not sent to jail for assault, but is released by disbelieving judges. Seventy percent of the men who try to gain custody of the children succeed. So the woman, not being able to support a family and fearing what will happen to her children, in half of all cases returns home.

Cyndee Pattison, a therapist who runs groups for men who batter women, says, "Most of the time the men don't understand that what they are saying or doing is offensive. It's like a reflex, something they've done all their lives." They try to minimize their actions and consequences by saying they just "had a little argument," even when the women required stitches.

Bible

World

CARMEL: The literal meaning of the word is "the park" or the well-wooded place. It is a mountainous peninsula which projects into the Mediterranean. It stands as a wall between the maritime plain of Sharon on the south, and the more inland, fruitful plain of Sharon to the north.

It is actually a range of hills extending 30 miles long from the Mediterranean Sea to the plain of Dothan. Mt. Carmel proper is the main ridge (1,740 feet) at the northwest end running 12 miles inland from the sea forming one border of Asher (Joshua 19:26). It is about 12 miles long from the sea until it stops abruptly in the hills of Janin and Samaria. Its highest point is about four miles from the east end at 1,728 feet above sea level. It is straight west of the Sea of Galilee. It interrupts a comparatively straight coastline, and forms the southern wall of the magnificent bay or gulf of Acre, the best natural harbor south of Beirut.

The limestone Carmel hills probably got their name from the luxuriant scrub and woodland that covered them. The stone is mostly soft white limestone, with nodules of flint. On the west it is chalk. On the northeast are rocks called "Elijah's melons"—light brown flint outside, hollow inside, and lined with quartz crystals or chalcedony, more often called geodes.

The forests have disappeared. Today, Carmel's shrubbery is everywhere, with rocky areas amidst jungles of oaks, evergreens, and numerous caves. Flowering and fragrant herbs abound, hollyhocks, jasmine, and various vegetable creepers (Isaiah 35:2). Hence it is the image of the bride's head with luxuriant tresses (Song of Solomon 7:5). This densely vegetated and little-inhabited region was a barrier with two main passes at Jokneam and Megiddo. Carmel's luxuriant growth was mentioned in Amos 1:2; 9:3, Micah 7:14, Nahum 1:4. The forbidding figure of Nebuchadnezzar of Babylon marching against Egypt was compared with the rocky grandeur of Carmel and Tabor (Jeremiah 46:18).

Joshua banished his enemies from Canaan including the king of Jokneam in Carmel (Joshua 7:22). Here Saul set up a monument after his victory over Amalek (1 Samuel 15:12). Here Uzziah had his vineyards (2 Chronicles 26:10).

To the East is a glaring white desert, without shrub or water, inhabited by wild goats and the partridge that David used to love to hunt (1 Samuel 24:2; 26:20).

Here Elijah stood against 850 heathen prophets and defeated them (1 Kings 18). Some think that Elijah used seawater to cover the sacrifice since water from any other source might be dried up from the drought. Some believe it occurred at the northeast range beside a perennial spring. This spring is 250 feet below the steep rocky plateau. Today it is in the form of a vaulted tank with steps leading down to it.

When Elijah went to "the top" of the mountain to pray for rain, Gehazi climbed the highest point overlooking the Mediterranean Sea to look for rain to end the drought. There he saw one small cloud coming out of the sea.

Elisha, Elijah's student and successor, visited there soon after Elijah was carried away to heaven (2 Kings 2:25). At one time he made his home there (2 Kings 4:25).

MAON: Abigail and Nabal's home town was Maon, and their ranch was on Mt. Carmel. Maon literally means habitation. Maon is a city in Judah near Carmel and seven miles southeast of Hebron.

Centuries earlier, the daughter of Caleb, Achsah, asked her father for this territory because she wanted something besides the arid southland (Negev) he'd given her. She wanted "springs of water," so he gave her this "field" or cultivated plain with "upper and nether springs." Maon was a descendant of Caleb, son of Hezron, tribe of Judah (1 Chronicles 2:42-45). Maon was the son of Shammai and the father of the inhabitants of Bethzur (1 Chronicles 2:45).

Around it is an unpopulated region of pasture land where David found refuge from Saul. David narrowly escaped Saul through the Ziphites' deception (1 Samuel 23:19,24,25). Saul was on one side of the mountain, David on the other, when a message announcing a Philistine invasion called Saul away. The rock that separated the pursuer and the pursued was called "Sela-hammah-lekoth."

The Maonites were mentioned in the official list of those who returned from exile in Babylon (Ezra 2:50, Nehemiah 7:52).

Introducing the Lesson

"Last week we talked about the prevalence of wife abuse. Today we are going to try to define it and talk about how to handle it the best way possible when we still have hope that things will work out, or she fears losing her children if she leaves."

Display chart entitled, YOU'RE BEING ABUSED IF YOUR MATE.... Read through the list.

"Next week we will talk more about what makes a man that way. But for right now, let's look at what this loving wife can do who chooses to stay. FIRST she needs to keep her values properly sorted out by recognizing what is truly right and wrong, not by his standards, but by God's standards. SECOND, since the abuser has extremely poor communication skills, there are perhaps some things she can do to help him develop them. Let's consider what God has to say to help in such situations.

Discussion Questions

8. **What can a wife do to help the children sort out their values and in turn help the husband/father sort them out?**

    1 Timothy 6:9,10: People wanting to be rich often drown themselves in foolish and hurtful things; the love of money is the root of all evil.

    Proverbs 15:27: Greedy people trouble their whole household.

Nabal loved his money more than anything in the world. Some husbands work late, on weekends, etc. believing their money and business career are the source of all family happiness.

Possible Class Response: She can teach her children not to try to buy friendship; also, not to associate with other children because of their designer clothes, swimming pool, large allowance, etc. When given gifts, she can single out the less expensive one that perhaps was made by someone in the family and say it means more than a million-dollar gift would. She can quote 1 Timothy 6:10 when the children start asking for more. When giving an allowance, even if only ten cents, she can tell the child they should give ten percent to God, for it all came from him to start with.

9. **Apply this to what an abused wife might try to do to help her husband.**

   1 John 4:20,19,18: In that order, it tells us (a) we cannot claim to love God if we hate our friends and relatives; (b) we don't necessarily love them because they deserve it, any more than God loves us because we deserve it; (c) If we're afraid those we hate are making us look bad, taking away the fear will take away the hate.

   Abusers truly believe people are against them and must be told the error of their ways. Other people's "sins" and shortcomings torment abusers and fill them with fear and hate. What types of love must an abuser feel to become loving?

   Possible Class Response: A wife can brag to people about her husband, and this will elicit responses from them. She can then tell her husband how much certain people like him, and positive comments they make about him. She can tell about people she was afraid of once and then found out they were "just ordinary people like us." She can leave love notes for her husband around the house, in his work clothes, etc. She can "cover for him" if he says something bad about someone by never repeating those things to them.

10. **How can a wife help such a husband tell her what he wants, starting with quickly obtainable things and working up?**

    Proverbs 18:19; 17:9: Once you offend a brother/sister, it's nearly impossible to break through the barrier of resentment. If, instead, one overlooks the offensive thing, the other person will love them for it.

    Abusers have great difficulty communicating, partly because they spend so much time telling what they don't want and how people do not want them to have what they want. They also have a tendency to want people to read their minds, which is usually impossible and leads to frustration and hurt feelings; and they don't like questions to learn the specifics of what they want.

    Possible Class Response: Whenever he does explain what he wants, she can say, "I appreciate your letting me know just what you want; it helps me to do thing for you better." Whenever he goes into a tirade about what isn't right, she can ask him point-blank, "What is it that you want?" If he gets negative again, ask him again what he does want done. Similarly, if there is an argument and it's just going in circles, ask him point-blank, "What is it you want to hear me say?".

11. **What can the wife of an abuser do to show him she believes in him?**

    Job 15:20: Suspicion and distrust turn an abuser inside out, and rule him his entire life.

    Corinthians 13:4-7: Love is not easily provoked, does not dwell on bad things, believes [the best of] all things [and people]. We think of others the way we think of ourselves.

    Possible Class Response: She can compliment him whenever she can. She can tell other people in his presence how proud she is of him (but not too much lest it sound phony to this suspicious man). She can talk with him about his dreams.

12. **What can the wife of such a man do to have good friends for herself?**

    Proverbs 4:14-17: We are warned not to associate with abusers, for they have no peace unless they have hurt someone.

    Possible Class Response: Good people who see good in others do not like to be around people who see only bad in others. Her good friends can spend time with her when he is gone to work and she is home, or for lunch if she works. They can send her notes and call her on the phone (but be careful; for he may be reading her mail and listening in on her calls).

13. **Tell what kindnesses she could show and to what kind of people in order to receive reinforcement outside her home that she is a loving and worthwhile person.**

    Ephesians 4:31,32: We should be kind to our fellow Christians.
    An abused wife's own self-esteem could go down to the point she too begins to lose hope in herself and others, and as a result becomes a form of abuser herself.

    Possible Class Response: She can do good things to other Christians who are strong and build others up easily. These good things could include sending notes, sending over a plate of cookies, complimenting someone on her new hairdo.

14. **In order to defend her name and get people to "go easy" on retaliating, what can she do?**

    Proverbs 22:1: A good name is more valuable than wealth.

    Matthew 5:9: Just as the Son of God was a peacemaker between God and man, we can be peacemakers between man and man.

    Included in the personal abuse received of her husband, Abigail had to endure the shame and consequences of his abusing other people, being one with him in marriage.

    Possible Class Response: She can cover for him and smooth things over when he's in the process of alienating someone. She can tell people he admires but doesn't have the nerve to tell, how much he likes them.

Good Work

Write a note to a woman you know who acts bitter or beaten down.

BEFORE CLASS:

A.   Gather up a small supply of church directories and local phone books.

B.   Obtain enough letter-size envelopes that each class member can have one.

C.   Obtain stationary. Use colored bond paper cut in half.

D.   Write on blackboard or poster board suggested things to write for those who have trouble wording what they feel.

"Just a note to let you know I think of you and appreciate the way you hang in there when life's little problems come your way. Let's have lunch/breakfast together someday. [Where] You are a special lady. God loves you and I love you."

DURING CLASS:

"We've been talking about what it is like to face physical or verbal abuse every day as a way of life. Perhaps it occurred as a child from a parent; or perhaps it is occurring now with a spouse. Some of you may be one of those people yourself, even though you have not said so. In that case, you know first hand."

"We need to reach out to each other, not knowing the pain each other bears. We just need to say, 'I love you and I want to spend some quality time with you'."

Hand out envelopes and stationery. "I have brought along a couple of phone books and several church directories. Select someone quickly so you'll have time to write a quick note. If you don't know what to say, I have written an example on the board that you may copy. The important thing is not the words but the intent of your note."

"You will have about eight minutes to find someone to write to, address the envelope and write the note. If the note is to someone the rest of us knows, you should keep it and mail it yourself. Otherwise, I can mail them for you."

"Let's all be quiet now and allow each other to think and write. When you are done, offer a silent prayer for the one you wrote while the others finish."

Concluding Remarks

When time is up and while the slower writers complete their notes, sing one verse of a song, possibly one of the following:

1. *Jesus Loves Even Me*
2. *Heavenly Sunlight*
3. *No One Ever Cared for Me Like Jesus*
4. *He Loves Me*

In a few minutes, your class will be returning to their day-to-day lives, and possibly even an abusive home life. End the class with fast-paced uplifting words of encouragement.

(Wait for one or two quick replies to each of the following.) "In just a few words, what advice would you give a woman to....

1. Teach her children and husband not to love money too much?
2. Help her husband communicate what he does want?
3. Show her husband he is loved by others?
4. Make sure she has friends who will lift her up?

Have a closing prayer, asking God's special blessings on women in difficult marriages, and thanking God for his love.

You're Being Abused if Your Mate....

- ☹ Constantly criticizes you and your abilities.

- ☹ Is overprotective or extremely jealous.

- ☹ Threatens to hurt you, the children, pets, family, friends.

- ☹ Prevents you from seeing your family or friends.

- ☹ Has sudden burst of anger.

- ☹ Destroys personal property.

- ☹ Denies you access to family assets, controls all finances, and forces you to account for everything you spend.

- ☹ Uses intimidation or manipulation to control you or your children.

- ☹ Hits, punches, slaps, kicks, or shoves you.

- ☹ Prevents you from going where you want when you want.

- ☹ Forces you to have sex when you don't want to.

- ☹ Humiliates and embarrasses you in front of others.

The New York Times

Inside the Hearts of Bible Women: Teacher's & Advertising Manual

Abused

Lesson Three: Abuse and Affliction—The Triumph

Lesson Aim
- ♥ **CREATE COURAGE FROM TRIALS**
- ♥ **UTILIZE A SUPPORT SYSTEM**

Scripture Outline

1 Samuel 25:32-35: David expresses his appreciation for Abigail's wisdom in keeping him from violence, and thanks her for her gifts of food.

1 Samuel 25:36: By the time Abigail gets back, Nabal is holding a celebration over his bounty and is drunk. Abigail wisely doesn't try to talk to him.

1 Samuel 25:37,38: The next morning Abigail tells Nabal that he was nearly killed yesterday by David. Terror strikes him, and he has an apparent stroke and is paralyzed. He lingers for ten days and finally dies.

1 Samuel 25:39-42: Some time later David sends servants to Abigail to propose marriage for him. She accepts and rides off into the sunset to meet him.

1 Samuel 27:1-7: David continues to hide from Saul who wants to kill him for imagined hurts, something Abigail well understands. She stands by her man. Finally, David takes his 600 soldiers to a nearby country to get rest from running. He is given the town of Ziklag for his men and their families to live in together. They stay there nearly a year and a half.

1 Samuel 30:1-6: While David and his men are away from home, Ziklag is invaded and their wives and children carried away captive. When they return to find them gone, the men cry like babies for their loved ones.

1 Samuel 30-7-18: David and his men head out to find who did this, find a young man willing to show them where the captors are camping, and rescue their families, including Abigail.

2 Samuel 3:3: After David becomes king, but while he is still reigning in Hebron, Abigail presents him with a son whom they name Daniel. He is David's second-born child.

Today's World

In the book, *The Day America Told the Truth,* the researchers developed a composite man from hundreds of interviews, the "American sociopath," and labeled him "a Werewolf in Pinstripes." He is in his late forties, in his third marriage, is a college graduate with a household income of some $75,000.

He is obsessed with hurting women and reads books on the subject. He also rents movies that are excessively violent. He often thinks of torturing and killing small animals and has, in fact, carried out his fantasies on many occasions. He thinks all men are vicious and repressed killers.

His three most important reasons for marrying his current wife are money, convenience, and sex. He feels, however, that sex with his wife is boring. He commits adultery often, having AROUND SEVEN AFFAIRS DURING EACH MARRIAGE. He selects women from strangers and old girlfriends, possibly from a local pub. He sees nothing wrong with it.

He thinks women are just money-grubbers. He stays with his wife for her money and so he won't have to divide up what he has with her.

***

An abuser expects other people to make him happy. If they don't, he blames them and punishes them. He also lacks assertiveness and cannot communicate his feelings. Therefore, as he gets more and more unhappy, he feels victimized; he blames the person he wants to gain the most happiness from, his wife.

He is self-destructive. He is afraid the marriage will end in ruin, then creates the kind of situation he most fears. He ends up like a puppet master who has tangled the strings of a marionette; she won't make him smile anymore, so he destroys it.

The personalities of abusers are usually quite charming and easy to like. They are not the overgrown bullies most people think they would be. Many are upset deep down that they are abusers, they don't want to do it, and they don't understand why they do. Most were brought up by fathers who were wife abusers. These actions are not the product of mental instability so much as of behavior they have learned.

The first step in cure is for the abuser to see himself as someone who actively chooses to batter; she does not make him do it. He must change his attitude that he is the victim; he must realize that he is the perpetrator. It's his own behavior that he can control and must be changed. He must learn that in a healthy relationship, there is no place for any kind of touch that is not done with love and care.

***

If a wife cannot create positive communication with her husband and the battering only gets worse, she may eventually leave him for her own safety. (Most are also committing adultery.) She often needs outside help such as some place to go until she can get on her feet.

Nearly always the wife will not tell anyone, even her closest friend or family, that she is being abused. She is too embarrassed to admit her own husband doesn't love her. Families can still usually tell the signs.

Some women have wished their families had run some kind of interference for them long before they did finally leave. But extended families usually respect the sanctity of the home, and seldom do. On the other hand, families can be at the sidelines ready to help.

The American Medical Association has new guidelines urging doctors to look for abuse. If they suspect battering, they must inquire about her safety and discuss options before she leaves his office.

Some states have now enacted laws whereby police officers called to a domestic dispute and seeing a physically abused woman, have the power to arrest him without his wife signing a complaint. These men are then usually put in jail with high bond to let them know what they are doing is serious and illegal. Then often judges give them choices of extended jail time or counseling; they nearly all choose counseling.

Bible World

David, too, had a tyrannical master. He was not a spouse; he was his employer, his king—Saul. Although he was a good soldier, Saul hired David to play the harp for him when he felt agitated....

"While David was playing the harp, as he usually did, Saul had a spear in his hand and he hurled it, saying to himself, 'I'll pin David to the wall.' But David eluded him twice (1 Samuel 18:10,11).

"That night David made good his escape. Saul sent men to David's house to watch it and kill him in the morning. But Michal [Saul's daughter, David's wife], warned him, 'If you don't run for your life tonight, tomorrow you'll be killed.' She let David down through a window, and he fled and escaped (1 Samuel 19:9-12). Then David... went to Jonathan [David's close friend] and asked, 'What have I done? What is my crime? How have I wronged your father that he is trying to take my life....there is only a step between me and death.'

"A cave was there, and Saul went in....David and his men were far back in the cave....Then David crept up unnoticed and cut off a corner of
Saul's robe. Afterward David was conscience-stricken for having cut off the corner of his robe. He said to his men, 'The Lord forbid that I should do such a thing to my master, the Lord's anointed, or lift my hand against him; for he is the anointed of the Lord.' With those words, David rebuked his men and did not allow them to attack Saul....

"Then David and his men went out of the cave and called out to Saul. 'My lord the king!' When Saul looked behind him, David bowed down and prostrated himself with his face to the ground. He said to Saul.... 'Look at this piece of your robe in my hand! I cut off the corner of your robe but did not kill you. Now understand and recognize that I am not guilty of wrongdoing or rebellion. Saul asked, 'Is that your voice, David, my son?' And he wept aloud. 'You are more righteous than I,' he said. 'You have treated me well, but I have treated you badly' (1 Samuel 24:3-17).

"But David thought to himself, 'One of these days I will be destroyed by the hand of Saul. The best thing I can do is to escape to the land of the Philistines' (1 Samuel 27:1).

"After the death of Saul....David and all the men with him took hold of their clothes and tore them. They mourned and wept and fasted....David took up this lament....Saul and Jonathan—in life they were loved and gracious....'Oh daughters of Israel, weep for Saul who clothed you in scarlet and finery....How the mighty have fallen in battle' (2 Samuel 1:1,11f,17-25)." *(Quoted from New International Version of the Bible)*

Introducing the Lesson

Today we're going to talk about creating courage during abuse and using a support system. The victim can become bitter and abusive herself, or she can show others how to be courageous in their own lives.

Wife abusers typically have similar personality traits. **Display TYPICAL PERSONALITY TRAITS OF ABUSERS.** Read through it.

If she believes her bitterness will cause her to lose her soul, or if she fears for her life or the lives of her children, she cannot stay with him. This kind of man also usually has several affairs during such a marriage. But it is extremely difficult for a woman to leave a marriage that is bad for her physically, emotionally, and spiritually. She needs a support system, but is almost always too embarrassed to tell anyone that the man she loves doesn't love her. At present, there are three support systems available to her.

1. Family or close friends should not turn their backs on her.

2. Physicians are now required by the AMA to discuss abuse and options to women they see in their offices that they suspect are being abused.

3. Some states are enacting laws allowing police officers to make arrests at domestic-violence calls without the wife pressing charges. The husband spends a few nights in jail for criminal (not civil) assault, then is given the choice of more jail time or counseling.

Again, as we enter our discussion, we must not try to guess if there are abusers in our congregation or among our friends. We are here only to learn how to be supportive of women in these situations. Nor can we make any decisions for her.

Discussion Questions

15. Do you know of a woman whose husband was spared punishment or retaliation for his wife's sake? Tell about it (no names, please).

1 Kings 11:10-13: Because Solomon began worshipping idols, God

said the dynasty of David would end, but not until Solomon's death "for David your father's sake."

When Abigail took David and his men the needed supplies and food, she asked that he remember her when he became king. She probably believed her husband's tongue would continue to bring her trouble.

Possible Class Response: A man in the church may not have been disfellowshipped in order to save his wife from humiliation. A man may have cheated someone out of a great deal of money, but there was no retaliation, for it would have made the family poor. A husband may insult people in public, but those insulted may keep silent as long as the wife is near, to avoid further pain to her.

16. What trait do the following verses say such trials develop?

James 1:2,3: We are to have joy when we are tried, for Satan has no need to put extra pressure on those who are already fallen; and it will develop patience in us.

Romans 5:3: We should rejoice in tribulation, for we are being treated the same way they treated our Lord; and it will develop patience in us.

Revelation 1:9: The Christians were companions in tribulation, and in the kingdom and patience of Jesus.

Possible Class Response: Trials develop patience. We learn that everything eventually passes away but God's Love.

17. This puts her and other women like her in the company of what world-renowned person?

Exodus 32:31,32: God chose Israel to love. Moses asked God to put him in hell rather than condemn the rebellious Israelites.

Possible Class Response: Abigail exercised a supreme type of love,

accepting the blame for her husband's sin. Moses wanted to take the sins of the Israelites on his shoulders and be sent to hell in place of them. Jesus not only wanted to, but he did take our sins and die for us. Then he overcame death, something else we couldn't do for ourselves.

18. Those who take advantage of a possible fear situation by choosing courage instead, have learned what?

2 Chronicles 32:7,8: Although we can only see ourselves standing up against wrong, God is fighting with us.

Possible Class Response: Fear rules the abuser's life, and eventually destroys it. Abigail had exhibited extraordinary courage—first by staying with her husband, and second by facing the enemies of his own making. God gave her courage, and God eventually gave her a reward.

19. **With such unsurpassing courage, who actually is the strong one in such a marriage?**

    Romans 15:1-5: The strong Christians should bear the infirmities of the weak, even when we don't want to. The God of patience and consolation wants us to treat others as he treats us.

    Possible Class Response: The abuser sees himself as strong and able to stand up to people. But he is actually saying that he cannot handle things very well and wants people to treat him with "kid gloves," to tip-toe around him and be extra careful so they won't hurt his feelings. This Abigail tried to do, and the wives of abusers try to do. They are the strong ones.

20. **The Christian wife can become a supreme example of being faithful to Christ when what happens? In what way (Ephesians 6:7)?**

    Abigail stood by her husband unto the bitter end—his death. A wife should insist on doing right, such as worshipping God, doing good works, reading the Bible, etc. An abuser eventually either is converted and glorifies his wife's dedication to God; or becomes so nervous around goodness he leaves and seeks another woman he can try to take down to his evil level.

    Acts 5:29: The Bible says that when the two conflict, we ought to obey God rather than man.

    Hebrews 3:6,14: We are partakers of Christ's suffering and glory when we hold fast our faith to the very end.

    Possible Class Response: We are to follow God's way, even if we suffer for it; in which case, those inflicting the suffering will wonder what we are so dedicated to. We are to take care of our obligations to our mate, even if he doesn't deserve it; we are actually doing these things to the Lord.

21. **Do you think her endurance in bearing up under her own persecution for years previously could have influenced David's proposal? For what other things might an abused wife be prepared in the future?**

    1 Corinthians 2:9: We cannot begin to fathom the great things God has prepared for those who love him no matter what happens.

    Possible Class Response: After Nabal's death, Abigail married David who was on the run to escape execution. He knew she was a strong-willed person with staying power, no matter how bad things went. He had to live in caves, and dodge Saul's pursuit to kill him for years. David knew Abigail would not desert him, no matter what.

22. **How do you think this affected their new marriage? What might have happened had she not?**

    Proverbs 17:27: When you understand others, you lift their spirit.

    Possible Class Response: Abigail understood exactly what David was going through by continuing to love the one who hated him—Saul. If she hadn't understood what David was going through, she might have done what Moses' Midianite wife did, and left him even before he freed the Israelite slaves.

23. **She could have become bitter and David wouldn't have wanted her; but instead she did what? How is this done?**

    Proverbs 3:3-6: Commit God's words to memory. Trust him more than you do yourself. In everything that happens to you, acknowledge that he is guiding your steps.

    Romans 8:28: Everything in our lives does not necessarily turn into what is best for us, but it can turn into some good for us.

    Possible Class Response: Our lives are like a puzzle that must be fit together, and the final result is good. Abigail had to go through a lot to finally be on the same mountain under the right circumstances for David. It takes God a while to rearrange our lives so even bad can be turned into good. Abigail remained patient and trusted in God.

24. **What would be the best philosophy of a woman in this position?**

    Philippians 3:13: We should forget about all those things that have happened to us in the past. We must let go of that excess baggage. We must always have faith in today and tomorrow.

    David was loved easily by all the people. Therefore, he was probably lovable at home too. He was a complete opposite to Nabal. A woman who has been abused in the past sometimes finds it difficult to adjust to a peaceful husband, having programmed herself to be on the defensive for so long.

    Possible Class Response: She must learn to believe in people's promises again, have confidence in their abilities, and trust them to see her emotions and be gentle with them. If she believes in, has confidence in, and trusts in God even while with her abusive husband, she will avoid becoming like him.

25. **What must a person do to hand judgment over to God and bring inner peace?**

    Through enduring persecution and trials, a person learns peace by allowing God to be the judge, saving themselves the agony of judging and passing sentence. David exercised this with Nabal and Saul.

1 Samuel 25:39: God kept David from killing Nabal and his family, for God punished Nabal himself.

1 Samuel 26:9: David refused to raise his hand against "the Lord's anointed" King Saul, even when he had opportunity, and even when Saul was trying to kill him.

Philippians 4:6-9: Hand everything over to God in prayer, and you will have peace that passes all understanding.

Possible Class Response: We must have a very active and enduring prayer life. We must never be far from God. We must trust that it is not ours to obtain revenge through temper and acting just like the abusive husband. God will take care of him. We must take care of our own selves and our own souls. We must not allow an abusive man to influence us in losing our souls over our attitude toward him.

Good Work

Send a note to someone who has suffered because of what someone else did.

BEFORE CLASS:

A1. Search for ideas of people to write. Check the library for articles listing cities and addresses of contact people such as newspaper editors.

1. People who are drinking polluted water or have developed Diseases because of toxic waste from industry

2. People who have lost their homes because someone set fire to them

3. Missionaries barred from a certain country because of illegal activity by previous missionaries

4. People blamed on the job for something a coworker or boss did

5. People individual class members know of

A2. Write a letter to the editor about social problems bringing sickness and death on people.

B. Bring enough stationery and envelopes to class for each member to have one. Pre-address several envelopes.

C. Write on blackboard or poster board suggested things to write for those who have trouble wording what they feel.

For Letters to Individuals: "I know you have been suffering because of what someone else did and through no fault of your own. I am so sorry this happened to you. God is sorry too. Just remember that when he sees you suffer, he hurts as much as when he saw his own son suffer for something he didn't do either. I just wanted to let you know that I am praying for you, and I care."

<u>For Letters to Editors</u>: "I am very concerned for all those who are suffering with [explain problem].... It was no fault of their own. Life doesn't seem fair sometimes. But to those of us who believe in Jesus, we believe he suffered for things he didn't do also. Yet he turned it around into a blessing for others. Perhaps the suffering and pain these people are going through today will not be in vain."

DURING CLASS:

"We've been talking about stick-to-it-ness in the face of suffering wrongfully. We've talked about what it takes to stick with a bad situation and try to make it into something good with the patience and love of God. There are people out there needing our encouragement."

"I have obtained a list of people who went through _____ and are still suffering for it. I also have the addresses of some nearby newspapers should you like to write the editor about the problem. We need to let these people know we really do care and God has not forgotten nor forsaken them."

Hand out pre-addressed envelopes and stationery. "Select someone quickly. If you don't know what to say, I have written examples on the board that you may copy."

"You have about eight minutes to write your note. When you're done, hand it to me and I will mail it for you. Let's all be quiet now and allow each other to think and write. When you are done, offer a silent prayer for the one you wrote while the others finish."

Concluding Remarks

When time is up and while the slower writers complete their notes, sing one verse of a song, possibly one of the following:

1. *Does Jesus Care?*
2. *God Moves in Mysterious Ways*
3. *All the Way My Savior Leads Me*
4. *Trust and Obey*

In a few minutes your class will be returning to their every-day lives, some to abusive homes. End the class with fast-paced uplifting words of encouragement.

(Wait for one or two quick replies to each of the following.) "In just a few words, what advice would you give a woman to....

1. Develop patience?
2. Develop trust in God?
3. Allow God to do the punishing or rewarding?
4. Remain a Christian?

Have a brief closing prayer for those who are suffering unjustly.

Typical Personality Traits of Abusers

- **He is usually quite charming and easy to like. He is sometimes nearly arrogant in an effort to cover up inner fears of others.**

- **He expects other people to make him happy. If they don't, he blames and punishes them.**

- **He is self-destructive. The marriage he dreads falling apart does so, due to his punishing it to make sure it doesn't fall apart.**

- **He sees himself as the victim and not the perpetrator.**

Katheryn Maddox Haddad

BEGUILING OCCULT
Witch of Endor

Lesson One: The Susceptible Ones

Lesson Aim
- ♥ UNDERSTAND WHY WE HELP OTHERS
- ♥ UNDERSTAND WHY WE WANT TO KNOW MORE THAN OTHERS

Scripture Outline

Leviticus 19:31; 20:6,27: The Law of Moses forbids seeking out those with familiar spirits and occultists. Anyone who seeks their advice is to be cut off from God's people. All occultists are to be stoned to death.

Deuteronomy 18:10-12: No one is to use or be an occultist. These are among the things the Canaanites are doing that causes God to guide Joshua and the Israelites to destroy them and take over their land.

Today's World

STATISTICS OF OCCULTISM: Is the occult alive and well or not? A survey of Americans across the country gave some interesting answers. Nearly half of us believe in ghosts. Nearly one-third of us believe some people have magical powers. About one-fourth of us believe in witchcraft. One in every twenty of us has actually participated in some ritual of Satanism or witchcraft.

Even though active, practicing Christians are less likely to believe in these things, social church-goers usually fit into national statistics as fairly typical. Therefore, if you have a congregation of 200 and three-fourths are fairly strong Christians, the remaining 50 would fit with the above statistics. That is, about 25 of them believe (but would never admit it to church friends) in ghosts, and 2 or 3 not only believe in the occult, but have at some time and some place during their lives participated in an occult ritual.

If you don't believe this, inquire around how many read horoscopes. Inquire around how many buildings have a 13th floor. How many people wear their lucky blouse or shoes for tests, business deals, or sports? How many believe there's some kind of force in the "Bermuda Triangle"?

How many people personally have met someone who claimed to have extra-sensory powers or powers of fortune-telling? Universities today have departments researching such things.

(The Day America Told the Truth by James Patterson and Peter Kim)

MODERN-DAY SUPERSTITIONS: A study reported in *Psychology Today* about 1980 found that 70 percent of all college students they surveyed resorted to some kind of magic: Wearing lucky socks, sneakers and blouses, using lucky pens.

Baseball player Jim Leyland famously refused to change his underwear during a Tigers winning streak in 2011. More recently, Richie Ashburn would sleep with his bat during a hot streak. Kevin Rhomberg refused to make right-handed turns because there are no right-handed turns on a baseball field. *(Friday-the-13th: Five Superstitious of MLB Players, Jan. 13, 2017)*

Trans World Airlines once reported that its load factor fell 5 percent on Friday the 13th. Members of the psychology department at Pierce College in Los Angeles became angry when their building was assigned the number 1300. They were afraid their superstitious students would refuse to take courses there. Some trace back the fear of 13 to the number of people who attended the Last Supper where Judas betrayed Jesus.

Money and the unknown future triggers superstitions among some in the stock-market arena as well as old-fashioned type gamblers. One stockbroker in Los Angeles says the market always does better if he's not in the office; so when things are going bad, he just leaves the office for a few days. Old-fashioned gamblers such as lotto players may bet on children's birthdays, license-plate numbers, odometer readings.

Horoscopes are printed in newspapers throughout the country; they wouldn't be there if people didn't read them. Books by modern-day prophets such as Jean Dixon abound in bookstores. Every New Year's season, predictions regarding politicians, movie stars, the weather, etc. abound in newspapers and on talk shows.

Anthropologist Donald Brenneis says "Human beings are always trying to make sense of the world." Superstitions arises anew in every generation in forms applicable to that age. They are a response to anxiety or universal longing for some kind of predictability about those aspects of life that are considered beyond human control. Superstitions reduce anxiety about such things by making the universe predictable again: life, death, love and money.

("Beyond Human Control," by Paul Ciotti, Los Angeles Times, 1988)

Bible World

ENDOR was a village about seven miles southeast of Nazareth. It was located in the territory belonging to the Tribe of Issachar, but actually belonged to the Tribe of Manasseh (Joshua 17:11). Israel's great victory over Sisera and Jabin took place here (Psalm 63:9,10). Today it is a small village at the foot of Mount Herman. It is rocky, and the hills around it are full of caves.

* * *

FAMILIARS: A Necromancer or one familiar with the dead, pretended to be able by incantations to call up the dead to consult them regarding things unknown to the living. The Eastern magi were especially famed for necromantic skill.

The necromancer was supposed to be the possessor of a conjuring spirit, that is, a spirit with which the dead were conjured up to make inquiry concerning the future (Leviticus 19:31). Such a person was called a witch such as the witch of Endor. However, it is evident from her exclamation that she was surprised at Samuel's appearance, thus indicating she was not really able to conjure up departed spirits or persons who had died.

The familiar spirit was supposed to be granted to the necromancer as a servant or attendant, and bound to him/her by the ties or obligations of witchcraft. To the spirits of the departed the necromancer lent a low, soft, almost whispering voice (Isaiah 8:19); 19:3). It is not certain that these mutterings and whisperings were produced by ventriloquism although this may be the case, as ventriloquism was one of the arts of ancient jugglers.

"In most parts of Greece necromancy was practiced by priests or consecrated persons in the temples: in Thessaly it was the profession of a distinct class of persons called *psychagogoi* (evokers of spirits).

* * *

WITCH: A woman supposedly having supernatural power by a compact with evil spirits (Webster).

Witches were not allowed to live (Exodus 22:18) because they defiled the people (Leviticus 19:31). God considered following witchcraft as "whoring" after them (Leviticus 20:6,27) and said it was for this abomination he allowed the Canaanites to be destroyed by the Israelites (Deuteronomy 18:10-12).

DIVINATION: The act or practice of trying to foretell the future or the unknown by occult means. A prophecy; augury. (Webster)

OCCULT: Hidden, concealed, secret, esoteric, beyond human understanding, mysterious, designating or of certain mystic arts or studies such as magic, alchemy, astrology (horoscopes).

ENCHANTMENT: The act of casting a spell over, as by magic; use of magic.

NECROMANCER: A person who claims to foretell the future through alleged communication with the dead; a conjurer, wizard, sorcerer.

When Pharaoh had a strange dream, his magicians couldn't interpret it, so Joseph did (Genesis 41:8,24). When Aaron performed his miracles before Pharaoh to prove he was from God, Pharaoh's magicians copied them. The hardest one to copy was putting lice on people and animals and they warned Pharaoh that they were competing with God. They couldn't copy any of the other miracles (Exodus 7:11f;20ff; 8:7;17ff; 9:10f).

Saul commanded that all who practiced the above arts be banished; but later he sought out someone with a "familiar spirit" to call up Samuel from the dead. That is one of the reasons he was killed (1 Samuel 27:8,11-15a; 1 Chronicles 10:13). King Manasseh used enchantments and witchcraft, and sought familiar spirits, provoking God to anger (2 Chronicles 33:6). Queen Jezebel practiced witchcraft (2 Kings 9:22). God said the "mistress of witchcrafts" sells families through her witchcrafts (Nahum 3:4).

Isaiah predicted Israel's captivity by the Assyrians because of the "multitude of your sorceries," the "abundance of your enchantments." That type of wisdom and knowledge perverted them and would destroy them (Isaiah 47:9-13). The Hebrews were ten times wiser than Nebuchadnezzar's magicians and astrologers (Daniel 1:19f). When Daniel was called on to interpret a dream for the king, he sarcastically asked, "Cannot the wise men, the astrologers, the magicians, the soothsayers?" (Daniel 2:1-12,27f).

Simon was a sorcerer who bewitched people of Samaria. When he saw the apostles perform miracles, he wanted to pay them to find out how they did it (Acts 8:9-13,18-23). Elymas was a sorcerer on the Mediterranean island of Cyprus. Paul told him he was a child of the devil and enemy of righteousness (Acts 13:8-10). In Philippi, a city of Greece, was a young lady who practiced divining the times for her masters who got paid for her service. Paul commanded that the evil spirit come out of her (Acts 16:16-19). While in Ephesus on the coast of present-day Turkey, some of the Jews started using Jesus' name to call evil spirits out of people. Among these exorcists were seven sons of a local priest who were all beaten by a man they tried to perform exorcism on. As a result, the people burned their books on "curious arts"—the total value of which was 50,000 pieces of silver (Acts 19:13-20).

God's people are not to believe every spirit, but try them to see if they are from God, not Satan (1 John 4:1). They prophesy lies in God's name (Jeremiah 14:14; 27:9f; 29:8f). Those who trust in divination (fortune-telling) are against God, for they are all lies and only seduce people from trusting in God (Ezekiel 13:6-10). People with familiar spirits and wizards that peep and mutter seek answers from the dead when there's a God in heaven who knows all (Isaiah 8:19). God makes diviners mad, and their wisdom that of fools (Isaiah 44:25).

Jesus said that people who claim to do miracles in his name and haven't followed his commandments work iniquity (Matthew 7:20-23). Among the works of the flesh is witchcraft, seditions and heresies (Galatians 5:19f). Murderers and sorcerers are among those who will not go to heaven (Revelation 21:8).

Introducing the Lesson

What are some superstitions we have today? (Encourage discussion.) This is a form of occultism when we trust in some other mysterious power other than God.

There are several forms of occultism. **Display DEFINITIONS.** Here are some definitions that will help us understand our lesson better.

Here are some statistics that will be of interest to you. **Display STATISTICS OF OCCULTISM IN AMERICA chart.** Although these figures are not as high for dedicated Christian people, they are just as high for social churchgoers. That means we have them among us.

One of the main reasons God allowed the Israelites to destroy the Canaanites and take over their land was because they relied on occultism instead of God.

Discussion Questions

1. **How can we test ourselves to determine our motives for helping others?**

   When we help others, we can have one of two motives. We do it to benefit others with personal joy a byproduct; or we do it for personal joy with others' benefit a byproduct.

   1 Corinthians 13:1-3: I may be such a wonderful Christian that I speak like an angel, I understand the scriptures with great depth, I give most of my paycheck to other people, and I'm willing to be tortured to death for Christ. But if I don't do it out of love, it is just garbage to God.

   Luke 17:10: After we've sacrificed to obey God and made him first in every part of our life, we shouldn't ask for extra praise or reward. We've just done what was expected of us.

   Possible Class Response: We could ask ourselves if we would keep doing the good works we do if those we did these things for never knew it was us who did them. Or if we are involved with organized church activities, would we keep doing them if others took the jobs we wanted and felt gifted to do and we were told only menial jobs were left for us. We could ask ourselves if we'd do good works out in the community if no one in the church knew about them.

2. **When we "mother" adults, what are we trying to make others think of us?**

   Luke 18:11,12: The Pharisee went to the temple supposedly to pray alone, but prayed so loud everyone around him could hear. Then he reminded God how much better he'd turned out than other people.

   Possible Class Response: As mothers we have told our children to eat properly and wear warm clothes. We comforted them when they cried and read stories to them. Mothers are bigger, stronger and wiser than children. When we do this with adults, we make them feel inadequate and us superior.

3. **Where in our lives do we catch ourselves needlessly analyzing things? What would cure people of this?**

   <u>1 Corinthians 4:5</u>: Don't judge things before the Lord does, for he knows things we don't; we'll be amazed by his wisdom compared with ours.

   <u>Proverbs 3:5</u>: No matter what happens, trust in God and his way, because he understands things we don't.

   <u>Possible Class Response</u>: Some people feel a need to control everything about their lives, and thus scrutinize and analyze everything in a frantic attempt to maintain that control. Often this happens as a result of a childhood filled with too much criticism or punishment, thus leaving the person trying to anticipate possible problems ahead of time in order to avoid them or justify them. Believing that others do not wish us harm would help stop this habit.

4. **Have we spent any time delving into the mysteries of the world? For those who do, what does it do to/for people?**

   <u>Ecclesiastes 1:16-18</u>: Solomon spent his life trying to understand not only wisdom, but also how the mentally deranged and immature fools think. He found it only brought him frustration and grief.

   <u>Genesis 3:5</u>: Satan convinced Eve that if she knew all the things God knew, she'd be happier.

   <u>Deuteronomy 29:29</u>: God has chosen what he wants us to know. Just like a protective parent, he has a reason for keeping the rest from us.

   <u>Possible Class Response</u>: Knowledge is usually considered power. But in investigating that which we can never know for sure, we usually end up more confused and more frustrated, because we've just created more questions. Where we used to have childlike faith, this inner peace is gone.

5. **How do we sometimes justify ourselves?**

   Our social motto today is, "If it accomplishes good, how can it be wrong?"

   <u>Proverbs 14:12</u>: We can choose bad activities for our lives and justify ourselves into believing they're okay, but it will still lead us to death.

   <u>Proverbs 16:2</u>: We can justify any bad activity we participate in, but it doesn't change God's laws.

   <u>Possible Class Response</u>: We justify harming our bodies, the temple of God, when we eat too much by saying the food is so good. We sometimes use our husband or children or company as excuses for not coming to church. We go along with lies at work rather than try to work with the truth or not work there at all.

6. **In searching the scriptures for answers to life, where should be our stopping point? What must we substitute for knowledge eventually?**

   The thing that can take us back to the level of a non-believer is believing we can understand why God said everything he did.

   Isaiah 45:9: Woe to the person who questions God. The clay doesn't tell the potter what to be made into.

   Hebrews 11:1: Faith looks around at what can be seen of this world with a resulting belief in what cannot be seen.

   Romans 8:24: Why have faith if we insist on seeing everything for ourselves?

   Possible Class Response: We can use a concordance to look up every scripture we can find on a subject and its variations. But when there are no more scriptures, we have to stop. Eventually, we must have faith in the unseen and unknown or quit being Christians.

7. **Have we ever felt extremely lonely? What types of things did we do to get people's attention?**

   Everyone feels lonely and alienated sometimes. Sometimes it was because we could not accept the fact that there were people or things we could not have in our lives. Sometimes it was because we did not understand how to mix with certain people. Sometimes we grasped at straws for people to notice us.

   Ephesians 4:14: Some people are easily led into movements of various kinds just to feel important. Some of these movements are led by con artists.

   2 Peter 2:1,3,14,17,19: False teachers disguised as friends of God rob people in the name of religion and get rich. They are greedy, and as useless as dried-up wells. They offer people freedom while they themselves are slaves to their own sins.

   Possible Class Response: Some may have walked around a mall just to be around people. Some may have told family members they were a little sicker than they really were. Some may have joined special-interest clubs or societies.

Good Work

Send a note to someone who seems to be a "loner."

BEFORE CLASS:

A. Gather up telephone books and church directories.

B. Obtain names of nursing-home residents, juvenile home residents, or similar home.

C. Write list of residents on separate envelopes or a sheet of paper.

D. Gather up stationary (bond paper cut in half) and envelopes.

E. On the blackboard or poster board, write the following:

"Although I hardly know you, I just wanted to let you know that I was thinking about you today. Sometimes life seems to be passing us by and we feel like observers. But you are still important to God who walks with you wherever you go. And there are those around you who appreciate your friendly smile and encouraging words. I am praying for you today."

DURING CLASS:

"We've been talking about people who are fairly intelligent and continually are searching for a special place in this world. Some people spend their whole life doing this, especially if they FEEL they are not usually accepted by the people around them."

"If you know someone like this, whether it is a temporary or permanent situation, please send them a love note today. If you do not, I have a list of the residents of the _____ Home for _____."

Hand out envelopes and stationery. "If you aren't sure what to say, I have written a suggestion for you on the board. Feel free to copy it if you like."

"You will have about eight minutes to write your note. When you are done, address the envelope and give it to me to mail. Let's all be quiet now and allow each other to think and write. When you are done, offer a silent prayer for the one you wrote while the others finish."

Concluding Remarks

When time is up and while the slower writers complete their notes, sing one verse of a song, possibly one of the following:

1. *Near to the Heart of Jesus*
2. *Blest Be the Tie that Binds*
3. *How Sweet How Heavenly is the Sight*
4. *What a Friend We Have in Jesus*

In a few minutes, your class will be returning home, either to emptiness and loneliness, or a busy household. End the class so the members don't forget each other during the week.

(Wait for one or two quick replies to each of the following.) "In just a few words, what should we do to....

1. Check whether we do good works just to be praised by others?

2. Stop trying to analyze everything that happens to us?
3. Check whether we are justifying wrong things we do?
4. Stop searching for what we humans cannot know?

Give the list of special-care home residents to person leading closing prayer. Have a special prayer for them all.

Occult Definitions (Webster)

WITCH: Obtains supernatural powers by a compact with evil spirits

DIVINATION: Fortune telling

OCCULT: Concealed, hidden, mysterious things beyond human understanding

ENCHANTMENT: Casting spells over someone

FAMILIAR: A spirit who serves someone, or someone who uses that spirit

NECROMANCER/SORCERER: A person who tells the future by communication with the dead.

Occultism Beliefs in America

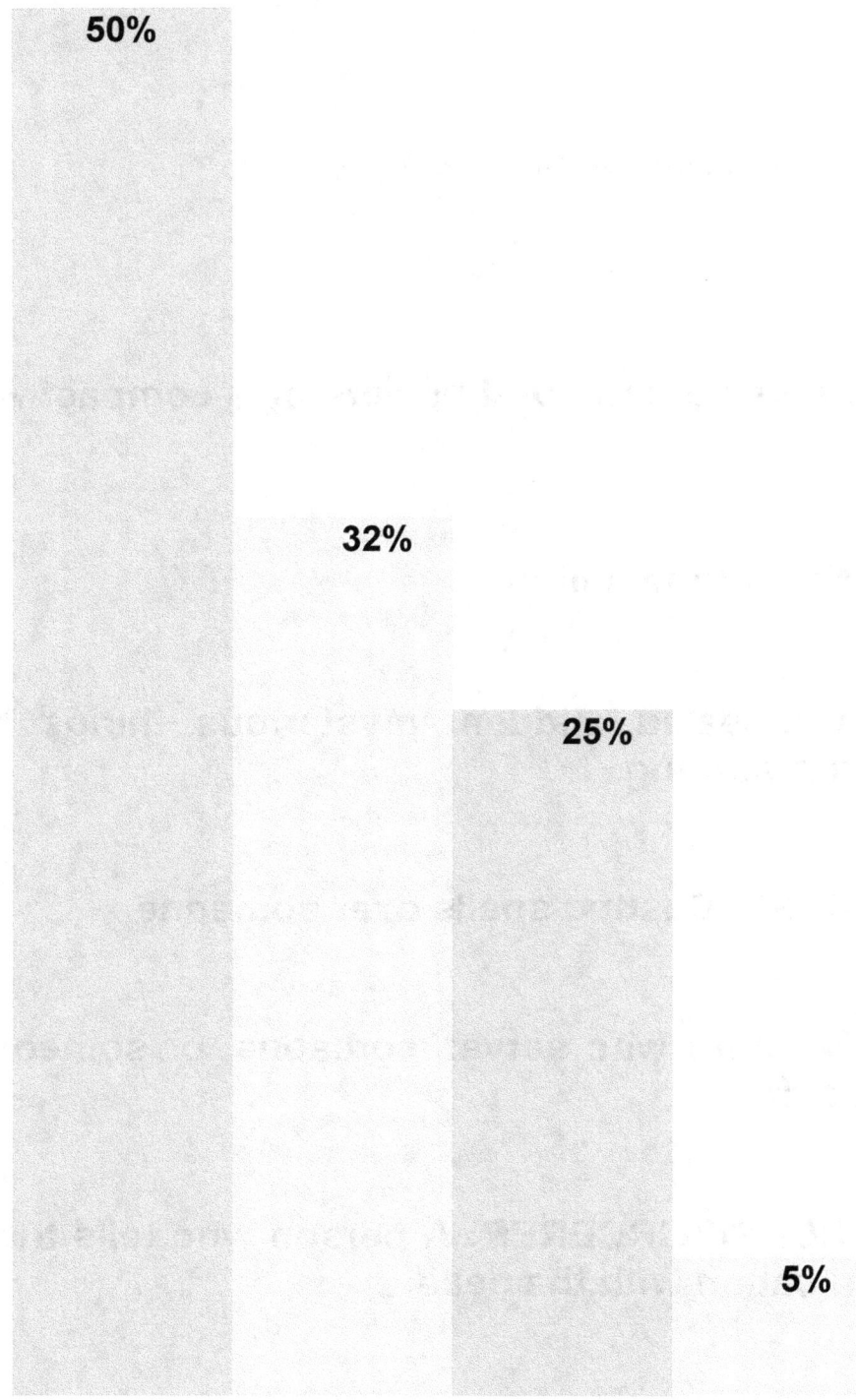

50% Believe in Ghosts
32% Believe in Magic
25% Believe in Witches
5% Participate in Occult Rituals

Inside the Hearts of Bible Women: Teacher's & Advertising Manual

Beguiling Occult

Lesson Two: Masquerade or Mystique

Lesson Aim

- ♥ DRAW THE LINE IN SEEKING ANSWERS TO LIFE'S MYSTERIES
- ♥ BE CAREFUL PEOPLE DON'T THINK WE ARE PROPONENTS OF THE OCCULT

Scripture Outline

<u>1 Samuel 15:13-35</u>: Saul spares people who worship idols, so the prophet Samuel tells him God is turning his back on the king. After that, Samuel never sees Saul again.

<u>1 Samuel 28:3</u>: Samuel dies and is buried at his hometown of Ramah. Saul has all those who practice the occult banished from Israel, but it is too little too late.

Today's World

There are probably very good Christian ladies in every congregation around the country who have been rainbow girls and worked in worthy projects for the community in the name of the Masons. It is not our intent to offend any of these ladies. However, if people knew just what the Masons stood for, they might decide to disengage themselves from them. The Masonic Lodge acknowledges that it "conceals its secrets from all except the Adapts and Sages, or the Elect, and uses false explanations and misinterpretations of its symbols to mislead those who deserve only to be misled" (p.104).

The quotations above and below come from *Morals and Dogma of the Ancient and Accepted Scottish Rite of Freemasonry, Prepared for the Supreme Council of the Thirty-Third Degree* by the Grand Commander and is 861 pages long. You will see that they ARE A RELIGION despite their denials, and that they accept only parts of the Bible and add to it what they consider the best of the religions from Egypt, China, Babylon, Greece and so on. Their God is a Moral Essence and goes by whatever name different religions wish to call him/it.

P.11: "The Holy Bible, Square, and Compasses...are called the Furniture of the Lodge....The Hebrew Pentateuch in a Hebrew Lodge, and the Koran in a Mohammedan one, belong on the Altar"

P.15: "In the East of the Lodge, enclosed in a triangle is the...Letter G...as the initial of the word God. The Blazing Star has been regarded as an emblem of Omniscience, or the All-seeing Eye, which to the Egyptian Initiates [to Masonry] was the emblem of Osiris, the Creator."

P.25: "Masonry is ordained of God to bestow on its volatiers, not sectarianism and religious dogma, not a redimental morality that may be found in the writing of Confucius, Zoroaster, Seneca, and the Rabbis, in the Proverbs and Ecclesiastes."

P.100: "The Hebrew allegory of the Fall of Man, which is but a special variation of a universal legend...."

P.163f: "The old theologies, the philosophies of religion of ancient times will not suffice us now....It sees with the eye of memory the ruthless extermination of all the people of all sexes and ages, because it was their misfortune not to know the God of the Hebrews, or to worship Him under the wrong name, by the troops of Moses and Joshua."

P.165: "Man never had the right to usurp the unexercised prerogative of God and condemn and punish another for his belief. Born in a Protestant land, we are of that faith....born in the Jewish quarter of Aleppo, we should have contemned Christ as an imposter; in Constantinople, we should have cried 'Allah, God is great and Mohammed is his prophet.'"

P.167ff: "We may well be tolerant of each other's creed; for in every faith there are excellent moral precepts. Far in the South of Asia, Zoroaster taught....And in the North of Europe the Druids taught....And thus said the books of India....Twenty-four centuries ago these were the Chinese Ethics....About a century later, the Hebrew law said....The same doctrine had been long taught in the schools of Babylon, Alexandria, and Jerusalem."

P.196: "The religious faith thus taught by Masonry is indispensable to the attainment of the great ends of life."

P.207: "The Deity of the early Hebrews talked to Adam and Eve...ate with Abraham...wrestled with Jacob...allowed Moses to reason him out of his fixed resolution utterly to destroy his people; he commanded the performance of the most shocking and hideous acts of cruelty and barbarity....Such were the popular notions of the Deity."

P.208: "The Supreme, Self-existent, Eternal, All-wise, All-powerful, Infinitely Good, Pitying Beneficent, and Merciful Creator and Preserver of the Universe was the same by whatever name he was called to the intellectual and enlightened men of all nations."

P.213: "Every Masonic Lodge is a temple of religion; and its teachings are instructions in religion."

P.226: Masonry, around whose altars the Christian, the Hebrew, the Moslem, the Brahmin, the followers of Confucius and Zoroaster can assemble as brethren and unite in prayer to the one God."

P.274: "This Redeemer is the Word or Logos, the Ormuzd of Zoroaster, the Ainsoph of the Kabalah, the Nous of Platonism; He that was in the Beginning with God, and was God, and by Whom everything was made....abundantly shown by the Gospel of John."

P.275: "Those truths were gathered by the Essense from the doctrines of the Orient and the Occident, from the Zend-Avest and the Vedas, from Plato and Pythagoras, from India, Persia, Phoenicia, and Syria, from Greece and Egypt, and from the Holy Books of the Jews. Hence we are called Knights of the East and West, because their doctrines came from both."

P.277: "The first Masonic Legislator whose memory is preserved to us by history was Buddha."

P.289: "The obligations of our Ancient Brethren of the Rose were to fulfill all the duties...took their philosophy from the Old Theology of the Egyptians, as Moses and Solomon had done, and borrowed its hieroglyphics, and the ciphers of the Hebrews."

P.290f: "The Cross has been a sacred symbol from the earliest Antiquity. It is found upon all the enduring monuments of the world, in Egypt, in Assyria, in Hindostan, in Persia, and on the Buddhist towers of Ireland. Buddha was said to have died upon it. The Druids cut an oak into its shape and held it sacred and built their temples in that form....But its peculiar meaning in this Degree [Masonic] is that given to us by the Ancient Egyptians....The Christian Initiate [into Masonry] reverentially sees in it the initials of the inscription upon the cross on which Christ suffered."

P.368: "Joseph was undoubtedly initiated [into Masonry]. After he had interpreted Pharaoh's dream, that Monarch made him his Prime Minister...married him to Asanat, daughter of Po, a Priest....He could not have contracted this marriage nor exercised that high dignity without being first initiated in the Mysteries."

P.379: "Blue Masonry...still retains among its emblems one of a woman weeping over a broken column...representation of Isis weeping at Byblos...while the God of Time pours ambrosia on her hair."

P.406f: "We know that the Egyptians worshipped the Sun under the name of Osiris. The misfortunes and tragical death of his God....Horus, son of Isis, and the same as Apollo or the Sun, also died and was restored again to life....In the Mysteries of Phoenicia...also the Sun, the spectacle of his death and resurrections....In Greece, in the Mysteries of the same God, honored under the name of Baccas, a representation was given of his death...descent into hell, his subsequent resurrection....The tomb of Apollo was at Delphis where his body was laid...over whom the God triumphs....In Crete, Jupiter...had also a tomb...with the skin of a white lamb....All these deaths and resurrections...under different names had but a single object."

P.526: "Masonry is a worship."

P.531: "What do the three Greek letters upon the Delta Iota, Eta, and Sigma represent? Three of the Names of the Supreme Deity among the Syrians, Phoenicians and Hebrews, IHUH, AL, SHADAI.

P.538: "What are the symbols of the purification necessary to make us perfect Masons? Lavation with pure water, or baptism."

P.539: "The fraternal supper, of bread and of wine....that once formed parts of the material bodies called Moses, Confucius, Plato, Socrates, or Jesus of Nazareth. In the truest sense, we eat and drink the bodies of the dead."

P.541: "In the early days of Christianity, there was an initiation like those of the pagans....The initiates were divided into three classes: Auditors...Catechumens...the Faithful."

P.625: "After a time the Temples of Greece and the School of Pythagoras lost their reputation, and Freemasonry took their place."

P.628: "What do you mean by the number 12? The twelve Articles of Faith: the twelve Apostles, foundation of the Holy City, who preached throughout the whole world for our happiness and spiritual joy, the twelve operations of nature, the twelve signs of the Zodiac."

P.655: "The cosmogony of the Hebrews attributed to Moses, that of the Phoenians...the Greeks... the Egyptians... the Cretans... Orpheus... the Persians... the Hindus... the Chinese... Iopas... Ovid: All testify to the antiquity and universality of these FICTIONS as to the origin of the world and its causes."

P.701f: "And this True Word [God's name] is with entire accuracy said to have been lost; because its meaning was lost even among the Hebrews, although we still find the name (its real meaning unsuspected) in the HU of the Druids and the Fo-Hi of the Chinese."

P.719: "Divine or human, inspired or only a reforming Essene, it must be agreed that Jesus' teachings are far nobler, far purer, far less alloyed with error and imperfection, far less of the earth earthly, than those of Socrates, Plato, Seneca, or Mohammed, or any other of the great moralists and reformers of the world."

P.726: "Religion is the crown of Morality, not its base. The base of Morality is in itself."

P.727: "The world, the ancients believed, was governed by Seven Secondary Causes; and these were the universal forces known to the Hebrews by the plural name of ELOHIM."

P.728: "The Cherub, or symbolic bull, which Moses places at the gate of the Eden world, holding a blazing sword, is a Sphinx, with the body of a bull and a human head."

P.730: "Christianity should not have hated magic; but human ignorance always fears the unknown."

P.732: "The DUNCES who led primitive Christianity astray, by substituting faith for science...."

P.733: "Nothing is better vouched for than the extraordinary performances of the Brahmins. No religion is supported by stronger testimony, nor has anyone ever even attempted to explain what may well be termed their miracles."

P.787: "The most potent of the names of Deity is ADONAI. Its power is to put the Universe in movement; and the Knights who shall be fortunate enough to possess it...."

P.800: "These things are entrusted only to the [Masonic] Holy Superiors, who have entered and gone out and known the ways of the Most Holy God, so as not to err in them, to the right hand or to the left. For these things are hidden."

P.801: "Every cross of Knighthood is a symbol of the nine qualities of a Knight of St. Andrew of Scotland. The Cross, sanctified by the blood of the holy ones who have died upon it; the Cross which Jesus of Nazareth bore."

P.809: "It is not one religion only, but the basis of all religions, the TRUTH that is in all religions, even the RELIGIOUS CREED OF MASONRY."

P.816: "The Templars, or Poor Fellow-Soldiery of the Holy House of the Temple intended to be rebuilt, took as their models in the Bible the Warrior-Masons of Zorobabel who worked, holding the sword in one hand and the trowel in the other."

P.819: "The Blue Degrees are but the outer court or portico of the Temple. Part of the symbols are displayed there to the Initiate, but he is intentionally misled by false interpretations. It is not intended that he shall understand them."

P.820: "But before his execution, the Chief of the doomed Order organized and instituted what afterward came to be called the OCCULT, Hermetic, or Scottish Masonry."

P.839: "The Occult Science of the Ancient Magi was concealed under the shadows of the Ancient Mysteries...and it is found enveloped in enigmas that seem impenetrable, in the Rites of the Highest Masonry."

P.842: "Magic unites in one and the same science, whatsoever Philosophy can possess that is most certain, and Religion."

P.843: "The Sohar, which is the Key of the Holy Books, opens also all the depths and lights, all the obscurities of the Ancient mythologies and of the sciences originally concealed in the sanctuaries."

P.844: "The Secret of the OCCULT Sciences is that of Nature itself, the Secret of the generation of the Angels and Worlds, that of the Omnipotence of God."

Bible World

In order to prove whether The Word of anyone is divine, we must see if it is historically accurate and scientifically accurate. Scientific truths are discussed in Lesson 3. The entire life of Christ was full of one fulfilled prophecy after another beginning with his exact date of birth and ministry and death, as found in Daniel 9:25-27. (These items are discussed in detail in the lessons on Priscilla.)

The admonitions of Jehovah are intermingled everywhere throughout the Bible with specific dates and places, people and events of world-wide historical significance. This is no accident, for its accuracy adds to the validity of the Bible's divine origin. Nearly every book in the Old Testament contains some prophecy of historical significance made at a verifiable time and fulfilled at a verifiable time. Some were made hundreds of years before the event.

One of great interest is that Isaiah foretold that the Jews 175 years later would be captured and then freed by a foreign ruler, and even gave his name—King Cyrus! Another great prophecy was that of Daniel when he foretold the great empires of the world that would come by the time of the Messiah's appearance—the Babylonian, Persian, Grecian, and Roman Empires.

We believe the Bible is true because (1) We can see today or read in reliable geography books about the cities and places mentioned in the Bible, (2) most of the people and events were written about in other reliable history books, (3) the scientific facts in the Bible were "discovered" to be true by our modern scientists, (4) Events about cities and people came true years after they were prophesied, (5) the books were kept long after the writers died and copied exactly word by word, (6) even though written over a 1600-year period by 40 authors, all of the books of the Bible go along with each other, (7) all books coincide exactly, and many tell about each other (300 O.T. quotes in N.T.).

Furthermore, there are more ancient manuscripts of the Bible than any other ancient document in the world.

Introducing the Lesson

The occult can be very deceiving. Just like the Witch of Endor and other witches of her time and our time, we can get caught up in something if we think it is for good. Witches today say their purpose is to do good and that they do not use the powers of Satan. They even perform miracles of healing on people in the name of good.

Remember, the word "occult" means hidden things, mysteries. We have many groups seeking answers to these hidden things of life. Often they deceive people by their good works. Believe it or not, one of these good groups is the Masons. The Masons have fooled a lot of us in the name of goodness. Some of us were even Rainbow Girls. They said they were not a religion but just wanted good for all mankind. (Read whichever of the parts from the book of Masonry listed above that you desire.)

So, with all the writings today on the spiritual world, how do we decide what is truth and what isn't? We must see if it is historically and scientifically accurate. We must do this with every book claiming to be of divine origin to prove whether it indeed is. We will discuss some scientific accuracies in a later lesson. So, what about the prophesies made in the Bible? **Display THE BIBLE IS REALLY FROM GOD**

BECAUSE.... and read. Display HOW THE BIBLE WAS PRESERVED and read. There are hundreds of prophecies made and fulfilled in the Bible. The Life of Christ was prophesied in great detail hundreds of years before he was born. Every prophet in the Bible prophesied something provable, in order to prove he was speaking the Word of God, and hoping the readers would pay attention better. Here are just a few representing the major and minor prophets in the O.T. ***Display PROPHESIES IN THE BIBLE.***

Since the Bible says we are to worship only the God described in its contents, we must reject any other religion or worship.

Discussion Questions

8. Have we ever read other explanations of the power of the mind, where we go after death, and such? Did this create answers or more questions? What did questioning such things lead to?

1 Timothy 1:3,4: Don't pay attention to philosophies that just create more questions, even about our faith.

1 Timothy 6:4: Some people who seem to be so wise don't know anything. They just bring up unanswerable useless questions, and argue over semantics. They just create envy by those who don't know their true nature and stir up more questionings about Satan that shouldn't even be thought about.

2 Timothy 2:23: The only thing such foolish questions accomplish is unsettled arguing.

Possible Class Response: There are books out about people "dying" for a few moments and being led by a bright light. There are articles and TV talk shows about extra-sensory perception. Around Halloween there are articles and shows about spirits coming back from the dead and exorcism.

9. When we read in the Bible about something that is wrong, there is a point in learning about the nitty-gritty of the sin that we must stop and forget it. What is that point?

Proverbs 6:27,28: Can a person embrace or walk on hot coals and not be burned?

1 Corinthians 10:14: Run from anything ungodly that might enslave your mind and heart.

Possible Class Response: When it takes over our thoughts day and night. When we find ourselves beginning to think it makes sense. When we start telling others about it and getting them to investigate it too. When we begin to visualize in our minds exactly what is going on in the sin, perhaps even visualizing ourselves doing it.

10. How can we overlook things ("justifying") in favor of one side or the other?

1 John 4:1: We're not to believe everything we hear just because someone says they're

from God. We're supposed to test them.

Possible Class Response: If the false teacher is wholesome and good looking, smiles a lot, kisses babies, and takes good care of the family. If the false teaching appeals to something we're afraid of or don't want to believe, such as whether or not hell exists if we have a non-Christian loved one. If the leader makes us feel more important than we've ever felt in our lives. If part of the money raised by this false teacher is used to help in a good social cause.

11. **God tells us about himself where? Satan tells us about himself where?**

Handling doubts in faith is difficult. It takes faith to believe both witchcraft and Christianity. The admitted source of witchcraft is Satan; the source of Christianity is God. Both claim to be incompatible with the other.

Revelation 3:16: We must make a decision. We cannot be lukewarm. This makes God sick.

Hebrews 11:1,3: Faith has both substance and evidence. To get the substance of God, we go to the Bible. To get evidence of God, we look at the physical world around us that he created.

Possible Class Response: God tells us about himself in the scriptures which have not changed over the thousands of years they have existed; they were built on each other harmoniously. There are no books in existence that reportedly were written by Satan. God created the physical world full of beauty and order. Satan did not create anything except disorder in people's lives.

12. **What are the questions we have about death? Could a Bible concordance help us? How?**

The unknown characteristic of death may lead people to seek answers in witchcraft.

Possible Class Response: We can look up every scripture in the entire Bible on a particular topic. When we're done, we will know everything God wants us to know about it. This can include word topics like death, angel, paradise, heaven, judgment, etc.

13. **Where are the dead? Do we know of any other book besides the Bible that can make scientifically and historically proven claims of foreknowledge?**

Where are the dead? It is only possible to know this for sure from someone who has been there and back. Only a few have written with this claim, among them Jesus Christ. You can only believe the one whose writing can be proven as not coming from man. Consider recent scientific discoveries in light of these statements made in the Bible over 4,000 years ago, yet not discovered by man until the past few hundred years:

John 26:7,8: God stretched the heavens over emptiness. He hung the earth on nothing.

Job 28:5: The core of the earth is fire.

Job 36:27-29: Rain comes from water vapor God draws up to the sky.

Job 38:22,24: The snow has treasures in it (nitrogen) that rain does not. There are currents in the ocean that ships use as paths.

Psalm 8:8: Another reference to the paths in the sea.

Isaiah 40:22: The earth is a circle, not flat.

14. **Do we ever feel as though we need to know more about the dead than the Bible reveals? Why?**

Even in Endora's time there were some indications in the scriptures written thus far as to where the dead are, and she could have been satisfied with them:

Genesis 5:24: Enoch is taken directly to God without dying.

Exodus 24:9,10: Moses, his brother, his nephews, and 70 elders see God; under his feet was a huge sapphire like our sky.

Exodus 32:32: Moses begs God to blot his name out of the book of life rather than Israel's.

Job 14:14: When a person dies, he undergoes a change and lives again.

Psalm 16:10: The righteous are not left in the grave.

Psalm 49:15: God takes the righteous soul out of the grave unto himself.

Hebrews 11:17-19: When Abraham started to kill Isaac as a sacrifice, he believed God would raise him from the dead.

Possible Class Response: When people have trouble letting go of their deceased loved one, they want to communicate with them, and will sometimes go beyond their sole belief in the Bible to some other belief. Sometimes we hear reports of people seeing or hearing ghosts, and they are given so much credibility, they influence us to want to find out if it is true. Some people are impatient with God and want to know as much as he does; this was what Satan appealed to when he tempted Eve.

15. **When can we know we have reached the point of commitment to a cause before others make that conclusion for us?**

A commitment has to be made eventually. It is easy to get a little involved with something out of curiosity, then before you know it, you are a proponent. That moment occurs when people around you get the impression you are a part of it.
Matthew 6:24: We cannot serve opposing masters, such as God and Satan. We will

hate the one and love the other.

James 4:4: Friendship with the world/Satan automatically makes us an enemy of God.

Possible Class Response: We can investigate a movement while away from the proponents and remain emotionally separate. We can talk to them in a friendly manner and accept them but not their belief, and even explain why. If we sat in on a meeting with them, we would be playing with fire. If we began to participate in even part of their meeting, we would be all but hooked. Also, if we began talking to others about the movement and telling only what we agreed with, without telling what we disagreed with, people would come to the conclusion we were "one of them."

GOOD WORK

Send a note to someone who has suffered a devastating loss of a loved one.

BEFORE CLASS:

    A1.   FOR LARGE AND MEDIUM CONGREGATIONS: Ask your minister for a list of the funerals he has preached during the past year. Make a list of the deceased, date, immediate family member (spouse, parent, child) and note, if possible, the circumstances such as car accident, a child, old age, etc.

    A2.   FOR SMALL CONGREGATIONS: Go to your library and read the obituaries for the past year. Make a list and note, if possible, the circumstances such as car accident, a child, old age, etc.

- B. Look up the families in the phone book if possible and write their addressed ahead of time on envelopes.

- C. On the glue part of the flap, write the deceased person's name, age, and date of death.

- D. Gather up stationary which can be colored bond paper cut in half.

- E. On the blackboard or poster board, write the following:

"Although it has been a [week, month, year] since _____ passed away, I know that you still miss him/her very much and always will. S/he will leave an emptiness in your heart that can never be filled. But your loved one is now in the loving hands of God. David said in 2 Samuel 12:22 and 23 that s/he cannot come back to you, but you can go to him/her. My prayer is that you will have comfort and peace until the day you are reunited."

DURING CLASS:

"We've been talking about our natural curiosity about where our loved ones are after death and our continued desire to communicate with them. Some people accept God's explanations in the Bible and some are not satisfied with that. There are people around us right now who are going through this turmoil in their hearts. Let's reach out to them and reassure them."

"I have pre-addressed some envelopes for you of some people who have lost loved ones this past year. On the glue of the flap is their loved one's name, age, and date of death."

Hand out envelopes and stationery. "If you aren't sure what to say, I have written a suggestion for you on the board. Feel free to copy it if you like."

"You will have about five minutes to write your note. When you are done, give it to me to mail. Let's all be quiet now and allow each other to think and write. When you are done, offer a silent prayer for the one you wrote while the others finish.

Concluding Remarks

When time is up and while the slower writers complete their notes, sing one verse of a not-too-slow song, possibly one of the following:

1. *Shall We Gather at the River?*
2. *Everybody will be Happy Over There*
3. *There's a Land that is Fairer than Day*
4. *Where the Soul Never Dies*

In a few minutes your class will be returning home, either to deal with the death of a loved one themselves, or a lot of activities with family. End the class with a lot of smiles and rather upbeat.

(Wait for one or two quick replies to each of the following.) "In just a few words....

1. Who tells us about the next world?
2. Where do we find out what he says about it?
3. Who went through death and returned to us to tell about it?
4. How do we know what the Bible says is true?

Give your list of loved ones to the person leading the closing prayer and remember them in a special, loving way.

The Bible is Really from God Because....

_We can see today or read about in reliable geography books all the cities and places mentioned in the Bible.

_Most of the people and events were written about in other reliable history books.

_The scientific facts in the Bible were "discovered" to be true by our modern scientists.

_Events about cities and people came true years after they were prophesied.

_The books were kept long after the writers died and copied exactly word by word.

_Even though written over 1600 years by 40 authors, all of the books of the Bible go along with each other.

_All books never have different facts, and many tell about each other (300 O.T. quotes in N.T.).

How the Bible was Preserved

1500 BC   Moses' O.T. books were kept in the Ark of the Covenant and the Temple.

400 BC   The O.T. prophets' books were kept in the Temple and copied.

300 BC   The O.T. was first put together in another language by 70 scholars.

50 AD   The N.T. books were sent to different congregations who copied them (Colossians 4:16).

300 AD   The N.T. books were put together in one book.

Prophecies in the Bible All Fulfilled
(A Few of Many)

Prophet	Prophecy	Made	Occurred	Yrs Later
Isaiah 14:1-27	Fall of Babylon	713 BC	536 BC	177
Isaiah 44:28;45:1	King Named Cyrus	713 BC	538 BC	175
Jeremiah 4	Fall of Jerusalem	626 BC	606 BC	20
Jeremiah 47	Fall of Philistines	605 BC	536 BC	69
Ezekiel 36	Israel's Regrowth	570 BC	538 BC	32
Daniel 2	4 World Empires	604 BC	27 BC	577
Hosea 5	Fall of Israel	750 BC	721 BC	29
Amos 6	Captivity of Israel	760 BC	721 BC	41
Obadiah	Fall of Edom/Esau	586 BC	582 BC	4
Jonah	Assyria to Thrive	785 BC	607 BC	178
Micah	Fall of Samaria	740 BC	721 BC	19
Nahum	Fall of Assyria	630 BC	607 BC	23
Habakkuk 1:12-2:20	Fall of Babylon	607 BC	536 BC	71
Zephaniah 2:4-3:8	Fall of Assyria	639 BC	607 BC	32
Haggai 2	Temple Rebuilt	520 BC	516 BC	4
Zechariah 2	Jerusalem Rebuilt	520 BC	444 BC	76
Malachi	John the Baptist	420 BC	25 AD	445

Beguiling Occult

Lesson Three: If It Were True

Lesson Aim

- ♥ **KNOW THAT WHAT IS NOT OF GOD IS AGAINST GOD**
- ♥ **FOLLOW GOD'S WAY TO REACH THE SPIRIT WORLD**

Scripture Outline

1 Samuel 28:4-6: The Philistine troops march on Israel, so King Saul gathers his entire army to fight them. He asks God's blessing, but he is no longer in God's favor and God won't help him.

1 Samuel 28:7-8: In desperation, Saul searches out an occultist, someone with a familiar spirit (someone "familiar" with the dead), even though he's ordered them all deported. They find one in Endor, he disguises himself, and goes to her with two of his men at night.

1 Samuel 28:9-11: Suspicious, she accuses him of doing this just to have her exposed and executed, but he promises nothing will happen to her. She relents, and King Saul asks her to bring up Samuel.

1 Samuel 28:12: When Samuel actually appears, she screams. Then she yells at Saul that he is really the king.

1 Samuel 28:13: No one can see Samuel but her. When Saul asks what she sees, she says it is some spiritual being ("a god"—KJV) rising up out of the ground.

1 Samuel 28:14: When Saul asks what this being looks like, she says he is old and has a cape around him, not much of a description. Saul says it must be Samuel, so bows with his face to the ground.

1 Samuel 28:15: "Samuel" speaking through the woman's voice ("familiar spirit") asks what Saul wants. Saul says he is afraid of the Philistines for God has left him, and he doesn't know what to do.

1 Samuel 28:16-19: "Samuel" says that tomorrow he and his sons will be killed and be where Samuel is.

1 Samuel 28:20: Saul falls sprawled completely on the ground in terror and exhaustion. Apparently the two men with him say he hasn't eaten since yesterday.

1 Samuel 28:21-25: The witch, a kind woman, begs Saul to let her give him some food to regain his strength. He refuses, so the two men and her both implore him until he relents. She kills a calf and cooks it and some bread for the men. They eat and leave during the night, still in disguise.

1 Samuel 31:1-5: Saul is wounded in battle, and fearing capture and torture, commits suicide with his own sword.

2 Samuel 1:10: An Amalekite wanting David's favor, claims he killed Saul, but actually all he did was witness Saul committing suicide. Saul is wearing his crown during the battle, so the Amalekite takes it and his royal armband and bring them to David.

Today's World

ASTROLOGY: Among organized astrologists are the School of Astrological Studies in England, the First Temple of Astrology and the Church of Light in Los Angeles. Astrological organizations include:

(1) American Federation of Astrologers (2) Astrologer's Guild of America (3) Scientific Thought in Astrological Research (4) Institute for Human Potential (5) Association for Research in Cosmicology (6) The Time Pattern Research Institute (7) American Astrology Association

Every day thousands of people in America read their horoscope. Throughout the history of man people have looked to the sun and moon, and possibly even worshipped them. Some modern scientists are trying to give credibility to astrology.

Links have been reported between the positions of celestial bodies and earthquakes, the stock market, birth rates, radio transmissions, menstrual cycles and murder waves in Miami. But every one of them have eventually being rejected after careful scientific study.

Planetary alignment has been blamed for many catastrophes. Some scientists warned that in 1982 the so-called "Jupiter effect" would trigger a major California earthquake. It didn't.

Another attention-getter of some scientists trying to prove astrology accurate, is the 10- and 11-year variations in number of sunspots. In 1987, *Science News* carried a story on this and interviewed Harry van Loon of the National Center for Atmospheric Research. "The number of polar bears, the length of women's skirts, the stock market: Everything imaginable has been correlated to the solar cycle," he mused.

Although there are links between such things as the gravitational pull of the moon on our ocean tides, not everything we're tempted to believe is true.

"Celestial Superstitions May Not Be So Loony" by Keay Davidson, San Francisco

Examiner, 1988.

WITCHCRAFT: According to the ***Encyclopedia of Witches and Witchcraft,*** there are about 50,000 practicing witches in the U.S. today.

That's about 1,000 per state and 10 per county on the average. There are also nearly 3,000 books in print on the occult sciences.

Dr. Raymond Buckland, one of America's leading practitioners of witchcraft says, "Witchcraft is a religion...witches do not believe in the devil...you can do basically whatever you like as long as you harm no one."

These are some of the American sects of witchcraft: AMERICAN DRUIDICS emphasize herbal medicine and healing, wearing black robes, the fatherhood of nature. ATLANTIONS stress positive public image. BOREANS worship the god Boreas and goddess Danu in secret ceremonies. TRADITIONALS create their own rituals and ceremonies. CELTICS resemble the ancient Celtic practices with intense reading of all phases of the craft. WELSH TRADITION-ALISTS are dedicated to the celebration of life-secrecy. AMERICAN CELTICS emphasizes couple and family participation.

Their God is the god of nature. Jesus is not the Son of God. They consider the goddess of birth and rebirth the highest deity. They believe in reincarnation. The "8-Fold Path" is (1) state of trance, (2) meditation, (3) dancing, (4) binding with cord, (5) drinking of wine, (6) flagellation, (7) rites and rituals, (8) the Great Rite.

Each coven has 13 members. It is ruled by a high priestess and high priest. Most experienced members start a new coven when the membership reaches 13. The high priestess then becomes "witch queen."

Their festivals are (1) Samhain (Halloween-November Eve), (2) Imboloc (February Eve), (3) Beltane (May Eve), (4) Lugnasad (August Eve), (5-8) four lesser Sabbats, (9-21) 13 Esbats (full moons).

SATANISM: Is Satanism alive and well in the United States? There are stories, rumors, and sometimes an actual proven report. Organized Satanism is small but existent. The San Francisco-based Temple of Set and the Satanic Church have several thousand members through the country.

Statistically, six out of every 10,000 violent crimes is attributed to Satanism. Such crimes are usually the result of one person's lone beliefs, or a small group of followers that person may have developed. The "Night Stalker" Richard Ramirez is an example of a serial killer who claimed the devil made him do it.

Seminars are offered all over the country for police departments on tracing the Satanist-based crime. A National Association of Chiefs of Police home-study text recommends that officers visit public libraries to record names of patrons who have borrowed books on the occult. Librarians in Louisiana and Florida say this occurs in their states. Robert Hicks, analyst with the Virginia Department of Criminal Justice, says that ritual-crime seminars are being pushed by the same fundamentalist Christian groups that also push censorship of offensive art, music, and books, and want to ban abortion.

Some communities have passed regulations or laws guarding against the occult. In Pasadena, Texas, school officials have banned clothing depicting the occult. Parents in several states are concerned about books on the occult, abortion, evolution and secular humanism. Right now there seems to be a trend toward increasing objections to occultism.

"The Devil Makes Them Do It," In These Times, Chicago, 1991.

DEMON POSSESSION: The ancient Greeks believed good gods could possess them, such as the cult of Bacchus and the cult of Eveusis. The Persians and Babylonians believed evil spirits that inhabit the universe often inhabited humans. The Zoroastrian religion reflected this.

During the Middle Ages, demon possession was closely related to the belief in witchcraft. People were possessed if they blasphemed, did immoral things, disregarded social rules, had frightening appearances, and so on. They thought witches had a pact with the devil.

Up until the time of modern psychology and modern medicine, most demon possession was attributed to those with either treatable mental problems, or illnesses. People even today remember when those unfortunate enough to have epilepsy were considered to be demon possessed. Some people in the U.S. today still practice Voodoo. As education increases, people learn to cure or work through the problems previously attributed to demon possession.

Bible World

SATAN was created one of the cherubim, an angel of great authority. His pride grew to the point he thought he was greater than God. There was war in heaven, and Satan (Lucifer) was cast out.

He is called the prince of this world, the god of this world, the prince of the power of the air. Satan made the earth and air his empire. Through lying and misrepresentation, he managed to secure the fall of man into sin. He bribes people to do wrong, just as he did with Jesus, by force, greed, selfishness, and ambition. He does not want anyone to be saved. He is the accuser of the brethren; for he does not have it within himself to be a forgiver. He sifts believers and we continually wrestle with him.

God allows him the power to test and sift us in order to prove that Good prevails over Evil. Satan heads a host of demons. He has been allowed the power of death only on earth. However, at the end Christ will bind him forever (1,000 years, which is the total of all-inclusive years [10] x all-inclusive years [10] x all-inclusive years [10]). He will be cast into a lake of fire forever.

See visual aid for scriptures on the above.

***

DEMON POSSESSION was considered an "invasion" of a human being by an evil spirit or power. Mental illness, physical illness, and delusions resulting from "symptomatic possession" was not demon possession.

Even in New Testament times when demon possession did exist, a clear distinction was made between demon possession and ailments of the mind and body. Matthew 4:24 says people brought to Jesus those sick with (1) diseases, (2) torments (birth defects), (3) those possessed with demons, and (4) those who were mentally ill.

Exorcism is the performance of special ceremonies, rituals, and continual incantations in order to eventually force an evil spirit to make an oath. This in turn forces that evil spirit to obey the <u>request</u> of the exorcist to leave the tormented person's body on its own.

<u>Christ never performed an exorcism</u>. He simply <u>ordered</u> the demon to leave (Matthew 8:16; Luke 11:20; Mark 1:25,34; 5:13; 9:25; Luke 10:17). Jesus' apostles did the same thing (Acts 16:18; 19:11-26). They didn't try to get the evil spirit to promise anything to them, for the spirit had no choice. They cast or threw the demon out.

Demon possession ceased in the apostolic era (Acts 5:16; 8:17; 16:16; 19:11-16; Mark 16:17f; 1 Corinthians 12-14; 13:10).

Christ was victorious over Satan (1 John 3:8; Matthew 4:1-10; Hebrews 4:15; John 12:31; Romans 6:23; Colossians 2:14f; Ephesians 4:8; 1 Corinthians 15:45; Ephesians 2:1f; Romans 8:35-39).

God had promised that Satan would be bound, and Jesus fulfilled that when he overcame death and started the church of the saved (Genesis 3:15; Zechariah 13:1-2; Luke 11:21-23; Revelation 20:1f; Luke 10:18; Romans 16:20; Colossians 2:14).

Satan now works primarily through indirect deception (2 Corinthians 11:13f; 2 Thessalonians 2:9f; James 4:7; Ephesians 6:12; 1 Corinthians 10:13).

Introducing the Lesson

Astrology is different from astronomy. Astronomy is a scientific study of the stars with telescopes to determine their size, location, and characteristics, just like biology does with growing things and geology does with minerals in the earth. Astrology is a superstition that the sun, moon and stars determine man's destiny. **Display ASTROLOGY chart and discuss.**

How many of you have ever personally known anyone who said she was a witch? How many of you have ever seen one interviewed on television? How many of you have sat down with your children and had a good laugh watching Bewitched? Did you ever know anyone who said they could tell the future with cards or palms? Today there are about 50,000 practicing witches in the U.S. or about 10,000 per state and 10 per county on average.

We also have Satanism. Satanists have their Temple of Set and the Satanic Church, both in San Francisco and have several thousand members around the country. Six out of every 10,000 violent crimes is attributed to Satanism, although usually these criminals are acting alone with Satan and not with an organized group. **Display chart on SATAN and discuss.**

Have you ever heard of anyone being demon possessed? Did you ever hear years ago that people with epilepsy were demon possessed? Of course it's just a treatable illness like any other illness. **Display DEMONS chart.** Demon possession seems to have existed only in Jesus' day so he could make an "open show of them" (Colossians 2:15). If anyone wants to study this further, I have other scriptures on this.

Let's talk about what the occult leads people to do and believe today, and how it can be overcome.

Discussion Questions

16. **What do you think are some of the reasons people become "mediums"?**

    Titus 1:11: Some people become mediums strictly for the money.

    Ezekiel 12:24: Some people become mediums to get people to like them.

    Colossians 2:18: Some people become mediums to show off greater mind power than others and make people think they can reach the unreachable.

17. **How is any form of the occult, whether astrology, telling the future, or bringing back the dead a betrayal of God, or is it?**

    The death sentence in the Law of Moses was reserved for people who sacrificed their children to idols (Leviticus 20:2), mediums (Leviticus 20:27), murderers (Leviticus 24:17), breakers of the sabbath (Numbers 15:32,35), idolaters (Deuteronomy 13:6-10), rebellious sons (Deuteronomy 21:18-21), and adulterers (Deuteronomy 22:22-24). Categorized, this penalty was specifically for betrayal of what creates life, what ends life, and the source of life—God.

    Hebrews 2:14,15: God represents life. Satan represents death.

    Possible Class Response: When we try to learn what is in our future, we are not trusting God to help us with whatever comes. If the foretelling is true, we cannot change it anyway. When we want to communicate with the dead, we are trying to live in both worlds and that is impossible except through prayer directly to God and no one else.

18. **If it were possible to bring up the dead, and since God condemns all forms of the occult, who else with superhuman powers would logically be the one making it possible for the dead to come back into this world this way?**

Job 1:12; 2:7: Satan can bring curses on physical things in this world including our bodies.

2 Corinthians 11:13,14: Satan can transform himself into an angel of light.

Ephesians 2:2: Satan is the Prince of the power of the air.

19. **Of all the examples in the Bible when God (not Satan) sent someone from the spirit world, from which direction did they come? Above (sky or ceiling) or below (ground or floor)?**

    Genesis 28:12,13: Angels of God came down to Jacob from heaven.

    1 Chronicles 21:16: The angel David saw was between heaven and earth.

    Daniel 7:13: Daniel saw the Son of man come down with the clouds from heaven.

    Luke 2:9-15: The angels who announced Jesus' birth came down from heaven.

    Matthew 28:2: The angel who announced Jesus' resurrection came down from heaven.

    Acts 1:10,11: When Jesus went to heaven, he went up into the sky.

    Revelation 10:1: An angel came down from heaven to the apostle John.

    Possible Class Response: Spirits from God always came from above, never up from the ground or floor.

20. **Is there any indication that they returned to death a few minutes later?**

    Whenever Jesus or a godly man raised someone from the dead, was it an inspirational occasion or one filled with terror and screaming?

    1 Kings 17:23,24: The widow's son left his bedroom and went to see his mother. Her faith in God was increased.

    2 Kings 4:32,37; 8:3-5: The mother praised God for raising her son from the dead. Seven years later, she and her son who was still living told the king about it.

    Luke 7:14-16: When the widow's son was raised, he went over to his mother, and people glorified God.

    Luke 8:54-56: When the girl was raised, she had a meal, and her parents were astonished.

    John 11:44,45; 12:1,2: When Lazarus was raised, he walked out of his grave, and several days later hosted a dinner for Jesus. It made people believe in Jesus.

Acts 9:41,42: The lady who was raised got out of her bed; and many believed in the Lord because of this.

Acts 20:9,12: When the young man fell out of the window to his death, after being returned to life, he went back to the assembly, and everyone was comforted.

Possible Class Response: They stayed alive indefinitely and made people happy.

21. **Did the image of Samuel give the type of news God would give or Satan would give?**

    John 8:44: Satan is the father of liars.

    Acts 13:10: Satan is deceitful.

    Acts 26:18: Satan represents darkness and causes us to sin. God represents light and causes us to be forgiven.

    2 Corinthians 4:4: Satan blinds people's minds to not believe in God.

    2 Corinthians 11:14,15: Satan masquerades as good when he is actually evil.

    Revelation 12:9,10: Satan leads the whole world astray. He continually twists around what good people do and accuses them of bad.

    Possible Class Response: He gave no hope such as repenting so he'd be spared.

22. **If Satan really did bring up this image who called himself Samuel, how can we know it was really Samuel, and how can we know what he said was truth?**

    John 8:44: Satan is a liar.

    Possible Class Response: We cannot know it was Samuel. Saul never saw him and the woman only described him as being old and wearing a cloak. And even if it was him, Satan never tells the truth.

23. **When you listen to Satan's message of accusations and doom instead of God's message of forgiveness and hope, you become whose disciple?**

    Revelation 12:9,10: Satan likes to tell God how bad his disciples are to get God to condemn them.

    Job 1:11: Satan wanted to prove Job was bad so God wouldn't love him anymore.

    Possible Class Response: Gloom and doom belong to Satan. God gives hope and life.

24. **Do you want to communicate with the spirit world? Try John 4:23,24 and Luke 11:2. Do you want to know how to direct our future? Try Psalm 23. Do you want to communicate with those who have died? Try Luke 16:22; 23:43 and Revelation 4:4. Do you want to enter a spiritual body? Try 1 Corinthians 15:35-**

37,44,49,52-54. Do you want to transcend worlds? Try John 14:1-6 and 2 Timothy 4:6-8.

<u>John 4:23,24</u>: God is a spirit, so we must worship him in spirit.

<u>Luke 11:2</u>: Pray and we can communicate with God in heaven.

<u>Psalm 23</u>: God will lead us safely through everything we do; no matter what happens, he will be there with us, even in death.

<u>Luke 16:22</u>: Angels will take us to those who have died before us.

<u>Luke 23:43</u>: Just like the thief was with Jesus in Paradise, we will also.

<u>Revelation 4:4</u>: Elders of the church will surround the throne of God and we will see them there.

<u>John 14:1-6</u>: Jesus is preparing mansions for us to live with him in heaven.

<u>2 Timothy 4:6-8</u>: When we die we will be given crowns of righteousness by God.

<u>1 Corinthians 15:35-37,44,49,52-54</u>: God will change our bodies and raise us from the dead to eternally live in the spirit world with him.

Is it possible to do the things the occult claims? Yes; but only if accomplished God's way.

Good Work

Send a petition to your local library objecting to books in favor of the occult (there are many and the numbers are growing). Explain why you think they are harmful to the readers (citizens of your town).

BEFORE CLASS:

    A. Go to your library and copy the list of books they have on the occult. Note those who are in favor of it and those who challenge it.

    B. Look up those books on the shelves and note how often they are being checked out. Ask a librarian who's worked there a while if s/he has noticed the age or types of people who check out these books.

    F. Also in your library, look up "occult" in the index of a newspaper as close to your town as possible. Photocopy at least one article of occult-related crimes, and write the date and newspaper at the top.

    G. Ask your library for a copy of a reference book that shows every book published in the United States by topic. Look up the occult and note the ISBN numbers, titles, authors, and publishers of books that are against the occult.

H. Obtain the address of your local library board, and possibly the head of the board.

I. Type a petition, something like the following, on a legal-sized paper:

"We, the undersigned, are concerned about the books in your library on the occult. Even though we feel certain you are not in favor of it, these books are being read [list how often]. Further, the occult is having its influence on our community and those nearby as you can see from the attached article(s) [list headlines and dates]. We understand it is healthy to represent both sides of an issue, but there seems to be an imbalance since we see ____ books in favor of the occult and only ____ books against it. We would like to suggest you order some of the books listed below."

[List of books against the occult}

Below the list, have the following headings across the top: PRINTED NAME, SIGNATURE, ADDRESS, DATE

Make several photocopies of your form.

DURING CLASS:

Tell about your findings on your trip to the library. Read through parts of any newspaper articles you found. Then read the petition you drew up.

Ask class members to sign the petition. Encourage them to take a copy of the petition to friends to sign.

Concluding Remarks

Sing one verse of a song, possibly one of the following:

1. *Onward Christian Soldiers*
2. *The Fight is On, Oh Christian Soldiers*
3. *Soldiers of Christ Arise*
4. *The Banner of the Cross*

In a few minutes your class will be returning home where the results of the occult in your community will not be evident. Send them away with a few reminders.

(Wait for one or two quick replies to each of the following.) "In just a few words....

1. Satan can masquerade himself as what?
2. Satan is the father of what?
3. Everyone that God sent to this world to communicate with us

came from which direction?
4. Who accuses us daily and predicts our failure before God?

Have a closing prayer. Pray especially that your petition will be heeded by your local library.

Astrology

12,000,000 Americans study astrology
150,000 are part-time astrologers
7,000 make a living at it

70% of our daily newspapers carry horoscopes
(35 dailies per state)

Among Churches of Astrology are
The Church of Light
The First Temple of Astrology

Satan

I John 3:8	Evil from the beginning*
John 8:44	A murderer from the beginning
John 8:44	Father of liars
Job 1:6	Satan goes to heaven sometimes
Luke 10:18	Satan was falling from heaven as the 72 preached (NAS is present tense)
Eph.2:2; 1 Pet.5:8	Earth and air his empire
Romans 5:12-14	Thru misrepresentation, secured man's fall
Genesis 3:14-19	Power destroyed through Son of Man
Matthew 4:8,9	Bribes with force, greed, selfishness, ambition
John 14:30; 16:11	Prince of this world
2 Corinthians 4:4	God of this world
Ephesians 2:2	Prince of the power of the air
Matthew 7:22	Heads a host of demons
Hebrews 2:14	Given power of death only on earth
Revelation 12:10	Accuser (unforgiver) of those God forgives
Job 1:6-11	Given power to test so good can prevail
Luke 31:32	Sifts believers
Revelation 20:10	Will be cast into lake of fire forever

*Beginning defined in John 1:1 – In the beginning was the Word. The Word was with God and the Word was God.

Satan's Angels

Gen.3:1; Rev.20:10	Have Satan as their leader
2 Peter 2:4; Jude 6	Kept not first estate, chained in darkness
Matthew 7:22	May be identical with demons

Demons

Matthew 12:43,45	Are spirits
Matt 12:26f; 25:41	Are Satan's emissaries
Mark 5:9	Their number makes Satan's power omnipresent
Matt 8:28; Mk 1:26	Are fierce
Mk 5:1-6, Lk 9:39	Cause self-destructive behavior
Matt 8:31, Mk 1:24	Recognize Jesus
Acts 19:15, Jas 2:19	Believe Jesus is Son of God
Matt 8:29; Lk 8:31	Know eternal fate is torment
1 Timothy 4:1-3	Seduce Christians to false humility
1 Timothy 4:1	Pull Christians from the truth
Ephesians 6:12-18	Christians' armor wards them off

Inside the Hearts of Bible Women: Teacher's & Advertising Manual

VIOLATED
Tamar

Lesson One: Innocent Trust

Lesson Aim
- ♥ **AVOID RAPE SITUATIONS**
- ♥ **KNOW HOW FAR TO TRUST**

Scripture Outline

<u>2 Samuel 13:1,2</u>: Amnon, David's oldest son, falls in love with his beautiful half-sister, Tamar. A typical rapist, he has poor problem-solving skills. So he just feels sorry for himself and makes himself lovesick.

<u>2 Samuel 13:3-6</u>: Their cousin, Jonadab (David's brother's son), sees Amnon moping one morning, and suggests if he wants to see Tamar, that he go back to bed, pretend to be sick, and tell his father that Tamar's cooking would make him well. David agrees to send Tamar.

<u>2 Samuel 13:7-10</u>: Tamar goes to Amnon's palace. He asks her to serve him in his bedroom and orders everyone out but her.

Today's World

The National Sexual Violence Resource Center reports one in five women and one in 71 men will be raped at some point in their lives. 91% of the victims of rape and sexual assault are female, and 9% are male. In eight out of 10 cases of rape, the victim knew the person who sexually assaulted them.

The FBI estimates only one-tenth are reported to the law. One out of every 12 male college students admit committing acts which meet the legal definition of rape (*MS Foundation Study*). The Rape Abuse Incest National Network reports that a vast majority of rapists will not go to prison. Out of 1000 rapes, 994 will walk free.

In New York, a woman took her two rapists to court, but they were found not guilty of wantonly assaulting her because jurors were shown a photo of her wearing makeup and what they interpreted as a sultry smile. In Florida, a man abducted and raped a young lady in a parking lot, but was found not guilty of his brutality by the jury because she was wearing a tank top and miniskirt. The attorney who tried unsuccessfully to prosecute this rapist said of the victim, "It's like the scarlet letter" is placed on her. She is turned into the abuser, and the rapist into the victim who was forced to give in to his "natural needs."

Many women never report their rape because, by reporting it they are humiliated and relive it over and over by endless examinations and questions. Sometimes even their own family and friends don't believe them. So, even though they are tortured with nightmares for months or years following, they don't pursue it further. "It's like you don't want to start any trouble," one woman said. Others don't pursue charges because "You don't want any publicity or people to know what happened to you." Twenty-two percent who don't go to the police fear reprisal by the rapist, and 17% don't report it because they don't want to go through the insensitive treatment they expect from the police department.

One housewife was raped by her doctor when she went in for a breast exam. She called the police and met them at a hospital where she was given a "rape kit" examination. Doctors examined her for trauma, secured semen samples and other physical evidence of rape. She said it was one of the most humiliating evenings of her life. "They sent a counselor down; the nurses kept asking me questions; I just wanted to run out of there." The doctor was acquitted. *(Newsday, "Date Rape")*

Many psychologists say that the emotional trauma can be more devastating for the victim when the attacker is a friend or relative. According to the American Humane Association, two-thirds of minor girls who are raped are attacked by a close family member or parent. This is one woman's story:

"From the ages of five to 13, I was molested by several male members of my family. The consequences of these acts were enormous in my life. I suffered the loss of my childhood innocence, and I was under constant emotional blackmail. You don't realize the constant brainwashing it takes to convince someone not to tell about the molestation, especially when the perpetrator begins his heinous acts with a five-year-old. Everything is so literal at that stage. I was told Mom would leave us if she knew, and that the current act was THE last time. It didn't end for eight years!"

Bible World

David was called "a man after God's own heart," because of his humility and continually going after God when times were good or bad, or when he was good or bad. Yet David was not perfect. He had family problems just like anyone else. Some he handled wisely. Some he did not. Here is an overview of the chain reaction of tragedies that occurred after the rape of Tamar, and a previous event that may have partially influenced it.

David was one of seven sons (one may have died young) and two daughters. Three of his brothers were soldiers in Saul's army. We don't know anything about the other three. He had five nephews that played significant parts in his life and that of his children. One brother had a son who killed the giant brother of Goliath; and another son, Jonadab, who urged cousin Amnon to pretend he was sick to get Tamar to come see him.

One of David's sisters had a military son who led Absalom's troops against father David; he later was forgiven and became Commander over David's army. David's other sister had a son who was a hero in David's army, saved his life, and even sneaked into Bethlehem to get David a drink of water from his home-town well.

This same sister had another son named Joab who became Commander of David's army. He was also close to Absalom and pleaded with David to let Absalom come home from exile and to relent and see his son. Later when Absalom rebelled, Joab killed him. Then he was fired and replaced as commander by his cousin (David's other sister's son, Amasa, noted above) whom he killed. Still later he helped one of David's sons, Adonijah, take the throne from his father as Absalom had. Both he and Adonijah, the two cousins, were killed by Solomon, a third cousin.

David had nine wives and several concubines. His first wife, Michal, was the daughter of King Saul. Saul was jealous of David's military popularity, so told the poor shepherd, David, he could have Michal if he'd kill 200 of the enemy. He hoped David would get killed in the process, but he didn't. Later Saul sent troops to kill David in his own home, but Michal found out, David climbed out the window. Michal then put straw in his bed to make it look like he was asleep when they searched the house. While David was in hiding, Saul gave her to another man to be his wife. When finally David found her, he demanded she return to him, and her husband followed her weeping and begging her not to go. Shortly after David was made king, he celebrated in the streets, she scorned him for degrading himself like that, so she never had any children. (1 Samuel 18:17-27; 19:8-17; 2 Samuel 3:14-18; 6:20-23)

He married his second wife while he was running from Saul, and she bore his first-born son, Amnon, who would become heir-apparent to the throne, and who later raped his half-sister Tamar. His third wife was Abigail, the widow of an abusive tyrant named Nabal, and she bore him his second son, Daniel. His fourth wife was Maachah, the daughter of the King of Geshur, who bore him Tamar who was later raped by half-brother Amnon. She also bore him Absalom who avenged Tamar's rape by killing Amnon, was exiled by his father, then tried to usurp his father's throne. His fifth wife was Haggith who bore him Adonijah who declared himself king when David was old, so was killed by his brother Solomon. His sixth and seventh wives had two sons we know nothing about. All these he married before moving to Jerusalem.

His eighth wife was Bathsheba. He was walking on his roof in the heat of the night and saw Bathsheba taking a bath on her own roof. Inquiring about her, he found she was married, but sent for her anyway and committed adultery with her. She became pregnant, so he had her husband killed and married her himself. A prophet, Nathan, told David the child would die because of their adultery and murder, and the sword would never depart from his family. (2 Samuel 11:2-17,26f; 12:14-25; 1 Kings 1:11-31; 2:13-21)

Bathsheba's next son was Solomon who became king after David. She had three other children we know nothing about except that Nathan was apparently named after the prophet, and became the ancestor of Mary, just as his brother Solomon became the ancestor of Joseph.

David had an unknown number of concubines by whom he had nine more children and about whom we know nothing. David's last wife was Abishag, a beautiful young virgin given to him in his infirmed old age just to sleep with him and keep him warm. After David's death when his son, Adonijah, tried to marry his father's widow, Solomon had him killed because it was against Jewish law to marry your father's wife. Being a "junior queen" (Bathsheba was David's favorite) would have helped establish Adonijah as king. (1 Kings 2:13-25)

Introducing the Lesson

Various studies around America show slightly varying figures, but they are overall fairly close. According to the FBI, a woman is raped every six minutes in the U.S. **Display EVERY SIX MINUTES.** Seventy percent were planned in advance (*Patterns of Forcible Rape*). The FBI estimates only one-tenth are reported to the law. One out of every 12 male college students admit committing acts which meet the legal definition of rape (*MS Foundation Study, 1988*). One out of every 7 Americans was raped as a child ["under age 18"] (*The Day America Told the Truth*). One in nine men and one in three women will be sexually assaulted during their lifetime. **Display WHO ARE THE RAPISTS and discuss.**

King David's oldest son committed incest with his half-sister, Tamar. This occurred just a few years after David committed adultery with Bathsheba. These two tragedies—that of father and son—set off a chain reaction of events that plagued the family for years to come **Display chart THE FAMILY OF DAVID.** Point out especially JONADAB, AMNON, ABSALOM, JOAB and TAMAR (bottom). Talk about the other cousins if you like.

We're going to talk about some difficult things. We are not here as counselors, but as fellow sisters either dealing with it in our own families, or trying to keep our families from ever having to deal with it.

Discussion Questions

1. **How can rape/incest throw a person off track in her life plans and relationships, even for years to come if she allows it to? How can Romans 8:28 help?**

   Proverbs 27:1: Don't brag about what you're going to accomplish in the future, because you don't know what might happen to interfere with those plans.

   Romans 8:28: God can take even bad things and work them around into something good.

   Possible Class Response: She often becomes distrustful of men and possibly all authority figures. She becomes a severe controller of everyone around her because she's afraid that if she doesn't, they'll control her. This seriously interferes with her career, friendships, and even her husband and children. Sometimes dreams for the future are thrown off because she becomes afraid to even leave her own home for very long at a time. As terrible as rape is, she must put it in God's hands and trust that someday and somehow he will be able to make something good come out of it all. She must keep loving and trusting her heavenly Father and realize it is Satan who caused it. Then she must hand the rapist over to God and release herself of the rapist's burden.

2. **What does Proverbs 25:28 mean as it relates to this situation?**

   Proverbs 25:28: People who lack self-control don't have anything to protect themselves from outside influences.

   Possible Class Response: People who lack self-control will end up hurting themselves and everyone close to them by it. Amnon's cousin did not tell him to go as far as he did (raping Tamar), but he urged him to be put into a situation that Amnon could not control.

3. **What changes people who are anti-social (Proverbs 16:6,7)? Do you think a rapist could ever make a turn-around because of this?**

   Someone lacking self-confidence thinks (s)he can't get things the same way other people do. A thief thinks (s)he can't earn enough money; an assaulter thinks (s)he can't change someone's mind without striking them; a murderer thinks the victim is against them; a rapist thinks women in general wouldn't want him, or even hate him, and he must punish them.

   Proverbs 16:6,7: By trying to follow God and truly love others as God does, even a person's enemies can become his friends.

   Possible Class Response: If anti-social people would at least try to "do unto others as you would have them do unto you," even for just a little while, they would find people respond to them better and they would have more friends and more peace in their lives. However, first they must deal with their own hurt. Who has hurt them so bad they don't want anyone else to be happy? People who harbor hurt always hurt people near them. They'll never be happy until they learn to both receive and give unconditional love.

4. **How would you warn women to show caution in visiting with men they know? What if she is living in the same house as her assaulter?**

   Matthew 10:16: When among wolves, be as wise as serpents and as harmless as doves.

   Possible Class Response: In someone else's house, try not to be alone in the house with a man. If it happens, stay near the door briefly, and then leave. At home, she should be careful how she dresses in front of her father and brothers, such as in shorty pajamas with no underwear. She could also put some kind of lock on her bedroom door herself so that entry would have to be forced and loud. She could nail her bedroom window down if entry is made there; or if not, she could make sure it is unlocked for fast exit if necessary. Not making it easy for the assaulter helps.

5. **We desire to let young ladies keep their innocence and trust in human nature as long as possible. How could you give them a gentle yet firm warning?**

    Proverbs 8:32,33: Sons and daughters must be instructed, and that includes warnings of dangerous situations.

    Possible Class Response: We do not have to go into detail with a girl. We can just tell her that her body belongs to herself and she is not required to let anyone else touch it. Touching her where she goes to the bathroom should never be allowed without her mother's consent and presence. We can tell her that anyone who hurts her is doing a bad thing, even if they claim they love her, for that is not true. We can teach her to run away from anyone hurting her. We can tell her who in her life she can go to in confidence if anyone ever hurts her and then threatens her. Usually this trusted confidant for a little girl would be a woman, not a man.

6. **What places should women not go for their own safety?**

    John 3:19,20: Men who do bad things love the darkness.

    Possible Class Response: Going out at night anywhere requires caution, even if there are street lights. Well-lighted public parking lots, even at malls and hospitals, can be dangerous. Covered parking lots should be avoided completely. Before getting in her car, she should glance under it and in the back seat. In the day time, women should avoid walking where there are not many people around; this could even include a park, cemetery, or such. Nearly deserted buildings should be avoided. Stairwells that are seldom used by others should be avoided.

7. **What types of things might a man say just to get a woman trapped in a car, a room, or a building? What types of response should she make? If a father or brother assaults her, he may tell her he'll get in trouble if she tells and she should protect him. Or he may say her mother will be killed if she doesn't cooperate. What can be explained to young ladies in general to get out of such situations?**

    Colossians 3:18: We are to follow what our husbands want us to do as would be fitting those who love the Lord.

    Possible Class Response: Women should watch for requests from men that do not make sense and not just automatically follow without thinking. A man might offer a woman a ride in the rain. He may ask her advice on how to decorate a particular room. He may tell her he has a surprise for her in a particular building. If she hesitates, he might tell her things like, "You can trust me," or "How long have you known me?" or "Have I ever hurt you before?" etc. Young ladies should be told that if men truly care for them, they will not take them into situations that frighten them. If they become frightened, they must say they are. Then they must leave, regardless of how much the man says she should trust him.

Good

Work

Have someone come to your group to explain self-defense techniques. Then call one or more lady friends who did not hear the speaker and share this with them.

BEFORE CLASS:

A. Contact a rape crisis center in your town or your local police department and ask if there is someone who specializes in self-defense talks who would make a talk to your group.

A. When the speaker is contacted, tell them you can allow 15 minutes for the speech, or 10 minutes for the speech and 5 minutes for questions.

B. Arrange audio-visual equipment the speaker may require.

C. Ask for printed material on self-defense that can be handed out.

D. If it is not included in pre-printed material, ask for some "Rules for Self-Defense" that you can type and photocopy for everyone before class.

DURING CLASS:

"We have been studying about being in situations that might make things a little easier for a possible rapist. We are going to omit writing a note of encouragement to anyone, as well as our usual song, in order to have time for our speaker."

Make a brief introduction and get right to the speech. Pass out printed materials while this person speaks.

Concluding Remarks

Sing one verse of a song, possibly one of the following:

1. *Abide with Me*
2. *The Lord is My Shepherd*
3. *Tarry with Me*
4. *Walking Alone at Eve*

In a few minutes your class will be returning home, possibly to family bickering we do not know about. Send them away with sweetness.

(Wit for one or two quick replies to each of the following.) "In just a few words....

1. Do you think it would be nice for a woman to buy herself a flower?
2. Do you have an audio recording of the Bible at home? If not, where else might you find one while not leaving the house?
3. Where is your favorite place to go for a walk in the daytime?

Have a closing prayer asking God to keep you and your loved ones safe. Also pray for those in your class who may have been or know victims of incest/rape, that God will give them peace.

EVERY SIX MINUTES

A FEMALE IN THE U.S.

IS RAPED

MANY DON'T REPORT IT

22% fear reprisal by the rapist

17% fear police and court displaced accusations

*Source: Victim Services Agency of New York City survey of 2,600 rape victims

Who Are the Rapists?

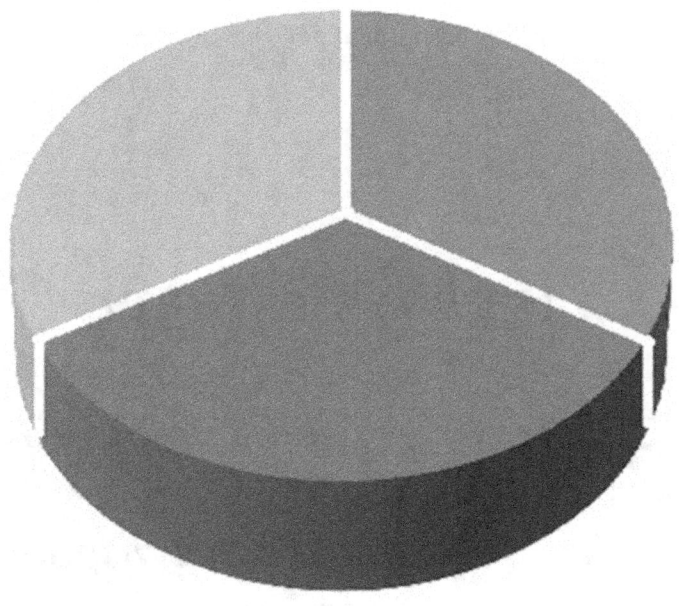

37%—Friends & Acquaintances
32%—Family Members
27%—Strangers

Family of David

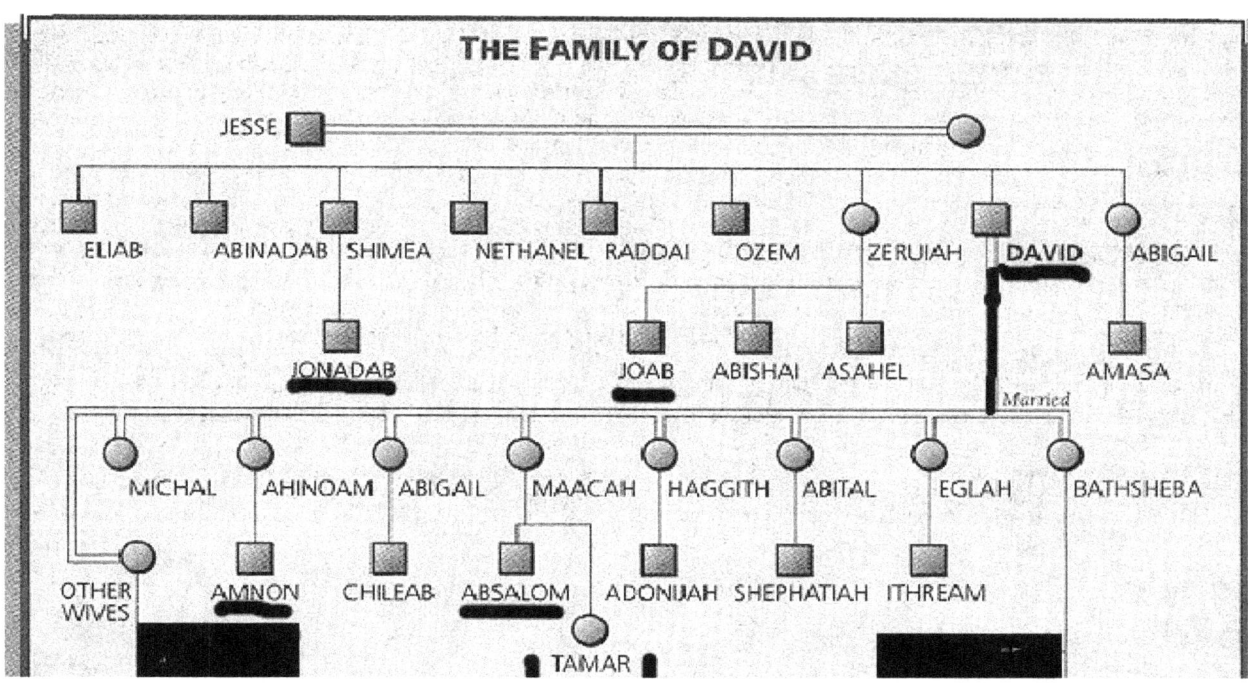

Katheryn Maddox Haddad

Violated

Lesson Two: Betrayal

Lesson Aim
- ♥ BE A COMFORT TO THE VICTIM
- ♥ CONSOLE ONE'S SELF

Scripture Outline

<u>2 Samuel 13:11-14</u>: Amnon grabs Tamar and pushes her down on his bed. She begs him not to shame her, but to just ask for her hand in marriage. He rapes her anyway.

<u>2 Samuel 13:15-17</u>: Tamar doesn't love him any more afterward than she did before, so Amnon's love turns to hate. He orders her out, but she begs him to marry her. He finally calls for a servant to throw her out and lock the door behind her.

<u>2 Samuel 13:20-22</u>: Tamar goes to her brother Absalom's palace and moves in with him. Absalom bides his time to take vengeance on what his brother did to his sister.

Today's World

Two-thirds of rape victims are molested by a close family member or parent. When they do, unless they obtain counseling, the victims heap some sort of abuse on people around them while they continue to carry the buried rage. Such behavior may include physical violence, sexual dysfunctions, obsessive/compulsive behavior, unfounded distrust in others to the point of paranoia, and self-destructive behavior alone or with others. Often they do not understand why their lives continue to be surrounded by abuse.

A child lives in a tiny world with just a handful of adults on whom s/he depends completely, and has no memories or past experiences by which to judge things. If this world betrays her, she has no other reality. Unless corrected by counseling, this impaired ability to judge continues with her through her life in varying degrees.

Furthermore, the invasion of her body as a child makes her feel so defenseless that she sometimes feels powerless to control how others treat her, so she may put herself in dangerous situations such as hitchhiking, feeling she will be harmed no matter what she does. Sexually, she is likely to either become frigid or preoccupied with sex.

The person abused as a child is the most-likely person as an adult to abuse or excessively control other children. *("The Incest Legacy,"* <u>Sciences</u>, *March/April 1986.)*

Although the courts are trying, many little girls are being left in horrible situations that can destroy the child. The parent must do everything possible to get the child away from the incestuous situation.

The Huffington Post reported in 2016 "How Mothers are Destroyed When They Try to Protect their Children."

Dr. Elizabeth Morgan spent two years in jail rather than tell the courts where her daughter was. When just a toddler her daughter showed signs of sexual molestation so the mother sought medical assistance. Eleven out of 13 doctors said she'd gone through sexual abuse, but the judge said it was inconclusive. He then ordered the child to spend two unsupervised weeks with her father. She declared her Christianity would not allow her to let her child be exposed to rape ever again.

Battered Mothers Custody (BMC) conference concluded that, if a mother knows her child is also being psychologically terrorized, beaten, and perhaps sexually abused, she will almost definitely lose custody if she dares mention this. She will be seen as a "parental alienator," as a vindictive and crazy liar.

Mothers Against Raping Children (MARC) has been organized to provide moral and physical support to parents with molested children fleeing from rapist relatives. *("Sanctuary for the Children," Atlanta Journal and Constitution)*

Bible World

Virginity is addressed in the Bible in a literal way and a figurative way. Figuratively, the Israel bride of God is like the virgin bride brought to her groom (Isaiah 62:5). Although put into captivity because of committing adultery with other gods, Israel was to be freed one day. Then, as a virgin bride in God's eyes, she would sing and dance again (Jeremiah 31:4). The church is espoused or engaged to Christ as a chaste virgin (2 Corinthians 11:2).

In the Law of Moses, priests were only to marry virgins. While others were allowed to marry widows, they were expected to punish new brides who it was found were not virgins. Proof of virginity was the husband producing a bloody cloth to her parents after the wedding night. Deuteronomy 22:13-21 says that if a man just decides he doesn't want his wife so declares she wasn't a virgin just to ruin her reputation and get rid of her, her parents could produce the bloody cloth, and the man will be fined a significant amount of money. However, if found to not be a virgin, she was to be stoned.

Stoning was also set aside for rape. If a man raped an engaged woman out in the country, it had to be assumed she cried for help, so only he would be executed. If a man had intercourse with an engaged or married woman in the city, it was assumed she did not cry for help which would have been heard, so she apparently went along with it. In that case, they were both stoned. If a man raped a virgin, he was to be fined and forced to marry her.

Isaiah and Jeremiah both predicted that the women of Israel would be raped when they were taken into captivity by both the Assyrians and Babylonians (Isaiah 13:16 and Lamentations 5:11). Zechariah said it did indeed happen (Zechariah 14:2).

God through Moses forbade people from having sexual relations with their father, mother, step-mother, sister, daughter, sister-in-law, step-daughter, granddaughter, half-sister, aunt, daughter-in-law, or neighbor's wife (Leviticus 18:6-20; 20:14-21). If they did, they were to be "cut off from Israel," possibly stoned. In the case of marrying both mother and daughter, they were all to be burned.

Introducing the Lesson

We are continuing our study of rape, but today it will focus some on incest. ***Display sign 2/3 OF ALL VICTIMS.*** Discuss to the degree you wish.

Talk about betrayal of trust and inability to make proper judgments of right and wrong. ***Display sign ADULTS MOLESTED AS CHILDREN.*** Discuss to whichever degree you desire.

It hasn't been too long ago that society was told it was the little girl's fault for tempting her father. Sigmund Freud said female patients who reported incest were only living out fantasies revealing sexual desires for their fathers. The Kinsey report said in 1953, *In many instances the [incest] experiences were repeated because the children had become interested in the sexual activity and had more or less actively sought repetitions of their experience.* In 1976, one of the Kinsey team, Wardel Pomeroy, said, *We find many beautiful and mutually satisfying relationships between fathers and daughters. These may be transient or ongoing, but they have no harmful effects.* In his 1974 *Guide to Psychiatry*, Myre Sim dubbed "promiscuous children" as eventually being able to "settle down to be demure housewives."

Although our society is now putting the blame where it belongs, with the stronger person who forces the weaker person, the process is slow. In the meantime, frantic mothers are running with their children rather than allow their fathers to continue molesting them. King David did not intervene even though he knew about it, and there were witnesses among Amnon's servants.

Sometimes the pain is nearly unbearable. Although rape victims need counseling, we will talk about how to help them by just being friends.

Discussion Questions

8. **How can you reassure a rape victim that God is of tender mercy, and still sees her as pure as she ever was?**

<u>Genesis 4:13</u>: Cain's punishment for killing his brother was to be separated from his family the rest of his life. He cried, "My punishment is greater than I can bear."

Matthew 19:24-26: When Jesus referred to a camel going through the eye of a needle, his disciples cried, "That's impossible." Jesus reassured them that with God nothing is impossible.

Possible Class Response: There is no comparison in the feelings of someone doing wrong voluntarily and someone being forced to commit a wrong. Someone having seared their conscience is hardly moved by consequences. But the tender conscience like a rape victim's reels under its own punishment. It is greater than she can bear. She must believe that for her it never was a sin in the first place, and there is nothing to forgive. She must believe that to God it never happened; to God she is still a "virgin".

9. **What are some topics a woman might begin talking about to try to avert a threatened rape?**

In SOME cases, possible rapists are talked out of their violence, usually by the victim remaining calm, getting off the subject, and reminding them of good things in their life. It is worth a try.

Proverbs 26:4: Don't answer a fool with his own foolish reasoning about his own foolish actions.

Possible Class Response: Tamar explained to Amnon she would marry him. She said he'd look like a fool to people if he raped someone he could have married. Today, if the rapist comes in through a window, she might have time to start talking to him with questions such as, "How did you get in here? I thought I locked that window." or "Do you have a sister? What is she like?" There have been cases where the rapist has changed his mind because the woman had the presence of mind to try to start a conversation. However, if it occurs outside where she is grabbed immediately, there would be no time.

10. **How would you use Proverbs 29:11 to save your life after a rape?**

Many rapists attack women to show hatred toward them, in which case the attack is random. Others do so because there is a stranger or a friend that they feel fanatic love for. They believe forced sex would force the woman to love them. When such a man sees the woman does not love him afterward, he becomes confused by her rejection, despises her, and even sometimes decides to end her life.

Proverbs 29:11: Fools tell everything they feel and all their opinions. A wise person keeps it to herself until she is away from the situation.

Possible Class Response: She should not pull a mask off. She could refrain from threatening to report him to the police. She could tell him she'll do whatever he asks if he won't do anything else to her. She might even say something like, "I know you've got some good in you. Please let me live" or "I have children at home to take care of. Please let me live."

11. **What ways of ministering to a victim's physical reactions might help her the most?**

Whether raped one time by a stranger, or often by a family member, she will cry uncontrollably, alternating between being hot with heavy perspiration and cold with chills. She'll alternate between hyperventilation and periodic stops in breathing, and alternate quickly between bitterness, resignation, and rage. This happens in varying degrees to various women.

Psalm 69:1-3: David felt like he was sinking in quicksand. He had cried so long he couldn't see and his throat was dry.

Psalm 69:19-21: God knew David's shame and he knew who dis-honored him. Reproach he felt from other people was breaking his heart. Those he used to eat with were now giving him bitter food to eat and vinegar to drink (figuratively).

Job 30:15,16: Job felt surrounded by terrors that pursued him like the wind. Peace in his life had vanished like a vapor. He felt like his soul was poured out and emptied. He felt like a big nothing.

Possible Class Response: Usually she needs another woman to be with her. She needs to be held and rocked and allowed to cry as much as she wants. We can put a blanket or coat around her when she is cold, and have a pot of hot tea or coffee available to her. We can have a cool washcloth nearby to wash her face when she is hot. A glass of ice water can be offered to her when she has breathing problems. We can pray aloud for her. We can sing to her some songs from the days of her innocence such as "Jesus Loves Me."

12. **How could Psalm 140:9-13 help a rape/incest victim?**

Hatred for the evil act haunts the victim.

Psalm 140:9-13: David prayed that God would take vengeance on his enemies - God would talk to them the way they talk to others, they would be cast into deep pits of fire. He also thanked God ahead of time for doing this, praised God, and expressed his continued faith that someday he and all good people would live with God forever.

Possible Class Response: Vengeance is God's and he will repay the rapist someday in his own way so that he can never hurt anyone ever again. She must acknowledge her rage, hand the rapist over to God, and then let go of him. Otherwise, he will rape her over and over in her mind the rest of her life. She must refuse to let him do this to her. Her job is to concentrate on accepting God's love and peace. All this will take time.

13. **The rape/incest victim shows signs of mourning in various ways and for various reasons - loss of innocence, loss of self-respect, loss of others' respect, etc. How could Romans 12:15b help?**

Job 6:1-15: Job said the weight of his grief was heavier than all the sand of the sea. His grief defied his vocabulary. It poisoned his spirit. Things he used to try hard to avoid now consumed him daily and he could not escape from them. The only way he could see to escape it all was to die. His so-called friends had left him and he was so very, very lonely.

Romans 12:15b: Weep with those that weep.

Possible Class Response: We can be accepting of her as she expresses her grief in whatever way she desires. If she cries, we can cry with her. If she sits and rocks, we can hold her and rock with her. If she yells in anger, we can yell in anger with her. We must give her the lead and stay with her, never letting go. We can be her friend and reassure her of that. We can tell her that nothing has changed between you and her, and nothing will ever come between your love for her or God's love for her.

14. **How could we help shield a rape/incest victim from curious onlookers or friends who hear about her rape? How about during a time of questioning by authorities?**

    Romans 15:1-3: We who are strong should bear the problems of the weak even though it puts difficulties in our life we don't want to deal with. We must put others first, even when it takes us out of our comfort zone. Christ took the scorn of others on to himself when it was we who had sinned.

    Possible Class Response: We can surround her with friends who can shield her, be buffers, and head off insensitive questions by the curious. We can encourage the curious to write her love notes instead of wanting to know the horrid details. When public authorities question her, we can try to stay with her, smile sympathetically, and possibly embrace her after difficult questions. If the authorities ask questions she is too embarrassed to answer or not sure how to word, we can help her with vocabulary. If things get out of control during questioning, we can be her spokesman and ask that she have a rest before they go on; if it occurs in her home, we can offer them something to drink while she regains control.

15. **What can family members do to help an incest victim work through the love-hate relationship she has with her father/brother/uncle/ cousin?**

    Psalm 41:9: My best friend who I ate with every day has become my enemy.

    Psalm 55:12-14: It wasn't a known enemy who did this; that would have been much easier to bear. I could have at least hid myself. Instead, it was someone I trusted and looked to for guidance.

    Possible Class Response: They should not justify his actions to the point that they do not defend her too. Too often the victim is given the burden. First she has to work through her feelings toward herself and the wrongness of what he did to her. Family members, in a way those outside the family cannot, can tell her he had no right to hurt her and betray her, even if he is part of the family. They can tell her that he was wrong, and she was right to tell what happened so he can't do it to anyone else. They can tell her it will be passed on to future generations if a strong person like her doesn't speak up and put a stop to it. Making her feel like a victor for telling it and putting a stop to it will help her overcome feelings of a helpless victim.

16. **If you were a victim and close to tears all the time, how would you want other people to act around you?**

    She may be repulsed by any object which reminds her of her rape. This after-shock can linger for days or even years if not dealt with. It is not easy for friends to be around her when she feels such consuming anguish.

Psalm 102:1-9: David prayed for God to not desert him. His heart was burning within him and breaking so that it was consuming his days. He couldn't sleep, he couldn't eat, and the only thing he drank was his tears. He felt like he'd been deserted in a desert.

Possible Class Response: An old poem says that if you laugh, the world laughs with you; if you cry, you cry alone. People work very hard to have calm in their lives, and they don't want other people's anguish upsetting this calm. However, we should not tell the victim to snap out of it because it's time to stop crying and put it behind her. We can, however, try to do things with her just to be a friend - have breakfast with her, go shopping with her, go to the zoo, etc. We can't work through the agony for her; she must do this herself and with a counselor. But we do need to be her friend while she does. If she cries even after she's talked it out, just smile and engage in small talk. If she doesn't stop, just say, "I know it hurts. I'm so sorry." Once you acknowledge it, go back to your small talk. She'll smile bravely and pull herself out in a few minutes. Believe in her courage and let her know you do!

17. **What might a victim do to help get through the nights and possible dreams?**

Job 7:3,4: For months I have dreaded the wearisome nights when I lay there tossing and wishing for day.

Psalm 6:6,7: At night I swim through my bed filled with my tears. My eyes are consumed with my grief.

Possible Class Response: She can have a night light; she can even leave every light in the house on to make it look more like daylight. She should have someone in the house with her. If not, she should have a phone in every room and possibly purchase an alarm to put around her neck that automatically notifies EMS. She can have books, a hobby, or something else nearby to do when she wakes up rather than lie there and cry. Some communities have a hotline that is manned 24 hours, and she could call there just to have someone to talk to. Most homes have alarm systems available to them now. She could have the phone number of Dial-a-Prayer or such. She can have naps during the day so she can have the energy to get up and read or do her dishes when the nightmares come.

Good Work

Invite a professional who understands rape/incest recovery to come talk to your group.

BEFORE CLASS:

A. Contact a rape crisis center, hospital, mental health clinic, or even a Christian counselor if you know one.

B. When a speaker is contacted, ask if they could speak to your group for about 15 minutes, or 10 minutes for the speech and 5 minutes for questions.

C. Arrange for audio-visual equipment the speaker may need.

D. Ask for printed material that can be handed out, and possibly enough to put in your church lobby for victims you do not know about who do not attend your class.

DURING CLASS:

"We've been studying about the emotional burdens carried by rape and incest victims, and how we can reach out to them in love. We are going to omit writing a note today so we will have time for a speaker. However, if you know someone who has been a victim, I hope you will write to her on your own time."

Make a brief introduction and get right to the speech. Pass out printed materials while this person speaks.

Concluding Remarks

This will have been one of the most emotionally-impacted lessons you will ever teach. Now your class has to go back out into the world and to their homes. They don't want to leave your class depressed.

Smile, say something like, "Well, we've learned a lot today. We're just grateful that the sun is shining, we have our loving families, and we have a God who loves us fiercely. So, no matter what happens, we are most blessed!"

Have a closing prayer asking God to give a special amount of love to victims of incest and rape.

Family Members

2/3 of all victims

are raped by

a close family member

or parent

Adults Molested as Children

Adults molested as children can exhibit any of the following:

control of people and situations
physical violence
sexual dysfunctions
obsessive/compulsive behavior
unfounded distrust in others
paranoia
self-destructive behavior
phobias
thoughts of suicide
eating disorders
multiple personalities

Katheryn Maddox Haddad

Violated

Lesson Three: Evasive Consolation

Lesson Aim
- ♥ RECOVER FROM RAPE
- ♥ HANDLE URGES FOR REVENGE

Scripture Outline

2 Samuel 13:23-28: Two years later, Absalom has a feast where he kills his brother, Amnon, for raping their sister Tamar.

2 Samuel 13:37,38: For three years, Absalom hides from his father in Gesher with the king, his maternal grandfather. Eventually David secretly longs to see Absalom, but won't admit it.

2 Samuel 13:39-14:24: General Joab, Absalom's cousin, figures out a way to get David to take Absalom out of exile. David allows Absalom to return to Jerusalem but sends word he is never to see his face again.

2 Samuel 14:25-33: After more two years (total of 7 years now), Absalom sends word to his father to either execute him for murder or agree to see him. They meet and kiss, but too late. The reconciliation is only external. Absalom also has a daughter by this time named Tamar.

2 Samuel 15:1-27d: Absalom steals people's hearts by saying he loves them more than his father does. He finally declares himself king, and David flees Jerusalem barefooted and crying.

2 Samuel 16:1-23: Absalom arrives in Jerusalem as king. He then puts a tent on the roof of the palace where David once lusted for Bathsheba and where the people on the street can see, and has his father's concubines brought to them there.

2 Samuel 16:20-18:8: Troops of father and son prepare to meet in battle, each led by two cousins. David asks his troops to go easy on Absalom for his sake.

2 Samuel 18:9-14: Absalom's hair catches on an oak tree and he is left hanging by it when his horse rides on without him. General Joab, his cousin who defended him as a young man, puts three darts in his heart. He is then thrown into a pit and covered

with stones. Messengers go and tell David.

2 Samuel 18:33: When David hears Absalom is dead, far too late he is heard as he walks away, "Oh my son Absalom, my son, my son Absalom...."

Today's World

REMEMBERING SO YOU CAN FORGET: Incest is a "cancer of the soul" that eats away at the victim's self-esteem and ability to trust other people. Without even remembering why, this can lead to thoughts of suicide, phobias, eating disorders, multiple personalities, physical violence, obsessive/ compulsive behavior. Often victims of incest don't even realize why they have personality problems because they have blocked out of their memories the incest. The book *Sybil* was written about a girl who was sexually abused by her mother and grew up with multiple personalities so she could keep the "bad girl" inside her hidden. An incest survivor might not start having flashbacks of the abuse until midlife.

CONFRONTING TO PUT THE BLAME WHERE IT BELONGS: Prosecuting rape has been very difficult through the years. Therefore, rather than wait for the legal system to press criminal charges, adult child-molestation survivors are now suing their sexually abusive parents in the civil courts. Some of the more well-known women who did so have been Roseanne Arnold, LaToya Jackson, and former Miss America Marilyn Van Derbur. Sometimes parents like Arnold's counter-sue their daughters for slander. It is easier to confront them in court if someone witnessed the act or the rapist admitted it to someone verbally or in writing.

One woman who took her father to court when she was 28 said he had sexually abused her over a two-year period, between ages 8 and 10. He stopped when an aunt walked in on them. Her mother blamed her, she recalled. She carried the guilt for years. Although there would be no prison sentence, she finally sued him so she could place all the guilt where it belonged. This young woman found out later that her own mother had been molested as a child. *If she had taken my molestation seriously, she would have had to take her own molestation seriously. My mother wasn't able to face it.* She had to be told repeatedly over the years that it was not her fault. Finally she said, *Even if I had been dancing naked in front of him, it would not have been my fault.*

In San Jose, California, a program has been started called Parents United, and has both molested and molesters (though never victim and their specific abuser). The group therapy session includes, in part, the victims telling off the molesters in an effort to release the blame from the victim and force molesters to take responsibility for their own actions. A 1991 study by Parents United and the state Board of Corrections showed that offenders who completed the program only became repeat offenders 5.6 percent of the time.

("Victims of Incest No Longer Keep Quiet," San Francisco Examiner)

FORGIVING SO YOU CAN LET GO: One young lady who was fondled by her boss and quit her job became so upset she no longer wanted to be touched by either her husband or children. *I'm a Christian. I know if I hold that totally against him and just* *hate him, it's going to hurt me more than it's going to hurt him.* She no longer shops at her favorite stores or eats at her favorite restaurants in that neighborhood for fear of running into him. *I really couldn't go up to him on the street and say, 'How are you doing?'. I'm still growing out of this.*

Some people believe forgiving is the same thing as condoning, and they don't even consider it. Those who don't come to some kind of resolution, sacrifice the joys in their life to keep the pain alive. For some, forgiveness is a resolution, an end to an emotional turmoil. To others it is letting go of the burden. It is a release that leaves them free of their anger and hurt and allows them to channel their energies into something else.

Hatred requires a great deal of energy. Beverly Flanigan, a therapist and social work professor at the University of Wisconsin has written a book, *Forgiving the Unforgivable* published by Macmillan. *I think that people who don't forgive injure or pollute themselves, or they may damage relationships of people around them....[those who did] forgave because they got so miserable, they thought they were either spiritually or physically going to die. They got up in the morning and felt so full of hatred, they recognized part of them was dying. When people hold on to the idea, they can hold retribution—get back, get back, get back at someone—they're still feeling terrible. They're still poisoning themselves.*

Forgiveness is not easy. It is complicated, especially if it involves someone loved and trusted—the ultimate betrayal. Forgiveness does not mean you condone with the rapist did. It means hoping he will turn his life around someday, then letting go of it and handing it over to God. We must. God said, *Vengeance belongs to me. I will repay* (Psalm 94:1).

FAMILY MEMBERS: Although support groups are cropping up everywhere for victims of rape, there is very little for the families. One such family is that of Abigail Browne who lived a privileged childhood in Boston and whose father was a partner in a prestigious law firm. When Abby went to work in 1983 for a school for disturbed girls, half of whom had been sexually abused, she began suffering attacks of excruciating pain that her physician could not identify. It lasted three years. Just before her father died, she began remembering her own incest. She recalled that from the time she was a toddler until a late teen, night after night he would get drunk and come into her bedroom. When she finally confronted it herself and told her husband, he had trouble accepting it. Her father was a model citizen and family man.

He wanted to help his wife. At first she couldn't stop talking about it. It just poured out of her. They read books like *Father-Daughter Incest* written in 1981 by Judith Herman, and *The Courage to Heal* written in 1988 by Ellen Bass and Laura Davis. In some ways her husband felt it was much easier for survivors than families. She found books and support groups. He had nothing until *Allies in Healing: When the Person You Love Was Sexually Abused as a Child* was written by Laura Davis. The families are indirect victims of abuse.

Couples facing the healing process have either separated for the sake of their own individual survivals, or stayed together but lived relatively separate lives. One couple said they went through separations of several months at a time, timeouts from sex, lots of crying, lots of humor, and realizing that if they had survived abuse, they could survive recovering from it. *"Incest: Living in the Aftermath," Boston Globe*

Bible World

The Law of Moses said that if someone causes you to go blind in one eye, you can put one of their eyes out; if someone causes you to lose your foot, you can cut their foot off (Exodus 21:23-25). If someone kills a neighbor's animal, the neighbor has to be repaid that animal. If someone kills a person, that person's family can have the murderer put to death (Leviticus 24:17-22). No matter what harm someone has done—if they cut off someone's hand, their hand should be cut off—or whatever it is, we are not to sympathize and withhold the punishment (Deuteronomy 19:19-21). However, Leviticus 19:18 commands that we are not to avenge or bear grudges, but to love our neighbors as ourselves.

Jesus repeated the eye-for-eye and tooth-for-tooth law and then retorted that if someone takes one thing from us, we should give them two. And he said it would be better to love than to hate our enemies. We should pray for them. (Matthew 5:38-44). He said that whichever way we judge other people, God will judge us (Matthew 7:1f). Paul in Romans 12:17-19 said we should not seek vengeance, quoting "Vengeance is mine; I will repay, says the Lord" from Proverbs 20:22.

Cities of refuge were built around the Israelite nation. People who had killed someone could flee there and be safe until taken to trial. If it was found they killed out of hatred, they were to be delivered to the avenger of blood (near relative) to be killed. But if it was found they killed by accident, they were allowed to remain in the city until the death of the high priest. After that, they were free to return home unpunished. (Numbers 35:19-29; Deuteronomy 19:4-13; Joshua 20:1-9)

There are several examples of vengeance in the Bible. God carried out vengeance on the Amalekites for killing part of his people soon after they left Egypt (Deuteronomy 25:17-19). Gideon exacted vengeance on the princes of Succoth for not feeding his army (Judges 8). Joab killed Abner after David had forgiven him, so David said Joab's house would be full of disease and murder (2 Samuel 6:21-23). These people either carried out God's vengeance, or declared the vengeance they deserved but which would be carried out by God. However, when Joab killed David's son, Absalom, David had Joab killed rather than let God take care of the punishment (although he may have been carrying out a sentence for murder).

✷ ✷ ✷

GESHUR was the homeland of Absalom's and Tamar's mother Maacah. It was located south of Damascus and on the east side of the Sea of Galilee (1 Chronicles 2:23). David invaded Gesher during the time he was running from Saul (1 Samuel 27:8). Although the Bible says he killed every man, woman, and child, that must have been in some limited sense. He later married Maachah, the daughter of Talmai, King of Geshur.

Introducing

the Lesson

Only after the attacks have ended can the possibility of healing begin. It is an extremely difficult process and is sometimes never attained by some women. There are basically three things a woman must do to heal. **Display STEPS IN HEALING THE HURT.** Explain each part to the degree you feel best. Professional counseling can help this process.

Vengeance must be handled carefully. God allowed it in the Old Testament only to the degree that it involved the breaching of HIS laws and the carrying out of HIS justice. Now, in the New Testament era, God does not even allow us to carry out HIS vengeance on sinners. Perhaps this is a great burden lifted from us, for we are not put in positions to cut off someone's hand because they caused a loved one to lose their hand and so on. Most of us couldn't stomach it. So, if we look at vengeance from this point of view, perhaps we should feel blessed that God no longer wants or expects us to carry it out. He will save us the anguish and do it himself.

Display REMEMBER GOD SEES YOU. Read and encourage with this.

Discussion Questions

18. What kind of positive thoughts and activities would help a rape victim rise above her tragedy (Psalm 55:4-6)?

Psalm 55:4-6: When our heart aches, when we're consumed with terrors of death, we just want to be like a bird and fly away from it all.

Possible Class Response: It takes courage to let go of something eating away at us. It is as though we are still punishing the person if we nurse our wounds; but all we're punishing is ourselves—over and over. She should seek counseling. A victim can also join a self-help group of other victims. She can direct her anger by aligning herself with a group who educates the public on what is going on with rape and incest in our country. She could spend time with little innocent children such as in a daycare center or even by teaching Sunday School to help remind her of childhood innocence and how quickly they forgive, so she can put such traits back into her life. She can begin a hobby or activity she always thought she'd like to do as a means of "becoming a new woman" and putting the rape behind her.

19. What can a family with guilt feelings for not protecting the victim spend their mental energy on instead of the guilt? Why?

Rape affects an entire family in some way. Some relatives wonder what they should have done to warn, teach, or protect the victim. They are experiencing a different form of guilt.

2 Samuel 24:17: When God punished the Israelites for something David did, he frantically prayed that they be spared and he punished.

Possible Class Response: They can rally around the victim and love her fiercely. They can ask the victim to forgive them for not protecting her more or warning her more, if this is how they feel; she will likely tell them it is not their fault and forgive them. If they can't heal, she never will either. As long as they feel guilty, they will feed her own feeling of guilt and victimization. By poking at the wound, they will just make it fester more. As long as it remains the major topic of conversation and activity, no one can let go and finally heal.

20. **What could you say to the people in a rape victim's family to help them deal with desires for revenge (Psalm 94:1)?**

    Hatred for the rapist is also strong among family and close friends, and sometimes strongest among the men. Vengeance takes hold.

    Psalm 94:1: It was said, then said again, Vengeance belongs to God.

    1 Samuel 26:8-10: David had to live in caves and run from place to place for years while Saul hunted him down to kill him. Yet, when David had a chance to kill Saul, he said that no matter how bad he was, Saul was God's anointed and God would punish him in his own way.

    1 Samuel 25:31: Abigail, whose husband abused everyone around him, wisely said that it would only bring grief and dishonor to anyone who sought vengeance; that is best left to God.

    Possible Class Response: How wonderful it is that God does not expect us to avenge wrongdoing like he did so often in the Old Testament. For instance, he told the Israelites to kill everyone in the Promised Land for their sins, and then take the land for themselves. God also allowed "An eye for an eye and a tooth for a tooth." We must look at it as a blessing to not have to dirty our own hands. We must look at it as a blessing that we can turn everything over to God who is bigger and stronger than we are. God knows our limitations, and he knows it would hurt us to take vengeance. David was told by God to kill many people who were idolaters, but when it came to building the Temple, he said it would be better if his son, Solomon, did that. There are tradeoffs. In this Christian era, God does not ask us anymore to take vengeance. He'll do it for us.

21. **Can vengeance ever be truly satisfied? How is it and is it not like punishment?**

    Proverbs 9:6,7: Stay away from fools and don't jeopardize your life. Those who seek vengeance against bad people only lower themselves and spin their wheels for nothing.

    Possible Class Response: Seeking vengeance is hollow. It will not undo the wrong that was done. It only allows the victimizer to hurt both the victim and those who love her over and over again endlessly. Punishing someone for wrongdoing also has as its goal boosting one's own ego that they are able to control even the "big bad guys." Our ego can make us take vengeance. Our Christianity can make us let go of our hurt.

22. **How would you apply Luke 9:54,55 to people trying to avenge a wrong-doing?**

Once vengeance begins, it snowballs. The avenger can be taken to the same level as the original evil doer.

Luke 9:54-56: When Jesus' disciples wanted to bring fire down from heaven on unbelievers, Jesus rebuked them and warned them to examine the vengeful spirit they had within themselves. He had not come to spread death.

Possible Class Response: We should not want to lower ourselves to the level of those on whom we seek revenge. It makes us as bad as them. It won't change the bad that happened. We would better use our energies helping the victim know that we love her now as much as if the incident never happened. We should use our energies to heal and help make her whole again, not bring even more tragedy to the family.

23. **David tried to close his eyes and hope the problem would go away by itself. This sometimes happens with the mother of a young lady being molested by a family member in order to keep her family together. What should this parent do?**

Philemon 18: Paul said that if a particular runaway slave he was returning to his owner had caused the owner any extra money, Paul would pay the debt.

Possible Class Response: She should take the problem onto herself as though the rape were hers. How would she feel if she was being tortured and killed daily, and everyone was trying to protect the killer? She must get help for her daughter by either making arrangements for her to live somewhere else, or by confronting her husband/brother/son. She must also try to get help for the man; and if he denies it, get counseling on how to deal with it. Then turn the matter over to the authorities and hope that they don't minimize it and let it go. The problem won't go away by itself. Future generations will be victimized; someone has to stop it.

24. **What is the ONLY way to get bitterness out of the lives of family members (Matthew 5:44,45)? Why?**

Just as you were violated physically, your family can get so caught up in so much bitterness that they rape each other's emotions (Galatians 5:15).

Matthew 5:44,45: We must love our enemies and do good to those who hate us. Jesus did as God's son, and we must as God's children.

Galatians 5:15: If we bite and devour each other, we will be eaten up by each other.

Possible Class Response: She must eventually put this in God's hands and out of her mind. She must separate the sinner and the sin. She must hope that someday this person can sincerely ask forgiveness of her and God, and make his life right for his eternal soul's sake. She can and should condemn this terrible sin, but not because it was against her so much as it was against God. If she keeps it in her mind, he will rape her over and over for the rest of her life. It will eat her alive. She cannot carry such burden. She MUST hand it over to God for him to carry out the vengeance. She MUST.

25. **Who must put a stop to vengeance seeking (Ezekiel 25:15-17)? How?**

Once vengeance gets out of hand, it spreads like a terrible disease.

Ezekiel 25:15-17: When we take vengeance from a spiteful heart carrying an old hatred, God will take vengeance on us.

Possible Class Response: Vengeance by us is wrong. God says that's HIS JOB. Vengeance is a sin. Someone in the family or a close friend must be the first to forgive the sinner for her sake, and turn him over to God's vengeance. If, for instance, he is taken to court and found not guilty, we still must somehow forgive. God is allowed to do certain things we're not allowed to do for our own inner peace and soul's sake. Whoever is the first to forgive must tell the others and tell them how and why.

26. **When victims and family get caught up in vengeance, in the end who will get the last laugh (2 Corinthians 2:10,11)?**

2 Corinthians 2:11a: We can't truly know what goes on inside the mind of someone except by putting those same things in our mind.

Possible Class Response: Once we lower ourselves to the level of the rapist by trying to hurt him, we will become just like him. The rapist who wanted to hurt this woman will be able to hurt her over and over. Rapists usually hate most of the people around them (they use pleasant personalities to manipulate people), so being able to continue hurting her family members too will bring him pleasure.

27. **What is the best way a victim's family and close friends can rally to her side and prove their love (Philippians 4:8 and 7)?**

Philippians 4:8 and 7: Spend your time thinking about things that are true, honest, just, pure, and lovely. This will bring you a peace from God that passes understanding.

Possible Class Response: We can continually reassure her how much she is loved now as much as ever. We can let her know she is still a pure virgin in our eyes and God's eyes. We can talk of positive things. We can bring her flowers, send her cards, write her love notes. We can sing to her and get her to sing with us. We can stop by and see someone with a baby and encourage her to hold it. We can give her a pet if she'd like one. We can take her to musical productions. We should surround her with every positive thing we can think of—not in a pushy way, for she has mourning to do. Gradually she will quit feeling the thorns and be able to see the rose.

Good Work

Write an undated note to a rape victim emphasizing the love of God.

BEFORE CLASS:

A. Contact a rape crisis center, hospital, mental health clinic, attorney or Christian counselor, and ask if you can pass on notes to rape victims that come to them for help. If you receive written permission, read their reply to your ladies class.

B. Gather up church directories and telephone books.

C. Gather up stationary (colored bond paper cut in half) and envelopes.

D. Write the following on the blackboard or poster board:

"[Although I do not know you,] I wanted to write to you and let you know that I am so sorry that you were raped. My heart aches for you and goes out to you in love. You did not do anything wrong, and God loves you as much now as he ever did. I wish I could undo it. But since we can't, please place it in God's hands and try somehow and someday to let go of the pain. My love envelopes you at this moment, and my prayers are offered as a healing ointment to your broken heart. Always remember, God's love will never, ever let you go."

DURING CLASS:

"We've been talking about the experiences of a rape and incest victim, and their efforts at healing. Believe it or not, there are probably victims in this very room right now, or someone who is close to a rape victim. Let's reach out to them and not forget them. Their agony can last a lifetime."

"_____, who deals with rape victims, has agreed to pass our letters along to rape victims if you do not know anyone you want to send your letter to. I received a letter allowing us to do this, and it reads as follows: [read letter]."

Hand out stationary. If you aren't sure what to say, I have written a suggestion for you on the board. Feel free to copy it if you like."

"You will have about five minutes to write your note. Let's all be quiet now and allow each other to think and write. When you are done, give your note to me, then offer a silent prayer for the one you wrote while the others finish."

Concluding Remarks

When time is up and while the slower writers complete their notes, sing one verse of a song, possibly one of the following:

1. *Jesus, Lover of My Soul*
2. *There Stands a Rock*
3. *O Love That Will Not Let Me Go*
4. *I am So Glad that Jesus Loves Me*

In a few moments, your students will be returning home, some to a bad situation, some with memories brought up during class, and some to the every-day responsibilities of happy families. So try to end the class as upbeat as possible. Smile!

(Wait for one or two quick replies to each of the following.) "In a few words....

1. What is something cuddly you could take to a woman needing extra "warm fuzzies" in her life?

2. Who does vengeance belong to?

3. The rape victim is just as pure as she was when she was born to whom?

4. What is something positive you could do for or with a victim to let her know how very much she is loved?

End the class with an uplifting and positive prayer of overcoming all through Christ who loves us.

STEPS IN HEALING THE HURT

REMEMBERING
so you can forget

CONFRONTING
to put the blame where it belongs

FORGIVING
so you can let go

Still Pure

Katheryn Maddox Haddad

UNFAITHFUL
Gomer

Lesson One: Beginnings of a Shaky Marriage

Lesson Aim
- ♥ KNOW THE FOUNDATION OF MARRIAGE
- ♥ WORK TO BUILD A SOLID MARRIAGE

Scripture Outline

Hosea 1:1: God speaks to Hosea during the reigns of Uzziah (52 years), Jotham (16 years), Ahaz (16 years) and Hezekiah (29 years), kings of Judah, and the reign of Jeroboam II (41 years), king of Israel, covering Hosea's whole life.

Hosea 1:2: God tells Hosea to marry a prostitute, the daughter of a prostitute, so he can truly understand God's pain when his people/bride "commits adultery" with other gods.

Hosea 1:3-5: God tells Hosea to name his first son Jezreel after the place where the sons of a previous king, Ahab, were killed by Jehu and the dynasty taken from his family. God is warning his wife, Israel, he will allow her to be taken from His family too—a kind of divorce.

Today's World

Here are some startling facts unearthed by the researchers of James Patterson and Peter Kim who anonymously interviewed people all over the United States in 1991. One out of every five children now loses his/her virginity before the age of 13. The researchers feel that this is a conservative figure. One Los Angeles elementary school teacher was quoted by the *Los Angeles Times* as responding to the question, "Whatever happened to childhood?" with "I'll tell you. Children are skipping it."

We thought the sexual revolutions of the 1960s and 1970s of "free love" were serious.

At that time three-fourths of the men had lost their virginity by the time of marriage, the same as their fathers and grandfathers. But the number of virgins at marriage dramatically reduced among women, from 57 percent of mothers, to 34 percent of daughters. Living together instead of marrying also became accepted. However, these baby boomers did not start sex earlier than their parents; they were almost always adults when they lost their virginity.

But of today's "baby busters" (18 to 24 years old), 61 percent said they'd lost their virginity by the time they were sixteen. More than 20 percent had lost it by the age of 13. Those who experience sex at age 12 or 13 do not do it for love. Only 10 percent gave love as their reason. They do not do it for pleasure either.

Overwhelmingly, the reason teenagers start having sex early is peer pressure with no effective counterforce from parents and schools. Teachers are basically saying, "If you're a virgin, fine. If you're sexually active, fine. If you're gay, fine." Some parents are saying it too. Some family television shows are reflecting this also.

Adults are making money by selling sex to young children anywhere from cosmetics, jewelry and clothes, to music tapes and posters. Most girls aged nine to eleven use nail polish, and in the next two years will add perfume, lipstick, blush, and eyeshadow. By age thirteen, many girls are spending over $250 a year on adult cosmetics.

(The Day America Told the Truth, by James Patterson and Peter Kim)

However, there is some good news. In 2016, *US News & World Report* an article stated U.S. teens are having a lot less sex, they are drinking and using drugs less often, and they aren't smoking as much, according a government survey of risky youth behaviors. Ten years ago, 47% of teens said they had had sex by age 16, and in 2016, 41% had.

"I think you can call this the cautious generation," said Bill Albert, spokesman for the National Campaign to Prevent Teen and Unplanned Pregnancy. Other attribute the fall to being on cell phones and playing video games as the preferred entertainment today.

Bible World

JEZREEL AND JEHU:

Jehu was the tenth king of Israel, and it was the ending of his dynasty in Jezreel that Hosea referred to in naming his first son.

The evil eighth king of Israel, Ahab, built an ivory palace in Jezreel (1 Kings 21:1). He had a neighbor, Naboth, with a field he wanted, and pouted because Naboth wouldn't sell it to him. His notorious wife, Jezebel, had Naboth killed so her husband could have his field.

Jezebel, introduced worship of Baal into Israel as well as the orgies of the goddess Ashtoreth Her husband, King Ahab, had a temple to Baal built in Samaria. She regularly had 450 Baal priests eat at her table. She persecuted followers of God and killed all God's prophets she could find, except 100 who were hidden by Obadiah (1 Kings 18:4; 19:14). Elijah then challenged hundreds of her prophets on Mount Carmel (1 Kings 18) and won when God brought down fire from heaven to burn up the water-laden sacrifice of Elijah. Then Jezebel's soldiers hunted him down to kill him.

Ahab was killed in battle, and his son, Joram, became the ninth king of Israel, continuing to live in the ivory palace in Jezreel with Queen Mother Jezebel. Jehu, a soldier in Ahab's army, was secretly anointed the new king by Elijah. Jehu had Jezebel killed by being thrown out the window of the palace tower (2 Kings 9:7,30-37). He also ordered killed all the Baal priests and worshippers who assembled in the temple to Baal. Then he broke down the image of Baal and parts of the temple, and turned the rest of it into an outhouse (2 Kings 10:18-28).

Jehu also killed Ahab's son, King Joram, and had his body thrown in the field of Naboth at Jezreel. Ahab had 70 more sons in Samaria. Jehu appealed to their servants to kill them, which they did. Then he had their heads transported to Jezreel where they were put in two piles by the city gate (2 Kings 10:1-11). Thus the idol worship Jezebel had introduced was finally avenged in Jezreel.

However, Jehu continued to worship the Egyptian calf, and to maintain temples at Bethel and Dan. God said he would destroy his dynasty, but not in his lifetime because of what he had done to end Ahab's dynasty and Baal worship. However, during Jehu's reign, the tribes of Gad, Reuben, and Manassah were captured by the Syrians.

Interestingly, God often used evil nations and people to do his avenging. God allowed the evil Assyrians to punish the Northern Kingdom for their idolatry, then punished them for their evil ways. God allowed the evil Babylonians to punish the Southern Kingdom for their idolatry, then punished them for their evil ways. God allowed evil Jehu to punish Ahab's house for Baal worship, then pronounced vengeance on Jehu's dynasty for what he did in Jezreel (Hosea 1:4).

POLITICAL/RELIGIOUS EVENTS DURING HOSEA'S LIFE:

Hosea lived in the Northern Kingdom after ten of the twelve Tribes of Israel broke away. After that, the southern half was usually called Judah because the tribe of Judah was the largest tribe in it. The northern half was usually called Israel, or Ephraim because Ephraim was the largest tribe in it. The two halves had their own kings.

Because the Temple was in the southern half in Jerusalem of Judah, and the northern kings didn't want their people to be swayed by southern influences, the northern kingdom went back to the calf worship of Egypt. They also accepted other idols as gods too (1 Kings 12:28).

Jehu's son, Jehoahaz, reigned as king 17 years. He maintained the calf worship. Elisha lived during his time. The king of Syria further weakened the kingdom by reducing his army to only ten chariots, fifty horsemen, and 10,000 foot soldiers. He asked God to help him, which God agreed to do, but in his son's reign (2 Kings 13:10).

Jehoahaz's son was Joram and he reigned 16 years. Although he continued worshipping the calves at Bethel and Dan, he respected Elisha and wept over him when he became deathly ill. Elisha predicted he would have three victorious battles against Syria. He also killed the king of Judah in battle.

Joram's son was Jeroboam II who was reigning during Hosea's lifetime. As prophesied by Jonah, he was able to restore the three tribes Syria had taken from Israel, and added other territories of Syria to his kingdom. The kingdom flourished and people were rich, but neglected the poor. Amos, who prophesied during this time rebuked Jeroboam for this.

Although the Northern Kingdom had two temples for golden calves, the calves were not worshipped as separate gods, but as symbols of Jehovah. "Subsidiary" temples and altars were located at Gilgal and Beersheba (Amos 4:4; 5:5; 8:14). Amos denounced the worshippers as hypocrites. Late in his reign, Isaiah prophesied the final destruction of Israel by the Assyrians because of their idol worship. Hosea lived during this time.

Jeroboam's son was Zechariah. He reigned only 6 months and was assassinated by the next king. Thus ended the dynasty of Jehu. Forty years later, Israel was taken captive by the Assyrians and forever became known as the "Lost Tribe of Israel."

Introducing the Lesson

Young people are losing their virginity at younger and younger ages. We might wonder what is motivating these children. **Display WHEN ARE AMERICAN CHILDREN LOSING THEIR IDENTITY.** Discuss briefly, then **Display WHAT CAUSES AN ELEMENTARY-SCHOOL CHILD TO ENGAGE IN SEX and discuss.**

How many are virgins when they marry? Our nation's average is 29%. The highest percent, believe it or not, of those who are virgins when they marry (36%) live in New York City and Washington, D. C. The lowest percent (21%) live in the western cattle areas and along the Pacific coast. This was the average thirty years ago and is still the average.

Hosea knowingly married a prostitute and daughter of a prostitute. Possibly he thought he could reform Gomer. But it didn't happen. For marriages to work, we need the proper foundation on which to build them.

Discussion Questions

1. **Tell of someone you know who lost their conscience (no names please).**

    <u>1 Timothy 4:1,2</u>: We can be seduced to believe lies about our actions. At first it may hurt our conscience, but the more we do the wrong things and like it, the less it will bother us. Eventually our hearts are covered with scar tissue and we have no feeling left as to the action's rightness or wrongness.

    <u>Possible Class Response</u>: People do not necessarily lose their conscience about everything. They may steal office supplies from work and say they deserve it because

their pay is too low. They may criticize other people all the time and say they deserve it because someone needs to straighten them out. They may be having an extra-marital affair and say their spouse doesn't give them the attention they deserve.

2. **Why is a marriage based on promises of future changes practically doomed to failure in the first place?**

    Proverbs 5:3,4: A suitor you don't really know very well can promise anything to get you to marry him, and then not do any of it.

    Proverbs 27:6: The person you think loves you may actually be your enemy; your friends will try to tell you the truth, even if it hurts.

    Proverbs 26:28: When someone lies to you, it means they don't really love you but rather they hate you. They can destroy you.

    Possible Class Response: People usually don't really change. When we think how difficult it would be for us to change an attitude or way of life, we can understand how difficult it would be for anyone else to change either. We need to watch their actions and not just listen to their words. If the prospective bride or groom can't give up seeing other men or women before marriage, they are not likely to after marriage either.

3. **How can different religious backgrounds create yet another terrible hardship on a marriage?**

    2 Corinthians 6:14: If you marry someone who prefers to follow their religious traditions or none at all instead of searching the scriptures, they will not understand your way of thinking and acting; your communication and activities will often be opposites.

    Possible Class Response: On Sunday morning, you will attend different places of worship and have a different group of friends. Or, one of you will attend church and have friends there, and the other will stay home and make friends among those who prefer recreation and entertainment on Sundays. Also, the latter will try to lure you to stay home "just this once" to sleep in, go to a company picnic, go camping with friends, etc.

4. **When we see a friend considering marriage to someone with an already troubled life, what could we say or do? If the wedding occurs anyway, should we stay away from it or attend?**

    Proverbs 17:17: Friends love each other no matter what happens. God gives us families to stand by each other, even in bad times.

    Possible Class Response: We can tell our friend they should not marry someone with a troubled life, hoping they can help them change. They should leave that up to less emotionally involved friends and counselors. We can tell our friend that they will have children someday, and do they want this person to be the father/mother of their children?

Children become like their parents; do they want their children to become like this prospective mate? Their soul and the souls of their children are too valuable to take chances with by marrying someone who could destroy them. We can assure them there is a Christian or someone who wants to be a Christian out there that needs a husband or wife like them. If they insist on marrying anyway, tell them you disagree, but will stand by them no matter what and will attend the wedding wishing them well.

5. **What is likely to happen to a marriage based on looks and material things, and with all the giving coming from only one side?**

    Ezekiel 16:1-32: When Jerusalem was born, she was abandoned to die. But when God saw her, he covered her up, washed her, clothed her in silks and ornaments and married her (1-14). Then her beauty "went to her head" and she began seducing other gods (15,26,28,29,32).

    Possible Class Response: When things get difficult or boring, the one who did all the receiving will just go elsewhere to fill their needs. A marriage must be based on both giving 100%, always thinking of the other person, a "mutual admiration society."

6. **What are some of the excuses unfaithful husbands or wives use today (Proverbs 12:20a)?**

    Gomer at first seemed to hide her infidelity and probably used various excuses to go into town to her lovers.

    Proverbs 12:20a: People who imagine bad things to do also scheme the things they will say to cover up what they're doing.

    Possible Class Response: I had to work late. I have to have a night out with the boys every week. My extra money is going into a special savings account for us. You're imagining things. You're just jealous/paranoid. You need psychological help.

7. **Why do people refuse to acknowledge the signs?**

    We know that Hosea did not acknowledge his wife's unfaithfulness at first by the names he gave his children.

    Proverbs 17:9: When you love someone, you try to think of only the good they do, not the bad. When you love someone, you refuse to believe anything bad about them unless it is proven to you. Even then, you don't repeat it to anyone in an effort to cover up for them.

    Possible Class Response: They do not want to break up the marriage they had planned to last for a lifetime. They do not want to break up the family. They do not want to believe their husband doesn't love them anymore. They hope it is a one-time fling that will die out and never be repeated. They are afraid that if they face their husband with the facts, he won't have to hide it anymore and will just go ahead and finish leaving her. They're afraid that if they confront their husband, irreversible things will be said that could finish destroying their marriage.

8. **How can having a baby bring couples closer?**

   Psalm 139:13-17: A little baby is so amazing with all its fingers and toes, its bright eyes, its little nose. A little baby must be God's masterpiece!

   Possible Class Response: A new baby created by a couple and given life by God can give them something in common that they both love. It can remind them how powerful love truly is. It can help them see each other in a new light, in a new role. People are generally more gentle around babies, and seeing that gentleness in each other can make it overflow into both their hearts.

9. **What is a marriage like with one a "party-goer" and self-centered, and the other person serious and concerned about others? How can such differences be reconciled? How long might it take?**

   1 Corinthians 7:12-16: The example of a Christian wife going out of her way to please her husband could be exactly what is needed for a husband to see that Christ wants what is best for people. He may become a Christian because of her example.

   Possible Class Response: The two have different friends and want to do different things for entertainment. Usually name-calling and ridiculing follow. A wife might ask a couple their age with her husband's interests to stop by a few minutes one day and introduce themselves without talking religion. If her husband likes the man, they could begin doing some entertaining things together. Sometimes the husband is converted in a few months this way. Sometimes it occurs after they've been married 50 years. Sometimes it never happens.

Good Work

Make a list of how to be "wise as serpents and harmless as doves" in choosing a marriage partner.

BEFORE CLASS:

A1. FOR LARGE AND MEDIUM CONGREGATIONS:

   Alternative One: Talk to the teacher(s) of your congregation's high school and/or college class. Tell them what you want to do and ask in what format they prefer the list: (a) one each on an index card; (b) the entire list photocopied for everyone; (c) what to do and what not to do.

   Alternative Two: If your congregation has a counselor on its staff, ask if you could give him the list of suggestions to give couples who come in for counseling.

A2. FOR SMALL CONGREGATIONS:

   Alternate One: Call a local high school counselor and ask if your class's suggestions could be used in a class on relationships, or given to couples who come in for counseling.

 <u>Alternative Two</u>: Call a private marriage counselor and ask if you could send your class's list of suggestions to give couples who come in for counseling.

B. Obtain enough index cards for two per student.

DURING CLASS:

"We've been studying about selecting a marriage partner who is not a Christian. Marriage is difficult even under the best of circumstances. There are young people all around us in the process of making these life-time decisions."

Hand out a stack of index cards. "I'd like each of you to take one or more index cards and write one suggestion on each one that you would give a young couple either considering marriage or in a new marriage. They will be given to....[whoever you decide on].

"You will have about five minutes to write your suggestions. Let's all be quiet now and allow each other to think and write. When you are done, give your cards to me, then offer a silent prayer for our young people or someone you know in a difficult marriage while the others finish."

Concluding Remarks

When time is up and while the slower writers complete their notes, sing one verse of a song, possibly one of the following:

1. *Take My Life and Let it Be*
2. *Let the Beauty of Jesus Be Seen in Me*
3. *How Sweet, How Heavenly is the Sight*
4. *Make Me a Channel of Blessing*

In a few moments, your students will be going back home, perhaps to a difficult marriage. But don't send them home depressed. End your class upbeat. Smile!

(Wait for one or two quick replies to each of the following.) "In a few words, what advice would you give young people who

1. Claim their future mate will change after they're married?
2. Are going to marry non-Christians despite all warnings?
3. Invite you to such a wedding?
4. Need to get acquainted with couples who attend church?

Have a closing prayer and remember the young people.

WHEN ARE AMERICAN CHILDREN
LOSING THEIR VIRGINITY?

**One-fifth lose their virginity
by the age of 13.**

**Two-thirds lose their virginity
by the age of 16.**

**Three-fourths lose their virginity
by the age of 25.**

Source: The Day America Told the Truth, by James Patterson and Peter Kim and CBN News 2016.

WHAT CAUSES AN ELEMENTARY-SCHOOL CHILD TO ENGAGE IN SEX?

Not love
Not physical urges

but

PEER PRESSURE

fed by
popular songs
and possibly incest

Source: *The Day America Told the Truth* by James Patterson and Peter Kim

Unfaithful

Lesson Two: Coping with a Tumultuous Marriage

Lesson Aim

- ♥ FACE UNFAITHFULNESS
- ♥ TRY TO HOLD IT TOGETHER

Scripture Outline

<u>Hosea 1:6,7</u>: The Israelites continue to commit spiritual adultery, and Hosea suspects Gomer is too. Gomer's and Hosea's second child is a daughter. So God names her Loru-Hamah as a warning to Israel that he will no longer have mercy, but will destroy her.

<u>Hosea 1:8-11</u>: Gomer's and Hosea's third child is a son. If each child was weaned after three years and there was nearly a year pregnancy, the younger children would be about 4 and 8 by now. Still the Israelites continue to worship other gods, and by this time it is obvious to Hosea that Gomer is a prostitute. So God names their son Lo-Ammi meaning, "You are not mine."

<u>Hosea 4 and 5</u>: God mourns for his own wife, Israel, who continues to commit adultery against him with other gods.

<u>Hosea 6-12</u>: God asks Israel to repent and renew her marriage vows.

Today's World

The New York Times investigated in 2016 why people bother to get married since 66% of people that Pew Research interviewed said sex outside of marriage didn't matter, and having children outside of marriage is becoming more common. According to a report by the National Marriage Project at the University of Virginia, 47 percent of American women who give birth in their 20s are unmarried at the time.

Many of today's young professionals marry as a status symbol of stability. They have often lived together and waited until both had good jobs and a nice apartment.

According to the National Center for Family and Marriage Research, 88 percent of

35- to 44-year-old women with four-year college degrees have married, compared with 79 percent of those without high-school diplomas. In fact, young adults without college degrees are increasingly likely to put off marriage and have their first children in cohabiting relationships, sometimes years before they marry. Nearly all of the increase in childbearing outside of marriage in the last two decades is from births to cohabiting couples, most without college degrees, rather than to single mothers.

So, how stable are these marriages? The Huffington Post reported in 2016 that 67% of married women are seeking an affair. But they have no desire to divorce. They claim they still love their husbands. At the same time, the percent of men who want affairs remains at 50%. They, too, claim to love their wives and do not want a divorce.

Bible World

GOLDEN CALF WORSHIP IN HOSEA'S TIME:

The primary idol of the Northern Kingdom of Israel after its split from the south was the calf. The calf or bull was worshipped as sacred in many Far East and Middle East nations. The one adopted by the Israelites was from Egypt (Joshua 24:14). The sacred bulls were Apis, Basis and Mnevis, and the sacred cows were Isis and Athor. Nature, and not the personal Creator God, was symbolized by bulls and calves.

Aaron built the first golden calf and announced, "Behold, the gods who brought you out of the land of Egypt" (Exodus 32:4). It is interesting that, in Moses' absence when the Israelites asked for a god, and Aaron obliged them, it seemed to be a form of compromise. For the word he used for "gods" is from the Hebrew Elohim, a title only used for Jehovah. He had made an image to represent Jehovah. In fact, he announced that the next day there would be a feast to Jehovah. Therefore, he was not breaking the first commandment not to worship other gods, but the second commandment to not make any graven images. This then led to worshipping the sun, moon and stars (Acts 7:40-42).

Apparently, the weak Israelites yearned for some visible symbol of their unseen Jehovah. Psalm 106:19,20 says they made a calf and changed their [God's] glory to the similitude of an ox.

Jeroboam, the first king of the Northern Kingdom, was exiled to Egypt before his ascension to the throne. There he would have become very familiar with the calves. He it was who built them in Israel so his subjects wouldn't return to Jerusalem to worship and turn against him (1 Kings 12:26-29). He even announced the same thing Aaron had, "Behold, your gods [Elohim] which brought you up out of the land of Egypt!"

Shortly thereafter, 1 Kings 13:1-5,33 says a prophet of God went to Jeroboam who was offering incense in Bethel. There he declared that a future king would offer the bones of these illegal priests on that same altar. Yet the northern kings continued to consult the prophets of the calves who regarded themselves as prophets of Jehovah (1 Kings 22:5,6).

Jeremiah compared the golden calf at Bethel to the idols of Chemosh in Moab (48:13). Amos said God would destroy the altar at Bethel (3:14), condemned both temples at Bethel and Gilgal where priests offered sacrifices every morning and people brought their tithes (4:4), and said the people of Samaria would fall because of it.

Hosea prophesied against the calf: "Throw out your calf-idol, O Samaria! My anger burns against them. How long will they be incapable of purity. They are from Israel! This calf a craftsman has made it; it is not God. It will be broken in pieces, that calf of Samaria (8:5,6). The people who live in Samaria fear for the calf-idol of Beth-aven. Its people will mourn over it, so will its idolatrous priests, those who had rejoiced over its splendor, because it is taken from them into exile. It will be carried to Assyria as tribute for the great king. Ephraim will be disgraced; Israel will be ashamed of its wooden idols (10:5,6). Is Gilead wicked? Its people are worthless! Do they sacrifice bulls in Gilgal? Their altars will be like piles of stones on a plowed field (12:11). Now they sin more and more; they make idols for themselves from their silver, cleverly fashioned images, all of them the work of craftsmen. It is said of these people, 'They offer human sacrifice and kiss the calf-idols' (13:2).

A king of Assyria took home with him the golden calf at Dan (2 Kings 15:29), and a later king of Assyria took the other golden calf at Bethel (2 Kings 17:6). The altars to the calves were destroyed by a king of Judah (2 Kings 23:4,15-20) after he dug up and burned the bones of the priests on them.

BAAL WORSHIP IN HOSEA'S TIME:

Hosea lamented, " 'She has not acknowledged that I was the one who gave her the grain, the new wine and oil, who lavished on her the silver and gold which they used for Baal....I will punish her for the days she burned incense to the Baals; she decked herself with rings and jewelry, and went after her lovers, but me she forgot,' declares the Lord....I will remove the names of the Baals from her lips; no longer will their names be invoked" (2:8,13,17).

"The more I called Israel, the further they went from me. They sacrificed to the Baals and they burned incense to images (11:2). When Ephraim spoke, men trembled; he was exalted in Israel. But he became guilty of Baal worship and died. Now they sin more and more; they make idols for themselves from their silver, cleverly fashioned images, all of them the work of craftsmen. It is said of these people, 'They offer human sacrifice and kiss the calf-idols'" (13:1,2).

When Israel was finally taken into captivity forever, 40 years after Hosea prophesied, it was written that Israel "forsook all the commands of the Lord their God and made for themselves two idols cast in the shape of calves, and an Asherah pole. They bowed down to all the starry hosts, and they worshipped Baal. They sacrificed their sons and daughters in the fire. They practiced divination and sorcery and sold themselves to do evil in the eyes of the Lord, provoking him to anger" (2 Kings 17:16f).

Places of worship were erected on hills where sometimes they offered human sacrifices (Jeremiah 19:5). The worshippers wore a particular kind of garment (2 Kings 10:22). They gashed themselves with knives at times to move his pity (1 Kings 18:26-28).

Baal's power was represented by the sun (2 Kings 23:5) and his female counterpart, Ashtoreth's, represented by the moon, Venus, and the stars. Monuments erected to Baal on hills were stone pillars, symbolizing his strength. Trees (in sacred groves) represented Ashtoreth's fruitfulness. Both represented procreation; Baal in vegetation, Ashtoreth in animals and humans.

The Baals and Ashtoreths were seen in the plural more than singular since they represented all of creation or nature. Therefore, they could be represented in almost any form and called by other names, even the name of Jehovah. Because of this, it was relatively easy for the Israelites to be drawn to this type of worship. The golden calves erected in Samaria seem to eventually have taken on an identity with Ashtoreth and sometimes Baal. (See the scriptures above.)

Introducing the Lesson

Today we're going to talk further about a difficult topic: Adultery. Although our discussion will center primarily around handling the pain if a husband has an affair, there is also the possibility of the wife having the affair. Just as we seldom if ever know when our friends are having marital problems, we almost never know if or which one is having an affair.

Today's lesson talks about trying to work through the problems and keep the marriage together. Based on a survey in the early 1990s and published in *The Day America Told the Truth*, on the average, 31 percent of Americans commit adultery, and the average relationship lasts one year. Further, 67% of all American married people are tempted at least once a week.

God's people were committing spiritual adultery against him as their spiritual husband. We see this carried forward in the New Testament when the church is called the bride and wife of Christ. God forgave and forgave, for he loved Israel.

Discussion Questions

10. **In what circumstances might children help? Why are children usually not the answer (Proverbs 11:29; Colossians 3:21)?**

    Proverbs 11:29: Those who cause trouble in their own house will end up with nothing and no one.

    Possible Class Response: Children sometimes mature people and make them reevaluate their priorities. They suddenly realize there is a little one depending on them for stability and support and physical needs. However, quite often the added responsibility makes an unstable person run from their obligations even more. They can even blame the child for their problems. And they may end up taking out their frustrations on the child.

11. **What do you think is a woman's motivation for going overboard with her**

makeup?

Ezekiel 23:40-44: These two sisters "painted their eyes and decked [themselves] with ornaments" in order to get the attention of strange men, and to commit adultery with them.

Possible Class Response: She feels she does not have the kind of love from a man that she wants. This may or may not be true. She feels incomplete without the love and admiration of a man/men. She is turning outward to find the love she wants to feel inwardly. She feels she is not being noticed, and is willing to do whatever is necessary to be noticed.

12. **Give some practical suggestions of substitutes and wholesome activities that could be followed by a woman who craves excitement?**

    Proverbs 7:10,11: This prostitute is described as loud, with stand-out-in-the-crowd clothing, and out on the street corner instead of at home.

    Possible Class Response: She could participate in rallies against abortion. She could organize parties for Sunday School classes so their teachers wouldn't have to do it. She could organize retreats for the ladies or couples of the congregation. She could teach students through World Bible Class. She could organize welcome potlucks for visitors or new members.

13. **What are the signs and symptoms of the hurt? Give some scriptures from the Psalms that could help a person through this terrible time.**

    Gradually Hosea began to acknowledge that his wife was being unfaithful. The King James Version of the Bible translates his new baby daughter's name as "not having obtained mercy" (1:6). Mercy is defined as "undeserved favor". He was not yet rejecting his wife, but only withholding favor. A betrayed marriage partner maintains the love but begins to withdraw because of hurt.

Psalm 18:	I will love you, O Lord, my strength....
Psalm 23:	The Lord is my shepherd....
Psalm 25:	Unto you, O Lord, do I lift up my soul....
Psalm 37:	Fret not yourself because of evildoers....
Psalm 40:	I waited patiently for the Lord....
Psalm 46:	God is our refuge and strength....
Psalm 56:	Be merciful...for man would swallow me; fighting daily...
Psalm 69:	Save me, O God; for the waters are come into my soul....
Psalm 71:	In you I put my trust; let me never be put to confusion....
Psalm 94:	O Lord God to whom vengeance belongs....
Psalm 121:	I will lift up my eyes...from whence comes my help....
Psalm 124:	If it had not been the Lord who was on our side....
Psalm 139:	O Lord, you have searched me and known me....

    Possible Class Response: The signs of the hurt are difficult to see if she is trying to hide them from friends. But she may become withdrawn and quit coming to church functions, especially coupled ones. She may become suspicious of other women.

Friends may see her look at her husband with eyes of sorrow. She may come to tears easily. She may compliment couples she knows on how loving they are to each other. She may push her husband's hand away when he tries to touch her. She may hang on to her husband more than usual in public.

14. **Give some examples of how a love for truth can be a deterrent to sin.**

    Hosea 2:7, 12, 13 seems to indicate that Gomer was having illicit affairs but gradually lost the interest of the men, possibly due to aging. So later she became a prostitute and was paid by individuals, and in Baal worship. She had to make up more and more stories to explain to her husband why she was gone so much and where her "rewards" or "goods for services rendered" were coming from.

    John 8:44: Satan is the father of liars.

    Possible Class Response: If telling the truth in all matters is important to us, we will avoid doing things we will be embarrassed over, have to confess and ask forgiveness for.

15. **Discuss what is necessary to forgive someone who shows no signs of changing. Try using "hating the sin but loving the sinner" as a possible guide. Tell what attitude steps must be taken.**

    This betrayed partner must have agonized alone with a pain worse than losing a mate by death. He must have truly experienced Jesus' command to forgive seventy times seven.

    Matthew 18:22: Jesus told his followers they must forgive 70 x 7. If 3 represents heaven (trinity) and 4 represents earth (4 winds), and 10 represents all-inclusiveness, then we must forgive a person no matter where they are and what they are doing, and do so indefinitely.

    Possible Class Response: This is extremely difficult. We might think of the infinite times God has forgiven us. We should think of the sin as against God instead of against us. We can defend God's hurt feelings with a sort of "righteous indignation" that does not involve self-destructive emotions as much as when we defend our hurt feelings.

16. **If we cannot make peace with the unfaithful partner, how can we still make peace with ourselves during such a time?**

    Hebrews 12:14,15: We must be at peace with all people. Not granting grace and mercy is the root of bitterness.

    Philippians 4:8: Center your thoughts on whatever is true, honest, just, pure, lovely, of good report, or virtuous.

    Possible Class Response: We should forgive so we can release that sin from our minds and the possible physical side effects it can create. An unforgiving woman can become bitter and it eats away at her physically and emotionally and spiritually. For her own sake, she must forgive and let go of her husband's sin each and every time he does it.

We can reinforce our own egos by reminding ourselves of God's unending love, and by associating with Christians as much as possible. We can read Psalms of praise to God and center our lives on positive things.

17.   Suggest some releases that do not hurt anyone.

Emotions are either very high or are buried during such a marriage. Since refusing to acknowledge the emotional infection is dangerous, the negative emotions must be let out.

Ephesians 4:26: Be angry and sin not.

Possible Class Response: She can join an aerobics class. She can jog. She can play handball and hit the ball as hard as she wants. She can clean house and mow her lawn or the church's lawn. She can become a scout leader.

Good Work

Write notes of encouragement, sympathy, and/or prayer to someone going through the possibility of a future separation or divorce.

BEFORE CLASS:

A1.   FOR LARGE AND MEDIUM CONGREGATIONS: Ask your minister or church counselor if the letters can be passed on to them.

A2.   FOR SMALL CONGREGATIONS: Contact a marriage counselor in the phone book and ask if your notes can be passed on by them to those they are counseling.

B.   Obtain local phone books and church directories.

C.   Obtain envelopes and stationery (half sheet of bond paper).

D.   Write the following on the blackboard or poster board:

For couples not sure if they should separate: "Although I do not know you by name [if not a personal friend], I wanted to say that marriage is very difficult for everyone. There is no one out there who can make a good marriage without patient hard work. My prayer for you is that you will find the emotional strength to keep trying to hold your marriage together. It's truly worth it. Pray together! Its power will amaze you. God's love can be your answer."

For couples who have already irreconcilably separated: "I am so sorry your marriage has not worked out for you. I know you intended it to last for your entire life. It is like an amputation, for you once loved your mate and still may. I wish I could take the pain away for you. There is a book in the Bible about a troubled marriage—Hosea in the O.T. God understands what you're going through and he loves you both."

DURING CLASS:

"We've been studying about troubled marriages. Even the 'ideal' marriage is difficult. Some of you may have had arguments with your husbands just this morning or last night. It touches us all. It is more serious for some."

Hand out stationery and envelopes. "If you know someone having marriage problems and they know you know, take this time to send them a note. I have some church directories and phone books for addresses. If you don't know anyone, _____, who does marriage counseling, has said s/he will pass your notes along to their counselees.

"If you don't know what to say, I have written a couple suggestions on the board. Feel free to use them. You will have about eight minutes. Let's all be quiet now and allow each other to think and write. When you are done, give your addressed envelopes to me to mail, then offer a silent prayer for this couple while the others finish.

Concluding Remarks

When time is up and while the slower writers complete their notes, sing one verse of a song, possibly one of the following:

1. *More Holiness Give Me*
2. *Take Time to Be Holy*
3. *Nearer My God to Thee*
4. *Close to Thee*

In a few moments, your students will be going back home, possibly to a troubled marriage or one that has already been ended. Send them home with hope and their egos built up. Smile!

(Wait for one or two quick replies to each of the following.) "In a few words, what would you advise a woman to do....,

1. Who wants excitement in her life?
2. To help her forgive and let go?
3. To build up her ego?
4. To let out her negative emotions?

Have a closing prayer and remember the marriages of those in your class and those you wrote.

Unfaithful

Lesson Three: Salvaging an Impossible Marriage

Lesson Aim
- ♥ **KNOW THE PRICE OF ONE'S SOUL**
- ♥ **COPE WITH MARRIAGE BREAKDOWN**

Scripture Outline

<u>Hosea 2:1-5</u>: Gomer has moved out of the house. Hosea sends his three children to go tell their mother he is divorcing her because of her adulteries and prostitutions.

<u>Hosea 2:6,7</u>: Hosea believes that when her lovers finally tire of her she will return to him.

<u>Hosea 2:8</u>: Hosea anonymously sends Gomer food and clothing and jewelry—probably for several years; he still cares for her, even when she doesn't love Hosea any more.

<u>Hosea 2:9-13</u>: That apparently doesn't work. So Hosea quits trying to support his ex-wife hoping she will return to him when she gets poor enough.

<u>Hosea 2:14-23</u>: Again years pass (remember the reigns of kings during these events in 1:1). Eventually Gomer is not even wanted as a prostitute and is to be sold as a slave. Unbelievably, Hosea wants her back, even as God wants Israel back. Hosea wants to betroth Gomer to himself forever (v.19).

<u>Hosea 3:1,2</u>: Hosea goes to the auction block and buys Gomer for 15 pieces of silver, the price of a slave.

<u>Hosea 3:3-5</u>: Hosea takes Gomer home with him, but as a slave (representing Israel's slavery in Assyria) and not a wife until she is able to repent. He is willing to take her back to himself as a wife.

<u>(Hosea 4-12</u>: See Lesson Two)

<u>Hosea 13</u>: God asks Israel to repent.

<u>Hosea 14</u>: Verse 4: "I will love [you] freely; for my anger is turned away." (Regrettably, Israel never repented, so the "remarriage" to God never took place.)

Today's World

In 2013 Schock and Bean conducted a survey of married people and found that as many as 73 percent said they are "making do" in their relationship. And 46 percent said they'd leave their spouse or partner to be with their true love.

According to *Huffington Post* in 2016, the number one reason for divorce is marrying for the wrong reason. Forty-four percent of Americans believe most marriages will end in divorce, and 60 percent think there's a possibility that, no matter how happy they are, their marriage might end in divorce.

An earlier research broke this down into subcategories. Also, 58% are divorced due to infidelity.

Bible World

PROSTITUTION:

Anthropologists have found that prostitution overall did not exist among primitive and rural communities. It did, however, exist in the more progressive and advanced cities. There the prostitution of unmarried girls seems to have been a common practice for usually three reasons: As a ceremony to sacrifice one's virginity, as a rite to earn a dowry, as a religious duty serving a goddess.

In Babylon at the eastern edge of the Middle East, Phoenicia/Canaan at the western edge of the Middle East, and Cyprus in the Mediterranean, women prostituted themselves as a religious duty at the temple of a goddess whose name varied with the locality, but was always the "Mother Goddess." Ashtoreth, the female counterpart of Baal, was usually this goddess in Jewish idolatry.

Herodotus recorded the Babylonian custom of requiring every woman, rich or poor, to sit in the temple of Ishtar and have intercourse with a stranger who signified his choice by throwing a silver coin of no matter how small value into her lap. The woman had then to accept the coin and have intercourse with the stranger. Once the rite had been observed, the woman was absolved from her obligations to the goddess. Elsewhere in the Middle East, however, prostitution was a permanent

service in a temple. The practice was considered a solemn religious duty.

In cases where prostitution was a rite of sacrificing one's virginity, the local priest was the one to whom she made her sacrifice.

In the huge temple of Aphrodite (Venus) in Corinth, there was a large staff of prostitutes in attendance to accommodate sailors frequenting the port. The priests of the temple pocketed the money. The brothel as we know it today seems to have taken over when temple prostitution declined.

In ancient Athens, brothels were run by the state and confined to certain parts of the city. They were forbidden in superior parts of the town. Prostitutes were required to wear a distinctive dress, and were not allowed to take part in religious services. However, there were independent prostitutes of the upper class who were also admired for their intellect.

In ancient Rome, female virtue was highly honored and preserved. Prostitution was considered disgraceful. Though not illegal, prostitutes were placed under stringent control, required to register with the police, had to wear distinctive dress and to dye their hair or wear yellow wigs, and were kept from various civil privileges. The state taxed prostitutes. In 4th century Rome, Theodosius closed down brothels and offered to pay out of his own pocket, the lost revenue.

The Jews stood apart from their surrounding peoples. Jewish fathers were forbidden to turn their daughters into prostitutes (Leviticus 19:29), and the daughters of Israel were forbidden to become prostitutes (Deuteronomy 23:17), but no specific penalty was attached to disobedience of this except in the case of a priest's daughter who was to be burned (Leviticus 21:9). Proverbs is full of warnings for young men not to go to prostitutes.

In Biblical history, Judah went to what he thought was a harlot, but ended up being his daughter-in-law. Rahab, who saved the twelve Israelite spies in Canaan, was a harlot. One of the Judges of Israel,

Jephthah, was the son of a harlot. Samson went to a harlot.

Jehovah called Israel harlots when they went "whoring" after other gods. The words translated "harlot" and "whore" in the Bible usually came from the same Hebrew or Greek word meaning fornication.

THE BRIDE OF GOD/CHRIST:

Isaiah said that their Creator was the husband of Israel (54:5,6) and he rejoiced over Israel as a bridegroom rejoices over his bride (61:10; 62:5). The entire book of Hosea is dedicated to this idea.

Trying one last time to warn the Israelites of their coming destruction, Jeremiah said the Israelites went by troops into the temples of idols' prostitutes and committed adultery against him (5:7). He went on to say that women who are divorced and go to other men, then want to return to their first husband, were like Israel who went after many lovers and then wanted to return to God (3:1,20), for they had done this over and over for hundreds of years since God brought them out of Egypt.

Ezekiel, who was later taken with the southern kingdom into Babylon, tried a last-minute warning. He said that the people had been like prostitutes and committed adultery against God by giving offerings to idols and building temples to them like brothels; so now, God was going to stone them and leave them for dead (16:30-43). And then when Ezekiel's wife died, God did not allow Ezekiel to cry so that he would understand just what God was going through and get this message across to the people (24:16-18).

Then something wonderful happened in the New Testament! Christ came and told us we were his bride! We could start all over again, as though all those terrible things in the Old Testament never happened! In Matthew 9:15 he said as long as our bridegroom was with us, we were happy. In John 14 he said he was going to prepare a permanent home for us. But even in his absence, Ephesians 5:23 tells us (the church, the Bride of Christ) he loves very much. And finally, in Revelation 19:7 we are told at the end of the world as we know it, our wedding feast will take place. The church is the bride, adorned for her husband (Revelation 21:2,9). On the very last page of our Bible it says, "The Spirit and the bride say, 'Come,' to which Jesus replied, 'Surely, I come quickly'" (Revelation 22:17,20).

Introducing the Lesson

The main reason given for divorce in America today is communication problems. Both husbands and wives complain they want to express their feelings and desires, but the other one won't let them. They also want their spouse to do so. **Display chart REASONS FOR DIVORCE IN AMERICA and discuss.**

God hates divorce, but allows it when fornication (any kind of sexual sin) takes place (Matthew 19:7-9). God himself experienced divorce with his people, and he knows the pain. God resisted it, but finally gave in to divorcing the Israelites because they wouldn't stop their adulterous idolatry. Today, many people keep a marriage together when one partner strays once or twice in a marriage; they forgive each other and go on with their lives. That is the best way.

But there are situations where the spouse never stops straying. Bitterness rises up, even to the point of wishing the offender were dead. Bitterness can destroy our souls. There is a point that we must put our eternal destiny ahead of a destructive marriage.

How do couples communicate after the divorce? Hosea waited for her, because he believed someday she would repent. It did happen late in their lives when she had lost her good looks and no one wanted her anymore. Most people can't do this. God was not willing to wait for the Northern Kingdom to repent during their captivity in Assyria, so left them there forever. He was, however, willing to wait for the Southern Kingdom to repent during their captivity in Babylon, so brought them back to Jerusalem.

Today we're going to talk about going through a divorce and what may follow.

Discussion Questions

18. At what point should a person pursue a divorce in order to save one's own soul?

The decision to divorce is a terrible one, separating from someone once loved with whom dreams were dreamed, children were created, and with whom there were at least some happy times. It is like pulling the switch on a life support system and letting the nearly-dead complete the death. God did not like divorce but allowed it for fornication as a way out.

1 Corinthians 10:13: When temptation becomes too great, God allows a way out before we sin.

Possible Class Response: God did not like divorce but allowed it as a way out. (There are various scriptures covering these allowances, which is an additional study.) Many women live with an adulterous husband and can forgive him and go on with her life. But if the circumstance goes beyond human ability to live with the hypocrisy, she may find herself losing her temper often, taking her frustrations out on innocent children, turning her back on the church, or wishing he were dead. She could lose her soul doing these things. When she reaches the point she believes she would lose her soul staying in the marriage, she should reconsider her priorities.

19. **After the divorce, how can a person secretly do things for the ex-partner out of concern but not as a gesture of reconciliation?**

Hosea 2:8: Gomer did not realize Hosea was sending her food and provisions, any more than the Israelites stopped to realize the gold they

were making idols out of and the food they were sacrificing to them were provided them by God.

Possible Class Response: There's not much a woman can do for an ex-husband, especially when he usually makes more money than her. However, if she thinks he needs medical or psychological help, she might send him information in the mail from various organizations. If he is not attending church, she might request that he be put on the bulletin mailing list.

20. **Discuss how people can be so easily fooled about what true happiness is.**

2 Peter 2:13-22: People speak swelling words that are empty to allure people to fleshly lusts. They feast and commit adultery but are unstable wells without water, clouds bumping about aimlessly. They promise people liberty, but they themselves are servants of corruption who eat their own vomit. Darkness of hell is reserved for them.

Possible Class Response: Sin often looks like fun or people wouldn't do it. It is difficult to distinguish what is innocent fun and what is sin without the Bible given to us by our Creator, the one who knows what is best for us. There was a time we were told smoking was wonderful, but gradually it is becoming extinct in the U.S. because we have faced how it was killing us. The more the people commit a sin, the harder it is to distinguish it as a sin. We become victims of mass hypnosis through the media. Often, only years of experience and self-destruction shows sin for what it is, and young people will usually not listen to such advice.

21. **A fool is someone who, if not in word, still has done what in deed? How do you think fear of failure or rejection drives one from peace to a life of turmoil?**

Gomer seemed to be more and more self-destructive. She literally fled from the peace of true love.

Proverbs 10:23: It is fun to a fool to do things that are wrong. They are self-destructive.

Proverbs 14:12: There are things some people do which seem to be right, but God knows that it will only lead to death.

1 John 4:18: People who fear rejection are tormented. Perfect love casts out fear.

Possible Class Response: A fool runs to self-destruction. A fool doesn't say so in words, but their actions speak loud and clear. Shakespeare said a coward dies a thousand times. Those who fear rejection do things to make everyone around them reject them wherever they go. It can even happen in a marriage.

22. **If Hosea had spent the rest of his life licking his wounds, could he have done this? Compare this kind of love with God's love after we reject him by sinning.**

    Years later, Hosea decided Gomer had gone far enough and perhaps now she was ready for the first step back up. He took his first step by remarrying her (2:19) and buying her back—redeeming her (3:2).

    1 John 4:19: We love him because he first loved us.

    Possible Class Response: People who feel sorry for themselves don't usually take the first step toward reconciliation. No matter how many times we sin, God comes running to us with open arms begging us to come back to him.

23. **Could observing a person well past their normal time limit of abstinence from a bad habit help us see if repentance and change had taken place?**

    Hosea 11:8,9; 13:9: Hosea took his adulterous wife back even though he was angry at what she'd done, because he was able to hand her actions and his anger over to God. Hosea saw that she had destroyed herself, and he knew he could help her. "How shall I give you up?"

    Possible Class Response: Sometimes people decide to remarry because the errant ex-spouse says he has changed. A former wife would probably know how long he could go without committing adultery: Six months? A year? Two years? Five years? If he remained faithful during this time, she might possibly consider remarriage.

24. **Is taking a person away from a bad atmosphere helpful or necessary to rejecting the bad ways?**

    1 Corinthians 15:33: Evil companions corrupt good morals.

    Matthew 12:43-45: When people get rid of a bad activity in their lives and don't replace it with something good, the same bad activity will return.

    Possible Class Response: Yes. It may be the husband enjoyed going out for drinks right after work. Expecting this husband who has done this every night for years to suddenly be content to go straight home and sit is unrealistic. Something just as much fun would have to be substituted for right after work, perhaps meeting his wife somewhere before going home.

25. **Should a person who hopes an unfaithful spouse will repent someday—perhaps late in life as Gomer did (Hosea 1:1)—wait for that person or remarry?**

Ecclesiastes 12:13: After spending his whole life chasing after wealth, women, and power, Solomon concludes following God is the entire essence of man.

1 John 5:3: God's commandments are not as difficult as we think.

Matthew 11:28,29: God begs us to come to him. Our burdens are so heavy, he is willing to take them in exchange for his which are light and easy to carry.

Possible Class Response: Paul said it is better to marry than to burn if someone needs the closeness of marriage (I Corinthians 7:9). Sometimes a woman needs a loving husband to help support her and her children, and to rebuild their self-esteem with kindness. Sometimes a woman much involved in the church meets a man also an active Christian, and they feel they can accomplish more for the Lord together than separately. Paul said single people can dedicate themselves to the Lord more (1 Corinthians 7:7,8). But each person must decide for herself.

Good Work

Write notes to someone who has gone through a divorce, possibly years ago. Tell them you admire their courage and their determination to hold their head high and continue to be a worthwhile Christian person.

BEFORE CLASS:

A. Gather up local telephone books and church directory.

B. Obtain envelopes and stationery.

C. Write the following on the blackboard or poster board:

"I know it has been a while since you have gone through your divorce, but that doesn't make it any easier. I know you loved your husband at one time, and making a life without him was hard sometimes. Still, I see you as a strong Christian woman in many respects who holds her head high, keeps her self-respect, and finds ways to have a fulfilling life. The church is the bride of Christ, so you belong to the most loving and caring individual in the universe."

DURING CLASS:

"We've been studying about marriages that have broken up. We did not cover what was a scriptural divorce, for that is another study. We just wanted to understand how these people feel and what they are going through. Everyone in this room knows people who have gone through a divorce, and perhaps you yourself have. We want to reach out to these people."

Hand out stationery and envelopes. "Write a note to someone who has been through a divorce, even if it was many years ago. I have phone books and church directories here for addresses. If you don't know what to say, I have written a suggestion on the board. Feel free to use it.

"You will have about eight minutes. Let's all be quiet now and allow one another to think and write. When you are done, give your addressed envelopes to me to mail unless you wish to keep the person's identity confidential. Then sit and offer a silent prayer for this person while the others finish.

Concluding Remarks

When time is up and while the slower writers complete their notes, sing one verse of a song, possibly one of the following:

1. *I am Praying for You*
2. *I Walk with the King*
3. *Make Room in Your Heart*
4. *What Shall it Profit?*

In a few moments your students will be going back home, possibly where there was a divorce. Send them back with courage and a smile.

(Wait for one or two quick replies to each of the following.) "In a few words....

1. What should a person put first—a sinful situation or their own soul?

2. What is true happiness?

3. Perfect what casts out fear?

4. No matter how many times we sin, God comes running to us to do what?

Have a closing prayer and remember those who have gone through divorce.

Inside the Hearts of Bible Women: Teacher's & Advertising Manual

Reasons for Divorce in America

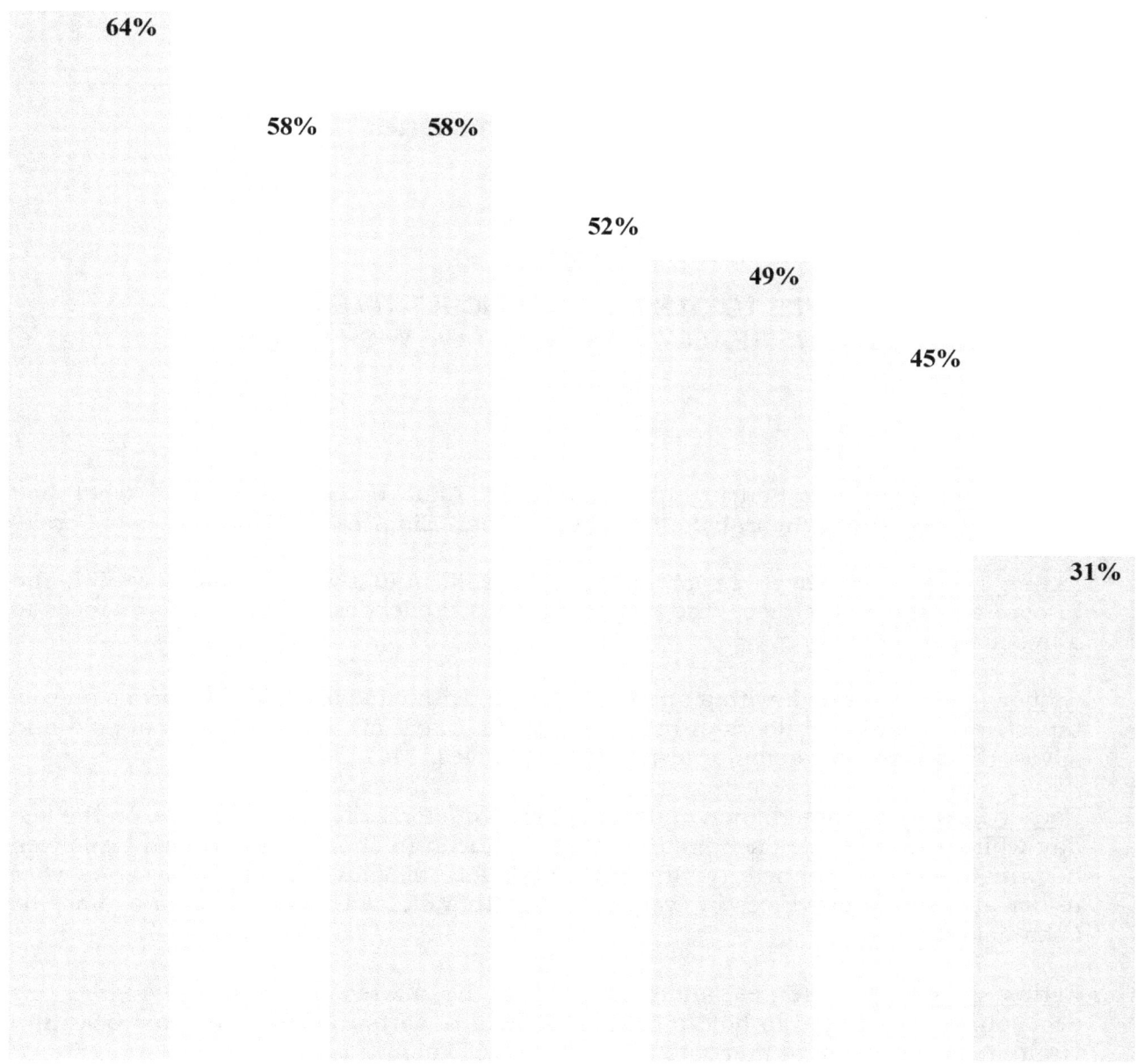

ALLOWED TO GIVE MORE THAN ONE REASON

Communication Problems – 64% **Spouse's Infidelity – 58%**
Constant Fighting – 58% **Verbal/Emotional Abuse – 52%**
Falling Out of Love – 49% **Unsatisfactory Sex – 45%**
Spouse Didn't Earn Enough – 31%

Katheryn Maddox Haddad

BEAUTY AND THE BEAST
Esther

Lesson One: Commoner

Lesson Aim
- ♥ **BE AN EXAMPLE TO OTHERS IN DIFFICULT TIMES**
- ♥ **MAKE SURE WE REALLY WANT WHAT WE WISH FOR**

Scripture Outline

<u>Esther 1:1</u>: King Aha-Seurus, also known as Aha-Xerxes, rules all of what had previously been both the Babylonian and Assyrian Empires - 127 provinces of Persia.

<u>Esther 1:2-4</u>: In the third year of his reign, to reaffirm just who is most powerful, and to plan an attack on Greece, the emperor invites the leaders of all those provinces to a five-month convention.

<u>Esther 1:5-9</u>: He ends it with a one-week festival with cups of gold, silver rings on wall tapestries, pillars and floors of red, blue, white, black marble, and beds of gold and silver. His queen has a similar festival for the wives.

<u>Esther 1:10-22</u>: Although men and women were customarily kept separate, on the last day while drunk, Xerxes sends for Vashti his queen to show off the crown he's given her and to show off her beauty. She feels uncomfortable and refuses. So he sends word to her and all his provinces in every language that she will never see him again. She is banished.

<u>Esther 2:1-4</u>: After Xerxes' anger dies down, he misses his wife and regrets his decision. He is advised to hold a beauty pageant of sorts to select the most beautiful virgin in the kingdom to marry to help him forget Vashti.

<u>Esther 2:5-7</u>: Mordecai is a descendant of a Jew who had served the last king in Jerusalem and been taken captive by the Babylonians. He works in the Persian palace. He is raising his young cousin, Esther, since both her parents had died.

<u>Esther 2:8-11</u>: Esther is chosen to go to the palace and enter the pageant. When Mordecai finds out, he sends word she is not to reveal her nationality. He goes every day to the courtyard of the women's house to inquire about Esther.

Today's World

Most Americans have no heroes. Only half of the people in New England and the western half of the Southeast do, which makes them the top area believing in heroes. Only one in five people living around the Great Lakes have a hero. (*The Day America Told the Truth*, p. 207)

People are fuzzy on what a hero does. The late historian Barbara Tuchman went to a "hero convention" once, and found those who do have heroes have them for strange reasons. The greatest hero at the time was a little girl who had fallen down a well and survived several days until rescued; yet she didn't actively do anything to be a hero.

Perhaps most Americans feel we have a good enough life compared with people in war-torn or famine-filled countries, so there are no situations requiring heroism. During wars, we always have national heroes. When we first conquered space, we had national heroes. That was about the last of our real heroes.

Author Ernest Hemingway in *The Old Man and the Sea* defined heroism as "grace under pressure." Perhaps we need to know enough about the pressures of each other's' lives that we can pick out some heroes. As long as we keep our daily challenges to ourselves, we don't know who of us are conquering, who are being heroes.

Bible World

By the time Esther was born, the Jews had been pawns in the hands of world leaders for some 250 years. Those national leaders who surrendered to hostile nations were led out with halters, as if for execution (1 Kings 20:32). Sometimes their thumbs, toes or ears were cut off (Ezekiel 23:25), or their eyes put out (2 Kings 25:7). Captives were sometimes suspended by the hand (Lamentations 5:12), made to lie down and be walked or driven over (Isaiah 51:23), put into forced labor (1 Chronicles 20:3). When a city was captured, the men were usually put to death, the women and children sold as slaves (Isaiah 47:3; 2 Chronicles 28:8-15), Psalm 44:12, Micah 1:11, Joel 3:3), or exposed to very cruel treatment (Nahum 3:5f, Zechariah 14:2, Esther 3:13, 2 Kings 8:12, Isaiah 13:16,18). Sometimes the people were exiled to other countries (Jeremiah 20:5; 39:9f, 2 Kings 24:12-16).

<u>Northern Jewish Kingdom:</u> Tiglath, king of Assyria, seems to be the first ancient ruler to practice the transporting of whole conquered populations to other parts of the empire. Among his first captives were the Jews who lived on the other (east) side of the Jordan River (1 Chronicles 5:26), and the inhabitants of Galilee (2 Kings 15:29) about 745 BC. Later Shalmaneser, king of Assyria, and Sargon II carried away over 27,000 Jews (2 Kings 17:3,5). Still later Assyrian kings took the rest of the Jews (excluding the poor) in the northern sector of Israel captive.

<u>Southern Jewish Kingdom</u>: Sennacherib carried into Assyria 200,000 Jews (2 Kings 18:13) around 705 BC. A hundred years later Babylon conquered and absorbed Assyria. Shortly thereafter in 606, Nebuchadnezzar (who would become emperor two

years later) exiled 10,000 noble Jews to Babylon including the king whose eyes were put out (Jeremiah 52:7-11) and Daniel (2 Kings 25:11), and appointed a puppet king in Jerusalem. In the seventh year of his reign (597 BC), he took 3,320 Jews to Babylon, new-generation upstarts, including Mordecai's great grandfather Kish, and the prophet Ezekiel. In the eighteenth year of his reign (586 BC), he got fed up with the Jews, took 832 middle-class Jerusalem residents to Babylon, and burned Jerusalem. In the twenty-third year of his reign (581 BC), he took 845 more middle-class Jews to Babylon, leaving behind only the very poorest and unthreatening country people.

Abraham's descendants were now back in the territory of Ur where he began his journey to establish a great kingdom for God. Had the plan failed? Had they returned to the land of Ur failures? While exiled in Babylon, the Jews were treated more like colonists than slaves. Ezekiel arrived in Babylon about ten years after Daniel. He began his prophetic writings about five years after his arrival. He lived with his family on the Euphrates river near the site of the Garden of Eden. Daniel referred to the Garden in his writings. He told the Jews they deserved what they got for disobeying God. But he said they'd return to Jerusalem someday, and left directions for rebuilding the Temple. He and Daniel undoubtedly knew each other.

Introducing the Lesson

We want to accomplish two things today. First, we want to resolve to be a good example to someone trying to overcome something we have overcome. Second, we want to make sure that what we think we want is what we really want.

Researchers have found that since we sent man into space, Americans have not recognized anyone as their hero. We have temporary heroes sometimes, but they do not last long. Hemingway defined heroism as "grace under pressure." Perhaps America has no heroes because we feel fairly content when compared with war-torn or famine-plagued countries. So, perhaps we need personal heroes to fit our own needs. Some women say Esther is their hero.

By the time Esther was born, the Jews had been pawns in the hands of foreign rulers for 250 years already. Gradually thousands of Jews were deported to Assyria. Eventually the Babylonians conquered Assyria and ruled the world. More Jews were then deported into Babylon.

Display DANIEL'S PLACE IN HISTORY. Among those early Jews who had been forced to go to Babylon was Daniel. Read through the chart. Probably Daniel was Esther's hero. Let's talk about it.

Discussion Questions

1. **Do you have a favorite Bible person whom you've loved hearing about all your life? Tell who it is and why.**

   1 Corinthians 10:11: The things that happened to the people written about in the Old Testament were for our examples.

Possible Class Response: (My favorites were always Esther and Joseph because they both did not become bitter, but turned around a bad situation into a good one to God's glory. From childhood, I often recalled Mordecai's words, "Who knows whether you are come to the kingdom for such a time as this?". Over and over, these words have caused me to have the courage to examine myself and then step forward and act, not leaving it for someone else. At this writing I am in my 50s. KMH)

2. **Give examples of how an event in our everyday life can be an opener to make a comment about God's concern for someone.**

   John 4:7,13,14: Jesus struck up a conversation with a woman from whom he asked for a simple drink, and was able to relate it to her soul - the waters of everlasting life.

   Possible Class Response: If the store clerk returns too much change, we can tell her our Christianity would be pretty worthless if we didn't try to be honest. If our neighbor is sick, we can take food over or wash her dishes, and tell her that Jesus loves us so much, we just want to pass his love on to someone else. If a friend calls and tells us some problem such as with children or marriage or finances, we can ask if we can pray for her right then, or tell her we will be praying for her.

3. **Have you ever wondered about anything exciting you'd like to see or do, never dreaming it would become a reality someday? Share it.**

   Psalm 73:23,24: God can not only make things exciting for us on earth, but someday he'll receive us to Glory!

   Possible Class Response: Perhaps in childhood you couldn't afford to go to camp, and someone at church volunteered to pay your way. Perhaps as a teenager you couldn't afford to go to a Christian college, but someone arranged for enough scholarships so you could go. In adulthood, some may wish to see some foreign country, so decide to go there on a religious mission such as "Let's Start Talking" which teaches people English using the Bible as a text. Some may enjoy camping, so may receive permission from the campground owner to hold a children's or ladies' Bible class once a week. Some may wish to go on a cruise, so arrange a fundraiser with a travel agency for a Christian institution with part of the fare being donated.

4. **Tell about an older woman who was an inspiration to you to stand up for right even when it was unpopular. What were the consequences?**

   Romans 8:31: We can gain courage to be the only one in a crowd to do what is right by remembering that if God is for us, we have the majority.

   Possible Class Response: This could be a teacher, a mother, a sister, a grandmother, someone we read about in the newspaper or a book. (I think Anita Bryant's standing nearly alone against homosexuality in Miami, having tomatoes thrown at her, being lied about, and losing her career as a result was an example of courage.)

5. **When you were younger, did you ever listen to advice of a group of people and then later wish you hadn't? What was your relationship with these people like**

afterward?

Exodus 23:2: Just because everyone does it on TV or among our friends at work, that doesn't make it right; we must continue to search the scriptures, pray, and do what is right—even if we have to change associates.

Possible Class Response: Some may have slipped off from their parents and gone with a group to do something their parents disapproved of. If they found out it wasn't the fun the crowd had promised it would be, they may have backed off from that crowd.

6. **Were you ever chosen for something pleasant you were not expecting? Talk about the fine line between agreeing with the other people's praise of you and praising yourself.**

   Proverbs 27:2: Let other people praise you. Don't you brag.

   Possible Class Response: They may have told us we were the prettiest, smartest, best leader, best speller, fastest, best organizer, best craftsman, best designer. We can thank them for their trust in us, but attribute much of our success to the encouragement or teaching of others, and the grace of God.

7. **If you were the poor person referred to in James 2:2,3, and were treated like the rich person suddenly, how would you probably react?**

   James 2:2-4: At church even, we tend to try to meet the person who is well dressed, well-groomed and wearing a big smile, and are afraid to make friends with the person who comes dirty, dressed poorly, and wearing a sad expression. This is wrong.

   Possible Class Response: We would probably be embarrassed and self-conscious. We'd not be used to success and need reinforcement by people around us that we were a worthwhile person and important to them. If the new friends stuck with us, we would gradually gain self-confidence and begin to clean ourselves up better, smile more, and perhaps even get a better job as a result.

8. **When you were younger, did you ever go to a home much finer than yours, or to a dinner with people you'd always thought superior to you in fame or fortune? Tell about your awkwardness among them. Did you find such things as which fork to use, when to bring up certain subjects, etc. a major task?**

   I Samuel 10:22-24: Young Saul had just been made king in private; but when they looked for him to crown him in a public ceremony, he was found hiding among some baggage.

   Possible Class Response: Some may have been invited to the home of a rich relative, or the president of an organization, or a reception for a celebrity, or a fund-raising banquet on behalf of some institution. Our first-time exposure to such is exciting and scary. Suddenly we can't find our mouth, we're all thumbs, and sometimes even forget our own name during an introduction. We may have even left early out of frustration.

Good Work

Write a note to a teenage girl telling her she has a wonderful life ahead of her. Encourage her to pray and trust in the Lord in all things.

BEFORE CLASS:

A1.   FOR LARGE AND MEDIUM CONGREGATIONS:

Obtain the names, ages and home addresses of girls in the teen and college classes of your congregation.

A2.   FOR SMALL CONGREGATIONS:

<u>Alternative One</u>: Obtain the first names of girls in a senior high school class and make arrangements to give the notes to a school counselor to pass on to them.

<u>Alternative Two</u>: Obtain the first names and ages of girls in a Christian home for troubled youth.

B.   Gather up stationary. This can be pink bond paper cut in half.

C.   Gather up envelopes and pre-address them.

D.   Make a list of these girls to give the prayer leader at the end of your class.

E   On the blackboard or poster board, write the following:

"I just wanted to send you a note to let you know you have a wonderful life ahead of you. Not everything will go as you plan, but go ahead and dream your dreams anyway, and some of them will come true. During disappointments, trust in God, and he will help you turn them into triumphs of a different kind. I am setting aside this week to pray especially for you. God will always love you."

DURING CLASS:

"We've been talking about standing alone in a crowd for right, and also about unexpected good things happening to us. There are young girls all around us who need reassurance that God does love them, and that he will guide their lives."

Hand out pre-addressed envelopes and stationery. "These are the names of girls from _____. If you aren't sure what to say, I have written a suggestion for you on the board. Feel free to copy it if you like."

"You will have about eight minutes to write your note. Let's all be quiet now and allow each other to think and write. When you are done, give your note to me, then offer a silent prayer for the girl you wrote while the others finish."

Concluding Remarks

When time is up and while the slower writers complete their notes, sing one verse of a song, possibly one of the following:

1. *How Shall the Young Secure Their Hearts?*
2. *Yield Not to Temptation*
3. *Farther Along*
4. *I Washed My Hands This Morning*

In a few moments, your students will be going back home where their own temptations and excitements await them. End the class on a positive note. Smile!

(Wait for one or two quick replies to each of the following.) "In a few words, what advice would you give young girls...

1. To get the courage to say no in a crowd?
2. To bring up God's love to a friend?
3. Who have won first-prize at something?
4. Who are going to meet their first important person?

Have a brief closing prayer. Hand a list of the girls you wrote to the prayer leader.

Daniel's Place in History

BC 606	**Jews are conquered by Nebuchadnezzar. Daniel, possibly a teenager, and other young intelligent men are the first to be taken to Babylon.**
BC 604	Nebuchadnezzar inherits the throne of Babylon.
BC 602	Daniel, maybe 20 years old, interprets Nebuchadnezzar's dream (Daniel 2:1). As a result, he is made governor of the province of Babylon (not the whole empire) by the young king.
BC 597	Mordecai's great grandfather, Kish, is taken to Babylon. Also taken is the prophet Ezekiel.
BC 590	Ezekiel writes of Daniel's example of godliness in a heathen nation (Ez. 14:14,20; 28:3). Daniel is about 30.
BC 586	Daniel's three friends are thrown into the furnace and live. Jerusalem is burned. Puppet King Zedekiah is taken to Babylon. Daniel is now about 35 years old.
BC 553	Nebuchadnezzar dies and his grandson Belshazzar becomes co-ruler of Babylon, making Daniel the "third ruler" (Daniel 5:16,29). Daniel is now about 65 years old.
BC 538	Darius, the Persian emperor, conquers and absorbs Babylon into the Persian empire. He makes Daniel ruler over one-third of the empire.
BC 537	Daniel survives the lion's den. He is now about 80 years old. Darius orders the entire empire to respect Jehovah.
BC 536	Cyrus, son-in-law of Darius, becomes emperor and allows any Jews who want to, to return to Jerusalem to rebuild their temple. Haggai and Zechariah lead 50,000 of them (Ezra 1-6).
BC 534	Daniel dies at about age 85 (Daniel 1:21).

Katheryn Maddox Haddad

Beauty and the Beast

Lesson Two: Queen

Lesson Aim

♥ KEEP UP OUR HEALTH DURING STRESS
♥ UNDERSTAND THE VALUE OF FASTING

Scripture Outline

Esther 2:12: Esther has daily beauty treatments for one year to soften her desert-dweller's skin and saturate it with ointments and perfumes.

Esther 2:13-15: When Esther's turn comes to be taken to King Xerxes, she tells others they are smarter than her and asks their advice what to take along. She does not take anything else. Esther knows that if she is not chosen, she must live out her years in a house of concubines (harem) and never see the king again unless he calls for her by name. Her humility makes everyone love her.

Esther 2:16-20: About three years after the beauty search began, Esther is chosen by this gruff king to be his new bride. She still does not tell her nationality.

Esther 2:21-23: Mordecai overhears a plot to kill the king. He tells Queen Esther who in turn tells King Xerxes in Mordecai's name. The rebels are hung.

Esther 3:1-7: Xerxes promotes Haman to prime minister. Mordecai refuses to bow whenever Haman comes near because he doesn't respect him. Haman's servants find out Mordecai is a Jew.

Esther 3:8-15: Five years after Esther is made queen, Haman bribes Xerxes and convinces him that the Jews want to overthrow his crown. So in the first month of that year, Xerxes by royal decree commands that all Jews including babies be killed on the 13th day of the last month of the year (to give time for the decree to be delivered to every province). Even the city where Xerxes lives wonders why Xerxes would command such a thing.

Esther 4:1-9: Mordecai begins wearing sackcloth to indicate his grief. When Esther finds out, she sends a messenger to him with a change of clothes so he won't give away his nationality, and to find out why the decree was made. Mordecai sends her a copy of the decree as written by Haman, and tells her to beg the king to save the lives of her people.

Esther 4:10-12: Esther sends word back to Mordecai that she can be put to death for going to the king without being sent for, and he hadn't sent for her in a month.

Esther 4:13-17: Mordecai sends word back to Esther that she will die one way or the other, for someone will tell that she is a Jew. "Who knows whether you are come to the kingdom for such a time as this." Esther then gathers her maids who are Jewish and they fast and pray for three days in preparation for her going to see the king. "If I perish, I perish."

Today's World

The number-one thing people in America would change about their bodies is their weight. A few are too thin, most are too fat. The Bible tells us not to eat animal fat (Leviticus 3:17; 6:12). Some fat is not very saturated and more easily digested. Other fat is saturated and causes a lot of trouble in our system. The American Medical Association recommends that we eat no more than 20 grams of saturated fat a day.

However, there is good fat with essential fatty acids; these are vital to our nerves and brain, various hormones, digestion, and are some part of every cell in our body. The principal sources of essential fatty acids are natural vegetable oils, especially safflower. The best sources on the grocery-store shelves are salad oils, mayonnaise, nuts, and peanut butter without hydrogenated oils. When two teaspoons of mayonnaise, sunflower seeds, peanut butter or dressing are eaten every three hours throughout the day, the stomach digests more slowly and more efficiently; and the blood sugar level influencing our appetite stays up.

Most dairy products, very high in nutrients, are also high in saturated fat; so we should purchase low-fat or skimmed milk products. A large glass of whole milk or two thin slices of cheese hits our fat limit for an entire day, whereas we can drink about all the skim milk we want (a quart a day is recommended).

Something else that digests fat is protein. The only food containing complete proteins and no saturated fats are skim milk, yeast, wheat germ, soy flour, and soybeans. Liver, eggs, heart, fish and seafoods are a close second. A minimum of 60 grams of protein should be eaten daily by women (80 by men).

What would be a good low-fat daily menu? Six ounces of fish, meat or chicken with the skin/fat trimmed off is acceptable. We can eat all the vegetables we want including baked potatoes and rice, nearly all the fruit we want, nearly all the bread we want including angel food cake. We can drink all the skim milk and juices we want.

* * *

MYRRH oil was, in our story, rubbed for six months into the skin of the girls waiting to be presented to the king. It is found only in Babylon, modern-day Arabia. It comes from small thorny trees found on parched rocky hills. In the spring, they have small white clustered flowers. The trunks are disproportionately short and thick. They have orange-brown bark which contains numerous resin ducts which, when split or cut, exude a yellowish fluid, myrrh. Upon exposure to the air, the resin hardens slowly into irregular lumps called "tears." Myrrh is harvested during the dry summer months.

Myrrh was brought by the wise men to Jesus at his birth. In medieval Europe, myrrh was regarded as rare and precious. Today it is used on costly incense, cosmetics and perfumes. Medicinally, myrrh possesses slight antiseptic, astringent, and stomach/intestinal healing properties. In the US, myrrh is used mostly as an aromatic and astringent mouthwash. The US imports about 20,000 pounds a year.

Bible World

Fasting was practiced throughout Bible times. It was also expected of Christians. Jesus said "WHEN you give...pray...fast," not IF (Matthew 6:2a, 5a, 16a). He said when he the bridegroom leaves, the church will fast (Matthew 9:15b). Jesus fasted once for 40 days—over a month (Matthew 4:1,2). Anna prayed and fasted daily in the Temple (Luke 2:37). The elders fasted whenever they sent out missionaries (Acts 13:2,3). Paul fasted whenever he established a church (Acts 14:22,23). Although fasting is normally done alone with no one else knowing about it (Matthew 6:16-18), husbands and wives are to dedicate themselves to prayer and fasting periodically (1 Corinthians 7:5).

Fasting was commanded because it reminds us that our minds are in control of our bodies, not the other way around (1 Corinthians 12:7), for the enemies of the cross serve the god of their appetite (Philippians 3:17-19). Isaiah commanded the people of God to afflict themselves in fasting to show humility before God (Isaiah 58:3). Fasting balances our pride for doing good (Luke 17:10), it acknowledges the death of our own will (Romans 6:11), and allows us to symbolically give sour lives for Christ, something we may literally face someday (Romans 12:1). It helps us understand hunger better (Matthew 5:6), for too often we eat until we hurt before we say we are full, when in reality we should only eat until the hunger pangs are gone. In a nutshell, fasting helps us understand the superiority of our spiritual nature over our physical nature; it puts things back in their proper perspective (John 6:27,33,63).

Jesus said in Matthew 6:16-18 that we should not tell anyone when we fast. Fasting is an act of self-restraint. It is a complete failure of self-restraint to show others our self-restraint! As an unknown poet once said:

> Let us keep our fast within,
> Till heaven and we are quite alone;
> Then let the grief, the shame, the sin
> Before the mercy-seat be thrown.

Just as a plant must begin its growth in darkness of soil, we begin our spiritual growth in the darkness of our own inner thoughts and prayers. And just as we can never safely expose the roots, we can ever show the exact process by which we develop our own spiritual roots.

How should we fast? Start in the morning when it's normally easy to skip breakfast anyway. Once the normal time of eating passes, the hunger pangs go away. However, we should drink water to avoid dehydration. If a person must eat periodically for health reasons, she can vary her fast by drinking juices and other nutritious drinks; but for the rest of us that would be hedging a little on the definition of "food".

What should we do during our fast? We should spend the day reading the bible, perhaps on a certain topic. We can read a few scriptures, meditate on portions of them to see if we are truly following them, and then pray about them. During our time of fasting and meditation, we will find that our thoughts go far deeper than normal and our introspection is far greater than at any other time. We will be astonished at ourselves! Sometimes we have to go on to work. If so, we should carry on as usual, but devote ourselves to reading and prayer on our lunch hour somewhere in private, in the car, and while we're at home.

Isaiah 57:15 sums up fasting better than any scripture in the Bible.
Only when we humble ourselves can God raise us up. He can raise us higher than we can. We are like a spring that, when pushed down the lowest, can then leap up to the highest!

Just one day of fasting will bring wonderful results. Two is fine also. We must break our fast gently so we don't shock our bodies. Before going to bed in the evening is the best time. We can drink a glass of milk or eat some toast or something bland. We won't be interested in food by this time, and our bodies won't be either, so go easy on it. The next day we will find our interest in food has declined and our interest in spiritual things has increased significantly. We feel resurrected!

Introducing the Lesson

Today we're going to talk about retaining both our physical health and our values during stressful periods of our lives. Most of us have physical symptoms under stress such as skin problems, getting ulcers, headaches, etc. We need to do what we can to maintain our health during this time.

Explain saturated fats. **Display FOODS THAT HIT OUR DAILY LIMIT OF SATURATED FAT chart.** Bring out highlights of the chart.

We need, during stress, to also give ourselves special quiet times. For instance, we can take long baths in bubbles or perfumed oils. Esther did. Myrrh was used for this purpose. (Explain Myrrh.)

Another form of quiet time is prayer and fasting. It was commanded in the Bible. Jesus said in Matthew 6:2, WHEN you fast, not IF you fast. Yet it's something we seldom ever hear about. **Display outline on FASTING.** Explain the chart.

Discussion Questions

9. **Beauty can be a real burden instead of blessing to a Christian woman. Why (Proverbs 31:30)? Give some examples.**

God made beauty. He likes it and approves of it. Heaven will be full of it.

Proverbs 31:30: Favor and beauty are vain and empty, especially as she grows older. A woman who lives a good life is forever admired by others.

Possible Class Response: A beautiful person can rely on beauty instead of a good life to gain favor of others; then as she grows old, she doesn't know how to gain favor any more and becomes frustrated. If she is beautiful and still tries to live a good life, others may praise her so much she has to continually fight the temptation to be conceited. She may also be frustrated that she does not gain favor because of her Christian life, but because of her beauty.

10. **Discuss how cleanliness and good nutrition influence our health and disposition. Then read Romans 12:1 and tell how these affect the purpose of our bodies.**

    Romans 12:1: We are to sacrifice our bodies to God over and over each day by using these bodies to do things on his behalf. We are the only hands, mouth, feet God has on earth.

    Possible Class Response: Soap is a germ killer, both on our bodies and in our homes. Foods free of harmful fat and with generous in vitamins and minerals keep our bodies strong so we can fight germs that are always around us. We should also be extra careful to guard against the type of problems that tend to affect us the most: Repertory (cover our heads in the rain), ulcers (take a nap every day), skin (use good lotions). And we should exercise in some way every day so our body organs and extremities do not grow weak through the years and to keep our metabolism up.

11. **If a leader seeks advice from a group they are leading, what does that group think of her after that? Share it.**

    Proverbs 12:15: Fools do whatever they want. Wise people seek advice of others and follow it.

    Possible Class Response: The group feels flattered, and then likes her even more for having that much confidence in them and boosting their own egos. Seldom does the group think she just doesn't know what she is doing; that occurs if she makes a decision and then flounders around. This is true asking opinions of her children, members of an organizations, students, people who work under her.

12. **Share some experiences where you were pleasantly surprised with the results of adopting Jesus' example.**

    Matthew 20:25-28: Worldly people try to dominate and dictate to those they are over. A wise leader goes among the people and shows them how to do their work.

    Possible Class Response: We taught our children to make their beds by doing it with them. to show them it is possible to find the floor under all the toys in their room, we sat in the floor with them, smiled, and picked up the toys one at a time long enough to make it come true. Some women may have been made chairman of a committee because no one else would do it, even though they didn't know what they were doing; so asked for suggestions of the committee members. Some may have been made a

Bible school teacher because no one else would do it, then asked the students what they'd like to learn.

13. **Tell of someone you have long admired from a distance without them even being aware of it. What does that tell us we should do with our own lives?**

    Genesis 39:4,5,21,22; 41:38-40: Joseph was made a slave, and volunteered to do whatever was necessary to make his master look good. He was made a prisoner and did the same thing. He was made the subject of a new king and did the same thing. He went from slave to prime minister.

    Daniel 1:9; 2:47,48: Daniel was one of Esther's Jewish ancestors who was taken to Babylon as a slave. He tried to do whatever would benefit the captor king who had destroyed his homeland. He went from slave to prime minister. His book of "Daniel" was undoubtedly left in the king's library after he died. He may have also taken the Pentateuch and the prophets with him into captivity and put them in the king's library.

    Possible Class Response: The ladies may have heard a speaker at a ladies retreat, heard about a missionary, read about a woman fighting a terrible disease or family tragedy.

14. **Did you ever stand up for right and it backfire on you? You thought you'd be appreciated, but instead things looked worse. How did you feel?**

    Exodus 2:111-14: Moses killed a cruel Egyptian taskmaster for beating a Jewish slave. since he was a prince, the Jews didn't trust him and thought he'd kill whoever he wanted, including them. He ended up being banished from where the people were that he wanted to help.

    Romans 8:28: When bad things happen to us, God can eventually turn them around and make something good come from them.

    Possible Class Response: A lady might have said December 25 wasn't really Jesus' birth and that we should celebrate his birth every day. A lady might have said the Bible doesn't tell us to celebrate Easter as Jesus' resurrection day, but every Sunday. In both cases, the word might have spread that she didn't believe in God, or she wasn't very religious. She might have used a position of leadership to suggest there be a prayer before an assembly, and people dropped out of the group/organization. They might have encouraged parents of children who were attending church to come with their children, and the parents no longer allowed their children to attend.

15. **Is it possible to have a misguided sense of modesty and thereby let people down when you are needed? How can you overcome this?**

    Genesis 45:5: Joseph was put in the kingdom of Egypt for such a time as this—to preserve life during a world-wide famine.

    Philippians 4:13: We can do anything as long as we depend on Christ for our strength.

Possible Class Response: This happens often. We tell ourselves we'd be doomed before we even tried, as Esther did. We tell ourselves people would be worse off than ever if we tried to do something, as Moses did. We can pray for God to be with us and give us strength. We can confess our fears to our friends, then ask them to pray for us. We can be prepared, if things turn out successfully, to give credit to God.

16. **Have you ever fasted? Tell what it did for you. If not, tell what concerns you about it and what would encourage you to try it.**

    Matthew 6:16: Jesus expected those who believe in him to fast.

    Isaiah 58:3-5: Fasting is a symbol of afflicting our souls before God so that he will hear us. It teaches the faster humility and greater reliance on God.

    Possible Class Response: Fasting takes our brains off the huge task of digesting food. It allows us to think more deeply and clearly about what is going on in our life. It helps us reevaluate our priorities. People are often afraid to fast because going without a meal is the first step toward starving to death; there is an instinctive fear of this in all living beings. We can tell ourselves, even though it is obvious, that we'll be able to eat again when the time is over. (We feel hunger when we miss the first meal, but that goes away the rest of the time. A one-day fast is good, and should be broken with a few bites of something bland just before bedtime.)

Good Work

Send a note to someone you have long admired and who perhaps does not even realize it. Thank them for their example and perhaps tell of a time their example encouraged your response to a difficult situation.

BEFORE CLASS:

Gather up telephone books, your church directory, and a directory of churches around the U.S. and the world. Also obtain the addresses of Christian colleges, the editors of various Christian publications, religious radio programs, and/or the organizations fighting for Christian principles in society.

Call the post office to find out what postage requirements are to various parts of the world.

Gather up envelopes and stationery (bond paper cut in half).

Write on blackboard or poster board a suggestion to write for those who have trouble wording what they feel.

"Although you do not know me [or this fact], I have long admired you because you _____. There were times when I did not know what to do, and then I remembered you. I asked myself what you would do. You have been very courageous and very dedicated. Thank you for your example. I have learned to love you because of this."

DURING CLASS:

"We've been talking about being put in difficult situations and more asked of us than we believed we could do. In many cases we were inspired by the example of someone else who may not even know we exist. Surely they, too, need encouragement sometimes. Let's send them a note of appreciation."

"I have address books here with me. On your envelope, write the name of the person you wish to write. Don't take too long to decide since everyone needs encouragement anyway. On the inside flap where the glue is, write the organization or state or country this person is/was associated with. While you write, I'll look up their addresses and write them on the envelope for you."

Hand out envelopes and stationery. "If you aren't sure what to say, I have written a suggestion for you on the board. Feel free to copy it if you like."

"You will have about eight minutes to write your note. Let's all be quiet now and allow each other to think and write. When you are done, give your note to me, then offer a silent prayer for the one you wrote while the others finish."

Concluding Remarks

When time is up and while the slower writers complete their notes, sing one verse of a song, possibly one of the following:

1. *A Charge to Keep I Have*
2. *Into Our Hands*
3. *Must Jesus Bear the Cross Alone?*
4. *Brighten the Corner Where You Are*

In a few moments, your students will be returning to a fairly predictable life, with opportunities passing by every day. Send them off with courage to stand up for Jesus!

(Wait for one or two quick replies to each of the following.) "In a few words, what should you do when....

1. You're asked by someone who knows your talents to lead a group And you are afraid to?
2. You can't get your group to do what you all decided to do?
3. You're the only one with the courage to stand up for right?
4. You've accomplished a good work and people are praising you too much?

Have a brief closing prayer for the people you admire, and ask God to help us be an example to others who may be watching us.

Foods that Hit Our Daily Limit of Saturated Fat

DAIRY
2 T. butter
2 T. margarine
Large glass (20 oz) of whole milk
Small bowl (1-1/2 c.) ice cream
1/2 c. grated cheese
4 eggs
3 T. salad dressing

MEAT
12 oz. meat/chicken with fat trimmed off
3 oz. ham or pork chop
1-1/3 c. chili with beans
2 hot dogs

VEGETABLES
2 c. mashed potatoes w/butter, cream
1 c. fried potatoes
30 potato chips
1/2 large avocado

BREADS
1 c. macaroni and cheese
2 c. spaghetti with meat sauce
2 c. cream soup
1 slice chocolate cake/icing
1"x2" piece of fudge
1/4 cup nuts
2 6" waffles, no syrup

FOODS WITH ALMOST NO SATURATED FAT (EAT ALL WE WANT)

Skim (1/2%) Milk
Nearly every vegetable, including beans, baked potatoes, rice
Nearly every fruit except olives and avocados
Nearly every bread including angel food cake

Fasting

WHO?

- Anna, the prophetess, prayed and fasted
- Jesus fasted once for 40 days
- Elders fasted when they sent out missionaries
- Paul fasted whenever he established a church
- Disciples are to fast when we pray
- Married couples are to fast and pray
- The church is to fast now that Jesus has left

WHY?

- Gets our bodies into submission instead of our appetites ruling
- Humbles us before God
- Balances our pride for doing good
- Acknowledges the death of our will
- Symbolically offers our lives as sacrifices
- Helps us understand hunger better
- Helps us understand the superiority of the spiritual over physical ; puts things back in proper perspective

RESULT:

- Only when we humble ourselves can God raise us up!
- God can raise us higher than we can!
- We are like a spring that, when lowest, can rise to the highest!

ARE YOU WILLING TO TRY?

Katheryn Maddox Haddad

Beauty and the Beast

Lesson Three: Hero

Lesson Aim
- ♥ **UNDERSTAND THE VALUE OF TACT**
- ♥ **STAND FROM THE CROWD FOR UNSELFISH REASONS**

Scripture Outline

Esther 5:1-8: Esther puts on her "Sunday best," goes before the king, and invites him and Haman to come to a banquet later that day. He keeps saying he'll give her anything up to half his kingdom. Building up the suspense, at the banquet she asks them to come to another banquet the next day.

Esther 5:9-14: Haman tells his wife and friends he's ecstatic that he now has so much power and wealth, and was the only other one invited to the queen's banquet; but Mordecai not bowing to him ruins everything. They convince him to have gallows built that night and ask the king to hang Mordecai on it; then he can go merrily on his way to the banquet.

Esther 6:1-14: That night Xerxes cannot sleep (can he hear the hammering too?) So a servant reads the royal chronicles to him, including where Mordecai saved his life by reporting an assassination plot. Since he never rewarded him, the next morning he asks Haman what he should do to reward a special unnamed person. Thinking it is him, Haman says that person should be given the crown. Then Xerxes tells Haman to give the crown to Mordecai, and Haman is humiliated.

Esther 7:1-10: At the banquet, Esther tells Xerxes someone condemned her and her people to die. Xerxes demands to know who did this so he can be killed, and she tells him it was Haman. The king goes to the garden to think, and while gone, Haman falls on the bed where Esther is to plead for his life; Xerxes returns and thinks Haman is assaulting his wife. Haman is hung.

Esther 8,9,10: Mordecai is made prime minister of the Persian Empire. The king's edict to kill all Jews cannot be rescinded, but he allows all Jews to arm and defend themselves so that they are not killed. This event becomes known as Purim and is celebrated by the Jews to this day.

Today's

World

In 2017, there were four woman governors in the US: Kate Brown (Oregon); Mary Fallin (Oklahoma), Susana Martinez (New Mexico), Gina Raimonde (Rhode Islands). The remaining forty-six are men. Twenty-one women are senators, with the rest (2 per state) being men. Eighty-three women serve in the House of Representatives out of the 435 total.

In major occupation groupings, women earn the following percent of what men normally are paid for the same jobs:

69.9% Managerial and professional specialty
66.9% Technical, sales and administrative support
71.9% Service occupations
64.8% Precision production, craft, and repair
69.3% Operators, fabricators, laborers
82.1% Farming, forestry, and fishing

71.8% AVERAGE

Around the world, women prime ministers, presidents or queens number 29. There are 197 countries in the world.

Would/do women make good leaders? According to a survey made by James Patterson and Peter Kim, American women are morally superior to men in every region in the country and on every moral issue. Women lie less, are more responsible, are far more honest at work, can be trusted more, fight less, do drugs/alcohol less, are more faithful in their relationships.

On the job, women are more loyal to the company who pays them than men. Women are much less likely to take office supplies home, to slander the boss, lie to the bosses or co-workers, leave early, or goof off. Less than half as many women as men believe the only way to get ahead is to cheat. Women are much less willing to compromise their values to get ahead, and somewhat more willing to quit as a matter of principle if they learn their company is doing anything illegal.

Bible
World

Esther's husband Xerxes was the son of Darius who allowed many of the Jews to return to their homeland after their 70-year ordeal. At this time, the Empire of the Medes and Persians included the entire civilized world except Greece. In Xerxes' third year, he assembled all his 127 provincial princes from Ethiopia to India (Esther 1:1-4). He made a great show of his treasury and strength, and together for five months they planned their invasion of Greece. Then he held a magnificent feast to plan and celebrate their up-coming conquest.

He sent for Vashti to show off her beauty as well as the magnificence of her crown. She refused to come and he banished her forever. At his advisors' suggestion, he ordered the most beautiful women in his empire be sought to be his new queen (Esther 2:1-4). With that order he then headed out to conquer Greece. Cyrus had failed and

Darius had failed. He would not.

After a 2-year journey, Upon learning Xerxes had finally approached their shores, the people of <u>northern</u> Greece surrendered out of sheer fright. Xerxes' army was reported by one ancient historian as 2,641,610 men supported by 1,207 warships and 3,000 smaller vessels. (Although most modern historians reduce the army by nine-tenths and the fleet by one half, they still presented a fearful sight.) He would now attack <u>southern</u> Greece. Xerxes ordered his engineers to build a bridge across a channel to Athens. After many weeks, it was completed. But before his army could use it, the bridge was destroyed by a storm.

The impulsive and enraged Xerxes ordered the sea beaten with 300 lashes, and his branders to brand it with fire. Then he had the overseers of the bridge builders beheaded. Again they tried. Two more bridges were built, this time by lining up 360 boats across the water, tying them together, and laying logs over them like a plank road. Walls were put up on both sides of the swaying bridges to hide the sea from the skittish horses and beasts of burden. It took his army four days to cross the channel.

Headed out to meet the Persian invaders were 7,000 Spartans, some of the mightiest warriors in the world. They fought valiantly for two days, and according to the Greek historian, Xerxes "leaped three times from his [portable] throne in agony for his army." But the tide turned and the Greeks could only struggle heroically against hopeless odds for their country. The Persians advanced further into Greece and finally killed the Spartan general. Next they took Athens which had previously been deserted by fear-driven residents.

Then a sea battle followed in the channel. Xerxes' ships were too large and too many, they got in each other's' way, clogged the channel, and lost the battle. Discouraged, Xerxes headed back to Persia and left behind his forces to keep trying. By now, the Grecians had 100,000 men and the odds were near even. The Persian fleet was defeated and the remainder of their army destroyed. The Grecian victory over the great Persian Empire was astounding. Xerxes arrived home in disgrace. But by then, he had a new distraction awaiting him.

An entire harem of the most beautiful women in his empire had been gathered. Each was being or had been beautified with skin treatments and taught royal demeanor for one year. An ancient historian says that he "consoled himself with the pleasures of the harem." In the seventh year of his reign (about a year and a half after his humiliating defeat), Xerxes finally chose Esther. "The king loved Esther above all the women....so that he set the royal crown upon her head, and made her queen" (Esther 2:16,17).

Little is known of Xerxes after this. He raised the taxes to rebuild the treasury now depleted from the war with Greece. He was murdered 13 years after marrying Esther. His murderer made Xerxes' son (Esther's step-son) Arta-Xerxes next king, and he reigned 41 years. He believed in only one God, hated vile worship practices, tore down temples of multi-god religions, and had high respect for the Jews.

Introducing the Lesson

Women today are overall more honest than men, according to a recent survey. **Display WOMEN, THE MORE HONEST SEX.** Point out parts of it. This shows that women are more willing to stand out from the crowd to protect their values. However, their opportunities for leadership positions such as Esther had, are small. **Display WOMEN IN MAJOR LEADERSHIP POSITIONS.** As a result, women must be extra careful we are as tactful as possible when we know we're right. Esther, certainly had to, for it might have cost her job and her life.

Esther took the challenge to stand up for moral responsibilities rather than live by hiding from them (though she would have eventually been killed anyway). **Display ESTHER'S PLACE IN HISTORY.** Her husband Xerxes had such a bad temper that when he lost a battle to the Greeks, he beat the sea with 30 lashes, and then branded it with a branding iron. Let's see how Esther handled this situation and changed a king's mind.

Discussion Questions

17. **Tell about a time you almost got off the track of helping someone because of an offer by someone else. How did you feel about it?**

    We humans can be easily distracted from a noble purpose even after fasting. Esther could have accepted the king's offer for half the kingdom considering the offer might never be made to her again.

    Matthew 4:1-10: Jesus had just been baptized, his divinity announced, and his ministry was now ready to begin. Then he went to the wilderness to meditate, and Satan tempted him to take shortcuts to accomplished what he wanted. First, he tried to cast doubts in Jesus' mind that he was the Son of God, so demanded he turn stones to bread to prove who he was. Or, he could cast himself down from the pinnacle of the Temple and live, then everyone would believe in him. Or he could receive the kingdoms of the world by just going over to Satan's side. Jesus was not distracted by any of these things.

    Possible Class Response: A lady may have decided to go see someone in the nursing home a couple times a day, but responsibilities with children, etc. distracted her. Someone else may have volunteered to help with VBS, but forgot to put it on her calendar and scheduled a vacation that week. A class member may have decided to take someone out for their birthday, but forgot and went somewhere else that day.

18. **Do you think when we show extra attention to people, they are likely to see themselves more for what they are? Have you ever heard a surprising introspection by someone you just did something extra nice to?**

    Esther's two banquets seemed to make both guests introspective of their position in life. Xerxes used it to see what else he could do to serve. Haman used it to make himself greater so others would serve him.

    John 13:34: After Jesus spent his life doing good to others, he told them to now do good to each other and to everyone.

Proverbs 25:21,11: If your enemy is hungry, feed her; if she is thirsty, give her a drink; thereby you'll heap coals of fire on her head and she'll feel guilty for the way she treated you.

Possible Class Response: Someone may have told a neglectful mother that she was a good mother, and that mother then confessed that actually she wasn't. Someone may have helped someone do housework, then complimented her on being a good homemaker, resulting in the latter saying that actually she wasn't. Sometimes a compliment helps a person feel secure enough and liked enough to tell what their shortcomings are and ask for help.

19. **Have you ever caught yourself just before you got into such difficulty? How did you feel after you reevaluated your priorities?**

    Greed eventually leaves us with nothing. If we run over enough people, others will begin to take a second look even at former friends

    Proverbs 9:6; 18:7; 25:6,7: Get away from fools and you'll live. A fool's mouth will destroy him. Those who brag how great they are will be put down and made to look ridiculous.

    Possible Class Response: Some may have bragged too much they could do something, someone took them up on it, then they were stuck because they really didn't know how. Sometimes it takes something like this for us to see ourselves and make a change in our lives.

20. **If you were being falsely accused, what would be your best defense? If you experienced this, share it.**

    Esther and Mordecai emphasized serving. Haman emphasized being served. She knew actions speak louder than words, and eventually it would be the queen's word against the prime minister's word. She knew, too, the outcome would mean death to one of them.

    John 3:18: Our deeds tell the truth about what we are.

    Possible Class Response: If someone ever lies about us, we should just be patient and not panic. We should go about our normal lives; people will remember how we acted in the past and will continue to watch us. They will make their judgments based on that. Some will even say, "I know this person and know she would never do what you accused her of."

21. **Once a person lies about you and people find out they**

    were deceived, how much are they likely to believe the deceiver in even innocent things after that?

    Ecclesiastes 7:1a: A good name is more valuable than anything else we possess.

Possible Class Response: People will not trust the deceiver any more, and are likely to stay away from this person for their own reputation's sake. This is especially true if they believed the deceiver to start with. They will feel betrayed.

22. **How many times could she submit her life like this? Does it become any easier? Have you ever known anyone to give up just before the completion?**

Although the enemy was now gone, the problem yet remained and Esther had to appear before the king once again.

Matthew 24:13: Those who endure to the end will be saved.

Possible Class Response: As long as Esther's courage continued, she could continue to approach the king. But, eventually she may have become discouraged. Her main motivation was that she might die if he didn't want her to see him, but she would for sure die if she didn't try. Some class members may have dropped out of school just before graduation. Or they may have fallen just before the end of a race.

23. **Is it self-conceit to think you as one person can make a difference? Are you willing to be on the watch from this day forward for the purpose for which you were born, small or great? Yes or no?**

The heroes of the Bible are lauded in Hebrews 11. Read together verses 33-38. Did they become heroes because things went easy or hard for them? What if Jesus' ancestors in Esther's day had never been threatened with annihilation? Can one person make the difference?

2 Corinthians 6:1: We are workers together with God!

Possible Class Response: We should remember that as Christians we no longer live, but Christ lives in us. Therefore, what we do is to bring honor to Jesus and his church, and not to ourselves. If we do not know for what purpose we were born, we should just keep stepping forward when needed and saying, "Yes, I'll do that." Maybe we'll never know our purpose until we see God. He'll be glad to tell us.

Good Work

Send a petition to someone in congress fighting for a good cause and tell him or her you support it.

BEFORE CLASS:

A. Call your local chamber of commerce or courthouse to find out the nearest phone number and address of a congressman's office. Then call or write, and ask for the issues they are supporting. Also obtain the address of the congressman's Washington office.

B. Select one thing your congressman supports that involves a Christian principal. It may be anti-abortion, jailing drug dealers, saving God's good earth, sending food to a hungry nation, etc. Take a writeup about it (his/hers, or your own) to class.

C. Gather up white bond paper and legal-size envelopes.

E. Write on the blackboard or poster board your congressman's Washington address.

F. Write on the blackboard or poster board some suggestions for those who have trouble wording what they feel.

---

1. "I am glad you are my congressman because you are fighting for _____. I am in full agreement with this. I just wanted to let you know that I am 100% behind you. God bless you."

2. "I have been reading that you are in favor of _____. This is a Christian principle that I, too, support. You have my vote on this issue. God bless you."

3. "I think God puts people like you in congress to stand for Christian principles, such as _____. We need more public servants like you."

4. "I am glad I voted for you, because you are standing for something that is close to my heart, _____. You are in my prayers. You are doing a good job; keep it up."

DURING CLASS:

"We've been talking about standing up for right even when we are afraid of the opposition. We have a congressman who has bravely stood for right, even though many criticize him/her for it. S/he needs our encouragement. Most of our elected officials truly do want to know what the people want, because they want to be elected again. We, as Christians, need to be supportive of good officials."

"I have received from Congressman _____ his/her opinions on the issue of _____. This is what s/he says about it: [Read what you obtained from your congressman.]

Hand out white bond paper and legal-size envelopes. "I have written Congressman _____'s address on the board. I have also written several suggestions of what you could say in your note of encouragement. Feel free to copy any one of them if you like."

"You will have about five minutes to write your note. Let's all be quiet now and allow each other to think and write. When you are done, give your note to me, then offer a silent prayer for him/her and the issue while the others finish."

Concluding Remarks

When time is up and while the slower writers complete their notes, sing one verse of a song, possibly one of the following:

      1.   *Stand Up, Stand Up for Jesus*
      2.   *Faith is the Victory*
      3.   *Onward Christian Soldiers*
      4.   *The Fight is On, Oh Christian Soldiers*

In a few moments, your students will be returning home to the routine needs and problems of their own personal life. Help them begin to be on the lookout for things they can come forward and do.

(Wait for one or two quick replies to each of the following.) "In a few words, what should we do when we're....

      1.   Falsely accused of something?
      2.   Asked to do something that no one else will do?
      3.   Tempted to quit just before fulfilling a task?
      4.   Tempted to give ourselves the glory for accomplishing something?

Have a brief closing prayer for the congressman everyone wrote and the issue involved.

Women: The More Honest Sex

	Men	Women
PEOPLE WHO BELIEVE IT'S ALL RIGHT TO LIE....		
To protect oneself	63%	52%
To keep one's job	56%	35%
To make oneself look better	28%	19%
To gain a small amount of money	25%	15%
To get even with someone	16%	8%
PEOPLE WHO HAVE STOLEN FROM....		
Store	27%	17%
Parent	25%	11%
Friend	19%	7%
Boss	15%	8%
Co-Worker	10%	1%
WORK ETHICS....		
Participated in unethical practices	23%	14%
Lied to boss	27%	18%
Drunk at work	15%	4%
Left early w/o telling anyone	19%	11%
LARCENY....		
Cheated on test/exam	43%	27%
Lied on job application	40%	26%
Borrowed money w/o repaying it	30%	16%
Exaggerated on insurance claim	27%	14%
Used expense account on personal friend	19%	5%
Expect to compromise values to get ahead	32%	20%
The only way to get ahead is cheat	19%	8%

The Day America Told the Truth, James Patterson and Peter Kim, p. 108f

Women in Major Leadership Positions

	Men	Women
United States Governors	46	4
US House of Representatives	352	83
US Senate	79	21

Presidents/Prime Ministers around the World

Women 29
Men 168

Esther's Place in History

BC 534   *Daniel dies at about age 85 (Daniel 1:21).*

BC 520   *Mordecai is probably born*

BC 495   *Esther is probably born*

BC 485   *Xerxes (Aha-Xuerux), son of Darius, becomes ruler of the Persian Empire.*

BC 482   *Vashti is deposed as Queen.*

BC 479   *Esther is taken to the palace, probably about 16 years old (Esther 2:16-20).*

BC 478   *Esther is chosen to be Xerxes' wife and Empress of the Persian Empire.*

BC 473   *Esther saves the Jews from massacre at about age 22.*

BC 465   *Xerxes is killed, having only been married to Esther for 13 years. Artaxerxes becomes emperor and Esther now becomes queen mother at about age 30.*

BC 457   *Esther's stepson, Artaxerxes, allows Ezra to leave Babylon and take a few thousand Jews back to Jerusalem. Esther is now about 40 years old.*

BC 444   *Esther's stepson, Artaxerxes, makes Nehemiah governor of the Jews and allows him to return and rebuild the walls of Jerusalem. Esther is now about 50 years old.*

Inside the Hearts of Bible Women: Teacher's & Advertising Manual

WHEEL SPINNING
Martha

Lesson One: Getting Organized

Lesson Aim

- ♥ **LEARN WHAT GETS IN THE WAY OF HOSPITALITY**
- ♥ **UNDERSTAND IMPULSIVE BEHAVIOR**

Scripture Outline

John 11:1-5: Martha is the sister of Mary who once washed Jesus' feet and dried them with her hair, and of Lazarus. They live in Bethany. Jesus loves them.

John 11:6-19: The sisters send word to Jesus that their brother, Lazarus, is deathly ill. He dies before Jesus comes, and their neighbors come to console them.

John 11:20-27: When word arrives, Jesus is near, Martha immediately runs out to meet him and laments that Lazarus would not have died if Jesus had arrived earlier. Jesus says he will rise again, and Martha says she knows he will on the last day. She also reaffirms her belief that Jesus is the son of God.

John 11:28-33: Martha returns to her house to tell Mary Jesus is coming. Mary goes out to meet him and says the same thing Martha did: He would not have died if he'd been here. Everyone cries for Lazarus including Jesus.

John 11:34-42: Jesus goes to the cemetery and orders the stone rolled away from the cave opening where Lazarus is laid. Martha objects that he's been dead four days and it will be smelly inside. When Jesus tells her she is about to see the glory of God, probably as the eldest sister she allows them to move the stone.

John 11:43-47: Jesus raises Lazarus from the dead to the amazement of everyone, including the jealous religious leaders who are told about it.

[This all occurred at a different time from our lesson. It is given here as background to Martha's deep faith in Jesus.]

Today's World

Nearly everyone has at some time dialed the telephone and then, when the person answered, with embarrassment had to ask, "Who is this? I forgot who I called." Most likely, while we were waiting for the other person to pick up the phone, we were writing ourselves a note to pick up the laundry, looking at the clock, checking the top button of our blouse, or our minds just drifted off.

How about driving somewhere that takes some length of time, suddenly we realize we're there, but don't remember how? We were so involved in other thoughts, we did not concentrate on our driving. And everyone has experienced going to another room to get something, and upon arrival, forgot what it was for. How about eating while we read, and suddenly realizing the food is gone without ever tasting it or remembering we swallowed it?

All of these experiences are due to an inability to concentrate on a particular subject because our brains become overwhelmed by many fleeting thoughts that range over several different subjects.

Everyone knows someone (or they may feel cursed with it themselves) who is unable to control her time. She can never get her laundry done, the family seldom sits down to the table together, she rushes into appointments at the last minute, at the end of the day she's exhausted and doesn't know what she did with her time. She'll explain that she starts to do something, forgets what it was, so starts doing something else. She just can't concentrate very long because other things take over. So her life is filled with numerous incomplete tasks. People tell her she needs counseling. She spends her life feeling like a failure.

If we were discussing children in the classroom, we would be quick to identify this child as having "Attention Deficit Hyperactive Disorder," or "Hyperactivity." Medical books call this "Minimal Brain Damage," or "Minimal Cerebral Dysfunction." The *Physicians' Desk Reference*, 41st Edition, gives indications for this problem as characterized by *distractibility, short attention span, hyperactivity, impulsivity. The diagnosis of this syndrome should not be made with finality when these symptoms are only of comparatively recent origin. Nonlocalizing neurological signs, learning disability, and abnormal EEG may or may not be present, and a diagnosis of central nervous symptom dysfunction may or may not be warranted.*

In late 1990, *The New York Times* reported that researchers may have found the cause of the problem. The National Institute of Mental Health at Bethesda, MD, found that adults who had suffered from attention deficit since childhood had markedly lower brain activity in the area which controls both mental and physical movement. They estimate that about 25 percent of parents with this problem pass it on to their children.

Healthline stated in 2016 that half of children with this affliction carries into adulthood. Dr. Gabrielle Weiss and Dr. Lily Hechtman of Montreal Children's Hospital followed 100 hyperactive children for 15 years into adulthood. Only about half had been able to work around their problem so they could lead productive lives.

One man explained that when a simple thing like a light goes out in a room, he has trouble focusing his behavior on changing the bulb. Instead, his mind is overwhelmed by all the possible problems, and he's likely to begin by examining the light switch.

Dr. C. Keith Conners of Duke University's School of Medicine in North Carolina, said, "It's very important to those of us in the field because we constantly fight a battle with those skeptics and nonbelievers who choose to pass this as bratty behavior caused by poor parenting."

Bible World

The name Bethany, where Martha and her family lived, means house or place of dates and figs. This is a small village on the slopes of the Mount of Olives. Today it is known as El-Azariyeh which means Lazarus. It is about two miles, or an hour's walk, east of Jerusalem, and is near the road leading to Jericho.

It was in Bethany that Lazarus and his sisters, Mary and Martha, lived. Lazarus became sick, and died before Jesus arrived. Then Jesus raised him from the dead (John 11:1-47). The following are the activities of Jesus in Bethany the last ten days of his life, and at his ascension into heaven.

TUESDAY: Jesus left Bethany for a little while and hid in Ephraim, but returned six days before the Passover. (John 11:54-12:1)

FRIDAY NIGHT: While Jesus ate at Lazarus' table, Mary took a full pound of spikenard and anointed Jesus' feet with it, and wiped it with her hair. Spikenard was from India and cost nearly a full-year's wages for the average person. Judas complained the money was wasted, but Jesus said she'd just prepared him for his burial. In the meantime, the Jews were plotting to kill Lazarus because he was living proof of Jesus' power over death. They were also plotting to kill Jesus. (John 11:1-47; 12:1-11)

SATURDAY: Sabbath rest in Bethany.

SUNDAY MORNING: Jesus' triumphal entry into Jerusalem took place. Crowds shouted "Hosanna!" and tossed palm leaves on the ground as a carpet over which he could ride. After speaking in the Temple, he went back to Bethany to spend the night. (John 12:12ff, Matthew 21:9,17)

MONDAY: The next morning, on his way back to Jerusalem, he and his disciples went up to a fig tree to get some breakfast, but it was bearing no fruit. It was wasting space. Jesus cursed it. Then he went on to the Temple where he cleansed it of money exchangers (to Temple currency). Then he returned to Bethany for the night. (Matthew 21:18-22; Mark 11:11-19)

TUESDAY: The next day he returned to the Temple where he spent the day teaching believers, and arguing with those sent by various religious and political leaders of the people (Matthew 21-23). When he left the Temple complex, his disciples pointed out all the grand buildings, and he said they would be destroyed, and then explained both the destruction of Jerusalem, and the end of the world. Two days later was the Passover. Jesus knew he would be crucified soon after it was over. (Matthew 26:1,2)

That night, Jesus went back to Bethany and spent it at the house of Simon who had previously been a leper but healed by Jesus. While eating dinner, a woman with an alabaster box of precious ointment anointed his head. The disciples criticized her for wasting the money, but Jesus said she was just preparing him for burial. (Mark 14:1-9)

WEDNESDAY: Jesus went back to the Temple to teach (Luke 19:35-40;47).

THURSDAY: The last supper was probably held in Jerusalem. Afterward, the disciples went back to the Mount of Olives between Jerusalem and Bethany, where Jesus begged God to not make him go through the agony of the cross. Then Judas arrived with the Temple soldiers. (Luke 22:39-48)

FRIDAY: Jesus was crucified.

ABOUT 47 DAYS LATER: On Jesus' last day on earth after his resurrection, he appeared out of nowhere to the eleven disciples and other believers gathered together in Jerusalem. There he showed them his pierced hands. Then he asked for food so he could eat in front of them, something ghosts don't do. He explained that he'd fulfilled all the prophecies about him in the Old Testament.

Then he walked the two miles with them over to Bethany. There he explained that the Comforter would come to them next. Then he lifted up his hands and blessed all those with him. While he blessed them, he began to rise up into the sky until he disappeared in the clouds. As they stood staring up into the heavens, two angels appeared to them reassuring them Jesus would return someday in the very same way he left them that day in Bethany. (Luke 24:33-53, Acts 1:8-11)

Introducing the Lesson

Have we lost the ability to be hospitable in North America? What is it creating? Year after year we attend church with people we never really get to know because we never have time. Year after year we intend to have a neighbor over to get better acquainted, and even invite to worship with us, but we never have time. We have relatives across town—brothers, sisters and cousins whose children are a foot taller every time we see them; and parents who are a little grayer every time we see them. We see them only on rare occasions when some one person in the group takes the responsibility to get everyone together; or perhaps when a relative comes in from out of town, wants to see everyone, so everyone gets together at one house for the sake of time.

The New York Magazine reported in 2015 that one-third of us have never met our next-door neighbor. In the 1970s, one-third of us regularly spent time with our neighbors.

Display THE PEOPLE NEXT DOOR. Is it lack of time? Is it lack of energy? Is it because we think everything has to be perfect with china out so people don't think we're uncouth? Do we spend all our time running back and forth to work, running back and forth getting our children to their activities, running back and forth to make sure we get to the church building for all its activities? Do we spend the remainder of our time in front of television sets?

The average person spends six and a half hours in front of the television in the summer and seven and a half hours in the winter, every day. **Display WEEKLY TV VIEWING OF AMERICANS.** In addition, CNN reported in 2016 the average American spends ten hours a day with a computer, i-pad or smartphone.

Discuss "Attention Deficit Disorder" in adults to the degree you wish.

One of the qualifications of a church elder is hospitality (Titus 1:7,8). A Christian widow supported by the church must be hospitable (1 Timothy 5:10). We must be hospitable to each other "without grudging" (1 Peter 4:9).

Discussion Questions

1. **Under what circumstances do we usually set our alarm clocks to get up earlier than usual?**

   Proverbs 31:15: The "worthy woman" rises before dawn to get breakfast ready for everyone.

   Possible Class Response: We get up earlier than usual if something special is going to happen that day. We may be leaving on a vacation and want to get an early start. Perhaps the weather is bad and we want plenty of time to get to work. We may want to beat the crowd to a park on a holiday. We may be expecting special company that day and have a lot to do to get ready for them.

2. **When we set our alarms to get up early, what kinds of things can nullify the extra effort?**

   Ecclesiastes 5:16: If we spend our time on unnecessary things, for all our efforts we'll only reap the wind.

   Possible Class Response: Sometimes we decide we have so much extra time, we can do something extra we'd been wanting to do such as fix an extra fancy breakfast for our family, or go out for breakfast, or transfer all our information from our old address book to our new address book. Or we can do a lot of things that "will only take a minute" such as mend the underside of our bedspread, read that magazine article we'd been wanting to get to, or make a Christmas list.

3. **In these busy times when many women work outside the home, what are some foods we can fix ahead of time and store to save us some work later when we have company?**

   Genesis 41:35,36: While there was plenty of food and a lot of time, Pharaoh had the extra food stored up in preparation for a coming famine.

<u>Possible Class Response</u>: We can fix cold drinks ahead of time as well as cold salads (keeping the ingredients separate). We can peel the potatoes and put them in water in the refrigerator. We can fix the bread, let it rise, and leave it on a counter. Deserts can almost always be fixed ahead of time. We can thaw the meat; or even select a meat that can be cooked several hours in the oven or a crockpot without much attention.

4. **What are some tactful ways we can get off the phone without making the caller feel they aren't important enough to talk to?**

On busy days, the phone is just as likely to ring as on ordinary days. Some people call just to talk and pass the time.

<u>Proverbs 16:20-22a</u>: If we handle things wisely, they will turn out good. We will be careful not to make people feel bad when we disagree with them, we will reassure them we understand their point of view, and we will use pleasant words.

<u>Possible Class Response</u>: If the person called just to talk, we can say something like, "I'm so glad you called. There were some things I wanted to share with you, but I'm right in the middle of something and can't do justice to it right now. Will you please forgive me if I call you back tomorrow? Wish me luck. I'll tell you about it tomorrow. Bye." Or, we can let her bring up a subject and respond in agreement without any other comments. When she pauses, we can just wait in silence and not respond with our own point of view. She is likely to tell her story briefly, and, without the interaction, say something like, "I guess you're, busy." We can agree we are and, "Let's get together tomorrow." Then hang up before she can get started on what the weather or sales are going to be like tomorrow.

5. **There are times on busy days that we have opportunities to do a good work, to encourage or teach someone. How should we handle these opportunities?**

We know Martha had great faith and probably looked for chances to help others.

<u>Luke 10:30-33</u>: A man was robbed and beaten and left on the roadside for dead. A priest [on his way to hospital visitation?] saw him but didn't stop. A Levite [on his way to church?] saw him but was afraid he'd be late, so he didn't stop either. Then an idol-worshipper came by, gave him first aid, took him to a hospital, left money for the bill, and went on his way.

<u>Possible Class Response</u>: We need to weigh the situation. If our company is very special and we are trying to practice hospitality as commanded in the Bible, we probably want to make things extra special. In that case, we should indicate our desire to help this person and see if we could do the good work or encourage/teach the next day, then tell them we love them and will be praying for them. However, if the matter is urgent, we should spend a little time with this person needing our help, then either cut out some of the special things we'd planned for company or call a friend/relative to come help us. But we shouldn't let the opportunity pass us by forever. It's a matter of prioritizing and then making adjustments to both responsibilities.

6. **Tell about a time you decided to do a major cleaning just before company came.**

How did it affect you? How did it affect your company?

Proverbs 24:3: A household is built with wisdom and discretion.

Possible Class Response: The author of this book in her younger years had a nasty habit of scrubbing walls, cleaning the carpet, washing curtains, or cleaning out cupboards the day special company was supposed to arrive. It's gotten her into trouble nearly every time. By doing what only indirectly affected her guests, she had to cut out something special that directly affected her guests such as a special dessert or writing love notes and putting them inside the cookies or whatever. One time, the company arrived while she was at the store buying something she forgot.

7. **Although fellowship can be inviting friends over for just coffee, what are some ways we can prepare ourselves ahead of time to demonstrate to our extra-special company how highly we think of them?**

   Esther 1:5-7: King Xerxes had a feast for his most-trusted governors and decorated the dining room with a white/green/blue color scheme, and got out his best gold- and silverware.

   Possible Class Response: We can have a pretty colored table cloth; if we don't want to spend much, we could buy a paper one, or a new and colorful shower curtain [with the holes and weights cut off], or even use a colorful sheet. We can put flowers or candles on the table. We can get out or borrow a punch bowl and have punch before or after the meal. We can fix coffee with an added flavor in it such as vanilla, mint, cinnamon, etc.

Good Work

Write down some tricks or recipe tips that can be prepared ahead of time. Exchange them with your discussion group and then pass them on to some young married women in your congregation.

BEFORE CLASS:

A. Obtain some brightly colored index cards, 3x5 or larger.

B. Fix up a shoebox with wallpaper covering it. (This is your way of getting them to recall the unique things they have done.) Cut a hole in the top.

C. Write a couple suggestions of your own on a couple of the cards.

D. Write your suggestions on the blackboard or poster board.

DURING CLASS:

"Fellowship in our home is a very important part of Christianity. We don't really get to know people in the church building. We have been talking about preparing things ahead of time when we have special company. I'm sure you have some unique ideas that you thought of or have been passed down in your family."

Pass out colored index cards. "Take as many as you like and write down some tricks or recipe tips that can be prepared ahead of time for when company comes. We will read them to each other and then pass them on to some young married women in our congregation who don't attend our class."

"You will have about eight minutes to do this. Let's all be quiet now and allow each other to think and write. When you are done, offer a silent prayer that you will be able to make more time to be hospitable yourself."

Concluding Remarks

When time is up and while the slower writers complete their notes, sing one verse of a song, possibly one of the following:

1. *How Sweet How Heavenly is the Sight*
2. *We are the Family, the Family of God*
3. *Take My Life and Let it Be*
4. *Blest Be the Tie that Binds*

"I doubt any of us practices hospitality the way we should. There are all kinds of reasons and excuses. Sometimes it's just because we can't turn off the TV. Let's just go around the room and share the reasons or excuses we have for not having company over as much as we should."

After you have done this, "Let's have a chain prayer in closing how. There is strength in numbers, so let's each one ask God to help us overcome whatever it is that keeps us from having our fellow Christians in our home more often. If you are not comfortable praying aloud, just squeeze the hand of the lady next to you."

Inside the Hearts of Bible Women: Teacher's & Advertising Manual

The People Next Door

45%

42%

27%

15%

45% Never Spent an Evening Together
42% Never Borrowed Anything From Them
27% Was Never in their House
15% Don't even know their name

Weekly TV Viewing of Americans

GENDER	AGE	TIME
Women	18-24	23 hours, 38 min
	25-54	30 hours, 34 min
	55-over	41 hours, 19 min
Men	18-24	20 hours, 50 min
	25-54	26 hours, 44 min
	55-over	38 hours, 05 min
Female	Teens	23 hours, 25 min
Male		23 hours, 01 min
Children	6-11	21 hours, 19 min
	2-5	26 hours, 14 min
EVERYONE	AVERAGE	29 hours, 05 min

Information Please Almanac

Wheel Spinning

Lesson Two: The Agenda

Lesson
Aim
- ♥ GET CONTROL OF OUR TIME
- ♥ ACCEPT OURSELVES WITHOUT COMPLAINT

Scripture Outline

John 12:1-3: Jesus goes to have dinner with Lazarus. Martha serves everyone. Mary washes Jesus' feet with expensive ointment and wipes them with her hair. [This occurred months after the events of today's lesson.]

Luke 10:38: Martha is apparently the eldest in the family, for Jesus and his apostles enter HER house. Lazarus, the only male, would have inherited everything, but Martha would still be in charge of the goings-on within the home.

Today's World

In her book, *Applied Christianity: A Handbook of 500 Good Works,* Katheryn Haddad included a chapter on "Keeping Your Home" for women who don't like housework and can't ever seem to get organized. Explaining Martha's problems, she recommended the following if you are a stay-at-home mom:

First, let's create a family for you. Let's assume you have four children—two school age and two preschools; and that your husband must leave for work no later than 7:00 AM.

You will want to get up at 6:00 to avoid a rush. Now there isn't anything so bad about getting up at 6:00 if you go to bed at 10:00—eight hours' sleep. You can arrange for a half-hour nap during the early afternoon to get more sleep to refresh yourself halfway through the day. Or if it's purely a psychological hangup, pretend you are living in England and it is really 11:00 AM!

Before you ever leave your bedroom, you should get dressed, fix your face and hair—which shouldn't take more than twenty minutes if you're not going anywhere. Then tidy up your room—make your bed (not more than 3 minutes) and pick up clothes and other miscellany (about 5 minutes)—yes, including your husband's clothes. How wonderful! It is now 6:30 and you already have one room clean and yourself fresh and pretty, ready to be presented to your awakening family!

At 6:30 wake up your children. Call them only once. If they do not get up after the first call, this means you have indirectly trained them to stay in bed by letting them get by with it. So discipline them immediately (not yelling though, for you have a gentle voice—Proverbs 31:26), and retrain them. Unless you serve pancakes or biscuits, it should not take you more than 15 minutes to fix sausage and eggs or oatmeal or something similar, with toast. Have your school-age children come into the kitchen and set the table for you.

At 6:45 the entire family should sit down to eat together. To start the day together as a family with your king at the end of the table will give a real feeling of closeness to your family and a warm sense of why and for whom your husband is faithfully going to work every day.

Now it is 7:00 and everyone says goodbye to the man of the house. Your preschool children probably will still be dabbling at their plates. Your school-age children can now take up to half an hour to get dressed.

At 7:30 they should be ready to tidy up their own room—make their own bed, pick up their clothes, and put away their toys. Everything should be off the floor but the furniture. If they are having trouble sticking with their chore, you may wish to set a kitchen timer to limit them to perhaps 20 minutes to clean up everything. When they are finished, compliment them and tell them their room looks very nice.

During the time between 7:00 and 8:00 when your older children are getting ready for school (this will have to be adjusted, of course, if they leave earlier), your preschool children can finish eating and then play while you wash the dishes/fill the dishwasher and clean up the kitchen. If one or both of your preschoolers is above age two, they can be taught to carefully take most everything off the table for you. It shouldn't take more than ten minutes to wash your breakfast dishes if you do them by hand, and another ten to dry them and put them away out of sight. Five minutes to wipe off the countertops, table and stovetops, ten minutes to sweep the floor, and ten minutes to mop it.

Your kitchen will take approximately 45 minutes to fix up; however, you will be interrupted by wiping off little ones' mouths and checking the older ones' rooms, so you should allow yourself an hour. Once you have done this, you will have a gleaming kitchen which you should not have to re-enter until noon (unless you wash or iron, etc., in there). Now whisk your school children out the door.

It's 8:00. You have been up two hours and have been very busy. Your husband is gone and your older children have just left for school. You now deserve a little break. Take out of the freezer the meat for the evening meal, then fix yourself a cup of coffee or glass of tea and sit down in a comfortable place. But be careful not to start something that will be hard to tear yourself away from, such as a novel. If your little ones bathe in the morning, they may wish to play in the tub during your half-hour rest, depending on their age.

At 8:30 take your little ones to their room to get dressed and do their share of cleaning up their room. If they are two, they are old enough to learn to make their own bed. Help them with it, but do not do it alone for them. Sit down somewhere in their room while they pick up their toys and clothes. It should not take more than 5 minutes to dress each child, and about 20 minutes to tidy up their room. Total, 30 minutes.

Now it is 9:00 and you've got most of your house clean and tidy already! Go into your living room or den. This room should require the least amount of your time. The previous evening your children should have put their books, shoes and toys in their room. Therefore, all that may be in the living room or den in the morning is newspapers, etc. If you knit or work on any project here, make sure there is a basket or some place to put it away. It should not take you more than ten minutes to straighten it up and quickly dust. You still have time to sort dirty clothes and put your first load in. (With a family of six, doing two loads a day will keep things manageable.)

9:30 and you are ready to clean up the bathroom. Try your best to keep it odor-free and sanitary. Clean out the sink, tub, and toilet daily so they are never really a hard chore. Be sure to clean around the bases of these appliances where bacteria usually grow the most quickly. then spray with a disinfectant. You will have fewer colds in your family doing this. Wipe off the mirror and chrome fixtures with window cleaner to make them really shine. Last, mop the floor with some kind of sanitizing agent. It shouldn't take you more than half an hour to clean up your bathroom, and put your second load of clothes in the washer.

10:00 and Eureka! You're done! Amazing!

Bible World

The humbler homes of the Jews consisted of just one room with clay-lined walls and dirt floors. Middle-class homes were made of kiln-dried brick. The wealthy had houses of limestone. Usually the flat roof was composed of layers of reeds cemented with lime for waterproofing, with openings in a low wall for water to run off.

It is believed that Martha's home was at least middle class. In that case, her rooms were arranged to form a courtyard in the center, with all doors opening onto it. Around the inside of the courtyard was usually a narrow covered walkway for rainy days.

Because of the mild weather in Palestine, much of the actual living was outside. Frequently the house had a courtyard stairway that led to the roof where much of the entertaining took place. In hot weather, it was customary to sleep on the roof. A portion of the roof was covered over to afford some protection from the intense rays of the sun. It was to such an "upper room" that Jesus and his disciples had the last supper, and where his disciples awaited him at Pentecost.

Inside the house, the walls would be plain or coated with lime. Walls of the rich were ornately decorated with wood, marble, and ivory mosaics. Windows were small to prevent the entrance of robbers, and frequently covered with latticework, since window glass was unknown then. The rooms were quite dark; therefore, each had a lamp which was usually placed on a shelf at the center pole of the room which supported the roof.

Most people ate baked wheat or barley cakes/biscuits. The village mill was operated by the women who usually ground together in pairs since it was arduous work (Matthew 24:41). It was important in preparing the grain for grinding that it be carefully sifted to remove the tares. Other parts of the meal would be a meat and vegetable stew. Each one helped himself from the common dish by a spoon or scoop formed by a piece of bread freshly torn from the loaf. It was an act of courtesy and reaffirming friendship to prepare such a "sop" and hand it to the next person at the table (John 13:26).

The main meal time came just after sunset when the day's work was done and people came in from the fields or the market. It was a time of family reunion. Cushions were placed on the floor around a low table. Amid the joys of family, the one hot-cooked meal of the day was consumed.

Introducing the Lesson

Some of us don't have company over because we think we must have beautiful china and a gourmet meal. We don't even have to have a meal at all. Or we may think our house has to be modern, our furniture without lumps and scratches, and our decor the latest trend. If we love ourselves as we should, we will be happy with what we have, even if it means comparing ourselves with poor people in Russia or China or Africa. If you are a lovable person, people will WANT to come to your home. We all would rather feel welcome in a poor home than awkward in a rich home.

We may be limited by income. But we are not limited with soap and water. We can have a house that is tidy and clean where people are more comfortable with us than in a rich house that is cluttered. In her book, *Applied Christianity: A Handbook of 500 Good Works*, Katheryn Haddad devotes one chapter to "Keeping Our Home." **Display HOW TO MAKE TIME FOR MYSELF.** Explain to whatever detail you desire. This is ideal, but shows the importance of time management even in our every-day life. If we get this under control, we'll be able to prepare for company more comfortably also.

Discussion Questions

8. **How can we avoid neglecting our families while preparing for company?**

    1 Timothy 5:8: Those who don't take care of their own families deny their Christianity.

    Possible Class Response: We can prepare for their needs as well as part of our company's dinner ahead of time. We can arrange for our family to go out to eat for breakfast without us, or allow the children to go somewhere special that afternoon. If we can't avoid neglecting them, we can spend extra quality time with them the few days prior to company coming. We can write love notes to our family ahead of time with perhaps an IOU for "one extra special day of your choice" for them to collect after the company is gone.

9. **Why do you think we try to impress people with being the best at something? Is it really for their benefit or ours?**

    Proverbs 16:18,19: Pride goes before destruction; haughtiness goes before a fall. It's better to be lowly with the right spirit than to associate with the proud who will fight over who has or gets the best.

    Possible Class Response: We must ask ourselves honestly why we are making things extra special for company. Are we trying to outdo someone else? Are we trying to show we are superior to others? If we have pottery dishes instead of china, or stainless flatware instead of silver, does that bother us? Praying to God about it helps. We can thank him for his blessings and promise to share those blessings with others as much as possible. Perhaps if our company compliments you on anything extra nice you have, you can say that God has blessed you far above what you ever thought he would, and you want to share these things.

10. **Have you ever tried a new recipe on company? What are the chances of it turning out perfect? Is a day with company the time to try it? Why?**

    Proverbs 13:16: If we're prudent, we'll do what we know will work out, and not make ourselves look like fools by guessing.

    Possible Class Response: Again, when the author of this book was younger, she tried out new recipes on company because she waited too long to try to come up with new ideas. About half the time they worked out. No, company should not be experimented with. We end up nervous and edgy about whether it will turn out and try to think up excuses if it doesn't. The company has to think of excuses for us, as well as try to find what does taste or look good. Everyone's embarrassed. It may discourage us from having company again for a long time.

11. **How can we organize a busy day ahead of time so distractions don't affect us and add to our burdens?**

    Jesus later told Martha she had been distracted with many things (Luke 10:40.

    Ecclesiastes 3:1: There is a proper time for everything.

    Possible Class Response: We should make out a detailed schedule and allow each duty sufficient time. We should make out the schedule several days ahead of time so we can insert things we might have forgotten. We need to allow time for travel if we're going to the store, cleaning each room, setting the table (do it early in the day), making meals for our family, doing the dishes several times, taking a restful bath, sitting with a cup of coffee/tea for a few minutes, and the time to make each dish. We should do as much as possible the day before such as house cleaning and shopping. Then we should spend the entire day company is coming doing nothing but setting the table, preparing dishes ahead of time, and getting ourselves ready. It will take twice as long as you think. Be sure to fit in your rest time before everyone arrives; it will make you a gracious hostess.

12. **Have you ever gone shopping on a rushed day to get something you really**

needed, but browsed first resulting in your not having time to get just what you went for? How did you feel when you got home?

Proverbs 31:27: The worthy woman supervised everything in her household in a responsible manner and did not get sidetracked.

Possible Class Response: Absolute frustration. When this happens, we do not feel good about ourselves, and we certainly don't feel like a "worthy woman." It throws us completely off if we are depending on the item we went to the store for. Then we have to change the menu or other arrangements. We don't feel good about ourselves, so we start snapping at other people. We end up not being a very pleasant hostess to our company.

13. **How can this "tortoise-and-hare" syndrome be avoided?**

Matthew 25:1-8: The parable of the bridesmaids shows half of them not preparing ahead of time for what they needed. They had to run out to the store to get oil when they're supposed to already be at the church. So the wedding goes on without them.

Possible Class Response: We can do early preparation for company, get over-confident and let the time slip up on us. We should make a detailed schedule, not leaving anything out.

14. **Making a new dress or new curtains or new table cloth, etc. just before company arrives is very tempting. Have you ever done this? Why? Consider Matthew 6:21. What was the end result of your last-minute endeavor?**

Matthew 6:21: What you spend your money on is where your heart really is.

Possible Class Response: If we ended up having to cut short the time spent on the meal or something directly affecting the company, we would have been putting ourselves first. We wanted OUR things to look better than usual, instead the COMPANY'S things looking and tasting better than usual. If we realized possibly half way into our project that we were going to be short of time after all, we probably tried to take short cuts and ended up not doing it right. If we truly thought we'd have time to do these things and ended up cutting short what we did for our special company, we probably felt frustrated and guilty.

15. **How can we decide just what is important so we can be gracious hostesses?**

Apparently, Martha had let a lot of important things go until the last minute, by what she said to Jesus after he arrived. Obviously she thought that everything she'd done that day was important. She had been too hard on herself and expected too much of herself.

Matthew 6:24: We can't put two opposing matters first. We can put love and the spiritual first or we can put the material first.

Possible Class Response: Some people think our company will come to our house and scrutinize everything in it. These people are self-conscious and don't feel people will accept them as they are. By doing this, we are putting our own feelings first instead of the feelings of the company. If the company cared that you didn't serve with china and crystal and silver, they wouldn't come in the first place. Company is always flattered they were remembered and invited. They know someone is putting themselves out for them, and appreciate the expression of friendship. They look forward to spending quality time, conversation, and laughter with their host family. This is why they are coming. Isn't that why we invite them? It should be.

16. **Tell of a time when you had to send someone else to the door to greet the guests and then to entertain them until you got dressed. How do you think it made your guests feel?**

    Because of much but poor preparation, Martha did not make a good hostess.

    Luke 12:36,37: The blessed are those who, when their special guests arrive, they hear their knock and meet them at the door. Then everyone will sit down and eat with joy.

    Possible Class Response: Some may have been just getting out of the bathtub. Some may have been rushing around to close the utility room door where they were doing laundry, or hide something they didn't get to. Some may have been at the store getting a last-minute item. Some may have been rushing to get the potatoes on. The guests always look forward to seeing the host and hostess. They felt special when invited. When both don't greet them at the door, they wonder what is more important—hiding the dirty laundry or giving a warm smile and greeting. They'd rather you look at them than the potatoes you're peeling.

Good Work

Write a sample schedule you normally keep the two days before having special company. Put everyone's sample schedules together and give to some young married ladies or a class of young marrieds. Include a note of love and appreciation for the young wives.

BEFORE CLASS:

A. Obtain line paper such as that sold in a tablet for informal stationery. Get colored just for fun if they have it.

B. Write down the schedule you normally keep before company.

C. Write the following on some nice stationery as well as on the blackboard or poster board:

"Having company is fun. Having special company for a nice dinner is a little extra work, but doesn't need to be harried. Young people today live such busy lives. Here is an example of how we in the ladies Bible class have learned to schedule our preparation time so we can be relaxed and happy hostesses, and have relaxed and happy guests. It isn't perfect, but it's worked for us. Maybe you've already worked all this out. But perhaps our little schedule will have an idea or two for you in it. It is sent to you in love for we know how much you love the Lord and those around you."

D. Make space on the blackboard or overhead projector transparency to write two days of schedule. Write in each hour of the day and leave a space to fill in during class.

DURING CLASS:

"We've been talking about scheduling our time when we have company so we can do everything we want to for them and still be relaxed and pleasant when they arrive. This makes everyone happy. And it encourages us to have company again. We've spent most of our time talking about special company for a nice dinner."

Hand out lined paper. "On the board is what I have written on stationary to be given to some young married ladies in our congregation. What we want to do in class now is to list what we usually do the day before and the day of having special company over. You will have five minutes to do this. Then we will combine our schedules. They will not be collected."

Let's all be quiet now so we can think and write.

When time is up, even though some may still be writing, line up someone to write down on paper what you write on the blackboard. Then go through each hour of the two days getting the consensus of the class members on what most of them do for your final list.

Concluding Remarks

While the "class secretary" finishes copying the schedule from the board, sing one verse of a song, possibly one of the following:

1. *Oh Thou Fount of Every Blessing*
2. *Count Your Blessings*
3. *I Want to be a Worker for the Lord*
4. *Give of Your Best to the Savior*

"We all are easily distracted by something, even when we have something very important to do. Let's go around the room and confess what distracts us."

After this is done, "Let's now have a chain closing prayer and ask God to help us overcome that which distracts us when we have more important things to do. If you are not comfortable praying aloud, just squeeze the hand of the lady next to you."

How To Make Time For Myself

6:00	Get out of bed, dress myself, make bed, pick up dirty clothes.
6:30	Wake up husband and children to get dressed while I fix breakfast.
6:45	Eat breakfast together as a family.
7:00	Wash dishes & clean off table/counters; school children tidy up rooms.
7:30	Send older children off to school; sweep and mop kitchen floor.
8:00	Take dinner meat out of freezer and sit down to relax.
8:30	Help younger children get dressed and tidy up rooms.
9:00	Tidy up den or living room; put first load of laundry in washer.
9:30	Clean fixtures in bathroom, sterilize, mop; put in second load of laundry.
10:00	THE REST OF THE DAY IS YOURS TO DO GOOD WORKS, STUDY, ETC. UNTIL YOUR CHILDREN COME HOME FROM SCHOOL AND HUSBAND COMES HOME FROM WORK.

Wheel Spinning

Lesson Three: Selfless Giving

Lesson
Aim
- ♥ **SET PRIORITIES**
- ♥ **REMAIN COOL, CALM, AND COLLECTED**

Scripture Outline

<u>Luke 10:39</u>: When Jesus arrives, Mary goes in to listen to him talk.

<u>Luke 10:40</u>: Martha stays in the kitchen and has too many things to do to get the meal finished and served. So she goes to Jesus, an old family friend by now, and indirectly blames Jesus for distracting Mary who she needs to help her.

<u>Luke 10:41</u>: Jesus says she's being too particular about too many things and it is just upsetting her.

<u>Luke 10:42</u>: Jesus then adds that Martha spending time with him is more important than the meal she's trying to fix.

Today's World

In her book, *Applied Christianity: A Handbook of 500 Good Works,* Katheryn Haddad talks in her chapter on "Keeping Our Homes" as though it were our privilege. Have we examined our attitudes toward housework? Here is what she says:

Do you consider yourself a slave to your house or the queen of your house? If you do not have to go outside of your home to work, you have not only a spiritual obligation here, but a wonderful privilege and opportunity that men do not have. They go out and earn money—cold, hard cash. They may or may not earn it doing a job they like or feel a personal interest in. And what's it all for? Food, clothing, a comfortable and attractive home. And you, Your Majesty, queen of your house, you have the honor and privilege of turning that cold cash into those things he is earning the money for—making them a reality. That's the fun part!

"But I still hate housework," you might declare after all this. "I know it's supposed to be noble and all that, and it is my Christian obligation, but to me it's nothing but plain drudgery and demeaning. Besides, I've got other more creative and satisfactory things to do."

Dear Queen, remember God is against confusion (1 Corinthians 14:33) and for order (1 Corinthians 14:40). He uses dirt as a symbol of sin (Isaiah 57:20) and cleanliness as a symbol of righteousness (Psalm 51:10). God uses bad odors as a punishment (Isaiah 3:24) and sweet smells as representative of sweet sacrifices (Philippians 4:18). Spots and blemishes represent the wicked, while white is pure and good (Isaiah 1:18).

Noble Lady of your palace, if you like creativity, then create! And since God uses symbolism, you use symbolism too. Use creative symbolism. Here's how:

Look at those dirty dishes. Wash each one as though it were a jewel in your heavenly crown to be made bright again. Look at the marks and dirt on your floor. Sweep it and mop it and put a little shine on it to give yourself and your family a little foretaste of the clean and shining streets of gold you will walk on in the heavenly realm. Look at your dirty oven. Wash it even as the Lord washes away your sins.

Look at those wrinkled clothes. Iron each piece as a work of art to see how smooth and silk-like you can make them for your royal household. Look at those torn clothes. Mend them as the Lord mends hearts when they are torn and broken.

Look at your dirty windows. Wash them and let the golden sunshine into your home, your life, your heart. Look at your messy bed. Pull the sheets and covers up nice and smooth, and then crown it with a bedspread the color of a gem from the very foundation of your heavenly home.

Yes, everything you do can remind you of the royal home that is awaiting you in heaven, and the royal realm of the home that is all your own, and with which your Lord has so greatly blessed you. *Whatever you do, work at it with all your heart, as working for the Lord* (Colossians 3:23).

You are the only one in your little world who can make your home into your family's fortress and palace. You are the only one, dear Christian lady, dear mother, dear wife, who is truly worthy (Proverbs 31) to do this for them. God bless you in this truly worthy good work that is as great as you are!

Bible World

Before the flood, people ate roots, vegetables, and fruits (Genesis 1:29; 2:16; 9:3,4). Jabal, who lived before the flood, raised cattle; so it is assumed people drank milk. During the post-Flood era, legumes (peas and beans) were eaten in abundance (Genesis 25:34). They also ate honey, spices and nuts (Genesis 43:11).

After the flood, they were allowed to eat meat from birds, land animals, and fish. However, the Law of Moses prohibited some as food. Overall, meat from animals who normally carried parasites or were parasites ("vultures") were forbidden. They were also not allowed to eat fat (Leviticus 3:16,17) or intestines.

They ate oxen, sheep, goats, calves, lambs, pigeons, turtle doves, antelope, deer, fish. Roasting on a spit was the oldest way of cooking, but by Jesus' time, they usually boiled, fried or roasted it (1 Samuel 2:15). When cooked in pots (1 Samuel 2:14; 2 Chronicles 35:13), it was taken to the table and served with broth (Judges 6:19). Usually meat was not served in steaks and roasts, but cut up and served with rice or squash, or wrapped in cabbage or grape leaves. Sometimes meat was salted and preserved in skin bottles, then cut in pieces and served as needed (Leviticus 11:22; Matthew 3:4).

They drank milk from cows, sheep and goats (Deuteronomy 32:14; Proverbs 27:27). Sometimes it was sweet, sometimes sour, sometimes thick or curdled. They also made butter from it (Proverbs 30:33).

At first, grain was eaten without cooking, and sometimes even today is mixed uncooked with some foods. If expecting to be gone all day, a laborer might take two loaves of bread, one filled with cheese and the other with olives. Sometimes grain was mixed into a broth with other vegetables to make a soup or stew. Vegetables included pulse, lentils, beans, onions, garlic, cucumbers, and green herbs (1 Kings 21:2; Proverbs 15:17).

They enjoyed honey from sweet grapes boiled to a syrup, wood honey of wild bees (1 Samuel 14:25; Matthew 3:4), or grape molasses used to boil figs. They also had raisins, dried figs (1 Samuel 25:18), date cakes (2 Samuel 16:1) and fresh fruits. Oranges and lemons ripened in the spring and lasted only a short time until the apricots ripened. After the apricots, the melons, plums, figs and pomegranates were ripe. Toward the end of the season, the grapes ripened and remained until the oranges were in season again.

***

The early inns such as what Joseph's brothers went to (Genesis 42:27) and Moses stopped at (Exodus 4:24) were just outdoor shelters such as a tent or cave. Rahab who kept the two Jewish spies in Jericho (Joshua 2:1) was a prostitute (the Hebrew word always being translated as harlot or whore), so they apparently stayed in a brothel. The first building set aside as an inn is found in Jeremiah 41:17 about the time the Israelites were taken into captivity. When Jesus was born, there was only one inn in Bethlehem (Luke 2:7 "the inn").

Therefore, hospitality was extremely important. People depended on private homeowners to provide them food and shelter. Lot in metropolitan Sodom took two men (angels) home with him so they wouldn't have to spend the night in the street (Genesis 19:2,3). A Levite traveling with his concubine and servant waited in the street for someone to offer to take them home (Judges 19:17-21). Inns were still not common in the early Christian era (I Timothy 5:10). Therefore, Jesus had to rely on friends at various towns to take him and his disciples in. Martha must have had at least a middle-class home to have housed as many people as she did.

Introducing the Lesson

Hospitality is important. Part of it involves keeping our house in order. Most of us confess that we don't like housework, never did like housework, and don't intend ever to like housework.

In that case, let me read a few words of encouragement. **Read whichever parts of APPLIED CHRISTIANITY found above that you like.**

What did Martha have to work with? They had about the same foods that we do today. The important thing is that Jesus and his disciples needed a place to eat. It didn't matter if it was on paper plates as long as they didn't go hungry.

There are many people in our lives today—people from church, our neighborhood, our extended family—that we need to be having in our homes. **Display Hebrews 13:2.** Perhaps if we use this as our motto, it will encourage us to be more hospitable.

Discussion Questions

17. **Tell of some similar personal experiences where you put yourself on a guilt trip over it all, and then became angry if someone else didn't share that "guilt trip" with you.**

    <u>1 Samuel 14:24,27-30,44,45</u>: Saul was mad at his enemy and couldn't eat, so he demanded no one else eat until he was avenged. His son, Jonathan, hadn't heard about it, so tasted some honey. When his father found out, he ordered Jonathan killed. The people convinced Saul to save him.

    <u>Possible Class Response</u>: Joy turns to panic because of poor preparation. Then tempers become short and we sometimes say things we shouldn't. Our plan to be such great hostesses backfires completely. Perhaps the recipe didn't turn out, or a food item came up short, or there was no time left to make desert so ice cream had to be substituted. We feel like failures as good hostesses. We become embarrassed in front of the company. It is hard for us to admit we didn't allow enough time for the unexpected as well as the necessary. It is easier to blame others for the fix we've gotten ourselves into.

18. **What is the difference in busy work and truly serving?**

    In the original language of the Bible, Luke says that what Martha was doing was encumbering herself with too many things (Luke 10:40-41). This is not what Martha said about herself—having to serve alone. Jesus never condemned serving. So apparently she was in the kitchen wearing herself out on non-essentials or essentials that should have been done earlier.

    <u>Possible Class Response</u>: We can lose our focus and play the part without getting down to the true reason we're doing something. In teaching a class, we may spend all our

time coloring a visual aid, and end up with little time to study. We can join a committee and spend all our time arguing about what dishes to keep in the church kitchen instead of deciding what potlucks to have and getting volunteers to be in charge. When having company, whatever directly affects the company is part of the serving. Washing curtains isn't. Making sure everyone has a fork is.

19. **How can we distinguish between temporal good and eternal good, and then arrange our time accordingly? Give examples of typical every-day choices.**

    The original Bible language says Mary chose that which was better (10:42). Jesus did not say what Martha was trying to do was bad; but there was something better to do with her time now (10:39, 42).

    Possible Class Response: One of the most obvious things that gets in our way is turning on the TV "to relax" at the end of a hectic day. We could do other things to relax like people did before TV such as read, call a friend on the phone, write a letter to a relative, address cards to some sick or shut-ins, read a book to our children. TV may relax us, but all we're doing is watching other people (pretend people) experience life while we sit on the sidelines. Something else that gets in our way is our choice of entertainment. We can go out to eat with just our family, or invite another family/friend to join us. On days when there is something special scheduled at the church building, we can ask ourselves what we'd do if we were paid to attend that function: We'd find the time to go. We can also recall times when we had to force ourselves to attend a special church gathering, but were glad after we arrived that we did.

20. **Tell about things in your life you have done to earn or "buy" other people's love in an artificial way. How will you change that?**

    A psychologist writing about shyness once said that we cannot be so intelligent, so talented, so witty, so anything to make us irresistible for others to love us. People do not love us so much for what we do or are, but for how we make them feel about themselves—how we love THEM. That love for them makes it nearly impossible to keep from loving us in return.

    1 Samuel 18:7-12: When people started singing the praises of David's battle victories over Saul's, Saul got jealous and afraid that David was taking people's love from him. Saul started trying to kill David so people would go back to admiring him the most.

    1 John 4:19: We love God because he loved us first and not because of his unspeakable power. Satan is powerful too, but we don't love him.

    Possible Class Response: Some get involved in church activities that are showy so others will tell them how great they are, and will avoid the quiet duties that need taken care of. Some buy a lot of gifts for their children or give them money to go to a lot of special events. Some neglect their families to help outsiders do things that aren't very important, because they will get more praise from the outsider than family members who she may think take her for granted. We change by asking ourselves if we would do what we are doing if no one ever knew about it. We could pray to God about it, and be comforted that he knows. We can learn the joy of loving others. We can learn the lesson, "Give and you will receive." We can remind ourselves that people don't love us for what we are, but because we love them.

21. **Tell about someone you know who is not exceptional in anything they do except what they do for others. How do you feel about that person? What will you do to be like that person?**

<u>1 Kings 17:12-16</u>: The poor widow during a famine took her last bit of food and gave it to Elijah the prophet instead. Then she expected to die of starvation. As a result, Elijah miraculously made her food multiply and last to the end of the famine.

<u>Possible Class Response</u>: Most people know of a "little old lady" who lives on Social Security and doesn't have much anymore. But she calls people to ask how they're doing and encourages them. She sends notes of encouragement. She bakes simple sugar cookies for children or newcomers. She stays after worship a long time to make sure she says something to everyone who is there. Sometimes there is a new convert like this, or a young person. Sometimes it is a woman who gave up a career so she could stay home and spend her time for others, even with lesser income. In all cases, the class will probably think of people with a childlike ready acceptance and love for others.

Write an invitation to your home to someone "just because I love you." Serve only something to drink. Spend time with them telling them how much you appreciate them.

BEFORE CLASS:

A. Gather up church directories and telephone books.

B. Gather up stationary (colored bond paper cut in half) and envelopes.

C. Photocopy enough calendars of this month and next month for all class members to have their own.

D. On the blackboard or poster board, write the following:

"Time goes by so fast and we get caught up in so many busy things. I have been wanting for a long time to have you over for a cup of coffee/some ice tea. We need to spend more time together. It seems the little bit of time I see you at _____ is not enough. I'd like to have a little bit of quality time with you, even if it's for just an hour. Please come to my home for coffee and rolls [if at breakfast, a good time for busy people] on _____ at _____. If you can't then, how about _____ at _____? Let's just set aside everything else and DO IT! Call me or I'll call you. We need this time together. I love you."

DURING CLASS:

"We have been talking about spending quality time with people and not allowing ourselves to be caught up in so many distractions in our lives. Life is busy enough just doing the important things. But we know that friendships are far more important than some of the things that occupy our time. We're commanded as Christians to be hospitable. That's one qualification of elders. Perhaps we can ask ourselves how we will want to be remembered after we die. That might help us make time for others."

"Let's send a note inviting someone to our home for a few minutes for coffee or tea, nothing fancy. Just plan to spend your time visiting in a more intimate way than we can in public meeting places."

Hand out envelopes and stationery. "It shouldn't be hard to word an invitation. But if you'd like to copy the suggestion on the board, please feel free."

"You will have about eight minutes to write and address your note. When you are done, give it to me to mail. Let's all be quiet now and allow each other to think and write. When you're done, offer a silent prayer for your friend while the others finish."

Concluding Remarks

When time is up and while the slower writers complete their notes, sing one verse of a song, possibly one of the following:

1. *Make Me a Channel of Blessing*
2. *Take My Life and Let it Be*
3. *Take Time to be Holy*
4. *Walking in Sunlight*

Have everyone tell what they plan to do with their friend in their home and how they decided to make time. Then have a closing chain prayer with each one asking God to help her follow through with this and have friends into her home more often. If anyone feels uncomfortable praying aloud, they may squeeze the hand of the person next to them.

Angels Unaware

"Be not forgetful to entertain strangers:

***for thereby some have entertained
angels unawares."***

Hebrews 13:2

Katheryn Maddox Haddad

TRUE TO THE END
Priscilla

Lesson One: The Price of the Search

Lesson Aim
- ♥ **SEARCH THE SCRIPTURES FOR OURSELVES**
- ♥ **SIFT OUT OUR OWN RELIGIOUS PRE-JUDGING**

Scripture Outline

<u>Acts 18:1-3</u>: Priscilla and Aquila are among the Jews run out of Rome by Claudius Caesar. They move to Corinth. Later Paul goes there on his second missionary journey and looks them up because he and they are both tentmakers. They invite Paul to live with them and he accepts.

<u>Acts 18:4-8</u>: During Paul's year and a half here, he writes his second letter to the Thessalonian congregation. He is also able to convert the chief ruler of the Jewish synagogue.

Today's World

There are approximately eleven major religions in the world today (2017). Christians in the loose sense of the word number approximately 2.3 billion. The Muslim faith numbers 1.6 billion. Hindus 1 billion; Buddhists 400 million; Sikhism 30 million; and Jews 20 million. Others of importance are the nonreligious numbering 1 billion; and atheists at 500,000.

CHRISTIANITY was started by one man, Jesus, who intended to have just one church. But today, Jesus' body (the church) has been divided into thirty-nine denominations, and those are even subdivided.

How do people choose their religion? Most choose their religion based on family and what they have been taught all their lives. They just assume those teachings are true. Otherwise, they choose by which place of worship is closest to their home, or provides good community services or social activities. Few are what we would call "seekers".

ISLAM is supposedly the fastest-growing religious group in the world. That is what their leaders claim. But most Muslims are embarrassed by their own religion and are looking elsewhere. Especially in the Middle East, more and more are learning to hate Islam. But they want God in their life somehow. They just want a different God.

Bible World

In order to prove whether a "holy book" of anyone is divine, mankind can check to see if it is historically accurate, especially in what it foretold. The Jews had for centuries looked for someone to restore the kingdom to Israel (Acts 1:6) as prophesied many times in the Old Testament. They longed for a king who would restore David's throne. They had been ruled by foreign powers over and over since they had become a nation. Even their own king Herod at Jesus' time was only half-Jew and often desecrated their religion.

So, how were they supposed to recognize the savior of their kingdom when he arrived? The Old Testament was full of prophecies telling them what to look for. People truly searching for the savior searched the scriptures so they would be sure to recognize him when he came. Priscilla was surely one of those who searched the scriptures.

The early Jews had to compare the scriptures to what they themselves had seen Jesus do, or they'd heard from friends that he had done. Probably the most amazing prophecy about him was in Daniel 9:25-27 which predicted six centuries before, the exact year Jesus' ministry would begin, how long he would preach, and when he would die.

Daniel, one of the first of the Jews to be taken into Babylonian captivity, and who lived until five or ten years before their release, prophesied that the Jews would be freed after 70 years. God had warned them back in Palestine that, if they didn't keep his sabbaths, he would force them to by making them stop their work for 70 years of sabbaths (2 Chronicles 36:21 and Daniel 9:24).

Daniel 9:24: Daniel created his own interpretation by saying that in 70 "weeks" the punishment/reconciliation of the Jews in Babylon would be completed. After that time, they would return and rebuild Jerusalem, the holy city. We know they were in Babylon 70 years (Jeremiah 25:11,12). So Daniel was using "weeks" as symbolism for years.

Daniel 9:25: Daniel predicted that from the time of rebuilding Jerusalem to the beginning of the Messiah's ministry would be 7 weeks plus 62 weeks, equaling 69 weeks. Multiplying these 69 week/years times the number of days in a week is 483 years.

Ezra was allowed to return and rebuild the walls of Jerusalem in 457 BC during the reign of Artaxerxes, a famous king whose reign is chronicled in secular history (Ezra 7:1,13,14). 483 years after 457 BC is 26 AD when Jesus began preaching. (Remember the calendar is off about 4 years.)

Daniel 9:26: After 62 weeks, the Messiah would be cut off and the sanctuary (Holy of Holies) severed. Verse 25 said his ministry would begin after 69 weeks. This verse cut it short by 7 weeks. Again, with weeks meaning years, the Messiah would be cut off after preaching 7 years. Read on....

Daniel 9:27: BUT in the middle of that week (7 years) was when he would make the ultimate sacrifice and cause all other sacrifices to cease. The middle of 7 is 3 and a half. Jesus' ministry began when he was age 30 (Luke 3:23), which would be AD 26. By tracing the number of religious feasts Jesus attended, we know that his ministry lasted about three and a half years.

Daniel, being prime minister of Babylon and then Persia most of his life, was revered. Surely his writings went into the royal library/archives. Since several prophets went with them into Babylonian captivity, he also had access to Moses' law and other prophets which surely he placed in the royal library during his lifetime.

Even the wise men from the east (Babylon area) knew the star when Jesus was born meant something. After all, Numbers 24:17 had predicted there would be a Star out of Israel who would hold the royal Scepter. Both the wise men of Babylon and the wise men of Herod knew this (Matthew 2:1-6) as well as the fact that he'd be born in Bethlehem. That's why Herod had all the boy babies in Bethlehem murdered. The Jews were not ignorant of the Messianic prophecies.

Priscilla and the other early converts had access to the same Old Testament scriptures that anyone else had. Many knew the scriptures but were in positions of power and did not want to give up their religious authority, much as many religious leaders do today. Some knew the scriptures and prophesies, but were afraid their religious leaders would make life difficult for them. Some knew the scriptures and prophecies, but didn't really care. Some didn't know the scriptures. Into all of these groups fall the people of the 20th century.

Introducing the Lesson

We say we want religious unity, but the Christian world keeps dividing itself. Jesus prayed the night before he died that all his followers would be one (John 17:21). This isn't happening. Instead, it's getting worse. **Display TOP DENOMINATIONS IN AMERICA chart.** Highlight whichever parts you desire.

Did Jesus tell us to be ONE if he thought it was impossible? We all have access to the same scriptures. We have access to the same scriptures the early Jews such as Priscilla had too. So what's the problem?

The Jews had longed for their Messiah to restore their kingdom to Israel's former greatness, the throne of David (Acts 1:6). They were tired of being ruled by foreigners and disbelievers. They wanted their Savior to free them of this. **Display FOREIGN RULERS OF JEWS and discuss.**

There are people in other world religions who are frustrated and want out. They want to worship, but they do not like their god. In the Hindu and Buddhist religions, they must live a perfect life and be reborn into this hard world over and over, and they are tired. Besides, their god has no personality; it is only the spirit essence of the universe.

Among Muslims, they are embarrassed over their own religion and do not like their god. They all want to find the true God; they all want to worship him.

The Jews had many scriptures describing the coming of this Messiah. They even knew the exact year he would come. **Display DANIEL 9:25-27 and discuss.** In fact, nearly every part of Jesus' life was predicted centuries before he was born. **Display JESUS' LIFE IN PROPHECY and discuss.** All the Jews had access to the same scriptures, but not all of them read them or accepted Jesus. All Christians today have access to the same scriptures, but not all of us read them or accept them fully.

Discussion Questions

1. **Tell about the first time you recall deciding to search for the truth for yourself and dedicate your life to Christ.**

   Acts 17:11: Those who are "noble" search the scriptures with an open mind and daily to see whether what they are taught is the truth. When they find the answer, they receive it readily.

   1 Corinthians 15:58: Once we decide to follow Jesus, we must make up our minds to stick with it no matter what happens. It is a life-long decision.

   Possible Class Response: Some may have been raised among the church and when they realized what the scriptures said to do to become a Christian, they did it. It was always assumed by them and their families they would. Some may have been taught by someone they dated and later married. Some may have searched the scriptures in private, and gone from "church to church" searching for what they saw in the scriptures, putting a great deal of effort and time into it.

2. **Tell about a time when you guessed someone was a Christian by their behavior. How did it encourage or discourage your search for what they seemed to have?**

   Philippians 1:27: Let your conduct always be complimentary and complementary to the gentle Jesus in whom you profess to believe and follow.

   Possible Class Response: They were not only honest and considerate and polite, but they went out of their way to help people. This may have been a co-worker, a neighbor, an in-law, even a stranger.

3. **Whose "philosophy" on how to become a Christian is the only one that counts? Read Acts 2:38, Romans 6:3,4 and 1 Peter 3:21. What is your conclusion? Is it a popular conclusion? Why?**

   Acts 2:38: To have forgiveness of sins, we must repent and be baptized.

   Romans 6:3,4: Just as Jesus died, was buried, and then raised to become our savior; so we die as sinners, are buried in the waters of baptism, and then are raised to become the saved.

1 Peter 3:21: In all good conscience, we must be baptized to be saved, even if it looks silly.

Possible Class Response: There are many philosophies in the world on how to become a born-again Christian—all the way from a simple decision in one's heart, to walking up the steps of a cathedral on one's knees with a prayer at each step. We often follow our family, assuming they searched the scriptures and knew the truth; that generation probably assumed the same thing of their previous generation. We also automatically believe preachers, not realizing they often teach the easy way to become a Christian so their congregation will be larger. Baptism is not popular because so many people have not done this, and our egos won't allow us to admit we are wrong.

4. **Tell about a time you felt closer to a Christian sister than you did a member of your earthly family.**

   Ephesians 1:5; 5:8,23: Being born means someone automatically enters a family. Being born again as a Christian means a person automatically enters God's family by a form of spiritual adoption.

   Possible Class Response: Some may have gone through a tragedy; their physical family's encouragement may have been superficial, while their Christian family's encouragement offered inner strength, hope for the future, and knowledge that our Creator will take care of everything. Others may enjoy going with other couples on vacations and find they do not have to argue over kinds of entertainment while with Christians.
   Others may prefer Christian friends just for visiting in each other's homes because the speech and jokes are clean, the topics of their conversation are wholesome, and their general viewpoints are positive and Christ-like.

5. **What can a wife do to honor a husband who is slower in accepting various precepts of Christianity than her?**

   Ephesians 5:22-25,31-33: Wives are to honor their husbands as the head of the home to be an example of how the church should honor Jesus as husband of the church.

   The fact that even Paul mentioned Priscilla's name before her husband's indicates she was possibly more outgoing than him, or perhaps was converted first.

   Possible Class Response: She can praise her husband in public to let others know the positive Christian traits she has seen in private that they ordinarily might not know. "When my husband asked the blessing before we ate a couple days ago...." or "The other day when we were reading the Bible together...." etc.

6. **Tell of ways people have tried to "spice up" what they consider boring worship and/or left out some things as "unnecessary." What do such variations do to God's pattern?**

   John 4:23,24: True worshippers worship God in both spirit and truth.
   Acts 20:7: Preaching and communion

1 Corinthians 11:24-26: Communion/Lord's Supper
1 Corinthians 16:2: Collection of money for the saints
Colossians 3:16: Singing psalms, hymns and spiritual songs
1 Timothy 2:1-8; 3:14,15: Prayers
Hebrews 10:24,25: We are to meet more and more as the Judgment Day comes closer.

Possible Class Response: Some have decided it would make the communion too commonplace to celebrate each week, so do it yearly at Easter, which spices up that holiday. Some have added musical instruments to the singing so it will sound better to them, despite God's obviously mentioning it in O.T. worship, and obviously leaving it out in the N.T. Some have added candle lighting to prayers to add atmosphere. Some take up collections more often than once a week so they'll get paid more or a pet project will more likely be paid for.

7. **Look up a topic in a Bible concordance and compare your conclusion with others. Do you think religious leaders complicate things? Do you believe it is possible for people to believe the Bible alike?**

   Romans 10:2,3,17: Philosophies on religion grow out of men's minds - each adding to the confusion. Most of it is due to zeal (sincerity) without knowledge.

   Possible Topics to Look Up: Astrologer, Bishop, Seal, Testament, Saints. It is suggested that, after each scripture is read, each person in class write down their own summary/conclusion of this verse without saying anything aloud. At the end, everyone should compare to see if their conclusions were the same.

   Possible Class Response: We can believe the Bible alike if we will all study it for ourselves and leave behind our prejudices. It is very difficult to leave prejudices behind because it is very difficult and almost impossible to see them for ourselves. Just a couple generations ago, good people who searched the scriptures had great difficulty breaking away from things we take for granted today: Calling Sunday the Sabbath; saying when we die we turn into angels (Lincoln referred to his angel mother); believing we should use "thee" and "thou" when speaking to God. But with an open heart, we can do it.

8. **Share smaller causes or projects you have had that were difficult, but were completed by sheer determination to see the end result.**

   1 Thessalonians 4:16,17: Our search for Truth is motivated by our desire to be saved.

   Possible Class Response: Some may have marched against abortion. They may have petitioned the government to remove immoral places of entertainment in their town. They may have written letters to TV stations and advertisers in protest of immoral program themes. They may have gone before a school board to defend prayers in the school or creationism as opposed to evolutionism. They may have learned to be scout leaders so their children could be in a Christian-based troop/den. They may have learned a particular school subject so they could help their children with their homework.

9. **What subjects in the Bible would you like to learn more about? Why? How can**

you go about it?

We do not have access to the apostles today to keep us on the right track to heaven. How can we substitute having them here in person?

Luke 1:1-4: We can read the letters left behind by those who knew the apostles.

John 20:30,31: We can read the accounts left behind by the apostles who had actually seen Jesus.

Revelation 22:18,19: We can stay away from writings of so-called Christians who add to or take away from the scriptures to our condemnation.

Possible Class Response: Many would like to learn more about heaven to clarify their ultimate goal. Some would like to study prayer to help them be closer to God. Some would like a quick survey of the Bible to help them put in order who came first - Moses or David, etc. Some would like to study homosexuality because of the AIDS epidemic, or euthanasia because of assisted suicides, or some other social issue.

10. **What can we do to avoid prejudicial statements toward each other during religious discussions?**

In religious discussions, we all have a tendency to tell the other person what they believe, thus confusing things even more.

Acts 24:5,6,12: The Jews continually followed and hounded Paul throughout his ministry because they believed Jesus had been a traitor to the Jews.

Possible Class Response: We can begin by praying together, and perhaps even holding hands during the prayer, so we can see each other approach the same God with unity of heart and purpose. We can read scriptures together that discuss things we both believe in: Jesus is the Son of God, we must worship him, we must do good to others. We can reveal our mutual vulnerabilities and humility by discussing things about our Christian life that are difficult to do such as forgiving our enemies, going to Sunday School on a beautiful day or when we have a cold, keeping a pure heart around people who speak with profanities. We could even tell each other the things we used to believe but changed our beliefs on. After this foundation is laid, we can discuss what we disagree with. Never tell the other, however, what they believe. If we bring up an untruth, we could say that their religious leaders have been teaching them this, but we should never say they believe it. We must allow them to save face for when they learn of a scripture that proves the opposite to what they'd formerly believed. Never back them into a corner. Always assume with them that you both are searching for the truth as equals.

11. **Recall a time when you believed something that was not really taught in the Bible. How can we "save face" when we admit a misunderstanding?**

1 Timothy 1:12-16: The great apostle Paul had previously been a blasphemer of God and murderer of Christians. He considered himself the chiefest of sinners. Yet he asked for forgiveness and received it. He spent the rest of his life making it up to God.

Possible Class Response: Some in your class may have believed women must wear a hat to church. Some may have thought Paul spoke in King James English and said "thee" and "thou". Some may have thought baptism was an outward sign that they'd already been born again. We can read the scriptures clarifying things for us and be excited about learning something new. We can say we can't wait to tell others. We don't have to say we were wrong; we only have to say the scriptures are right.

12. **What must the new Christians quickly do in order to not let these old friends pressure them into reneging on the Truth (Hebrews 10:22-26)? Changing friends is not easy. If you have ever done so, tell how you did it.**

When Crispus, the Jewish synagogue ruler, became a Christian, what do you think he was treated like by lifetime friends with whom he ceased to worship?

Hebrews 10:22-26: They must meet with their new Christian friends as often as possible—at the church building, in each other's homes, going out for coffee together, etc.—more and more all the time.

Possible Class Response: Friends from the religious group someone left may have called and sent notes encouraging them to come back to the church. When they didn't, those same former friends may have resorted to phone calls warning them of hell, and perhaps even hate notes. Friends who someone may have formerly gone out with on Sunday mornings to go boating or for some other form of entertainment may have begun calling them goodie-goodies and holier than thou. The important thing is to change friends quickly.

Good Work

Write a note to someone you know who seems to have many questions about God but not the answers. This person is likely to not even be attending church anywhere due to confusion. Tell them you have noticed this searching in their life and are praying for them.

BEFORE CLASS:

A. Gather up several copies of your local telephone book.

B. Ask for a list of people who visited your congregation from various denominations.

C. Gather envelopes and stationery (bond paper cut in half is fine).

D. Write on the blackboard or poster board a suggestion for class members who are unsure what to say:

Visitors to your congregation: "I am pleased that you chose to visit and participate in our congregation's worship recently. You may be searching for a group of believers who continually search the scriptures to come as close to pleasing God as possible. If that is the case, we hope your search will stop here and that you will give us the opportunity to show you that we believe we are the people, the church, you are looking for. Our preacher, elders or I [if you feel comfortable doing it] would be happy to search the scriptures with you in private. Call us."

<u>Friends who have brought up God to you</u>: "Recently you were talking to me about why [God allows evil, people die young, preachers always want money, there are hypocrites in the church, etc.]. Such things bothered me in the past too. I learned a great way to read the Bible and find out for myself the answers to these hard questions. How about us getting together over coffee and searching the scriptures together? I'm not real good at this yet, so perhaps I could bring one of my friends who showed me how to do this. I'll call you in a couple days."

DURING CLASS:

"We've been studying about breaking away from old religious beliefs and our confusing search for truth. We all run into someone sometimes who is searching. If not a visitor at worship, it may be a friend who's just suffered a tragedy."

"We may be the only link to truth they ever meet in their lives. That's a scary responsibility. But let's gather our courage, trust in God, eliminate something from our schedule we don't really have to do, and reach out to a searcher for truth."

Hand out stationery and envelopes, and scatter telephone books around the room. "If you aren't sure what to say, I have written a couple of suggestions for you on the board. Feel free to copy one if you like."

"You will have about eight minutes. Let's all be quiet now and allow each other to think and write. When you are done, give the letter and addressed envelope to me, and offer a silent prayer for the person you wrote while the others finish their notes.

Concluding Remarks

When time is up and while the slower writers complete their notes, sing one verse of a song, possibly one of the following:

1. *Seeking the Lost (omit chorus)*
2. *Do All in the Name of the Lord*
3. *The Ninety and Nine*
4. *Ye Must Be Born Again*

In a few moments your students will be returning home and to all the activities going on there. It will be easy for them to set aside well-intentioned Christian duties such as calling a friend searching for a better understanding of God. So end the class by giving everyone one last boost.

(Wait for one or two quick replies to each of the following.) "In a few words, what should we do to....

1. Find out if we've been taught the truth?

2. Make friends of other Christians?
3. Lay a common foundation before studying about our differences with others?
4. Help those we teach save face?

Have a closing prayer, remembering especially those who are truly and honestly searching for the truth in a confusing religious world.

Top Denominations in the U.S.

1. The Catholic Church	67,515,016
2. Southern Baptist Convention	16,306,246
3. The United Methodist Church	7,995,456
4. The Church of Jesus Christ of Latter-day Saints	5,779,316
5. The Church of God in Christ	5,499,875
6. National Baptist Convention, U.S.A., Inc.	5,000,000
7. Evangelical Lutheran Church in America	4,774,203
8. National Baptist Convention of America, Inc.	3,500,000
9. Presbyterian Church (U.S.A.)	3,025,740
10. Assemblies of God	2,836,174
11. African Methodist Episcopal Church	2,500,000
12. National Missionary Baptist Convention of America	2,500,000
13. Progressive National Baptist Convention, Inc.	2,500,000
14. The Lutheran Church – Missouri Synod (LCMS)	2,417,997
15. Episcopal Church	2,154,572

Top World Religions

Christianity	**2.3 billion**
Islam	**1.6 billion**
Hinduism	**1.0 billion**
Buddhism	**400 million**
Sikhism	**30 million**
Judaism	**20 million**

Foreign Rulers of the Jews

1st Time	1800 BC	Egyptians for 430 years (Exodus 12:40)
2nd Time	1300 BC	Mesopotamians 8 years (Judges 3:8-10)
3rd Time		Moabites 18 years (Judges 3:14,15)
4th Time		Canaanites 20 years (Judges 4:2-4)
5th Time		Midianites 7 years (Judges 6:1,11)
6th Time		Philistines 18 years (Judges 10:7-18; 11:1)
7th Time	1100 BC	Philistines 40 years (Judges 13:1-25)
8th Time	750 BC	Assyrians forever (2 Kings 7:6,18)
9th Time	600 BC	Babylonians 70 years (2 Kings 25:21;Dan 9:24)
		Persians as part of the above (Daniel 2:39)
10th Time	350 BC	Greeks (Daniel 2:39)
11th Time	200 BC	Romans (Daniel 2:40)—See below
	168 BC	Pig sacrificed in Temple
		Alter to Jupiter erected in Temple
		1000 Jews tortured to renounce their religion
	167 BC	Maccabean family led revolts (living in caves)
	37 BC	•When Herod the Great arrived to rule as King of Jews, they closed the gates of Jerusalem.

- For three years he surrounded Jerusalem, trying to starve the Jews into submission.
- Finally he attacked and killed thousands.
- Herod built the Samaria with temple to Caesar in it, and forced 6000 Jews to inhabit it

KING HEROD'S FAMILY:
- Killed first son
- Made teenage brother-in-law high priest but later had him killed
- Killed his favorite wife because she was mad he'd killed so many in her family
- Killed his mother-in-law because she was mad he'd killed her daughter, son and father
- Had two more sons killed for treason.
- Son tried to poison him, so had him imprisoned & executed 5 days before his own death at age 70

Exact Year of Jesus Predicted

DANIEL 9:25-27

```
    7      Week-years
 + 62      Week-years
   69      Week-years
 x  7      Days in a week
  483      Years from rebuilding
           Jerusalem to Messiah
            introduced
```

```
 457 BC    When Jerusalem was rebuilt
 -483      Years to Messiah introduced
  26 AD    When Jesus began to preach,
           remembering the calendar is
           off about 4 years
```

Jesus' Life In Prophecy

Foretold	**Event**	**Fulfilled**
Genesis 22:18	Descendant of Abraham	Matthew 1:1
Psalm 89:3f,27	Descendant of David	John 8:42
Daniel 9:24-27	Year born, preached, died	Luke 3:1,2
Isaiah 7:14	Mother a virgin	Matthew 1:23
Micah 5:2	Born in Bethlehem	Matthew 2:6
Jeremiah 31:15	Babies killed after his birth	Matthew 2:16-18
Hosea 11:1	Lived a while in Egypt	Matthew 2:15
Malachi 3:1	Messenger would announce him	Matt 11:10
Isaiah 40:3	Messenger from wilderness	Matthew 4:10,1
Psalm 91:11f	Angels comforted at temptation	Luke 4:10f
Isaiah 35:5,6	Healed people	Matthew 11:5
Psalm 78:2	Spoke in parables	Matthew 13:35
Zechariah 9:9	Rode donkey into Jerusalem	Matthew 21:4-7
Psalm 41:9	Betrayed by a friend	John 13:18
Zechariah 11:13	Betrayed for 30 pieces silver	Matthew 27:5-7
Zechariah 11:13	Silver bought pauper's grave	Matthew 27:5-7
Isaiah 52:7	Did not speak at trial	Matthew 27:12-24
Psalm 69:21	Given gall/vinegar at death	Matthew 27:34
Psalm 22:18	Gambled away his garment	Matthew 27:35
Psalm 22:8	Mocked for trusting God	Matthew 27:43
Psalm 22:1	Words to God before death	Matthew 27:46
Psalm 31:5a	Words to God at death	Luke 23:46
Psalm 34:20	Bones unbroken-against custom	John 19:32-36
Zechariah 12:10	Side pierced	John 19:37
Isaiah 26:19	At death, the dead rose	Matthew 27:52f
Isaiah 53:9	Buried in tomb of rich man	Matthew 27:57-60
Psalm 45:8	Anointed with myrrh/aloes	John 19:39
Psalm 16:10	Body did not corrupt	Acts 2:31
Hosea 6:2	Rose from death on third day	Luke 24:46

True to the End

Lesson Two: The Price of Sharing

Lesson Aim
- **COURAGEOUSLY STAND FOR CHRISTIAN UNITY**
- **HELP OTHERS READ THE BIBLE FOR THEMSELVES**

Scripture Outline

Acts 18:9-17: Paul leaves when the Jews cause riots again, and takes with him Priscilla and Aquila.

Romans 16:4: Priscilla and Aquila offer their own lives to save Paul's.

Acts 18:18-21: They establish the church in Ephesus, then Paul leaves for his home congregation to report on his second missionary journey.

1 Corinthians 16:19: The church at Ephesus meets in Priscilla's home.

Acts 18:24-28: Priscilla and Aquila hear Apollos preach John the Baptist's teachings, and explain to him in private that the Messiah did come, was put to death, and was raised to eternal life; Apollos is baptized.

Acts 19:1-23: Paul returns to Ephesus and possibly moves back in with Aquila and Priscilla. He stays two years and writes his first letter back to the congregations at Corinth and Galatia. He sets up a preachers' school here (v.9), and sends for Timothy to help him. He casts out evil spirits, does other miracles.

Today's World

Missionaries have gone all over the world and thought they were taking the gospel of Jesus to them for the first time. But sometimes they found these people worshipping in the same simple way Christians of the first century did. They have been found on almost every continent—Europe, Africa, Asia. They had copies of the scriptures centuries earlier and did not remember who brought them there. It didn't matter anyway. They had the scriptures and could read for themselves. Almost always, despite cultural and language differences, they worshipped the same way and didn't know each other existed.

These pockets of Christians were overshadowed by the church leaders at Rome who decided there needed to be a world headquarters to let people know what to believe. Finally, a man of prominence stepped forward to say he wanted to restore the church the way it was originally. His name was Martin Luther. The *Encyclopedia Britannica* says that in 1515 he "turned to the direct study of the Bible." It was difficult for him to work through even his own prejudices, just as it is for us today. So his study took time. In 1522 he said "the word of God must be the agent of reform." Here are just two examples of the result of years of his personal Bible study.

BAPTISM: "*Taufe* is called in Greek *Baptismos*, in Latin *Mersio*; that is, when they *immerse* something entirely into the water, which goes altogether over it. For also, without doubt, the word *taufe* in German dialects comes from the word *tief*, that what one would baptize, he sinks deeply into water. That also signification of Baptism demands; for it signifies that the old man and sinful birth of flesh and blood, should be completely drowned through the grace of God; as we shall hear. Therefore one ought to do enough for this signification, and give a right, perfect sign."

INFANT BAPTISM: "The sophists in universities have fabricated the story that young children are baptized without personal faith, namely on the faith of the church which the sponsors confess at the baptism; whereupon in and by virtue of the baptism, the little child receives forgiveness of sins....From this poison and error guard yourself, even

though it were the expressed opinion of all the Fathers and Councils alike. For it does not exist, has no foundation for itself in the Scripture....In addition, it is directly contrary to the forgoing chief scripture where Christ says 'Who believes and is baptized, the same shall be saved' and so forth. The brief conclusion is: Baptism helps no one and is to be given to no one except he believes for himself, and without personal faith no one is to be baptized....It is my sincere counsel and judgment that one straightway desist, and the sooner the better, and never more baptize any child, as that we no longer mock and blaspheme the most blessed majesty of God with such baseless tomfoolery and jugglery."

NAME OF THE CHURCH: "I pray you leave my name alone and call not yourselves Lutherans but Christians. Who is Luther? My teaching is not mine. I have not been crucified for anyone...how then does it befit me, a miserable bag of dust and ashes, to give my name to the children of Christ? Cease, my dear friends, to cling to these party names and distinctions; away with them all; let us call ourselves only Christians after him from whom our teaching comes."

(Excerpts from *Changes in Worship Since the First Century* by Katheryn Maddox Haddad where original citations are given)

* * *

The following is from THE CATHOLIC CYCLOPEDIA, *published in 1960.*

CELIBACY: "This freedom of choice seems to have lasted during the whole of what we may call the Vacandard, the first period of the church's legislation; i.e., down to about the time of Constantine and the Council of Nicea....Although it is true that at the close of the fourth century, as we may learn from St. Ambrose, some married clergy were still to be found, especially in the outlying country districts, many laws then enacted were strong in favor of celibacy" (Vol. 3, p.485).

"The incidents of the long final campaign, which began indeed even before the time of Pope St. Leo II and lasted down to the First Council of Lateran in 1123....The attack was conducted along two distinct lines of action. In the first place, disabilities of all kinds were enacted and as far as possible enforced against the wives and children of ecclesiastics. Their offspring were declared to be of servile condition, debarred from sacred orders, and, in particular, incapable of succeeding to their fathers' benefices. The earliest decree in which the children were declared to be slaves, the property of the church, and never to be enfranchised, seems to have been a canon of the Synod of Pavia in 1018" (Vol. 3, p.486).

"Finally, in 1123, at the First Lateran Council, an enactment was passed...which while not in itself very plainly worded, was held to pronounce the marriages contracted by sub-deacons or ecclesiastics of any of the higher orders to be invalid. This may be said to mark the victory of the cause of celibacy. Henceforth, all conjugal relations on the part of the clergy in sacred orders were reduced in the eyes of the canon Law to mere concubinage" (Vol. 3, p.486).

THE FIRST CHURCH: "There is no clear evidence in the New Testament for a monarchial (one person ruling) episcopate, this office, which was firmly established by the early decades of the second century" (Vol. 2, p.595).

"An old tradition that Peter spent 25 years in Rome is quite unacceptable. All that can be said with certainty is that he went to Rome and was martyred there" (Vol. 11, p.204).

"Pope and παπας appeared in Christian literature from the beginning of the third century as a title used of bishops, suggesting their spiritual paternity. From the third to the fifth century the name was applied to all bishops, but in the sixth century it began to be reserved to the bishops of Rome. The practice of restricting the title to the Roman bishops has been universal in the Western Church since the eighth century" (Vol. 11, p.572).

BIBLE READING: "Innocent III in 1299 warned the people that, though the desire to study the Scriptures was commendable, it was wrong to study them apart from the Church's teaching authority and to presume themselves superior to the priests in Scriptural studies....Indiscriminate reading of the Bible with independent interpretation was forbidden by Pius IV in 1564" (Vol. 2, p.515).

"Bible reading, private and liturgical, is strongly encouraged as a means to spiritual perfection, although it is not necessary for salvation....On December 13, 1898, he [Leo XIII] granted specific indulgences [works of repentance] for reading the Scriptures" (Vol. 2, p.518).

"The decree on the sources of [divine] revelation published in session IV [April 8, 1546, Council of Trent] contain a list of the canonical Books of the Old Testament and New Testament and decreed that the apostolic traditions on faith and custom that 'have been transmitted in some sense from generation to generation down to our times' were to be accepted 'with as much reverence' as Sacred Scripture" (Vol. 14, p.272).

Bible World

<u>Written by Justin Martyr a few years after the Apostle John died regarding early-church worship</u>: "We always remember one another. Those who have, provide for all those in want. And on the day called Sunday there is a gathering together in the same place of all who live in a city or a rural district. The memoirs of the apostles or the writings of the prophets are read, as long as time permits. Then, when the reader ceases, the person presiding in a discourse admonishes and urges the imitation of these good things. Next we all rise together and send up prayers.

"As I said before, when we cease from our prayer, bread is presented and wine and water. The person presiding in the same manner sends up prayers and thanksgivings according to his ability, and the people sing out their assent saying the 'Amen.' A distribution and participation of the elements for which thanks have been given is made to each person, and to those who are not present it is sent by the deacons.

"Those who have means and are willing, each according to his own choice, gives what he wills, and what is collected is deposited with the person presiding. He provides for the orphans and widows, those who are in want on account of sickness or some other cause, those who are in bonds and strangers who are sojourning" (*Apology I, 67*).

<u>Written by Tertullian a few years after the Apostle John died regarding baptism</u>: "We are little fishes, in accordance with our *ichtys* Jesus Christ, are born in water. [The fish was the "password" of early Christians looking for each other when Christianity was punishable by death.] It has assuredly been ordained that no one can attain knowledge of salvation without baptism. This comes especially from the pronouncement of the Lord, who says, 'Except one be born of water he does not have life'....Baptism itself is a bodily act, because we are immersed in water, but it has a spiritual effect, because we are set free from sins....There is no difference whether one is washed in the sea or in a pool, in a river or a fountain, in a reservoir or a tub, nor is there any distinction between those whom John dipped in the Jordan and those whom Peter dipped in the Tiber" (*On Baptism, 1,4,7,12*).

<u>Written by Polycarp who history says was a friend of the Apostle John</u>: "And the elders are to be compassionate, showing mercy to all, turning back those who have strayed, looking after all the weak, not neglecting widows or orphans or poor....Likewise the deacons are to be unblamable before his righteousness as servants of God and Christ and not of men....Wherefore it is necessary that...you be subject to the elders and deacons as to God and Christ" (*Philippians 5 and 6*).

Introducing the Lesson

We all have wonderful friends who believe in God but don't worship anywhere. We have wonderful friends who worship with one of the many denominations, believing unity in the Christian world is impossible so may as well be accepted.

We also have friends who either do or don't worship anywhere, who have read things in the Bible that are inconsistent with their religious leaders' teachings, and have given up hope of finding anyone "out there" who agrees with them.

People today are educated and independent thinkers, and want to work out their own salvation, but think they're alone. Their own denominations' leaders felt alone too, but tried to do something about it. They studied for themselves. ***Display WHAT LEADERS OF MAJOR DENOMINATIONS SAID ABOUT BAPTISM.***

People mistakenly took the words of these sincere people trying to study themselves out of denominationalism, made creeds out of them, and even called themselves after their leader or a particular doctrine against their will. ***Display CREEDS: THOUGHT QUESTION.***

We can ask our friends if there is anything about the Bible they've always been curious about. If so, get with them with a concordance and show them, through their own chosen topic, how to study the Bible for themselves. ***Display DO YOU HAVE A BIBLE CONCORDANCE.***

Priscilla went through a similar experience reaching out to Apollos who was teaching people part of the gospel, but not all of it because he didn't know it all.

Discussion Questions

13. Sometimes when we try to share God's truth with people, they become angry and assume we are their enemy. Share some Psalms or other Bible passages that have encouraged you in such times.

Exodus 34:6: When God showed Moses his glory, he described it as being merciful and longsuffering.
Psalm 103:10: God does not deal with us according to our sins.
Isaiah 30:18: In the process of being gracious to sinners, God is exalted.
Matthew 23:37: Jesus told Jerusalem that even though she'd killed his prophets, he longed to gather her under his sheltering wings.
Romans 9:22,23: God puts up with us when he should be angry, and shows mercy instead in order to reveal the riches of his glory.
Romans 15:5: The God of patience and consolation wants us to treat each other the same way.
1 John 4:19: We love God because he first loved us.

Possible Class Response: Do not encourage scriptures about being persecuted for righteousness sake. Making the ladies feel like martyrs will not encourage them to keep trying.

14. Even the strongest Christian has been known to get discouraged and nearly give up. Tell of such an instance you know of (no names please), and how some weaker people misunderstood and gave up on their own

faith. Who actually were the weaker people using to determine their faith (2 Corinthians 10:12)?

2 Corinthians 10:12: Weak Christians compare themselves with how they themselves used to be or with other Christians, and sometimes with non-Christians.

Possible Class Response: Discouragements usually come when people are involved with church groups/committees making decisions together. Sometimes emotions run high, egos get wounded, and weaker ones drop out of the committees or even the church. Discouragements can come from being the only one in the church willing to do a good work such as taking meals to the sick. Discouragements can come from getting small children ready for Sunday School on cold dark Sundays and having to keep them quiet during worship with no husband to help.

15. **As a fairly new Christian, how can a person find and apprentice herself to an older Christian?**

Jesus apprenticed his twelve apostles, and also a group of 70 disciples. Barnabas apprenticed Paul. Paul apprenticed Timothy.

1 Corinthians 11:1: We are to be followers of Paul insofar as he was a follower of Christ.

Possible Class Response: Find out who in the congregation are teachers. (Most people do not teach all the time.) Also find out who the deacons' and elders' wives are. Go to them and ask them if they will call you the next time they go to visit someone to take food/encourage in sickness/console in death/have a Bible study with.

16. **Name some ways you can use your home in which to teach God's truths and principles of love. Be imaginative and try to think of something in which your unique interests could be utilized in this way.**

Romans 12:6-8: Each of us has a different gift and talent. Some can teach, some can minister to physical needs, some have a large home.

Possible Class Response: We can invite neighborhood children over during the summer to sit on our porch, eat some of our cookies, and listen to a Bible story and learn some Bible songs. We can have adult neighbors in once a week for coffee to search the scriptures together on various topics out of the concordance. We can have large groups of Christians over to have fellowship away from the church building. We can have people over on holidays who do not have families nearby.

17. **What are other ways we can explain to people that our religious opinions do not matter, only God's? What can we do to have readily available to us God's answers to their questions?**

1 Corinthians 1:12,13: Paul condemned the Christians who claimed to follow the teachings of various preachers. He said Christ wasn't divided, and these preachers did not die for them.

<u>Possible Class Response</u>: We can explain that if a creed is more than the Bible we don't want it, and if it's the same as the Bible we don't need it. Many people believe things they do not realize are opinions, but think they're found in the Bible. We can humbly search the scriptures with them to locate the verses that they believe are there. Then, with a sense of humor and sympathy, we can laugh and say something about, "At least we don't have to worry about that one." We can also tell about something we once thought was in the Bible but wasn't. We can use a concordance and take all personalities and opinions away. With that we are all equal.

18. What are some other times of doubt?

There are some people we try to teach who are not logical because they seem afraid of the truth or just don't like the truth. We need to be patient, remain friends, and watch for a time when their wrong beliefs are making their circumstances worse.

<u>Acts 26:14</u>: Paul could only be stopped from putting Christians in prison and to death by something drastic: Jesus not only spoke directly to him, but he also made him blind for several days.

<u>Possible Class Response</u>: We may have faced doubt in some of our beliefs when we became critically ill or were in an accident and nearly killed. Often a sudden catastrophe makes people who do not profess Christianity at all to reassess their values. Some people begin to doubt their beliefs when their own church leaders take advantage of them such as getting rich on the contributions of lower and middle-class followers.

19. Name some common points of faith that are close to the truth but not quite there, and discuss the steps you could take to show someone to a fullness of that truth.

We can listen to other preachers on the radio or TV and listen for points where they are very close to the truth.

<u>Acts 18:24-28</u>: Apollos taught that the Messiah would come soon and people should repent. Priscilla and her husband invited him home with them, and exclaimed, "He has already come! He was killed but he proved his superiority over death by rising again! Jesus is the one you've been talking about! Praise God!" Apollos was baptized into Jesus Christ.

<u>Possible Class Response</u>: Confessing Jesus and then being baptized is a common area many fall short in understanding. Attending worship every week is another point. Taking the Lord's Supper every week is another. Having local elders and not district bishops over them is another. We can sit down with the person and ask what their understanding of the topic is and write it down as we go. We can ask them if we understood them correctly. We can tell them we'd like to study it further and would they join us. Then we can get out a concordance and look up all the scriptures on the topic we can find, writing down mutually agreeable summaries of each scripture. Then we can tell them we seem to see that a particular scripture says so-and-so, and ask if

they do also. We can be mutual truth seekers together.

20. If we have a Bible study group of men and women in our home, how small should it be to keep it private and personal? What special effectiveness would you want?

1 Corinthians 14:34-36: Women should not believe they understand the scriptures better than the men. Although they often receive it quicker, they are to not be speakers in the church assembly, but talk about it at home.

Possible Class Response: The size of home Bible studies is a matter of judgment. It should be such that everyone has opportunity to say as much as they want without being misunderstood. It should be intimate enough that people get to know each other on a personal basis - each other's fears and excitements, highs and lows, faiths and doubts. Many times women can be much more effective encouragers in a home setting.

21. Tell about someone you know who was taught many years before finally becoming a Christian.

2 Timothy 4:2: We are to teach in season (when expected) and out of season (when not expected).

Isaiah 28:9,10: We are to teach one thing at a time and gradually build on each one.

Possible Class Response: The author knew of a man who was converted just before he was married. He spent the next thirty years teaching his parents by mail. His mother was converted right away. When his letters would come, she would read part of it to his father, he'd get mad and leave the house. After a while he'd come back and say, "All right, what else did he say?". It often took a week to read one of his letters! Finally in his old age he, too, became a Christian as a result of his son's steadfast teaching and wife's steadfast example.

Good Work

Begin a correspondence with a radio evangelist with the goal of finding a common faith and then teaching them more fully. Assume they want to know the truth. Do not be defensive.

BEFORE CLASS:

A1. Call a nearby Christian radio station and ask for a listing of their programs.

A2. Call or write some of your local radio stations and ask for a listing of their Sunday programs.

B. Listen to the station for a full weekday or Sunday and write down the names and addresses usually given out at the end of each program. (You may need help with this.)

C.   Make a list of each program, the preacher, their address, and the radio station you can hear them on. You may wish to comment on what the preacher seems to emphasize.

D. Gather envelopes and pre-address them, addressing two the same if you have a large class.

E.   On the inside flap where the glue is, write what this preacher's emphasis seems to be or a false teaching, and a scripture condoning or opposing it. Use your concordance.

F.   Gather stationary, either full or half-size white bond paper.

G.   Write on the blackboard or poster board a suggestion for class members who are unsure what to say:

"I have heard you on the radio and am impressed by your dedication to getting your message out to the people. Many people are searching for the truth, as I continue to do and I know you do. I appreciated what you said on [date] about _____ and agree wholeheartedly. Also, I may have misunderstood you when you said _____ because the Bible tells me in [scripture] that _____, which is different. Will you please write to me and share with me your views. I cannot make a contribution to your effort; but I do want to study this with you. I am praying for you."

DURING CLASS:

"We've been learning about how to study with other people and bring them into a closer understanding of God's will for our lives. There are many people out there who are only religious for social or power purposes; but there are others who are very sincere and doing the best they can. They need our help."

"I have a list of religious programs broadcast locally and have addressed some envelopes to them. You may never hear from them, but then again, you may. If only ten percent are sincerely searching, it will be worth our effort. Remember, you do not have to debate them on the spot; you will have time to prepare your answer to them with our elders or anyone else who might help you. Who knows? He may become a modern-day Paul."

Hand out stationery and envelopes. "If you aren't sure what to say, I have written a suggestion for you on the board. Feel free to copy it if you like. On the inside flap of the envelope I have written what this preacher emphasizes, and any questionable teaching I may have heard. I have also written a Bible verse that condones or condemns it."

"You will have about eight minutes. Let's all be quiet now and allow each other to think and write. When you are done, give the letter to me, and offer a silent prayer for this preacher while the others finish their notes."

Concluding Remarks

When time is up and while the slower writers complete their notes, sing one verse of a song, possibly one of the following:

1. *Give Me the Bible*
2. *Sowing the Seed of the Kingdom*
3. *Arise! The Master Calls for Thee!*
4. *A Charge to Keep I Have*

In a few moments your students will be returning home, perhaps a little uncertain they can follow up with a powerful denominational preacher, and possibly hoping he will not reply to their letter. So end the class by giving them all a shot of encouragement.

(Wait for one or two quick replies to each of the following.) "In a few words, what can we do....

1. When we come across someone who dropped out of the church because of a weak Christian example?
2. To use our home to encourage others?
3. To encourage someone who hasn't found ALL the truth on a subject?
4. To encourage ourselves to keep plugging along in teaching a friend?

Give the list of radio evangelists to the person leading the closing prayer. Have a closing prayer calling these evangelists by name and asking God to open their minds and hearts to his word.

What Leaders of Major Denominations Said about Baptism After Studying the Bible for Themselves

John Calvin—Presbyterian: "The word baptize signifies to immerse. It is certain that immersion was the practice of the primitive church."

Martin Luther—Lutheran: "Baptism is a Greek word and may be translated immerse. I would have those who are to be baptized to be altogether dipped."

John Wesley—Methodist: "Buried with him in baptism...alluding to the ancient manner of baptizing by immersion."

Wall—Episcopalian: "Immersion was in all probability the way in which our blessed Savior, and for certain the way by which the ancient Christians, received their baptism."

Brenner—Catholic: "For thirteen hundred years was baptism an immersion of the person underwater."

Macknight—Presbyterian: "In baptism the baptized person is buried under the water. Christ submitted to be baptized, that is, to be buried underwater."

Whitfield—Methodist: "It is certain that the word of our text, Romans 6:4, alludes to the manner of baptizing by immersion."

CREEDS

THOUGHT QUESTION

*If your creed contains more
than what is in the Bible,
you shouldn't have it.*

*If your creed contains the same
as what is in the Bible,
you don't need it.*

**HAVE YOU READ YOUR DENOMINATION'S CREED?
DON'T YOU THINK YOU SHOULD?**

DO YOU HAVE A BIBLE CONCORDANCE?

IF NOT
Beg, borrow (but don't steal) one
TODAY!

DON'T LET ANYONE TELL YOU WHAT TO BELIEVE

READ THE BIBLE FOR YOURSELF!
Make your own decisions
on what to believe!

THIS WILL BRING RELIGIOUS UNITY TO THE WORLD
BELIEVE IT OR NOT!

Katheryn Maddox Haddad

True to the End

Lesson Three: The Price of Salvation

Lesson Aim
- ♥ SACRIFICE FOR JESUS IN SOME WAY EVERY DAY
- ♥ STICK WITH THE CHURCH (BODY OF CHRIST) NO MATTER WHAT

Scripture Outline

Acts 19:23—20:1-3: Paul barely survives the riots caused by Demetrius the silversmith of the goddess Diana. He escapes to Macedonia where he writes Timothy back in Ephesus. He then goes on to Corinth.

Romans 1:11; 16:3,5: Priscilla and her husband return to Rome shortly thereafter because Claudius Caesar has died. The church again meets in her home. Paul writes the congregation in Rome while in Corinth and says how much he longs to see them. Six years after this letter, Nero burns Rome. Priscilla and Aquila flee Rome again and move back to Ephesus.

1 Timothy 1:3; 2 Timothy 4:6-8,19: A couple years later Paul arrives in Rome in chains and nearly deserted. Just prior to his death, he writes to Timothy, Priscilla and his other close friends back at Ephesus and says goodbye until they meet again in heaven.

Today's World

Through the centuries there have been parts of the world where the Bible and Christianity were illegal. Foxe's Book of Martyrs is full of people being imprisoned and tortured to death from the first century up to the seventeenth century. Some tortures were too horrible to even speak of.

Up to the late twentieth century, the only way to get the Bible to these places was to smuggle them in. We have all heard the stories of people putting false bottoms in their wagons or vehicles to fill with Bibles. Others hid them under cartons of imported food or dry goods. Still others printed special Bibles with tiny print the size of cigarette packs. Hundreds of smugglers and those they were helping were discovered and hung or shot.

Today, thank God, we have the internet. Websites like Bible League and You Version provide Bibles in different languages. But, once they become Christians, what then? They become illegal owners of Bibles and illegal Christians.

The author who teaches English using the Bible over the internet right now knows a woman in Kurdistan whose mother-in-law locked her in a bedroom a full week and beat her every day to get her to return to Islam. (It did not work.) A man in Palestine had his computer confiscated, and a few months later was fired from his position of professor of his universe. A man in Afghanistan was threatened with imprisonment if he did not pay a bribe; he and his wife and children escaped to India. The wife of a man in Iraq left him, took the children, and had the men in her tribe beat him. The life of a man in Afghanistan has been threatened and right now his wife and children are hiding in a different province, and he is in hiding in yet another province far from them.

All these have been shown the evidence through prophecies fulfilled of entire kingdoms and of the promised Messiah. Plus they are convinced that the "Christian God" really does love them, something no false god in the world either claims or acts like. One of the men wrote the author just last week, "In a short time I will be with Jesus in heaven."

Do any of these want to escape to the Western World? Absolutely not. They are determined to stay and help their countrymen learn about the only true God, even if it means imprisonment or death.

Bible World

The Bible says in Hebrews 11 about Abraham who agreed to kill his only son, believing God would bring him back to life. About Moses who left palace living for living in a desert the rest of his life. It speaks of many others who "were tortured and refused to be released so that they might gain a better resurrection. Some faced jeers and flogging, while still others were chained and put in prison. They were stoned; they were sawed in two; they were put to death by the sword. They went about in sheepskins and goatskins, destitute, persecuted and mistreated. The world was not worthy of them. They wandered in deserts and mountains, and in caves and holes in the ground."

Bible World

Polycarp, according to history, was about 30 years old when his close friend, the Apostle John, died. He was born and died in Smyrna. *Below is part of a letter he wrote to the church in Smyrna:*

"Blessed therefore and noble are all the martyrdoms which have taken place according to the will of God (for it behooves us to be very scrupulous and to assign to God the power over all things). For who could fail to admire their nobleness and patient endurance and loyalty to the Master, seeing that when they were so torn by lashes that the mechanism of their flesh was visible even as far as the inward veins and arteries, they endured patiently, so that the very bystanders had pity and wept."

Below is part of what Polycarp's friend wrote about events surrounding his own martyrdom:

"Herod the captain of police tried to prevail upon him saying, 'Why? What harm is there in saying Caesar is Lord and offering incense?' But he at first gave them no answer. When however they persisted, he said, 'I am not going to do what you counsel me'....Being taken to the stadium, there being such a tumult in the stadium that no man's voice could be so much as heard....The proconsul tried to persuade him to a denial saying, 'Have respect to your age....Swear by the genius of Caesar; repent and say, 'Away with the atheists [people who believe in only one God]'. The magistrate pressed him hard and said, 'Swear the oath and I will release you; revile the Christ.'

"Then Polycarp with solemn countenance looked upon the whole multitude of lawless heathen that were in the stadium, and waved his hand to them; and groaning and looking up to heaven and said, 'FOURSCORE AND SIX YEARS HAVE I BEEN HIS SERVANT, AND HE HAS DONE ME NO WRONG. HOW THEN CAN I BLASPHEME MY KING WHO SAVED ME?'

"The proconsul said, 'I have wild beasts here and I will throw you to them, except you repent.' But he said, 'Call for them.' Then he said to him again, 'I will cause you to be consumed by fire if you despise the wild beasts, unless you repent.' But Polycarp said, 'YOU THREATEN THAT FIRE WHICH BURNS FOR A SEASON AND AFTER A LITTLE WHILE IS QUENCHED; for you are ignorant of the fire of the future judgment and eternal punishment, which is reserved for the ungodly. BUT WHY DO YOU DELAY? COME, DO WHAT YOU WILL.' Saying these things and more besides, he was inspired with courage and joy....the proconsul was astonished.

"These things then happened with so great speed, quicker than words could tell....When the pile was made ready, divesting himself of all his upper garments and loosing his girdle, he endeavored also to take off his shoes....he had been treated with all honor for his holy life even before his gray hairs came. Forthwith then the instruments that were prepared for the pile were placed about him; and as they were going likewise to nail him to the stake, he said, 'LEAVE ME AS I AM; FOR HE THAT HAS GRANTED ME TO ENDURE THE FIRE WILL GRANT ME ALSO TO REMAIN AT THE PILE UNMOVED, even without the security which you seek from the nails.'

"Then he, placing his hands behind him and being bound to the stake, like a noble ram out of a great flock for an offering, a burnt sacrifice made ready and acceptable to God, looking up to heaven said:

"'Oh Lord God Almighty, the Father of Your beloved and blessed Son Jesus Christ...I bless you for that you have granted me this day and hour, that I might receive a portion among the number of martyrs in the cup of Christ unto resurrection of eternal life, both of soul and of body, in the incorruptibility of the Holy Spirit. May I be received among these in your presence this day, as a rich and acceptable sacrifice....You are the faithful and true God. For this cause I praise you, I bless you, I glorify you through the eternal and heavenly high priest, Jesus Christ, your beloved son, through whom with him and the Holy Spirit be glory both now and for all ages to come. Amen.'
the fire. And a mighty flame flashing forth, we to whom it was given to see....there was

in the midst, not like flesh burning, but like gold and silver refined in a furnace....And so we afterward took up his bones...and laid them in a suitable place."

(The Apostolic Fathers, translated by J. B. Lightfoot, pp. 103-115)

* * *

Although, as far as we know Priscilla did not suffer martyrdom, she did what she could. She offered her home for use by the church. The preacher, Paul, was a guest in her home for extended periods of time. Also Christians met in her home to study and to worship. Below are writings admiring some early Christian women:

NONNA: "She who was given by God to my father became not only his co-worker, but even his leader, drawing him on by her influence in deed and word to the highest excellence; judging it best in all other respects to be excelled by her husband according to the law of marriage, but not being ashamed in regard of piety to present herself as his teacher....

"What time or place for prayer ever escaped her? To this she was drawn before all other things in the day.... Who reduced the flesh by more constant fast and vigil? Or stood like a pillar at the all-night and daily psalmody.... Who was a better patron of the orphan and the widow? Who aided as much in the alleviation of the misfortunes of the mourners?.... Her voice was never to be heard in the holy assemblies or places except in the necessary and liturgical words of the service" (*Oration XVIII, "On the Death of My Father," 7-9, by Gregory Nazianzus, about 350 AD*).

[Nonna was born to Christian parents and converted her husband. Although wealthy, Gregory says all her property did not suffice for what she would have liked to give away so that she would gladly have sold herself into slavery if there had been the opportunity in order to give more to the poor.]

ANTHUSA: "When [my mother] perceived that I was meditating this step, she took me into her own private chamber and, sitting near me on the bed where she had given birth to me, she shed torrents of tears [of joy and relief], to which she added words more pitiable than her weeping, in the following lamentable strain: 'My child, it was not the will of Heaven that I should long enjoy the benefit of your father's virtue. For his death soon followed the pangs which I endured at your birth, leaving you an orphan and me a widow before my time to face all the horrors of widowhood, which only those who have experienced them can fairly understand. For no words are adequate to describe the tempest-tossed condition of a young woman who, having but lately left her paternal home, and being inexperienced in business, is suddenly racked by an overwhelming sorrow, and compelled to support a load of care too great for her age and gender....My foremost help indeed was the grace from above" (*On the Priesthood, i.5 by John Chrysostom, about 350 AD*).

"Once while I was still a youth, I know that my teacher expressed admiration before many for my mother. He asked of me the age of my mother and the length of her widowhood. When I said that she was forty and there were twenty years since my father's death, he was astonished and exclaimed aloud to those present, 'Bless me, what women these Christians have!'" (*Letter to a Young Widow, i,2 by John Chrysostom, about 350 AD*).

[Anthusa taught John the scriptures at home, and made sure he had the best possible education.]

MARCINA: "She furnished food for her mother from her own labor, and in addition, she shared her mother's worries. Her mother had four sons and five daughters.... When the care of rearing the children and the responsibility of educating them and establishing them in life was over...and turning her [mother] aside from all that she was used to, she led her to her own standard of simplicity....

"Among them was seen no anger, no envy, no hatred, no arrogance, or any such thing; neither was there in them longing for foolish things like honor and fame and vanity, nor a contempt for others; all such qualities had been put aside.... Their one concern was the Divine; there was constant prayer and an unceasing singing of hymns distributed throughout the entire day and night so that this was for them both their work and their rest from work....

"When her lofty understanding had been tried by the different attacks of grief, the genuine and undebased quality of her soul was revealed in every way.... She remained like an undefeated athlete, in no way overcome by the onslaught of misfortunes" (*Life of Macrina by Gregory of Nyssa about 350 AD*).

[Marcrina's paternal grandparents had their possessions confiscated because of their confession of Christ. When her mother died, she gave her share of the family inheritance to the church. She gathered many women around her to teach them the principles of Christian living. Because of her many bereavements, she often stood by families in times of trial.]

MARCELLA: "I shall not set forth her illustrious family, the glory of her ancestors, and her descent through consuls and praetorian prefects. I shall praise nothing in her except what is her own and the nobler, because, despising riches and rank, she has become the nobler by poverty and humility.

"She was left an orphan by the death of her father, and seven months after her marriage she was deprived of her husband....Of gold, she refused even a signet ring, hiding it rather in the stomachs of the poor than in purses....

"Her zeal for the divine Scriptures was unparalleled....Her fasts were moderate: abstaining from meat, and knowing the scent of wine more than its taste, for her stomach's sake, and frequent infirmities....

"She never met me without asking some question concerning the Scriptures. Nor would she at once acquiesce but she would put forward questions to the contrary, not to be contentious but so that by questioning she might learn answers to the objections which she perceived could be raised. What virtue! What intelligence! What holiness! What purity I found in her! (*Letter CXXVII "To Principia" 1-5, by Jerome about 350 AD*).

[One of Marcella's converts as a result of Bible study in her home was Paula. Paula gave so extensively to the poor that her relatives warned her that she was leaving nothing for her children. She replied that she was leaving them a better inheritance in the mercy of Christ.]

Introducing the Lesson

For the most part, we are not making time for Christianity in our everyday lives in any way. Some of us feel guilty about it but have to work out of our homes and we have no energy left at the end of the day. Weekends are spent with house cleaning and upkeep and doing the grocery shopping.

Tell about Christians in the Middle East today and other stories you may have heard. Tell about Polycarp's martyrdom. Then tell about the simple yet dynamic sacrifices early Christian women made to help the church. End by quoting the Christian man in Afghanistan on the run: "In a short time I will be with Jesus in heaven."

That's where sacrifice comes in. Although today in America we are not usually persecuted for our Christianity or even our Christian values, making time for Christian works seems nearly impossible. Is it? We need to MAKE TIME to reach out with a telephone call, a note, inviting new Christian friends over after church, inviting neighbors over for coffee and Bible study. **Display ARE YOU WILLING TO SACRIFICE.** MAKING TIME is a sacrifice. Are we willing to do it for Jesus?

Discussion Questions

22. **Tell of a personal experience or one you heard of where people were helped from your wealth or poverty. Share any struggles you may have had with it. Have you ever missed a meal to help someone?**

    Philippians 3:8: Paul lost all of his wealth including his home. He had to live with other people and worked only enough to buy himself food and provisions. All he lost he considered manure compared to what he gained.

    Possible Class Response: Some may have been down to their last five dollars and didn't know how they were going to pay their bills (the $5 certainly wasn't enough anyway), and gave it to the church. Some may have suddenly been given a very high-paying job so they could afford a nice big house or car. To guard against their good fortune being used selfishly, they decided since they were blessed with it by God, they would use their house or car to his glory by inviting people over for fellowship or study, or taking people to the doctor or picking people up for church, etc.

23. **Were you ever surrounded by a group you tried to teach and they "ganged up on you" with false religious accusations (friends, stranger, even family members)? How did you feel in front of them?**

    1 Peter 2:23: Jesus didn't talk back, argue, or threaten.

    Possible Class Response: Most of us would want to run. You could quietly listen to them, and then tell them that since you listened to them without interrupting, you would like them to listen to you without interrupting. Afterward, you could write the scriptures down you had referred to, and rather than allow yourself into an argument, quietly hand them the scriptures to talk about another time after they'd looked them up.

24. **Have you ever prayed with others over the phone or in a home over a special problem? How did it make you feel? What was the outcome?**

    Colossians 1:9: Even as we must rearm ourselves daily with God's word, we must empty ourselves of our burdens and transform them into praise in our daily prayers.

    Possible Class Response: They may have been hesitant, but afterward were glad they did. Praying immediately when someone tells us a problem lets them know we consider it important enough to set everything aside and go to God about it immediately. Anyone who has done this has felt good about it afterward. Often others will hear about it and be encouraged to go to them with their own problems and prayer requests.

25. **Name an obstacle to your Christianity that you have complained about and decide how you can rejoice and grow from it.**

    Philippians 2:14-16: Just as a coach puts obstacles in front of runners to strengthen them, so God allows us to run into obstacles to our salvation. And just as the coach cheers those who face the obstacles, overcome them, and run even better and faster; so too God cheers us when we overcome and become stronger Christians as a result. We can complain about the obstacles or rejoice.

    Possible Class Response: Some may have husbands who will not attend worship with them; they can encourage others in like circumstances. Some may feel extremely tired after work on Wednesdays and not wish to attend the evening Bible study; they can remind themselves they would attend if it were for money, and heaven is much greater than that. Some may have to work with people with foul mouths; they can show people by their example how to express themselves positively with pure speech.

26. **Tell about any laws you disagree with and try to see some good in it. Also reconcile these laws with Galatians 5:22,23.**

    Galatians 5:22,23: There is no law in the world that punishes love, joy, peace, patience, gentleness, and temperance.

    Possible Class Response: Pro-abortion laws are terrible. But they allow Christians an opportunity to show how dedicated they are to saving life and God's desire for all people to live now and eternally. Pornography is bad, but it gives Christians the opportunity to provide a contrast with good speech and good magazines and good movies that make people feel good about themselves. The worse something is, the more stark the contrast with God's way, and the more obvious the difference in his way is shown. Laws that are "almost good" are difficult to contrast with God's way.

27. **Do you know people who have been in pain but continue to tend the needs of others? How does this help you forget your own difficulties?**

Matthew 25:35,36,40: Whenever we help someone else, even if it is as simply giving a glass of water, or as complicated as visiting them in prison, we are doing it to Jesus.

Possible Class Response: Mothers all know the experience of getting out of a sickbed to fix a meal for the family or get the children off to school. Some may have visited people in the hospital who were spending their time encouraging other patients who were not as bad off as them, or even encouraging the doctors and nurses.

28. **Tell of a time your burdens got so unbearably heavy you handed them over to Jesus, then got a brave smile and spread the love of God instead.**

    Matthew 11:28-30: Jesus said that his burden of helping others in a physical and spiritual way is very light. But we can't and won't reach out to others as long as we hang on to our own burdens. Our own burdens are much heavier than his, and he wants us to just give them to him to carry for us.

    Possible Class Response: Various tragedies will have been experienced by various class members. They may have used these events to understand and reach out to others and show them the peace God can give them in such turmoil.

29. **Discuss how you would like to react if you were told to renounce God or be tortured or executed. How do you think making such a determination now can help you with your Christian dedication both now and in the unknown future?**

    Romans 8:17;31;35-39: If we share Christ's suffering, we will share his glory. If the whole world is against us and God is for us, we have the majority. Nothing can separate us from the love of Christ, not even torture or Satan's servants on earth. Only by overcoming a great obstacle can we become overcomers. In Christ we are more than overcomers; we are conquerors!

    Possible Class Response: We can imagine various bad things people could do to us, then imagine ourselves enduring the shame, the embarrassment, the isolation, the pain. We can decide what we would do if we were made a shame and embarrassment to others, what we would do if isolated from everyone for months or years, what we would do if unbearable pain were inflicted upon us. We can picture Jesus standing beside us sharing in our affliction. We can remind ourselves it takes only a moment and we can be in the presence of Jesus our Savior.

30. **Describe how you think you will feel when at last, at the end of your Christian life, you are released from this body and rush to the arms of Jesus.**

    Philippians 1:20-24: Paul said that no matter what was done to him, he would not be ashamed nor would he be afraid what anyone could do to him. Even if it meant death, his executor would just be helping him join his Lord in heaven all that much sooner.

    Revelation 14:13: Most blessed are we who die in the Lord; after all we have been through, we'll be able to rest in glory.

    Revelation 7:9-17: Multitudes standing before the throne of God dressed in white, shout "Salvation to our God!", bow in worship, then declare: "Blessing! and glory! and wisdom! and thanksgiving! and honor! and power! and might! be unto our God forever and ever! Amen!"

<u>Possible Class Response</u>: Bliss! Release! Relief! Consolation! Unspeakable joy! Faith at last a reality! Doubting gone! Ultimate happiness!

Good Work

Write a note to an elderly Christian. Tell them how you have admired their dedication and how marvelous you know it will be when at last they get to live with Jesus forever in heaven.

BEFORE CLASS:

A1. Obtain the name and address of a Christian nursing home. If you do not know where one is, look in a *Churches of Today* book or some other such publication. Ask your preacher for assistance. Ask the nursing home for the names of their residents. (They may wish to only give first names, which is okay.)

A2. Obtain the names of the elderly members of your congregation. Your preacher or church secretary would be able to help.

B. Gather up some local church directories and telephone books.

C. Gather envelopes and stationery (colored bond cut in half).

E. Pre-address some envelopes. Leave some blank for those who have an elderly friend or relative they would like to write.

F. Write on the black board or poster board a suggestion for class members who are unsure what to say:

"I just wanted to let you know how much I appreciate the dedication to God you have had all these years, even when things were difficult. Although death is frightening to all of us, I know you are looking forward to the day when you can at last be with Jesus who has loved you and stood by you for so long. Won't it be wonderful! You will be with Jesus forever in heaven. If you get there before me, I will be a little jealous. God bless you and keep you with him forever!

DURING CLASS:

"We've been studying about being steadfast in our faith no matter how discouraging and bad things get. For our reward is not here on earth anyway; it is beyond our grave in glorious heaven.

"We all know elderly people who have been Christians for a long time. If you do not, I have a list of elderly Christians who live at _____ nursing home. Their fight is almost done, the race is almost over. They are nearly Home. Let us send these

Christian soldiers a letter of appreciation and encouragement.

Hand out stationery and envelopes. "If you aren't sure what to say, I have written a suggestion for you on the board. Feel free to copy it if you like."

"You will have about eight minutes. Let's all be quiet now and allow each other to think and write. When you are done, give the letter to me, and offer a silent prayer for the person you wrote while the others finish their notes.

Concluding Remarks

When time is up and while the slower writers complete their notes, sing one verse of a song, possibly one of the following:

1. *We Shall See the King Some Day*
2. *How Beautiful Heaven Must Be*
3. *Sing to Me of Heaven*
4. *Face to Face*

In a few moments your students will be returning home to their regular routine. Encourage them to view everything they will be returning to as a tool for Jesus to use along the way to heaven.

(Wait for one or two quick replies to each of the following.) "In a few words....

1. How should we use the blessings God gives us?
2. What should we do with obstacles in the way of God's goodness in the world?
3. How can we encourage others while it is we who are sick?
4. What will it be like when at last we arrive in heaven?

Give the list of Christians in the nursing home to the person leading the closing prayer. Pray for them and for persecuted Christians being faithful to death, and thank God for the wonderful reward he holds for us at last at the end of our life.

Question

ARE YOU

WILLING TO

SACRIFICE?

Thank You

Thanks for reading my book! I'm so honored that you chose to spend your precious time with my research. You are appreciated. I'm an independent author who relies on my readers to help spread the word about stories you enjoy. Would you take a few minutes to let your friends know on Facebook, Pinterest... wherever you spend your time online?

Also, each honest review at online retailers means a lot to me and helps other readers know if this is a book they might enjoy,

I welcome contact from readers. At my website (below), you can do so. You can also sign up for my newsletter (below) to be notified of half-price books and new releases.

About The Author

Katheryn Maddox Haddad grew up in the cold north and now lives in Arizona where she does not have to shovel sunshine. She basks in 100-degree weather with palm trees, cacti, and a computer with most of the lettering worn off.

She has a bachelor's degree in English, Bible, and history, from Harding University, a Master's Degree in management and human relations from Abilene Christian University, and part of a Master's Degree in Bible from Harding University, including Greek studies. She served as a social worker for the states of Virginia and Illinois.

She spends half her day writing, and the other half teaching English over the internet worldwide using the Bible as textbook through World English Institute. She has taught some 7000 Muslims, mostly in the Middle East. Students she has converted to Christianity are in hiding in Afghanistan, Iran, Iraq, Yemen, Jordan, Somalia, Sierra Leone, Uzbekistan, Tajikistan, Indonesia, and Palestine. "They are my heroes," she says.

In addition to her seventy-seven books (non-fiction, novels, and storybooks), she has written numerous articles for *Gospel Advocate, Twentieth Century Christian, Firm Foundation, Christian Bible Teacher, Christian Woman,* and several world mission publications. Her weekly column, *Little-Known Facts About the Bible,* appeared several years in newspapers in North Carolina and Texas.

Buy Your Next Book Now

CHRISTIAN LIFE
Applied Christianity: Handbook 500 Good Works
You Can Be a Hero Alone
Worship Changes Since 1st Century + Worship 1sr Century Way
The Best of Alexander Campbell's Millennial Harbinger
Inside the Hearts of Bible Women-Reader+Audio+Leader
The Lord's Supper: 52 Readings with Prayers
http://bit.ly/Christianlife

BIBLE TEXT STUDIES
Revelation: A Love Letter From God
The Holy Spirit: 592 Verses Examined
Was Jesus God? (Why Evil)
365 Life-Changing Scriptures Day by Date
Love Letters of Jesus & His Bride, Ecclesia
Christianity or Islam? The Contrast
The Road to Heaven
http://bit.ly/BibleTexts

FUN BOOKS
Bible Puzzles, Bible Song Book, Bible Numbers
http://bit.ly/BibleFun

TOUCHING GOD SERIES
365 Golden Bible Thoughts: God's Heart to Yours
365 Pearls of Wisdom: God's Soul to Yours
365 Silver-Winged Prayers: Your Spirit to God's
http://bit.ly/TouchingGodSeries

-SURVEY SERIES: EASY BIBLE WORKBOOKS
→Old Testament & New Testament Surveys
→Questions You Have Asked-Part I & II
http://bit.ly/BibleWorkbooks

HISTORICAL RESEARCH BIBLE
for Novel, Screenwriter, Documentary & Thesis Writers
http://bit.ly/32uZkHa

GENEALOGY: How to Climb Your Family Tree Without Falling Out
Volume I & 2: Beginner-Intermediate & Colonial-Medieval
http://bit.ly/GenealogyBeginner-Advanced

Connect With The Author

Website: **https://inspirationsbykatheryn.com**

Facebook: **bit.ly/FacebooksKatherynMaddoxHaddad**

Linkedin: **http://bit.ly/KatherynLinkedin**

Twitter: **https://twitter.com/KatherynHaddad**

Pinterest: **https://www.pinterest.com/haddad1940/**

Goodreads:
https://www.goodreads.com/katherynmaddoxhaddad

Get A Free Book

Sign up for Katheryn's monthly newsletter with half-price books for the whole family and insider tips on what's coming next.
http://bit.ly/katheryn

Join My Dream Team

Members get the first peek at my newest book and have fun offering me advice sometimes. I have a point system of rewards for helping me get the word out. Check it out here:
http://bit.ly/KatherynsDreamTeam

www.ingramcontent.com/pod-product-compliance
Lightning Source LLC
Chambersburg PA
CBHW081738100526
44592CB00015B/2226